S0-BSA-814

WITHDRAWN

From Dreyfus to Vichy

From Dreyfus to Vichy

The Remaking of French Jewry, 1906–1939

Paula Hyman

New York   Columbia University Press   1979

The author wishes to thank the *Jewish Journal of Sociology* and the *YIVO Annual of Jewish Social Science* for permission to reprint material which appeared in their publications.

The photograph on the dust jacket is by the courtesy of the YIVO Institute for Jewish Research.

Library of Congress Cataloging in Publication Data

Hyman, Paula, 1946–
    From Dreyfus to Vichy.

    Bibliography
    Includes index.
    1. Jews in France—History—20th century.
    2. France—History—20th century.   I. Title.
DS135.F83H95   944'.004'924   79–14401
ISBN 0–231–04722–3

Columbia University Press
New York   Guildford, Surrey

Copyright © 1979 by Columbia University Press
All Rights Reserved
Printed in the United States of America

DS
135
.F83
H95

To my parents
Sydney and Ida Hyman

84719

84722

Contents

Illustrations appear as a group following p. 178

Contents

List of Abbreviations

ACIP	Archives of the Association Consistoriale Israélite de Paris (Paris Consistory)
A.D.	Archives Départémentales de France
A.I.	Archives israélites
AIU	Archives of the Alliance Israélite Universelle, Paris
A.N.	Archives Nationales de France
Brandeis	Special Collections, Brandeis University Library
CAHJP	Central Archives for the History of the Jewish People, Jerusalem
C.C.	Archives of the Central Consistory, Paris
CZA	Central Zionist Archives, Jerusalem
EIF	Archives of the Eclaireurs Israélites de France, Paris
HUC	Special Collections, Hebrew Union College, Cincinnati
JSS	Jewish Social Studies
JTS	Archives of the Jewish Theological Seminary, New York
MAE	Archives of the Ministère des Affaires Etrangères, Paris
NP	Naye presse
PH	Parizer haynt
REJ	Revue des Etudes Juives
TJ	La Tribune juive
UI	Univers israélite
YIVO	Archives of the YIVO Institute for Jewish Research, New York

Preface

Every book of history is the product of many encounters in the world of scholarship. It is a pleasure to have the opportunity to acknowledge publicly the assistance of those who have contributed, directly and indirectly, to the writing of this work.

I have had the good fortune to study Jewish history with teachers who prodded the imagination and suggested the manifold possibilities of historical investigation. As an undergraduate I was introduced to the excitement of the field by Mordecai Wilensky at the Hebrew College of Boston and by Yosef Yerushalmi and Isadore Twersky at Harvard. At Columbia University, where I pursued my graduate studies, I profited from the erudition and guidance of Gerson Cohen, Ismar Schorsch, Arthur Hertzberg, Robert Paxton, and Zvi Ankori. As the supervisor of my master's thesis, Gerson Cohen taught me the arts of research and writing, and rewriting. His profound lectures continue to stimulate my thinking. Ismar Schorsch generously offered me of his time and his sophisticated insight into modern European Jewry. I benefited also from Arthur Hertzberg's ability to isolate the questions worth asking as well as from his provocative answers. To Robert Paxton I owe whatever French history I have mastered. His close reading of my dissertation and its revisions never failed to yield helpful suggestions.

To Zvi Ankori, in particular, I am grateful for the probing questions and critical comments which helped me shape the dissertation upon which this study is based. An historian of great insight and a writer of style, he challenged my assumptions and demanded clarity of expression. Working with him transformed the writing of a dissertation from an obligation into the culmination of a learning process.

I am appreciative as well of the advice of numerous colleagues and friends. Richard Cohen, Morris Dickstein, Roger Errera, Harriet Freidenreich, Arthur Hertzberg, Ismar Schorsch, and Allan Silver read the manuscript in whole or in part and offered useful advice. My knowledge of French Jewry has been immeasurably enriched in particular by my ongoing international dialogue with Richard Cohen as my understanding of modern Jewish history has grown from years of local conversations with Ismar Schorsch. Phyllis Cohen Albert, David Ellenson, Todd Endelman, Emmanuel Etkes, and Marion Kaplan, also helped me to clarify specific issues. The late Zosa Szajkowski shared with me his extensive knowledge of French Jewry and the sources available for its study. Finally, Deborah Dash Moore not only provided a careful page by page critique of the manuscript; her friendship, support, and intellectual stimulation were crucial to the writing of this book as well as to my development as an historian.

Many research institutions graciously made their facilities available to me. I am grateful to their staffs, and in particular to M. Gérard Nahon, archivist of the Central and Paris Consistories; to Mme. Yvette Levyne, librarian of the Aliance Israélite Universelle; to Dr. Menahem Schmelzer of the Jewish Theological Seminary; to Dina Abramowicz, Ezekiel Lifschutz, and Marek Web of the YIVO Institute for Jewish Research; to Hillel Kempinski of the Bund Archives; to Dr. Simon Schwarzfuchs of the Central Archives for the History of the Jewish People; and to Dr. Michael Heymann of the Central Zionist Archives. The research for this book was funded in part by generous grants from the National Foundation for Jewish Culture and the Memorial Foundation for Jewish Culture, for which I express my appreciation.

This book also owes much to my supportive family. My husband, Stanley Rosenbaum, not only encouraged me in my work; he also collaborated in the daily chores which prove such a distraction from work and listened patiently to endless discussions of French Jewry. Our children, Judith and Adina, provided much diversion, when it was needed and when it was not, as well as proper perspective. Our devoted babysitter, Mary Schweizer, made it possible for me to be a historian as well as a mother. Finally, to my parents, Sydney and Ida Hyman, who set me on my way and instilled in me a love of learning and a passion for Jewish history, I dedicate this book in love and gratitude.

Paula Hyman
April 1979

From Dreyfus to Vichy

1.
The Legacy: France and Her Jews

Since 1808 the motto of the consistories has been "Religion and Father-
land." One could add a keynote of conduct: "Utility, Steadiness, and
Discretion." Though neither spoken nor written, it has been the practice.

Georges Wormser
Personal Communication, Oct. 27, 1972

Introduction

In the years immediately preceding the Dreyfus Affair, French
Jewry enjoyed the reputation of being the most successfully assimilated and most stable Jewish community in Western Europe. Its population was culturally French and relatively homogeneous, for the
more traditional Jews living within the small towns and villages of Alsace were now, however reluctantly, German citizens. French Jewry
had developed an institutional and ideological consensus which permitted an appearance of public serenity and self-satisfaction. Individual French Jews—Léon Blum, Henri Bergson, Emile Durkheim, to
name but three—were achieving recognition in their chosen fields in
the highest strata of French academic and cultural life. And they
were able to do so without denying their Jewishness, without converting to Christianity. Despite the rise of anti-Semitic publicists, the
major issues of the nature of Jewish integration into French society
appeared to have been resolved.

During the next fifty years, however, French Jewry and its status
were radically altered. With the influx of immigrants from Eastern
Europe, the majority of the Jewish population of France became—
and remained until the years following World War II—a population
of foreigners. In an age of growing xenophobia and increasing emphasis upon rootedness in French tradition and culture as the
prerequisite for claiming French nationality, the foreign origins of
close to two-thirds of France's Jews raised anew questions about the
assimilability of Jews within French society. Within the Jewish community itself, the immigrants also called into question the nature of

Jewish patterns of assimilation and identity by introducing the secular
and ethnic components of Jewish identity in Eastern Europe. They
taxed both the financial resources and the tolerance of native Jewry.
Moreover, beginning with the Dreyfus Affair of the 1890s and cul-
minating with the troubled years of the 1930s, French Jews observed,
from the sidelines, the intensification of anti-Semitism as an ideological force within French society. The self-confidence of French Jewry
ebbed, not only vis-à-vis the immigrant newcomers, but also with respect to France itself.

To outside observers, French Jewry appeared to have failed the
crucial tests confronting Western Jewish communities of the twentieth century: the challenges of integrating the immigrants and combating anti-Semitism. Indeed, historians and political critics have accused French Jewry of political passivity in times of crisis.[1] They
have charged France's Jews with an assimilation so profound and destructive as to constitute self-delusion at best, moral cowardice at
worst.

Such a condemnation of French Jewry seems entirely reasonable at
first glance. French Jews were certainly not alone among the Jewish
communities of the West in facing the problems engendered by mass
immigration and rising anti-Semitism. The American and British
Jewish communities dealt with similar problems, and far more successfully. To the historian falls the task of explaining why the response of French Jewry was so hesitant and ambivalent: why French
Jews counted so many individual successes amidst communal failure,
and why there were so many flamboyant and creative intellectuals
and so few decisive leaders. Equally is it the historian's concern to ex-
amine how immigration remade the French Jewish community. For
by the eve of World War II the French Jewish community was transformed. The institutional and ideological consensus which had characterized native Jewry in the late nineteenth century had been shat-
tered. In its place a diversity of Jewish institutions and political
strategies flourished. New political and cultural ideologies, like Zionism and Jewish Communism, challenged older patterns of assimilation and won adherents, especially among the younger generation, in
the interwar years. Just as the first World War swept away the social

and political patterns carefully constructed by the masters of nine-teenth-century Europe, so the French Jewish synthesis, which en-joyed a temporary renewal in the period after the Dreyfus Affair, was fatally weakened by the new conditions of the interwar Jewish com-munity.

The remaking of French Jewry in the encounter of native Jews with Jewish immigrants from Eastern Europe took place in a milieu which differed substantially from that of America, long virtually the sole laboratory for the study of Jewish immigrant adaptation. The constellation of social, political, and cultural forces which can be labeled the "national context," as well as the monolithic structure of the Jewish community in France, shaped twentieth-century French Jewry just as surely as American social attitudes like Progressivism and the voluntary and localist nature of the Jewish community in the U.S. influenced the development of American Jewry. Unlike America, and even Great Britain, France made no claims to cultural pluralism. That was a fact of which French Jews were well aware, and were eager to impress upon their immigrant brethren. Indeed, French Jews felt they had evolved a synthesis which took into ac-count France's lack of cultural pluralism. For French Jews had been marked by the peculiar and contradictory legacy of the century be-tween the French Revolution and the Dreyfus Affair.

The Impact of Emancipation

It is impossible to understand the responses of French Jewry to the new conditions of the twentieth century without comprehending the centrality in its collective consciousness of the Revolution and the emancipation which came in its wake. French Jewry is, in fact, a child of the Revolution. As a result of the revolutionary upheaval in the concept of the nation-state, the 40,000 Jews resident in France in 1789 became the first in the West to achieve full emancipation—that is, acceptance as equal citizens with all the civic and political rights and obligations which citizenship entailed.[2] Moreover, the terms of emancipation, as articulated in the early years of the Revolution and during the reign of Napoleon I, set standards for the sociopolitical and institutional structure as well as the ideology of French Jewry, which remained unchallenged until the twentieth century. The French´Jewish community was transformed from an autonomous corporate *kehilla* to a consistory.

It has been forcefully argued that the emancipation of the Jews was a logical necessity of the ideology of the Revolution and of the socio-economic changes which gave birth to the modern nation-state.[3] All corporate groups had been dissolved, and the autonomous corporate status of the Jewish community could not persist unchanged. In addition, the universalist concept of natural rights, which replaced that of privileges, extended to all mankind, Jews included. However, despite the egalitarian tone of much of the rhetoric of the Revolution, the debate regarding the emancipation of the Jews was prolonged and acrimonious because of doubts as to the willingness and ability of the Jews to assimilate within French society and fulfill the obligations of citizenship.[4] Thus, the wealthy and socially acculturated Sephardi merchants of Bordeaux and Bayonne were the first to be granted the rights of citizenship, on January 28, 1790, while their more numerous, poorer, and unassimilated brethren of Alsace were not emancipated, and then reluctantly, until September 27, 1791.

Both the pre-Revolutionary progressive literature on the Jews and the debates in the National Assembly expressed the conviction that emancipation would at the least stimulate the complete social and cultural assimilation—or "amelioration"—of the Jews, and at best facilitate their conversion.[5] The degraded socioeconomic state of the Jews, it was widely held in enlightened circles, was a result of persecution; therefore, the cessation of persecution and legal disabilities would lead to the rapid improvement of Jewish manners and morals. The Jews would, in fact, soon become indistinguishable from other Frenchmen.[6] In the 1787 Metz essay competition on the subject "Are there means of making the Jews happier and more useful in France?" Adolphe Thiéry optimistically forecast in his prizewinning entry, "We can make of the Jews what we want them to become, for their faults and vices derive from our institutions."[7]

What the Jews were expected to become was individual Frenchmen of the Jewish faith. As one of the proponents of Jewish emancipation, Clermont-Tonnerre, declared during a debate in the National Assembly, "To the Jews as individuals—everything; to the Jews as a group—nothing. They must constitute neither a body politic nor an order; they must be citizens individually."[8]

If the expectations of the proponents of Jewish emancipation were limited to a vaguely phrased aspiration for social amelioration, they were made explicit by Napoleon I. Disappointed at the failure of the Jews to alter their socioeconomic behavior substantially, and disturbed by charges of rampant Jewish usury in Alsace, Napoleon undertook to resolve the Jewish question in France by making clear the political terms of Jewish emancipation.[9] In the Sanhedrin which he convened with great theatricality to elucidate the relationship of French Jews to France and of Jewish religious law to French civil law, the carefully selected delegates of French Jewry declared their absolute loyalty to France and her law and denied the validity of the national, or political, elements within Judaism.[10] Judaism was to be a creed like all others, divested of political law and sanctions.[11] And French Jews were to declare, with evident exaggeration, that their primary sociopsychological loyalty was to their fellow Frenchmen, rather than to Jews in other lands.[12]

Moreover, Napoleon fervently hoped—though in vain—that the Sanhedrin would adopt his goal of one intermarriage for every two endogamous Jewish marriages as the ultimate solution to the Jewish problem. Furthermore, Napoleon imposed the "Infamous Decree" of 1808, which restricted Jewish commerce and moneylending, to compel the assimilation of Jews into the French economy.[13] Finally, by establishing a consistorial structure for French Jewry, parallel to the one legislated for French Protestants, Napoleon made it clear that within the French polity Jews, like Protestants, were to be considered as no more than members of a religious denomination. As the official administrative bodies of French Jewry, the consistories were defined in legislation as centralized religious institutions under state supervision, called upon not only to administer the Jewish community but also to serve the needs of the French state by preaching patriotism and recruiting soldiers.[14] Appropriately, "Fatherland and Religion" became the slogan of the Central Consistory, while its rabbis were state functionaries. The consistories remained quasi-governmental bodies until the separation of Church and State in 1905 and then served as a model for the voluntary organizational structure of French Jewry in the period following the separation.

The Napoleonic era thus signaled in theory the severance of national and religious elements within French Judaism, setting a precedent for the process of emancipation in all Western countries. It defined the limits of Jewish identity and political activity within France, and determined the institutional structure of French Jewry. The period of emancipation had taught its eager Jewish pupils that they were expected to assimilate within French society until they could be distinguished from other Frenchmen only in that they worshiped in the synagogue rather than the church. As a group, political neutrality became their watchword, for they had learned that collective Jewish politics, except to serve the needs of the state or defend their own equality, would be suspect in the eyes of Frenchmen. Indeed, it had come to seem so to the Jews themselves. During the nineteenth century French Jewry thus gradually developed a social and ideological consensus based upon the terms of their emancipation. That ideology was propounded within the Jewish community by its foremost intellectuals, prominent rabbis, and major lay leaders. By the end of the nineteenth century, it was virtually unchallenged as the dominant public position of French Jewry.

While there were important regional and class variations in the pace of acculturation, their generally rapid cultural assimilation enabled French Jews to accept with little difficulty the terms of their emancipation. As a group they fulfilled the cultural expectations of the proponents of their admission on an equal basis into the French polity, for they accepted much of the Enlightenment critique of the social and cultural inferiority of their own community. However, French Jews saw no conflict between their recognition of the necessity for acculturation and their concern for group survival as Jews; or in Uriel Tal's terminology, between integration and identity. Assimilation, they felt, did not demand obliteration of Jewish identity but rather its transformation, its privatization, in accordance with the standards of the larger community. They could be, and desired to be, both Frenchmen and Jews. In fact, as Phyllis Albert has pointed out, they retained many characteristics of what we would call ethnic solidarity.[15] However, the ideology of emancipation compelled them, particularly in the latter part of the century, to express that solidarity in religious terminology.[16]

Within two generations French Jews, had, in fact, attained what one sociologist has labeled behavioral assimilation, or acculturation—but not structural assimilation, or the total obliteration of their group distinctiveness.[17] They spoke French, attended French schools for the most part, worked in many areas of the urban sector of the economy, and participated in French cultural life; but they retained the social structure of their religious, charitable, and cultural institutions. Moreover, they maintained primary group relations. Despite the persistence of ethnic solidarity, French Jewish leaders, like those in other newly emancipated Western Jewish communities, were eager to deny any notion of dual loyalty and became ardent spokesmen for a public ideology of assimilation, summarized succinctly by the historian Théodore Reinach:

> The Jews, since they have ceased to be treated as pariahs, must identify themselves, in heart and in fact, with the nations which have accepted them, renounce the practices, the aspirations, the peculiarities of costume or language which tended to isolate them from their fellow citizens, in a word cease to be a dispersed nation, and henceforth be considered only a religious denomination.[18]

In celebration of the centennial of the Revolution, French rabbis echoed Reinach and proudly proclaimed the success of Jewish assimilation. As one declared, "We have adopted the customs and traditions of a country which has so generously adopted us, and today, thanks to God, there are no longer any but Frenchmen in France."[19] Thus, by the end of the nineteenth century, the self-definition of French Jews was expressed ever more consistently within the acceptable framework of a religious, rather than ethnic, subculture. In this French Jews shared the approach of other Western European Jewish communities. What they all failed to appreciate was the fact that the religious definition of the community involved a large measure of self-deception. For many nonobservant Jews continued to identify as Jews and were considered so by the Jewish community, much to the bewilderment of Gentile society.[20]

The Political Ideology of French Jewry

The rapidity and relative completeness of Jewish emancipation in France enabled French Jews to enjoy a sense of security unparalleled in the other countries of continental Europe. The temporary discriminatory measures decreed by Napoleon I were allowed to lapse in 1818, and in 1831 the state assumed the responsibility of paying the salaries of rabbis along with those of priests and ministers. By 1846 even the last vestige of discrimination, the oath *more judaico*, was formally abolished, and French Jews were equal, at least in theory, to other French citizens.[21] Despite the changes in regime and sporadic local incidents of popular anti-Semitism, the citizenship of French Jews was never seriously jeopardized during the nineteenth century. Consequently, throughout the nineteenth and early twentieth centuries, in contrast to their German counterparts, French Jews were spared the necessity to organize and engage in overt political activity in order to acquire equal rights. Indeed, they established no defense organizations of the type which existed in Germany by the end of the nineteenth century, though the consistories did protest discriminatory practices against French Jews in the courts and the educational bureaucracy.[22] Instead, they were able to identify with the French political system and express confidence that its rule of law would ensure their continued equality. Although French culture was suffused with Catholic concepts and symbols, French Jews selectively adopted the liberal principles of the Revolution as the basis of French national culture, ignoring pre-Revolutionary traditions as atavistic. Furthermore, under the impact of the ideology of emancipation, the major institutions of the French Jewish community espoused a policy of political neutrality except in the defense of equality or of purely religious interests. Thus, they denied the legitimacy—indeed, the very existence—of political, as distinct from religious, Jewish interests. Hence the communal behavior so often characterized as passivity.

True, French Jews established the Alliance Israélite Universelle in 1860 to defend the interests of persecuted Jews in foreign countries and to promote their civic emancipation. However, the Alliance did not interfere in domestic political issues and at the end of the nineteenth century did not consider French anti-Semitism as worthy of attention, even while the Dreyfus Affair raged. When the Alliance spoke of solidarity with Jewish brethren, it consciously patterned itself after an association of Protestants and attempted to parallel the concern expressed by the French government for Catholics within the Ottoman Empire. In fact, after its early years of activism in the 1860s the Alliance was but another example of how French Jews identified themselves with French culture and policy. For the Alliance diffused French culture in its educational network, introduced foreign Jews to modernity in its French guise, and served French political aims abroad.[23]

Even the growing visibility of anti-Semitism in the last two decades of the nineteenth century did not disturb French Jewry's professed sense of political security. Most French Jews seem to have perceived little evidence of discrimination in their personal lives and in their relations with their fellow Frenchmen.[24] Moreover, French Jews saw anti-Semitism as a German import. Since anti-Semitism was not officially espoused by the government, its recrudescence was seen as a weapon seized upon temporarily by the political extremes to undermine social and political stability. While deploring the manifestations of anti-Semitism, French Jews remained confident that the parties of order would ultimately prevail and that French political institutions could be relied upon, and could be called upon, to defend the rights of all French citizens.[25] As Zadoc Kahn, the Chief Rabbi of France, declared in 1889, "France will not repudiate her past, her traditions, her principles which constitute the best of her moral patrimony. . . . As for us . . . we will continue to love our country . . . and bear witness, in all circumstances of our gratitude and devotion."[26] To Jewish spokesmen anti-Semitism was not a Jewish question but merely one aspect of the general problem of maintaining a stable and

well-ordered society, a problem of concern to all proper members of
the bourgeoisie. French Jewry, thus, was able to link the eradication
of anti-Semitism to the general welfare of the French nation.

For the most part bourgeois in life style and aspirations, if not
always in income,[27] in the first decades of the Third Republic
French Jews supported the Republican Opportunists who promised
an orderly regime congenial to middle class economic interests. Because their citizenship was rooted in liberal concepts of state and law,
it was natural for French Jews, as individuals, to place themselves
squarely in the Republican camp throughout the nineteenth century.[28] The French Right, with its adherence to the concept of the
organic Christian state and its intransigent opposition to the liberal
Republic, scarcely offered them an alternative.[29] The French Left
also had a tradition of anti-Semitism rooted in anti-capitalist sentiments, and its ideology contradicted the class interests of most native French Jews.

The nature of French politics also facilitated the political neutrality
of the Jewish community as a collective group. Ethnic politics did
not exist in France, and pressure groups in general were few. The
Third Republic has been characterized as a "stalemate society" with a
poor associational life.[30] Religious groups were not expected to participate actively in politics. The incursions of the Catholic Church
into the political process, for example, were vigorously combated by
Republican forces. In fact, French Jews found themselves politically
isolated in the polarized atmosphere of the early years of the Third
Republic, where religious convictions and political stance often converged.[31] Anticlericalism characterized the Republicans, with whom,
as we have noted, French Jews most naturally identified as defenders
of the ideology of the Revolution. In the clerical struggle, however,
many Republicans placed Jewish institutions in the enemy camp,
merely because they were organs of a religious community. To its
surprise, French Jewry discovered that its unchosen political bed-
fellow was the Catholic Church, itself the major victim of anticlerical
wrath. But the Jewish community could never throw in its lot with
the royalist, anti-Republican, and heavily anti-Semitic Church
(which blamed the anticlerical campaign on the Jews).[32] This poli-

ticization of the religious issue in France, and the resulting political isolation of the Jewish community, fortified the ideology of the emancipation, which had enjoined French Jewry from political activity as an organized community.

The Dreyfus Affair, paradoxically, also confirmed French Jews' decision to remain collectively politically neutral. While the anti-Semitism unleashed by the Affair may have temporarily shaken the faith of French Jewry in the readiness of French institutions to uphold the ideals of the Revolution, its eventual happy outcome seemed to the Jews to vindicate their political inaction and reliance upon nonsectarian organizations and the political process. During the Affair, the spokesmen for French Jewry carefully refrained from public activity on behalf of Dreyfus, relying instead upon the dilatory support of the Republicans and some Socialists. Although Chief Rabbi Kahn attempted quietly to organize a committee against anti-Semitism, his initiative failed because of the lack of support among French Jewry.[33] For French Jews saw the Affair not as a matter for Jewish political action but as a clash between Republican and anti-Republican forces, which would be resolved by the general polity. To the Jewish community the Dreyfus Affair thus appeared as an unfortunate aberration in the relatively untroubled experience of Jews in France.

The National Context: Jews in French Public Opinion

If emancipation and the French political system provided French Jewry with a measure of political equality enjoyed by no other European Jewish community, there was a darker side to the Jewish experience in France. While French Jews dismissed anti-Semitism as a serious threat to their status, they were not unaware of its existence. They recognized that as adopted children of France they would have to repeatedly prove their devotion and worthiness as French citizens. Moreover, they were sensitive to their image among the molders of French opinion. In large part, in fact, French public opinion set limits upon the political activity of French Jewry and influenced their

attitudes to Jewish immigrants and to such seemingly internal Jewish
matters as Zionism, the nature of Jewish identity, and Jewish cultural
expression.

French Jews were perplexed by the chasm which divided their self-
image as loyal French citizens, devoting their talents to their beloved
homeland in so many spheres of activity, and their image in French
literature and the press. As Rabbi Abraham Bloch, who would die as
a chaplain in World War I, passionately declared in a sermon of
1889. "[The Jews] have embraced [arts, letters, politics, the military,
industry, and commerce] with avidity and love, and not without success, better to show how they cherish their new homeland [and] to
make themselves more worthy of her love and protection."[34] But the
Jew who became increasingly visible in French literature and the
press was anything but the selfless and dedicated patriot. Distinctive
negative images of Jews—in particular, the Jew as alien and as exploitative capitalist—were shared across much of the political spectrum.
A related image—the Jew as vicious corroder of French traditions and
strengths, as veritable destroyer of the moral and political order—was
propagated most often by the publicists of the Right, in both its traditional Catholic and new nationalist forms.

These dominant images of Jews came to the fore in the last two decades of the nineteenth century, but they survived, albeit in muted
form, into the twentieth. While the heated passions of the Dreyfus
Affair, which had transformed the Jewish question into a national
issue, cooled in the decade before World War I, the negative stereotype of the Jew persisted for a number of reasons. The diffusion of
nationalist sentiment into new sectors of political leadership, even
among formerly passionate Dreyfusards, created a climate in which
xenophobia and concern for true national identity could flourish.[35]
Furthermore, the Jews who were most visible in France, in particular
the great banking families of the Rothschilds, Herzes, Reinachs, and
Bischoffsheims, were of relatively recent German origin. The influx
of immigrants from Eastern Europe also reinforced the image of Jew
as foreigner. Finally, the rise to prominence of Jewish intellectuals
critical of bourgeois values confirmed for many Frenchmen not only

that Jews "thought differently" but that they were, in fact, saboteurs of French values.

European culture has been obsessed with the Jew as dissenter and outsider. It is no surprise, then, to discover that the Jewish characters which people the works of a wide variety of late nineteenth and early-twentieth-century French writers, both secular and Catholic, fit into this category.[36] Particularly after the Panama Scandal of 1892 and the Dreyfus Affair, French writers concerned themselves with examining the essential separateness of the Jew and his role in modern French society. Political publicists as well pictured the Jew as the foreigner within, the quintessential, unassimilable alien.

For Catholic, secularist, and anti-Semite of both camps, the primary characteristic of the Jew was his alienation and uprootedness, which was a product of his long heritage of religious (and hence cultural) difference. Even the baptized Jew, particularly if his conversion was not due to a true religious experience, was destined to retain some aspect of his Jewish identity and thus remain apart. Proust's Swann, for example, was considered a Jew although his family had converted to Catholicism two generations before.[37] As Paul Claudel noted in his play Le Père Humilié (1917), "It takes a lot of water to baptize a Jew!"[38] For the Catholic writer, whether overtly anti-Semitic like Georges Bernanos, or not, like Paul Claudel, the survival of the Jew as a separate entity, as witness to the truth of Christianity, was drawn from traditional Catholic theology. Likewise, the images of the Jew as usurer and traitor and of Jewry as the chosen but cursed people were deeply rooted in medieval Catholic thought.[39] However, the secular writer as well still depicted the Jew as essentially foreign, despite his acknowledged superior intelligence and understanding of the French soul. Even such sympathetic writers as Emile Zola and Anatole France saw the Jew's separateness and will to survive as a stigma and sign of obstinacy.[40] For the Catholic, the ultimate goal remained the conversion of the Jew; for the secularist, his complete absorption within French society; for the anti-Semite, restriction of his freedom and economic activity.

In addition to their religious dissent, the Alsatian origin of the majority of French Jews was another sign of their foreignness. Alsatian Jews were perceived as Germans, and their migration into France after the annexation of Alsace-Lorraine by Germany in 1871 was depicted as a German invasion.[41] Edouard Drumont, France's leading anti-Semite, disseminated the image of the Jew as the newcomer to France and the quintessential German.[42] Because of the popularity of this image, the major Catholic paper *La Croix*, which together with its sister publication *Le Pèlerin* had a circulation of some 500,000 in the 1890s, liberally dotted its pages with cartoons of grotesquely ugly Jews mangling the French language with their German accents.[43]

Among the most influential figures in propagating the perception of the Jew as foreigner in respectable circles was Maurice Barrès. An important literary and political personnage and member of the *Académie Française*, his works were immensely popular from the late 1880s through World War I. While he became a racist and champion of right wing politics during the Dreyfus Affair, his impact as a writer and proponent of the *culte du moi* for many years enabled him to bridge Left and Right, and he influenced even the young Jewish socialist, Léon Blum. His appeal was therefore not limited to the circles of the radical Right.[44] As the major proponent of the doctrine of integral nationalism, Barrès provided a theoretical formula for hostility toward French Jews.

For Barrès national feeling was instinctive. It was born of rootedness for generations in French traditions and in French soil. As he wrote in 1902,

> The Jews do not have a country in the sense that we understand it. For us, *la patrie* is our soil and our ancestors, the land of our dead. For them, it is the place where their self-interest is best pursued. Their intellectuals thus arrive at their famous definition. '*La patrie*, it is an idea!' But which idea? That which is most useful for them—for example, the idea that all men are brothers, that nationality is a prejudice to be destroyed. . . . You will not deny that the Jew is a different kind of being. . . .[45]

The Jew to Barrès was that most unfortunate of creatures, a *déraciné* (a rootless person), and as such, Jews were not truly French.[46] Rather, as Barrès had noted in one of his earliest political campaigns in 1889, "[though] assimilated to native Frenchmen by the Revolution, . . . the Jews have preserved their distinctive characters."[47] They were foreigners, and foreigners, Barrès asserted, "do not have their heads made the same way as ours."[48]

Taking Barrès' antiforeigner animus to its logical conclusion, his fellow integral nationalist Charles Maurras, future founder of the rightist and anti-Semitic Action Française, proposed that French citizens who were not truly sons of France be stripped of their citizenship. In an article which appeared in 1894 he labeled these cosmopolitan Frenchmen of foreign origin "métèques" (metics) and suggested that they be granted the status of tolerated resident aliens, like the metics of ancient Athens.[49] Since they were not French, they could not aspire, at least for three generations, to either the privileges or responsibilities of full citizenship. Only with the passage of time would the processes of intermarriage and—in the case of Jews and Protestants—conversion accomplish the complete fusion of the metics into the French national body. Until that process had been completed, they should be restricted in their capacity to take advantage of political and economic opportunities in France—such as owning land and holding office—and to undermine the virtues of the true France.[50]

Maurras transformed anti-Semitism into the rallying cry of the New Right. However, it was Barrès, again, who in the 1890s launched an attack upon foreign workers in France which had far-reaching consequences for French Jews. The foreign workers who were flooding France and depriving native Frenchmen of jobs and wealth, Barrès asserted, were introduced by that "international financial feudalism" which was dominated by Jews.[51] Barrès therefore described his program to exclude foreign workers in order to protect domestic labor from foreign competition as "a meeting point of anti-Semitism, socialism, and the patriotic current."[52] Moreover, his corollary that access to naturalization be limited also bore anti-Semitic undertones. It was through naturalization, "this fissure," Barrès noted, "that so many of the worst Jews had come to us."[53]

This antiforeigner campaign subjected Jews to criticism not only as the insidious importers of foreign workers, but also as immigrants themselves. The first sizable group of eastern European Jews had arrived in France in the wake of the Russian pogroms of 1881–82. While their numbers were relatively small, by the time of World War I there were at least 25,000 immigrant Jews in Paris alone. Concentrated in a few neighborhoods and industries, immigrant Jews drew a great deal of public attention, most of it unfavorable. As more and more Jewish immigrants settled in France, the French Jew was tarred with the unpopular qualities of his newly arrived coreligionist.

If the image of the Jew as foreigner was widespread in significant sectors of French opinion by the beginning of the twentieth century, the image of the Jew as capitalist had even deeper roots in French political thought. It was an image shared by Right and Left in the nineteenth century. In fact, the traditional identification of Jew as capitalist served to make the French Left either indifferent to the Jewish question or overtly hostile to the survival of Jews as a social entity. Even during the Dreyfus Affair, when much of the Left began to recognize the danger of anti-Semitism, it continued to share the widely accepted view that fusion with the general population was the only real solution to the Jewish problem in France. In the postrevolutionary socialist society of the future, there would be no need for separatist religious groups. Thus, French Jews could not look to the Left for unqualified support of their own position that assimilation and Jewish group survival were both compatible and desirable.

The earliest fathers of French socialism, Charles Fourier and Pierre-Joseph Proudhon, left as a legacy to the movement their anti-Jewish attitudes.[54] As George Lichtheim has remarked, the linkage of anti-capitalism and anti-Judaism among the early socialists was not accidental. In their antipathy to bourgeois liberalism, Fourier and Proudhon saw the Jew as the major beneficiary of the political upheaval which had unleashed the despised market economy. Moreover, the prominence of usurers and private bankers among their Jewish contemporaries combined with lingering medieval prejudices against usury and unproductive capital to yield the sentiment that even among capitalists the Jew was the most exploitative.[55] French Jews thus paid a price for the coincidence of their emancipation and the emergence of capitalism.

The disciples of Fourier and Proudhon shared their masters' anti-

Semitism. In 1845 a follower of Fourier, Alphonse Toussenel, wrote
one of the first anti-Semitic classics in France, grandiosely entitled
Les Juifs, rois de l'époque. While later disciples often used "Jew" in-
terchangeably with "capitalist,"[56] the traits attributed to the Jew were
ethnic as well as economic. Moreover, Jews who were not capitalists
were not carefully excluded from attack. Certainly the use of "Jew" as
the shorthand for capitalist fed popular anti-Jewish prejudices, despite
protestations to the contrary. Even Jean Jaurès, who rejected racism
throughout his life and was to risk his career as the most prominent
socialist convert to the Dreyfusard cause, asserted about Jewish financiers that "their long association with banking and commerce had
made them peculiarly adept in the ways of capitalist criminality."[57]
In fact, many French socialists were willing to exploit popular anti-
Semitism as a means of attracting the masses to socialism. Before the
Dreyfus Affair Jaurès himself refrained from attacking anti-Semitism
as a movement and depicted anti-Semites as sincere but misguided.[58]
Some socialists went further and saw even the racist anti-Semitism of
an Edouard Drumont as politically useful. What emerged as opposition to specifically Jewish capitalism could, they believed, be transformed into anti-capitalism plain and simple.[59]

Animosity toward the Jew as capitalist thus linked Right and Left
theorists in late nineteenth century France. Both focused upon the
Jewish "financial feudality" as the source of French problems. Anti-
Semitic attitudes were diffused both among French workers sympathetic to socialism as well as among the lower middle classes who saw
in the teachings of Drumont and Barrès protection for their own
eroding position. While the excesses of the Dreyfus Affair led to an
official dissociation of French socialism from the rabid anti-Semitism
of the radical Right, anti-Jewish hostility survived among workers,
who continued to invoke Rothschild as the capitalist *par excellence*.
At the Socialist Unity Congress of 1900, persistent hostility toward
Jews emerged when one sector of the audience loudly added "anti-
Jewish" to a description of the Party as democratic, republican, and
anti-clerical.[60]

The political middle in France, heir to the ambivalence of the
philosophes toward the Jews, was not immune to attacking the Jew as

capitalist. For example, when Georges Mandel was expelled from the
Radical party in 1911 for breach of party discipline, local leaders justified his dismissal by accusing him of being the agent of Jewish financial interests.[61]

However, the significant locus of anti-Semitism had shifted with
the Dreyfus Affair to the Right. Anti-Semitism became associated
ever more strongly with anti-Republicanism and with support for
Catholic clericalism. The anti-Semitism first popularized by Drumont in the 1880s continued to appeal to the small shopkeepers, artisans, and businessmen who feared the mysterious and crippling
power of big capital. The Jew, already suspect for his foreign origins,
became the readiest symbol for the uncaring new order which was
victimizing the non-rising members of the middle class.

That Jews could use capitalism to exploit hardworking, real
Frenchmen and gain control of the French economy was, to leaders
on the Right, perhaps the most horrifying aspect of the capitalist
Republic. Following Drumont's lead, Barrès pictured the Jews as the
anti-nationalist "conquerors" of France. Their money had enabled
them to "infinitely surpass the normal proportion to which their
numbers would entitle them" in the army, judiciary, the ministries,
and local and national administration.[62] Barrès was not alone. Even
Romain Rolland, who found much in Jews to admire, noted in his
novel *Jean Christophe* that "for the time being they do occupy a position out of all proportion to their true merit. . . . The Jews are like
women: admirable when they are reined in; but with the Jews as with
women their use of mastery is an abomination."[63]

Representatives of the Right, much of the Catholic press, and anti-
Semites of all camps saw the Jewish "domination" of French life as
far more insidious and pervasive than mere economic exploitation.
They viewed the upward mobility of the Jews and their presence
within the French administrative system, and especially in such cultural spheres as journalism, the arts, and letters, as threatening because of their fundamental assumption that even seemingly assimilated Jews were not truly French. Drumont's assertion that Jews were
quick to pick up Parisian jargon but always retained their own style
and accent was extended to the spiritual realm as well:[64] the Jews

were undermining the fundamental values of French society. The French veneer of assimilated Jews was considered to be woefully superficial. Within the depths of their being, French Jews had their own distinctive and alien culture. It was this assumption to which Barrès gave concrete expression in *Les Déracinés*. Jews endangered French culture because they "threatened to transform Frenchmen into copies of themselves, undermining the psychological integrity of the nation."[65]

For many on the Right that erosion of traditional French culture had begun with the Revolution. It was "Jewish" values—democracy, the rights of man, anticlericalism—as Charles Maurras was quick to point out, that had been imposed upon the French nation during the Revolution, and perpetuated by Republicans. "The ancestors of the Revolution," he noted darkly, "spring from the Jewish spirit."[66] Contemporary Jews merely continued to uphold and profit from the principles of rationality, equality, and democracy which denied the emotional and irrational elements of the French national tradition.

Even French liberals contributed to this perception of the Jew as eroder of certain traditional French values by suggesting that Jews, as a group, had a sensibility particular to themselves. With this critical sensibility they could offer new insights to the French people and spur them to greater moral sensitivity and cultural creativity. To Jacques Lacretelle, author of two novels about an intelligent young Jew named Silbermann, the Jew represented the values of the mind in a society succumbing to the cult of force.[67] Romain Rolland, too, saw the Jew as the bearer of reason and expressed the ambivalence so characteristic of all writers who perceived Jews as a distinct group: "The Jews have been true to their sacred mission, which is, in the midst of other races, to be a foreign race, the race which . . . is to link up the network of human unity. They break down the intellectual barriers between the nations, to give Divine Reason an open field."[68]

The outstanding liberal exponent of a special role for the Jews in France, however, was Charles Péguy, the mentor of the pre-World War I generation of French intellectuals. A philo-Semite, he devoted twenty issues of his great journal, *Cahiers de la Quinzaine*, to some aspects of the Jewish question. He also opened its pages to numerous Jewish contributors, among them Edmond Fleg, Joseph Reinach, Julien Benda, André Suarès, and André Spire.[69] Alone among Catholic writers, Péguy was not intent upon converting the Jews. Rather, he defended the Jews of his own time against anti-Semitic calumnies. Neither money nor politics, he argued, was any different for Jews than for non-Jews. In politics, Péguy noted, "the great majority of Jews [were] . . . like the great majority of other voters. . . . They feared trouble."[70]

While Péguy expressed great sympathy for the plight of modern Jews and cleared them of any fault in the lamentable degeneration of the Dreyfus Affair from "mystique" into "politique," he continued to insist upon the survival of a Jewish mission—one hardly conceived to facilitate their acceptance into modern societies.[71] For Péguy the Jews remained "the prophetic race."[72] True, only a small minority of them followed their own prophets, but it was this very capacity to bring forth prophets who would speak the truth to a reluctant world that explained the meaning of Jewish existence: "Being elsewhere— the great vice of that race, the great secret virtue, the great vocation of that people."[73]

For Péguy there was a Jewish mystique, which was to be distinguished from the Jewish politics of silence. Péguy defined the Dreyfus Affair as an explosion of that Jewish mystique, rather than of Jewish politics; further, he defined the Jewish mystique as "Israel follow[ing] in the world her resounding and sorrowful mission."[74] Ironically, while Péguy accepted French Jews as Frenchmen (more wholeheartedly than either Lacratelle or Rolland), his insistence that the Jews' mission was to be a prophetic people and to disturb society by calling for justice again set the Jews apart. There were many in France who were ready to reject the Jews along with, and because of, their prophets.

While Jewish prophets were rare indeed in France of the late nineteenth and early twentieth centuries, Jewish intellectuals and politicians were not averse to airing their views on the major issues of the day. Jews were particularly prominent as reviewers, critics, and art collectors, in short, as cultural middlemen (as Romain Rolland noted approvingly in *Jean Christophe*).[75] Jews in France, both native and foreign, could also be seen in the forefront of radical cultural and artistic movements. Léon Blum, for one, scandalized bourgeois society in 1907 with the publication of *Du Mariage*, the most widely read of his many books. Though he dedicated the book to his wife and touted his own happy marriage, Blum advocated premarital sexual experimentation for young women as well as men.[76] To Catholics and conservative members of the middle class, Blum's critique of bourgeois marriage customs constituted an attack on the heart of morality—healthy family life.

Blum was only one of several Jews—among them Alfred Naquet, Joseph Reinach, and Georges Mandel—who were prominent anticlericals.[77] That sizable bloc of Frenchmen who considered the church as one of the pillars upon which French culture rested were particularly offended when Jewish political personalities attacked the church's power and influence. It was convenient to label the anticlerical campaign a Jewish plot, as Sorel did,[78] for example, though anticlericalism had figured prominently in Radical (and, to a lesser extent, Socialist) politics for almost fifty years. Still, when Blum or Mandel's political positions were criticized, not infrequently their Jewishness entered into the debate.

Moreover, in the two decades before the first World War, Jews played a considerable role in the vitality and excitement of Parisian cultural life. Such Jewish poets as Gustave Kahn, Catulle Mendès, and Ephriam Mikhaël took part in the symbolist and decadent movements. Few would have suggested, even then, that Jews had created the Paris school of artists, or that radical cultural criticism was limited to Jews.[79] However, in a society sensitive still to religious and ethnic differences, the Jewish (and foreign) origins of, for example, Marc Chagall, Chaim Soutine, Amadeo Modigliani, or Gertrude Stein were duly noted. This was ironic, for the vast majority of Jewish intellectuals, radicals, and artists were marginal Jews. Unaffiliated with the organized Jewish community, they took little part in Jewish activity of any sort. Most saw themselves as French intellectuals or artists of Jewish origin. Yet it was these marginal Jews who represented Jewry to the French public. Jewish artists, left-wing Jewish in-

tellectuals like Léon Blum and Julien Benda, Jewish scholars like
Emile Durkheim and Lucien Lévy-Bruhl—who were in the forefront
of new academic disciplines—all symbolized the disturbing intellec-
tual ferment so often associated in the popular mind with Jews. As
Georges Sorel once noted, they represented an assault upon tradition,
a brilliance untempered by concern for hallowed institutions. To cite
Rolland once again, "Unfortunately, the past does not exist for the
Jews."[80]

Many believed that the Jewishness of bohemian artists and radical
politicians, critics, and literary figures was no mere accident or coincidence. Rather, the affinity of Jews for modernist cultural movements and revolutionary political activity was directly attributed to
the secularization of the traditional Jewish opposition to Christian
western culture. Jews had found new means to undermine their ancient enemies. Historically excluded from Christian society, Jews
were now seen as availing themselves of the benefits afforded by liberal society to mount a new attack upon the values dear to the
French bourgeoisie. It mattered little that the majority of French
Jews cherished bourgeois values of family, property, and patriotism
with the ferocity of parvenus eager for acceptance. To Frenchmen
who *a priori* considered Jews alien, the more exotic or radical the
Jew, the more authentically and prototypically Jewish he seemed. No
wonder, then, that the Jewish radical or artist loomed larger than the
conventional Jewish small merchant, minor civil servant, or respectable consistorial leader.

In reality French Jewish intellectuals were not producing their
oeuvres to take their revenge upon the traditional Christian values so
dear to the French bourgeoisie. Rather, Jews in France were comfortable with the cultural and social life of bourgeois society. Emile
Durkheim's sociology, for example, is not the product of an intellectual stimulated by marginality and adrift in society but of a figure
rooted in the stability of his own milieu.[81] True, Jewish intellectuals
were often less restrained by traditional modes of thought, be they
Jewish or Christian, than their Gentile contemporaries. That liberation from tradition of all sorts was one of the effects upon nineteenth-
century European Jews of rapid modernization and acculturation.

Yet the popular image of the Jew is ironic precisely because Jewish intellectuals were both creative and integrated individuals, not the vindictive and rootless beings their antagonists depicted.

Aware of the popular negative image of Jewry, leaders of the organized Jewish community in France measured their own decisions against possible repercussions in the larger society. Like most Jews of the time, they shared the assumption that proper Jewish behavior, combined with efforts at educating the public, would gradually eradicate the anti-Semitic stereotype of the Jew. Perhaps more than Jewish leaders elsewhere, they preferred to rely on a low social profile rather than on antidefamation efforts.

Their sensitivity to the image of the Jew as foreigner and as saboteur of French values was reflected, as we shall see, in their attitudes to immigrant Jews from Eastern Europe. (They preferred to ignore the deep-rooted animus against the Jewish capitalist, for they were unwilling to associate anti-Semitism with their own economic pursuits.) As far as consistorial leaders were concerned, it was crucial that the immigrants quickly adopt French habits and culture to avoid implicating French Jews in their own foreignness. The visibility of Yiddish signs in shops and of immigrants drinking tea rather than wine in cafés was thus perceived as particularly threatening because of the French social and cultural climate. Likewise, even the non-political cultural Zionism of the immigrants, with its intimations of ethnic separatism, seemed to native Jews liable to reinforce the convictions of so much of French society that the Jews remained basically unassimilable. Clearly, no sector of French society appeared willing to tolerate an unassimilable bloc. Finally, native Jewish leaders abhorred the leftist political orientation of immigrant politics, and not primarily because they were themselves members of the moneyed bourgeoisie whose own material interests were at stake. More importantly, they saw in immigrant Jewish revolutionaries a threat to their own status as Jews. For the very existence of Jewish radicals might confirm the view that all Jews sought to rip asunder the fabric of society. The immigrants, the controversial politicians, the bohemian artists thus all cast into doubt the carefully cultivated respectability and patriotism of the organized French Jewish community.

The National Context: The Loss of Confidence

The image of Jews in French public opinion reflects the larger political and cultural mood of France in the Third Republic, a period when French elites were shaken by self-doubt and a sense of constricted possibilities. Growing French sensitivity to the Jews as an alien element within the national body and to the possible pernicious effects of immigration was but one aspect of a larger concern with the capacity of France to maintain its position within Europe. In part, this sense of unease was rooted in demographic facts of which the French public became aware with the census of 1890. Alone among the major European powers, France had entered a period of stagnant population growth. In a stable population the cultural as well as demographic effects of immigration are heightened. Convinced of the superiority of their own cultural heritage, Frenchmen feared being swamped by immigrants whom they might fail to assimilate fully. Hence their obsession with the need for complete and rapid fusion of immigrant populations within France.

Economic factors as well shook the confidence of the French. Because of a lack of coal and the persistence of traditional values inimical to industrialization, France lagged behind both Britain and Germany in the development of an industrial economy and resisted the assimilation of new technological information. As John B. Wolf has remarked, "The French themselves became acutely aware of the gap that was appearing between their economy and that of their more advanced neighbors when the [Paris] World Fair at the opening of the twentieth century dramatically called attention to the technological and industrial development elsewhere."[82] Discussions about the decline of French *élan vital* which first appear at that time are an expression of French anxiety at the prospect of becoming a second-rate power.

France of the Third Republic was thus in a mood of retrenchment. There was little room for generosity to newcomers or for receptivity to those who might challenge the status quo. The renewed emphasis on decadence, which assumed a prominent place in French literature in the 1880s—coincident with the rise of the new anti-Semitism—sig-

naled a loss of confidence in France's ability to maintain its greatness
not only in the economic sphere but also in the arts and in politics.
Even those, like Romain Rolland, who admired Jews for their energy, for their capacity to get things done as cultural middlemen or
capitalist entrepreneurs, were uneasy at the prospect of "excessive"
Jewish influence. Jewish accomplishments, it seemed to them, occurred at the expense of others. Jews could succeed, in part, because
true Frenchmen had lost the *élan* necessary for the competition. Furthermore, the very qualities of entrepreneurial drive which Jews exhibited in their rise into the middle classes were themselves culturally
suspect, even in twentieth-century France.[83]

Such a constricted mood certainly characterized French students
in the decade before and the period immediately after World War I.
While an impressionistic survey of French students published in
1913 stressed the rebirth of patriotic fervor, it also acknowledged the
anxiety evident in the widespread criticism of its own optimism: "You
speak of patriotism, of early marriages, of a Catholic renaissance
. . . and here are the facts: France is becoming depopulated, the
seminaries lack priests, recruitment for Saint-Cyr [the military acade-
my] is more difficult each year. . . ."[84] Moreover, the very nationalism in which the survey exulted often expressed itself in hostility to
foreign competition. Abandoning France's tradition of hospitality to
foreign students, in April 1913 a conference of French medical
students called for a ban on foreign students in the medical faculties
and the exclusion of foreign holders of French medical diplomas
from practice in France. In an economy characterized by slow
growth the upwardly mobile foreigner was a threat.[85]

It was French Jewry's misfortune that large-scale Jewish immigration from the East occurred during the latter part of the Third Republic, when the social mood was so bleak. Although France recognized a need for immigrants following its significant loss of
manpower during World War I, that recognition always coexisted
with ambivalent feelings toward the newcomers. Expressions of paternalism, anxiety, and of a desire for social control and rapid assimilation of the immigrants were common. Fast upon the arrival of the
masses of Jewish immigrants, France experienced the severe eco-

nomic crisis of the 1930s, which brought to the fore the social and
psychological malaise visible even in the early years of the Third
Republic. In a period which witnessed an erosion of faith in parlia-
mentary politics, in the army, in the capacity of the French economy
to bounce back, immigrant Jews from Eastern Europe, visibly different and extremely politicized, were easy targets. Highly sensitive to
the cultural and political values of their homeland (at least where the
immigrants were concerned), native Jews mirrored the suspicion and
loss of *élan* of the larger society.

The Nature of the Community

   Like the lessons of emancipation and the impact of national context, the communal structure of French Jewry promoted political
quietism. Hierarchical and increasingly centralized, the consistorial
system enjoyed a monopoly upon Jewish religious association. In
theory, no public religious service could take place without the approval of consistorial authorities. Moreover, the seventy-four local
Jewish communities in France and Algeria at the turn of the century
depended for spiritual and financial guidance upon the eleven departmental consistories, and especially upon the Central Consistory, located in Paris. The Central Consistory wielded enormous power. It
administered France's only rabbinical school, confirmed the appointment of local rabbis, and named all departmental grand rabbis. Furthermore, the Central Consistory made all policy decisions affecting
French Jewry as a whole and disbursed funds to those local communities which were not self-supporting.[86]
   Throughout the nineteenth century the consistories had become
increasingly dominated by laymen rather than rabbis.[87] In fact, a
small number of upper bourgeois Jews, with the members of the
Rothschild family at their head, administered the institutions.
Though membership was theoretically open to all adult males, a
membership fee was required. Only a small proportion of the eligible
joined the consistories, therefore, and a still ·smaller proportion participated in consistorial elections. The slate endorsed by the consis-

torial leadership was almost always elected, so that the leadership of the consistories was a self-perpetuating oligarchy.[88]

That oligarchy equated the Jewish community with the local consistory. Native leaders were convinced that they had a right, sanctified by a century of governmental support, to be the sole spokesmen for French Jewry. Indeed the legitimacy of the consistorial leadership, its ideological position, and its claim to speak for all Jews in France were not seriously challenged after 1870. An abortive effort had been initiated at mid-century to introduce religious reforms into French Judaism, thus challenging the traditional leadership. However, the proponents of Reform—who, incidentally, were of the same class as the leadership of the consistories—were deprived of an issue when the Central Consistory adopted many of their proposals.[89] Although the centralization and oligarchic nature of consistorial leadership did not go unnoticed, particularly by lower class, more observant Jews who wished to retain their independent *minyanim* (prayer meetings), alternative spokesmen for French Jewry failed to win power.[90] Indifference to consistorial affairs and criticism were common; articulate ideological opposition was not. Consistorial leaders, therefore, were conservative. In their eyes, the ideological and institutional structure of the community had proved itself, even though there were so many unaffiliated Jews. Newcomers would simply have to adapt to the existing institutional framework.

By the end of the nineteenth century the French Jewish community could be described as relatively homogeneous in class, ethnicity, and ideology. Eager to escape from the economic confines of the pre-emancipation period, French Jewry had benefited from the commercial and industrial development of nineteenth-century France. French Jews ranged from clerks, small tradesmen, and middle class professionals, to members of the Jewish financial aristocracy presided over by the Rothschilds; virtually all, however, were of the bourgeoisie, be it *petite* or *haute*.[91]

The community had also become increasingly urbanized, as Alsatian Jews moved first from their small town communities to the major centers of Alsace and Lorraine, and from there to Paris. With the loss of Alsace-Lorraine to Germany in 1871, Paris became the

undisputed center of French Jewry, attracting the numerous Jewish
refugees who could not bear to live as German citizens.[92] By the turn
of the century two-thirds of the 80,000 Jews in France lived in Paris
and her environs.[93]

As the process of assimilation proceeded, the differences between
the descendants of the Ashkenazi Jews of Alsace-Lorraine, who predominated, and the far fewer Sephardi Jews of the South had become
blurred, particularly in Paris. While each group retained its ancestral
rite of worship, religious customs, and local pride, the sociocultural
differences between the groups had been virtually eliminated. With
the ideology of the emancipation accepted by all French Jews, regardless of their origin, a unified Franco-Jewry had come into being.

Standing on the threshold of the twentieth century, that Franco-
Jewry had developed a set of institutions and a definition of Jewish
identity which it declared to be the sole forms acceptable in France.
Its self-definition as a purely religious group, albeit with historical
traditions and ethnic memories, was primary. Hence, its institutions
were confined to the functions ascribed to religious bodies: the administration of religious services, the practice of charity, and the organization of religious education. French Jewry articulated no tension between French and Jewish culture; the principles of Judaism
and the ideals of France were found to be identical. The existence of
a Jewish culture which transcended religious beliefs and practices was
denied, even though nonpracticing Jews were still considered coreligionists and often took part in Jewish philanthropic efforts as a
nonreligious expression of their Jewishness. One served France, according to the accepted ideology, by being a good Jew and one served
Judaism by being true to France.[94]

The Breakdown of the French Jewish Synthesis

Although in the 1880s and 1890s native Jews paid little attention to
the newcomers in their midst, the uniformity of the turn-of-the-cen-
tury French Jewish community was already weakened with the settlement, primarily in Paris, in the years following the Russian pogroms,

of approximately 8,000 Eastern European Jews.[95] In the period between the resolution of the Dreyfus Affair and the outbreak of World
War II, a much larger influx of immigrants transformed French
Jewry in terms of population, ethnicity, institutions, and social
classes. And, as a result of these demographic and social changes, as
well as the political experiences of the interwar years, the ideology
and institutions accepted virtually unanimously by French Jewry
since the mid-nineteenth century were publicly challenged and modified, particularly by the interwar generation of youth. For the ideology of emancipation proved incapable of providing a solution to the
social and political problems of the post-Dreyfus period.

Though not recognized as such by contemporaries, 1906 was a
turning point in many ways. While it saw the Dreyfus Affair finally
laid to rest with the rehabilitation granted its protagonist-victim by
the *Cour de Cassation*, and thus symbolized the restoration of
French Jewry's security and tranquility, it also ushered in a time of
change.

In 1906 the separation of Church and State went into effect. It
struck down the hitherto accepted principle of state support for religious institutions and undermined the consistorial monopoly over
Jewish life in France. With the legal framework for institutional
diversity established, new Jewish institutions could be—and were—
organized independent of the consistories. A "congregation of strict
observance," formed by native Jews from Alsace-Lorraine who found
the traditional Judaism of the consistories too lax, was incorporated in
1906, choosing not to affiliate with the Central Consistory. Likewise,
France's first Reform congregation, the *Union Libérale Israélite*,
which had been rejected by the Paris consistory in 1905, secured
legal recognition as a religious organization in 1907. It provided an
alternative form of Jewish expression for the disaffected upper class
assimilated Parisian Jews who had turned away from the consistory.[96]
Immigrant Jews as well could now legally set up their own religious
associations and select their rabbis free of consistorial supervision.[97]
One group of observant immigrant Jews from the Russian Empire,.
for example, banded their nine smaller congregations into a religious
association called *Agoudas-Hakehillos* (the Union of Congrega-

tions).[98] The erosion of the consistorial monopoly thus stimulated institutional activity and religious pluralism, or denominationalism, a new phenomenon in French Jewish life.[99]

The new law's limitation of the consistories to religious activity, narrowly and rigidly defined, also diminished the attractiveness of the consistories to many French Jews. Since philanthropic activity and social action alike were considered beyond the pale of the legitimate conduct of religion, nonreligious French Jews—and they were the majority—had little incentive to affiliate with the consistory and, at best, only occasional contact with either the religious institutions or titular leadership of French Jewry.[100] Paradoxically, while religion remained the technical basis for Jewish identity in France, it had clearly lost its hold over most French Jews. The membership of the consistory of Paris (France's largest), which had a population ranging from approximately 60,000 in 1905 to 200,000 in 1939 to draw upon, varied from a low of 3,321 in 1907 to a high of 7,114 in 1932.[101] Many French Jews avoided the synagogue, except for *rites de passage*, and some even for those; the numbers of marriages and funerals performed under consistorial auspices indicate that civil marriages and nonreligious funerals were not uncommon.[102] Furthermore, the number of organized Jewish communities and of Jewish officiants declined after the separation of church and state. Before 1905 there had been 74 communities in France and Algeria affiliated with the Central Consistory; by 1931 there remained about 50. Before 1905 France alone had been served by 30 consistorial rabbis; by 1931 that number had been reduced to 17.[103] Religious institutions in general were on the decline, and Jews who wished to express their Jewish identity in socially acceptable but not explicitly religious ways affiliated with institutions other than the consistories. Though the consistories retained power and prestige far beyond what their membership figures would suggest, new institutions were established to serve the social, cultural, and religious needs of Jews in France, often in ways alien to the mentality of the native Jewish leadership.

The bearers of social change were Eastern European immigrants and their children. While France had received relatively few immigrants in the years following the Russian pogroms of 1881–82, in

1906 there was an upsurge of Jewish immigration from Russia, as a result of the failure of the Revolution of 1905 and of the governmental repression which followed. Between 1906 and 1939 an estimated 150,000 to 200,000 Jews settled in France. More than 75 percent of these new immigrants came from the countries of Eastern Europe, approximately 15 percent from the Levant and North Africa, and some 5 to 8 percent from Central Europe.[104] The East European immigrants brought with them a folk culture, customs, and ideologies alien to French Jewry. The blatant ethnicity as well as the cultural and political interests of the immigrants could not be accommodated within the religiously defined community. Moreover, eager to perpetuate their traditions, the immigrant groups established their own institutions, which challenged the long-standing claim of the consistorial circles to speak for all of French Jewry.

The French Jewish community which confronted the crises of the 1930s was very different from and far more complex than the community which had faced the Dreyfus Affair. In the interwar period French Jewry, in fact, became two communities, united neither in acknowledged spokesmen nor in proposed strategies to deal with the fierce xenophobia and anti-Semitism which arose as responses to the economic depression and the social tensions of the 1930s. The experiences of the interwar years and the new constellation of French Jewry converged to erode the French Jewish synthesis which had been established during the nineteenth century. Though most of the changes in post-World War II French Jewry have been attributed to the impact of the Holocaust, the establishment of the State of Israel, and massive immigration from North Africa, in fact they were set in motion in the years preceding the war. For the growing diversity of France's Jews in the first four decades of the twentieth century reopened, for the first time since the emancipation, the question of the nature of Jewish institutional and political activity in France.

2.
The Golden Age of Symbiosis

The changes that mass immigration was initiating were not apparent to French Jews until after the First World War. Although Jewish immigrants were settling in Paris in uncomfortably large numbers and straining the resources of native philanthropy, they appeared to French Jews as a nuisance—as clients seeking assistance, not as claimants to partnership in French Jewish life. Furthermore, they were seen as temporary settlers who might move on to the welcoming shores of America or return to a less hostile Russian homeland.

In 1906 French Jews had something other than immigrants on their mind. They were caught up in the exhilaration surrounding the reversal of Dreyfus's conviction. For French Jewry the end of the Dreyfus Affair marked the symbolic commencement of an era of tranquility and security which lasted through World War I. French Jews felt themselves once more an integral part of the French nation and were convinced that the spectre of anti-Semitism would haunt them no longer. They knew they had achieved a synthesis of French and Jewish interests, and the French government acknowledged this as well.

The symbiotic relationship of France and her Jews found expression both in the personal successes of individual Jews and in the communal behavior of French Jewry. The relationship between French Jews and their homeland was never more beneficial. As individuals, Jews took advantage of the educational and economic opportunities available to them and attained prominence in the arts, in academe, and in commerce. By doing so, they made considerable contributions to the intellectual and economic life of France. In the prosperity of the pre-war years, they flourished.

As a community French Jewry also thrived. Just before World War I, there were even signs of what was called a Jewish Renaissance, as some French Jews found the political and cultural climate more conducive to the expression of their Jewishness. Though religious indifference remained a matter of concern for the organized Jewish community, communal institutions basked in quiet stability while communal leaders expressed their renewed sense of security by defending Jewish interests resolutely and with greater assertiveness. They also found means for the community to serve France by disseminating French culture abroad. Particularly through the schools of the Alliance Israélite Universelle, as the government was well aware, French Jewry indoctrinated important and strategic Jewish communities in Egypt, Morocco, the Balkans, and the Levant with love of France and her culture.[1]

During the war the atmosphere generated by the *union sacrée* confirmed in French Jewry its sense of respected membership in the family of France. The war offered France's Jews an opportunity to prove their patriotism not only on the battlefield but also by volunteering to seek support among American Jews for French political interests. They could point with pride to the fact that the French government encouraged, and welcomed, their efforts as an agent of French interests.

The years 1906–18 can thus be seen as a golden age for French Jewry, as the last act of the French Jewish synthesis of the nineteenth century. While the seeds of future social problems had already been sown both within the Jewish community and within the larger society, they were not to sprout until the conclusion of World War I.

The Restoration of Tranquility

The Dreyfus Affair had led to no major changes in either the institutions or the mentality of the organized French Jewish community, though it did bring some Jews back to Judaism. The felicitous, if long-delayed, conclusion of the Affair confirmed in French Jewry its love of and confidence in its native land. As an editorial in *Archives israélites* noted, "The Dreyfus Affair has concluded for the Israelites and its conclusion would make us love even more, were that possible, our dear country."[2] The policy of political neutrality had worked so well for the organized Jewish community that its leadership was content to mark the passing of the Dreyfus Affair with newspaper editorials alone. Narcisse Leven, president of the Alliance Israélite Universelle and a member of the Central Consistory, suggested that the latter body send a letter of congratulations to Captain Dreyfus; his proposal was tabled as inappropriate.[3] In a retrospective evaluation of the Dreyfus Affair a writer for the *Univers israélite*, focusing on the impact of the crisis on the nation and on the Jewish community, expressed the prevailing sentiment of the organized Jewish community. The Affair, he commented, "had particularly fortunate results for our coreligionists, for in giving birth to the Dreyfus Affair, anti-Semitism had died."[4]

Although most French Jews seem not to have realized it at the moment, the obituary for French anti-Semitism was premature. True, it had declined from its peak during the years of the Affair; nevertheless, it retained its appeal in the conservative and nationalist circles which considered themselves the real victims of the Affair. In 1908 Charles Maurras began to publish the royalist and anti-Semitic daily *Action Française*. The paper preached an integral nationalism to be achieved by regulating or expelling those alien elements— prominent among them, the Jews—who were undermining French society because they lacked French roots and sensibility.[5] The same year witnessed the formation of the *Camelots du Roi*, auxiliary youth gangs of the *Action Française*, who hawked the movement's paper, demonstrated at republican ceremonies, and disrupted plays of Jewish dramatists. The most famous campaign against a Jewish playwright occurred in 1911 when the *Comédie Française* produced *Après Moi* by Henri Bernstein. The *Camelots du Roi* exploited the fact that Bernstein had deserted the French army in his youth. After a series of virulently anti-Semitic demonstrations, Bernstein, under official pressure, withdrew his play. In 1910 the gangs also disfigured the commemorative statue erected in Nîmes to the prominent Jewish Dreyfusard, Bernard Lazare.[6]

In the years preceding World War I, the *Camelots du Roi* intensified their activity. They were particularly active in the Latin Quarter of Paris, disrupting courses of Jewish professors. In 1911, for

example, after riots with republican students, they forced the resignation of the Jewish dean of the Faculty of Law, Lyon-Caen.[7] And yet,
while a number of Jewish intellectuals and professionals, among
them André Spire, Henri Franck, Jean-Richard Bloch, and Edmond
Fleg, took note of the persistence of an anti-Semitic movement in
France and gathered each Sunday at Spire's home to take lessons in
sword and pistol,[8] their attitude did not reflect the public mood of
French Jewry. Though the Alliance Israélite did donate, secretly,
2,000 francs to the League of Rights of Man for its campaign against
the anti-Semitic press, neither the Jewish newspapers nor the minutes
of the major communal institutions reveal much concern with anti-
Semitism in the years 1906–1914.[9] The *Univers israélite*, for example, took note of Lyon-Caen's resignation, "as a result of the
recent incidents," in a terse three-line communiqué printed at the
back of the issue among miscellaneous news reports.[10] With governmental power securely in the hands of the Dreyfusards, anti-Semitism could be dismissed, in the words of the English-language Paris
Daily Mail, as the "political weapon wielded by two minorities. . . .
the *Action Française* . . . and a few revolutionaries."[11]

Jewish leaders reacted vigorously, rather than languishing in indifference or waiting for non-Jewish protectors, when they perceived legitimate Jewish interests to be threatened. This reflected the sense of
security experienced by French Jewry. The defense of Jewish religious interests and the redress of instances of discrimination were,
as we have noted, exempted from the unofficial ideological ban on
Jewish political activity. Moreover, the Jewish community rightly expected the French government to treat its Jewish citizens equally with
all others. Therefore, between the end of the Dreyfus Affair and the
outbreak of World War I, the Central Consistory engaged in political
activity occasioned by two issues: revision of the "Blue Laws" and the
complicity of the French government in Russian discrimination
against French citizens of the Jewish faith.

In 1906 the Chamber of Deputies and Senate had under consideration legislation proscribing business activity on Sunday. Throughout
1906—when the bill was being formulated and passed—and 1907,
the Central Consistory deliberated what means would be most effec-

tive in securing the exemption of observant Jews from the Sunday Blue Laws.[12] The Central Consistory was not averse to active lobbying on this issue. A delegation was sent to the Senate Commission which was dealing with the legislation; letters were written to the historian Théodore Reinach to interest him in the matter; a report was submitted to the Commission of Labor of the Chamber of Deputies.[13] Debate within the Central Consistory focused on arguments to be presented in behalf of the Jewish position. There was considerable opposition, articulated particularly by Narcisse Leven and the president of the Consistory, Baron Edouard de Rothschild, to posing the question on religious grounds. Rather, it was suggested, the issue should be formulated as a matter of liberty of conscience; everyone should be permitted to choose his own day of rest.[14] This preference for appealing to the universalist principle of individual liberty is understandable. As a minority, Jews have, whenever possible, attempted to subsume their own particular interests under those general principles which have been found acceptable by the majority population. A liberal government was expected to respond more favorably to a matter presented as deprivation of individual rights rather than as special treatment for Jews.

In the end, both elements found expression in the Consistory's approach to the legislative commission. Its report, drafted by Isaie Levaillant, stressed liberty of conscience and the right to work as well as the demands imposed by Judaism on its faithful adherents. The law as passed in 1906 allowed no exceptions for Jews; they would have to close their businesses two days a week. In summation the report stated, "We ask simply that just as the various needs created by business interests or the public interest have been taken into account through numerous exceptions, one should equally take into account, through a new exception, the necessities imposed upon Israelites by the practice of their cult."[15] Although objections to this report had been raised within the Central Consistory on the ground that it overemphasized the religious question,[16] a letter briefly summarizing the report's arguments was transmitted to the appropriate legislative commission in December, 1907.

The fact that the report was not communicated in full provided the

Univers israélite with a reason for publishing a critical article, charging that certain members of the Central Consistory had been anxious to suppress the report. "One is an Israelite, of course, but one shouldn't be too obvious about it," noted the correspondent sarcastically. "Don't speak of the Decalogue to the deputies; it wouldn't be well taken."[17] The paper called upon all Jews, the consistories, and the rabbinate to take further measures to defend the Jewish Sabbath. Indeed, the Central Consistory did discuss the need for establishing a special commission that would approach the government with a view to gaining its support for the desired exemption of observant Jews from the Blue Laws.[18] That such an outspoken article could appear in the pages of the Jewish press and that the Central Consistory would involve itself in a legislative battle over the matter is extremely revealing. It gives ample indication of French Jewry's confidence that such behavior was politically acceptable and of its decision that the potential response of anti-Semites was no deterrent.

Even more striking was the political activity of the Central Consistory in response to the discrimination suffered by French citizens of the Jewish faith in Russia. In order to travel or reside in Russia, a French Jew had to have his religion stamped on his French passport. If not a merchant, he also required special permission for a visa. While in Russia, he was subject to a three-month limitation of his stay, restrictions on his mobility, and to discriminatory monetary levies.[19] French Jews felt particularly indignant about their government's compliance with Russian requests regarding passports and visas. They felt that they were being denied the equal protection of French laws to which their proudly vaunted citizenship entitled them. In March of 1909, therefore, the Permanent Section of the Central Consistory established a subcommission to study ways of bringing the question to the attention of government circles.[20] Its report detailed Jewish grievances against the French government and expressed its shock at the complicity of French authorities: "The instructions given to establish this sort of collaboration are in such violent disagreement with all the principles which guide governmental policies . . . that we cannot keep from thinking that they were obtained by surprise and ordered inadvertently."[21] Having endorsed the report, the Central Consistory decided to broach the matter with the Minister of the Interior, who was responsible for the delivery of passports. Since the issue was an international one, affecting Jews of many countries, efforts were also made to gather information, through the Alliance Israélite Universelle and through rabbinic contacts with the Chief Rabbi of England, about negotiations with the Russian government on this matter.[22] Finally, on December 19, 1909, a delegation of the Central Consistory, headed by the Baron Edmond de Rothschild, paid a visit to Aristide Briand, president of the Council of Ministers, to protest the discrimination against French citizens of the Jewish faith.[23]

This political activism on the part of the major organization of French Jewry was not successful. The Franco-Russian alliance was too important an aspect of French foreign policy to be endangered for the sake of France's Jewish minority. All that the Minister of Foreign Affairs, Stephen Pichon, was prepared to promise on December 27, 1909, during a debate in the Chamber of Deputies, was to enter into negotiations with the Russian government with a view to achieving a satisfactory interpretation of the treaty of 1905.[24] The issue, still unresolved, was again discussed by the Central Consistory in 1912, while the Alliance Israélite protested the matter to the French government during World War I.[25] The leaders of the Central Consistory expressed the hope that the question would be resolved by the new commerce treaty between the U.S. and Russia. Eugène Sée, who was handling the matter both for the Central Consistory and for the Alliance, was prepared to continue his efforts with the French government, but he noted the latter's reluctance to approach the Russian government on this matter.[26]

In spite of the less than satisfactory outcome of its intervention, the active and public concern evinced by the Central Consistory represents a sharp break with the quietism it had maintained during the years of the Dreyfus Affair. True, the Central Consistory continued to rely primarily on the traditional Jewish policy of *shtadlanut*, personal and discreet contact of prominent members of the community with governmental figures. However, unlike Jewish political activity in the pre-emancipation period, the political action of the Central

Consistory was based not on the application of Jewish economic pressure to buy privileges but on the exertion of political and moral pressure to protect rights. French Jews assumed that there existed a social and political consensus that condemned discrimination against French citizens, whatever their faith. Therefore, they expected governmental circles to recognize that the legal order had been violated and to redress that social injustice.

The leaders of organized French Jewry were acting as insiders, confident of their membership in the social and political order, though cognizant of the continuing lapses of that order. As one rabbi stated in a widely circulated public speech, "We are French, not only through affection and by choice, but also by temperament."[27] The election of Henri Bergson as the first Jewish member of the Académie Française on February 12, 1914, symbolized for the Jewish community of France its final acceptance as a member of the family. The last bastion of exclusivity, "the last and highest citadel of the national tradition," had admitted a Jew into its ranks. French Jewry had contributed to French culture at its summit and hence could bask in this confirmation of its sense of belonging.[28]

Anticlericalism and the Decline of Tradition

For the vast majority of French Jews, the period of social and political tranquility was accompanied by religious and cultural indifference. The official leadership of the Jewish community could not speak for those who found their Jewishness to be a social stigma and psychological burden or for those who had abandoned Judaism in the name of universalism. Concern mounted in consistorial circles about the extent of civil marriage among Jews, the number of synagogue seats left unrented and unoccupied, the general inability of French Jews to read Hebrew, and the spread of the free-thinking ideology associated with the anticlerical sector of republicanism.[29] Such indifference, it was posited in the Jewish press, stemmed from a misunderstanding of the fundamental nature of French Judaism: "Living in the midst of the war against clericalism and ignorant of the true spirit of Judaism, they [i.e., Jews who chose not to join the Consistory] believe . . . that the religion of Israel tends to impose on its adherents a political line of conduct and to cause a particular system of government to prevail."[30]

A community which claimed religion as the sole legitimate basis of Jewish identity faced two fundamental problems in twentieth-century France. It found it difficult to counteract the free-thinking spirit of the age and to appeal to the majority of Jews, who were nonobservant. Justifying its separateness in religious terms was particularly constricting in the period of republican anticlericalism. Its institutions—except, perhaps, for the philanthropic—would not attract the secular Jew. Indeed, even Jewish philanthropy depended upon a sense of solidarity with coreligionists which was waning among those who were either indifferent to Judaism or, worse still, conscious of their Jewish origins only as a liability. French Jewish institutions could offer to the nonbelieving Jew no rationale for remaining Jewish without unmasking the basic fiction that the Jewish community could be defined solely in terms of religion.

The situation of mass indifference which confronted the religious leadership of French Jewry stimulated vain attempts at creative religious reform within the framework of traditional Jewish law. In the pre-war years, much time and imaginative thinking was mobilized in attempts to stem the tide of secularism. The meetings of the Association of French Rabbis were devoted to discussions of how to come to terms with the reality of sparse participation in local religious life and how to stimulate greater interest. Proposals were considered with a view to lowering the number of persons legally required for a *minyan* (the quorum for public prayer) and to counting women as eligible for at least part of that quorum.[31] Equally reflective of the religious status of French Jewry was the 1911 decision of the Association of French Rabbis to admit uncircumcised male children to courses of religious instruction (while denying them authorization for the celebration of the *bar-mitzvah*). Reserved for later discussion was the question whether the marriage of an uncircumcised Jew could receive the blessing of a religious ceremony.[32] In order to encourage religious marriages the rabbinate, at the prompting of lay leaders,

lifted the traditional ban on weddings during the mourning period
between the 17th day of Tammuz and the first of Ab (which falls during the summer months) and authorized their celebration with customary pomp and ceremony.[33]

On the other hand, to stimulate interest in religious affairs, both
the lay leadership and the rabbinate proposed a series of minor li-
turgical reforms, such as the abridgement of religious services, recita-
tion of more prayers in French, and the institution of the triennial
cycle in the reading of the Torah.[34] French Jewish leadership did not
insist on more innovative reforms, realizing that the opposition to
them of traditional immigrant rabbis could undermine the very legitimacy of the French rabbinate among the immigrant population.
Moreover, they felt that French Jews, though not personally observant, wanted whatever Judaism they sampled to remain traditional in
form. Looking to the future, the French rabbinate recognized the
need for improving the poor state of Jewish education.[35] The late
nineteenth and early twentieth centuries had witnessed the decline of
sectarian Jewish schools. Moreover, the structure of the French public school system, with its long hours and rigorous standards, retarded
the development of intensive Jewish education. Instruction was provided a few hours a week in the *lycées* for those students who
requested it, but the anticlerical temper of the times, combined with
the suppression of the government subsidy in 1908, limited the effectiveness of that mode of education.[36] Little improvement was noted
before the advent of World War I. In 1913 a young rabbi was still
lamenting the indifference of Jewish youth to Judaism.[37]

The Return of the Intellectuals

Despite the widespread indifference to their religion among the
masses of French Jewry, a new element of symbiosis emerged after
the Dreyfus Affair. It took the form of the unprecedented return of
prominent Jewish intellectuals to Jewish cultural interests. So striking
was this phenomenon that the activity which the returning intellec-

tuals organized and inspired occasioned prophecies of a revival of Judaism in France. In 1913 the *Univers israélite* announced,

> This new affirmation of Jewish personality, this sort of resurrection of French and universal Judaism is signaled notably in Paris by a variety of efforts, of organizations, of institutions touching upon all the branches of human activity: creation of study groups, circles of artisans, societies to stimulate Jewish literature, committees for religious publications and observance of the sabbath . . . , in short, a series of measures appropriate to invigorating our anemic cult. [38]

This assessment of the revival of Jewish activity is substantiated by a review of the Jewish press and publications. *Foi et réveil*, a new intellectual Jewish periodical founded "to present in a simple and attractive manner the principles and aspirations of Judaism and to revive or maintain in the hearts of Israelites love of and respect for our faith," made its first appearance in 1913. [39] Moreover, two issues of a *Revue hébraique*, specifically devoted to Hebrew and to ancient and modern Jewish literature, were published by the *Cercle Hebraea* of Paris, a group of intellectuals of immigrant origin and Zionist sympathies. [40] Most significantly, between 1906 and 1914 the work of a number of consciously Jewish writers first saw the light of day. André Spire's *Poèmes juifs* was published in 1908; Jean-Richard Bloch's early stories on Jewish themes in 1911; Henri Franck's "La Danse devant l'arche" appeared in Péguy's *Cahiers de la Quinzaine* in 1912, and Edmond Fleg's collection of poems, *Ecoute, Israël*, in 1913. [41]

This proliferation of writings on Jewish themes was a new phenomenon altogether. While by the last half of the nineteenth century Jews had been well represented among French intellectuals, they had avoided public reflections about their Jewishness. Assimilation had "resolved" the Jewish question for them; in their own eyes they were French intellectuals, no different from the rest. The anti-Semitism unleashed by the Dreyfus Affair, however, compelled a number of Jewish intellectuals, with André Spire as their eldest statesman, to explore the meaning of their differentness in French society.

Born in 1868 into an upper middle class Jewish family engaged in the glovemaking industry, André Spire was an assimilated Jewish poet and successful civil servant. If he had any special identity, it was his sense of himself as a son of the province of Lorraine. His Jewishness was neither important nor particularly problematic in his youth, for he was indifferent to religious matters.[42] Nevertheless, in the twentieth century Spire was to become a prominent intellectual critic of the Jewish establishment and an articulate Jewish nationalist.

Spire recognized the significance of the Dreyfus Affair as the turning point for Jewish intellectuals like himself. His pride as a Jew had been aroused by the anti-Semitic attacks of the Drumont circle and of the anti-Dreyfusards. His discovery of the impoverished Eastern European immigrant proletariat during a trip to London in 1902 and his reading of Israel Zangwill's *Chad Gadya*, a novel of an immigrant Jewish youth whose assimilation leads ultimately to despair, triggered his active interest in Zionism and Jewish culture.[43] As Spire himself later related of the period beginning with the Dreyfus Affair, "French Jews who had lost all contact with Jewish life, who were ignorant of virtually all of Jewish history began to study them with fervor. Instead of seeking, as before, to hide their Jewish souls . . . [they published] Jewish poems, Jewish novels, Jewish dramas and comedies."[44]

Edmond Fleg's spiritual odyssey confirms Spire's analysis. The son of an observant Jewish family of Geneva, Fleg had abandoned his faith in his teenage years. Devoting himself to his secular studies, he found that the Jewish culture with which he was familiar was no match for the sublime treasures of Western culture. He no longer felt himself to be a Jew.[45] "It was the Dreyfus Affair which revived my Judaism," declared Fleg in an interview many years later. "I already had a literary career; one of my plays had been performed at the *Comédie Française*, another at the *Opéra*. I abandoned all that, devoured as I was by the Jewish question. I read all I could on that subject and I published my works."[46] Fleg's prolific literary creativity on Jewish themes, his publicly articulated Zionist sympathies, and his active work with the Jewish scout movement were to make him in the interwar period the mentor of those Jewish youths who were seeking a return to their roots. Though he was less directly involved in political activity, Fleg, like Spire, became a voice to be reckoned with from outside the conservative ranks of the native Jewish leadership.

By 1914 a French Jewish literature, imbued with both French and Jewish concerns and sensibility, had come into being. It continued to flourish through the interwar period. Jewish writers, with Fleg and Spire in the forefront, had found their experience as Jews to be a valid source for a creative contribution to French culture.

The renewed interest in Jewish culture on the part of French Jewish intellectuals expressed itself not only in literary creativity but also in the formation of groups devoted to the study and propagation of Jewish culture. In a period in which French intellectuals assumed ever more prominently a public role, their Jewish counterparts, too, shouldered the responsibility of moral leadership which they had formerly shunned. Although they did not frequently challenge consistorial circles, throughout the period from 1906 to 1939 they did offer, through their group activity and individual leadership, the possibility of an alternative; a nonreligious form of Jewish identity. Particularly in the interwar years they also took upon themselves the defense of Judaism and articulated independent positions on vital Jewish questions at a time when consistorial leadership was becoming increasingly cautious.

The most prominent and ambitious of the pre-World War I intellectual Jewish groups was the "Amis du Judaïsme," founded in 1913 by an illustrious group of intellectuals, among them the symbolist poet Gustave Kahn, the jurist Victor Basch and the composer Darius Milhaud (both professors at the Sorbonne), Grand Rabbi Israel Lévi, Jacques Hadamard (professor of mathematics at the *Collège de France*), Salomon Reinach (member of the Institut), and Edmond-Maurice Lévy (the librarian of the Sorbonne).[47] As the successor organization to the Society for Jewish History and Literature, established the year before by students who styled themselves "Heroes of the Jewish Renaissance," the "Amis du Judaïsme" appealed to all those, Jews and non-Jews alike, who wished to study Jewish thought and culture of the past as well as the present and enrich themselves "by examining moral and social questions in the light of Judaism."[48] Judaism, as seen by these distinguished thinkers, was a source of intellectual and moral wisdom, a patrimony to be proud of, and one which all Jews had the duty to cultivate. Because the group hoped to attract Jews of differing levels of religious commitment and interest, it declared itself to be religiously neutral and organized itself along the lines of disinterested, but morally valuable, study so attractive to French intellectuals.

Admittedly it was anti-Semitism which had stimulated the interest of many of the irreligious intellectuals in their Jewish heritage.[49] However, they had come together not to engage directly in battle against discrimination, but to declare publicly the positive value of Judaism as a constituent of *universal* culture—hence the appeal to non-Jews. By invoking thus *Judaism's* general value, they expected to enhance the status of the *Jews* as the heirs and bearers of Jewish culture. As Gustave Kahn, president of the society, stated in its 1914 general assembly, the Amis du Judaïsme wanted "to penetrate the life of Judaism, propagate it, and consequently justify it."[50] Thus, interest originally generated by anti-Semitism flowered independently of constant anti-Semitic pressure. As Salomon Reinach noted in his speech at the initial meeting of the group, "Even when anti-Semitism has ceased . . . Judaism must not therefore disappear. . . . Judaism is the noblest and most considerable moral personality which Humanity has ever known, first because it is the most ancient in existence today . . . and then because . . . Judaism represents that which must impose itself one day on all consciences, the ideal of justice."[51] Because anti-Semitism constituted no immediate threat, Jewish intellectuals were free to study Judaism and express their Jewishness in literary forms rather than in direct self-defense.

The Position of Jews in French Society

The attempt to establish the respectability of Jewish culture in France was natural for French Jews, for they had achieved prominence—anti-Semites would have said notoriety—in so many sectors of French life. For individual Jews France, far more than Germany, remained a land of opportunity and integration.

Despite the claims of Drumont and his sympathizers and successors, the French economy was not dominated by Jews. However, the visibility of wealthy Jewish banking families (like the Rothschilds and Péreires) and of Jewish industrialists lent credence to anti-Semitic charges and conveyed the impression that French Jews as a whole had prospered under capitalism as the solid French peasant and burgher had not.

There are no statistics on the professional distribution of native French Jews on the eve of World War I. Whatever information is available is descriptive and impressionistic in nature. All of it indicates that native Jewry was overwhelmingly middle class; the Jewish working class which came into existence in France between 1880 and 1914 was almost without exception composed of immigrants from Central and Eastern Europe.

Native Jews were engaged in large numbers in banking and commerce. At the top of the social scale were the great banking families of Paris, the Rothschilds, Péreires, Lazards, and Finalys. According to one estimate, one-third of Paris bankers were Jews.[52] While by 1914 many of the Jews in this highest economic stratum had assimilated totally into the upper layers of French society and abandoned any formal identification with the Jewish community, the Rothschilds were the dominant figures in Jewish communal life. The presidency of both the Paris Consistory and the Central Consistory had virtually become a patrimony of the Rothschild House. The Rothschilds were both the spokesmen for and the symbol of French Jewry, living proof of the fact that Jews could totally assimilate in the country's culture and society, and yet remain loyal to their ancestral Jewish heritage.[53]

Not all were Rothschilds, though. Most native Jews moved in more modest economic circles. Within the world of finance, they worked as agents and stock brokers. In commerce they were concentrated in several lines of supply, most notably the garment industry, leather goods, jewelry, and furniture. They served as cloth and silk brokers, wholesalers in furs and leather skins and machinery, and as retail merchants in cloth, clothing, jewelry, and furnishings.[54] Native Jews also invested in and operated factories, particularly in the garment and light machinery industries.[55]

By the end of the nineteenth century a large sector of the native

Jewish middle class had left finance and commerce for the professions, the lower and middle levels of the civil service, and politics. Each weekly edition of the *Univers israélite* ran a column entitled "Nominations et distinctions" which chronicled the professional advancement of French Jewry by publicizing the honors meted out to individual Jews. It is clear that by 1900 the *embourgeoisement* of native French Jewry was an accomplished fact. Doctors, *lycée* instructors, and professors abounded, along with the more numerous *négociants* and industrialists admitted as *Chevaliers de la Légion d'Honneur* or *Chevaliers du merite agricole.*[56] With the admission of André Spire, Léon Blum, and Paul Grunebaum-Ballin to the *Conseil d'Etat*[57] even the highest ranks of the civil service had been infiltrated by Jews. Furthermore, while Jews constituted less than .25 percent of the French population, in the years between 1906 and 1914 the three to six Jews in the Chamber of Deputies ranged from .5 to 1 percent of the Chamber. Only within the ranks of the police and the army officer corps, where traditional prejudices were strong, were there few Jews to be found.[58] French Jewry took quiet pride in these respectable accomplishments.

The column of "Nominations et distinctions," it was stated, was not printed out of boastfulness. Rather, it was meant to provide "facts and examples" in order to repudiate the anti-Semitic lies about the inferiority of the Jews.[59] French Jews felt that the contribution of their manifold talents to the French economy merited general approbation and signaled the success of their emancipation and of their symbiosis with French society.

Jews were particularly prominent in the intellectual world. With the Dreyfus Affair French intellectuals assumed a position of unprecedented leadership on both sides of the struggle, and within Dreyfusard circles, as well as within the university, Jewish intellectuals were represented far beyond their proportion in the general population. Individual Jewish professors, such as the philosopher Henri Bergson, the sociologist Emile Durkheim, the anthropologist Lucien Lévy-Bruhl, and Léon Brunschwicg, to name but a few of the most outstanding, helped shape the mentality of pre-war French youth.[60] Of Bergson it has been stated that he "was in a very special sense the presiding spirit of the generation of [Péguy's] *Cahiers*, and [Daniel] Halévy . . . has recounted how [Bergson's] teaching, after first casting its spell on his students at the *Ecole Normale*, had later taken by storm all those who . . . had flocked to his lectures at the *Collège de France*." [61] While it would be difficult by any standards to characterize the thought of these men as "Jewish," the very fact of their Jewish origin has much to say about the intellectual predilections of Jews and the opportunities for their professional success in the French society of the period.

Péguy's circle, in particular, attracted numerous Jews. Those of his disciples who were least sympathetic to Jews—Georges Sorel for one—attributed Péguy's philo-Semitism to his economic dependence upon Jewish benefactors and readers. [62] From its early days many of the subscribers to the *Cahiers* had been Jews, and Jews frequented Péguy's bookstore. Péguy himself acknowledged of the Jews, "It is they who provide me with a living." [63] Not only were Jews responsible for the success of the *Cahiers*; they were also instrumental in establishing *L'Humanité*. It was Halévy, Blum, Lévy-Bruhl, and other wealthy Jews in Jaurès's circle who exploited their family connections with Parisian bankers to acquire loans which provided the financial backing necessary for the enterprise. [64] Likewise, Jews were active in publishing. Ironically, the publication of Sorel's *Reflections on Violence*, for example, was partly financed through the efforts of André Spire and Daniel Halévy. [65] Moreover, some of the more fashionable literary salons were conducted by intellectuals of Jewish extraction. [66] While the ideology of emancipation had mandated a rather quiet Jewish group presence in French life, the reality of emancipation had enabled individual Jews to rise to prominence.

The Jews and the War

It was the wholehearted participation of Jews in France's war effort during World War I rather than their professional accomplishments which served to reinforce their sense of security and belonging and to put into abeyance some of the popular suspicion of the Jews. Even a former antagonist like Maurice Barrès admitted that the war helped to integrate the Jews more firmly into French life. For Barrès acknowledged for the first time that "many Israelites, settled among us for generations, and centuries, are natural members of the national body."[67] Moreover, he recounted the heroic exploits of native, immigrant, and Algerian Jews. While Barrès qualified his endorsement of Jewish patriotism by adding that the Jewish commitment to France was intellectual rather than instinctual[68]—and Barrès favored instinct above intellect—that qualification was overlooked by the leadership of French Jewry.

The war provided the Jews with an opportunity to write in blood their love for France and to engage in political activity on behalf of the fatherland. The *union sacrée*, which called upon all Frenchmen to put aside their differences and devote themselves to *la patrie*, became the watchword of Jewish institutions: they saw in the Jewish contributions to the war effort—which they publicized—the most persuasive proof of, and argument in behalf of, their equality as Frenchmen. Even when the *union sacrée* began to disintegrate, French Jews stubbornly clung to it.

For French Jewry the war demonstrated the full commonality of French and Jewish interests. If France longed for the return of the two lost provinces of Alsace and Lorraine, the longing of the Jews was especially personal and deep, for Alsace-Lorraine was the heartland of their community.[69] If the triumph of the French cause meant the diffusion of the spirit of justice and liberty, was it not this very spirit that had brought about the Jews' own emancipation as well?[70] Even France's alliance with anti-Semitic Russia was welcomed: Russia, so went the argument, would aid the French war effort and might be influenced, through its association with France, to improve the treatment of its own Jewish subjects.[71]

Patriotism and religion marched arm in arm throughout the war. Memorial services were organized for fallen Jewish soldiers, not only to demonstrate the part played by Jews in the defense of the fatherland, but also, according to Rabbi Israel Lévi, to strengthen patriotism "by joining to it religious sentiment."[72] In an era in which patriotism had become sacred, the alliance of patriotism and religion enhanced the image of Judaism as well.

French Jewish institutions enjoyed close cooperation with the government. Thirty-seven rabbis served in the chaplaincy which was organized for each army corps, ministering particularly to regiments with numerous Jews and to the wounded in hospitals, and visiting German Jewish prisoners of war. [73] The government accepted the procedure instituted by the Central Consistory to identify the Jewish dead and replace the crosses on their graves with simple markers. [74] The Chief Rabbi of France, Albert Lévy, noted with great satisfaction that his letter to the Minister of War, asking that arrangements be made to facilitate the celebration of the Jewish holidays by Jewish soldiers had yielded favorable results. [75]

The *union sacrée* on the battlefield, particularly the close cooperation of Jewish and non-Jewish soldiers and chaplains, was hailed in the Jewish press and in consistorial reports. Chief Rabbi Lévy singled out for comment the actions of a priest who had mimeographed and distributed Rabbi Joseph Cohen's note on the Jewish holidays, while the story of Chaplain Abraham Bloch, who was killed in action while bearing a crucifix to a wounded Catholic soldier, was given wide publicity. [76]

With patriotism approved as apolitical, the Central Consistory determined to serve French interests in its special capacity as official leader of French Jewry. It felt it could best do so by working among its coreligionists, particularly those in the U.S., who were being courted by German propaganda. [77] Thus, in October of 1915 the Central Consistory published an "Appeal of French Israelites to the Israelites of Neutral Countries" and, along with the Alliance Israélite Universelle, in January of 1916 established the French Information and Action Committee among Jews of Neutral Countries (Comité français d'information et d'action auprès des Juifs des pays neutres). Deliberately nonsectarian in composition, the Committee was composed primarily of Jews prominent in academic circles and of liberal non-Jewish deputies. While its president was a former government minister, Georges Leygues, its vice-president and secretary, Sylvain

Lévi and Jacques Bigart, were active in the Alliance Israélite (Bigart was its secretary-general).[78]

Both the Appeal and the Committee sought to remind the Jews of neutral countries of what they owed to France, "the initiator of the emancipation of Israelites throughout the world," and to lay the blame for anti-Semitism on Germany, "which was renowned for having created anti-Semitism with scientific pretensions."[79] The major problem was how to explain away the treatment of Jews by France's Russian ally. An early draft of the Appeal asserted that anti-Semitism had implanted itself in the East because the Russian bureaucracy was impregnated with the German spirit. The draft stressed that "our brothers in Russia [were] victims of a plague of Germanic origin." The final version went a step further and mitigated even these mildly anti-Russian statements. It noted that "reassuring signs have already appeared; the victory of the great liberal powers of the West, united with Russia for the defense of right, cannot fail to achieve the emancipation of our brethren in Russia."[80] Faith in France, thus, was proposed as the solution to the problem of Russian Jewry; Jewish and French political interests were contended to be the same.

As one of its fund-raising letters stated, the Committee had no specifically Jewish goals. It sought "only to serve the national interest."[81] Toward that end, it sponsored a delegation, headed by Professor Victor Basch of the Sorbonne, to the United States to conduct propaganda with the aim of influencing Jewish public opinion to support the Allied cause.[82] After meeting with Jews as divergent in class and opinion as Columbia University professor Richard Gottheil, the banker Jacob Schiff, and Dr. Goldfaber of the *Jewish Daily Forward*, Basch relayed information on the attitude of the various sectors of American Jewry toward Russia and the Allied cause to such governmental leaders as Raymond Poincaré and Pierre Berthelot.[83] The Minister of Foreign Affairs also corresponded with Bigart regarding the work of the Committee.[84]

Jewish opinion in France welcomed the political activity of the Central Consistory and of the French Information and Action Committee as public manifestations of French Jewry's patriotism.[85] There appears to have been little concern that the assertion of a special political tie with foreign Jews contradicted the assimilationist policy of French Jewry or implied that the Jews were not French citizens like all others. Only Rabbi Maurice Liber, writing under his pseudonym "Judaeus" in *L'Univers israélite*, opposed the propaganda campaign among Jews of neutral countries. Noting that Jews played only a minor role in France and in Europe in general, he felt that the sole issue that might legitimately draw together both French and foreign Jews was the fate of their coreligionists in war-torn Eastern Europe. [86]

The French government, however, saw the usefulness of, and welcomed, the special political activity of its Jewish citizens. The government authorized the activity of the French Information and Action Committee. [87] Moreover, during 1915 and 1916 it subsidized the visits of no fewer than three French Jews—Nahum Slousch, Victor Basch, and Octave Homberg—to the United States and assisted them in their propaganda and information gathering activities among American Jews. [88] As Jusserand wrote to Briand in support of Basch's trip, whose ostensible purpose was to deliver a series of lectures at the San Francisco Exposition, "The intention of M. Basch is to show [American] Jews that anti-Semitism is a German product, without roots in France and that with the progress of ideas, a radical improvement of the lot of Russian Jews was to be expected." [89] To make Basch's message more effective with Jewish leaders, who were widely suspected of Zionist sympathies, the Ministry of Foreign Affairs informed Basch that "you can add confidentially that in the course of discussions . . . between France, England, and Russia on the subject of the eventualities which will arise in Asia Minor . . . the defense and extension of the liberty of the Jewish colonies of Palestine will not be forgotten by France and England. . . . What you can affirm is that France brings to the question the most decided sympathy for the suffering of the Jewish race wherever it is oppressed and active liberalism towards the demands of one of the intellectual ferments of the world." [90] In a similar vein, Octave Homberg, a representative of the French Ministry of Finances in the U.S., was expected "to study the feelings of the Jewish world with regard to the Allied cause and to determine to what degree these sentiments were really affected by the Jewish question in Russia." [91]

In other areas as well, both within France and in North Africa, the government was willing to take advantage of Jewish personalities. To conduct propaganda among Jews in Alsace-Lorraine Rabbi Mathieu Wolff was selected as a governmental emissary.[92] Similarly, to carry out its "Jewish policy" in North Africa, the government placed particular emphasis on the Alliance Israélite Universelle. As a governmental report noted, "In favoring a slow and prudent evolution in the direction of our civilization . . . and in facilitating . . . the French naturalization of elite individuals who have . . . furnished proof of their attachment to France, in this goal we can profit from the assimilationist tendencies of French Jewish groups and of the Alliance Israélite Universelle whose schools have already contributed much to the diffusion of our culture."[93]

For French Jews this active collaboration with governmental bodies to serve the French war effort and to realize French aims abroad was the ultimate symbol of the mutual benefits of French Jewish symbiosis.

The War and the Jewish Question

While war enabled French Jews to demonstrate their patriotism and justify their sense of full integration in and identification with France, it also raised two facets of the Jewish question. There was anti-Semitism of the old style, which at times reared its head during the war. Though never seriously disturbing French Jewry's self-confidence, this occasional breakdown of the *union sacrée*, had to be confronted. Moreover, the fate of the Jews of Eastern Europe, caught in the war zone and suffering under regimes which denied them full citizenship, became an international issue which drew the attention of French Jewry.

Since the *union sacrée* represented the incarnation of patriotism, French Jewish spokesmen, convinced that they were doing their share for France, were particularly sensitive to the injustice of anti-Semitic slurs during the war and felt justified in invoking the *union sacrée* on their own behalf. The real antipatriots, so they pointed out, were those who attempted to destroy the *union sacrée* through anti-Semitism. In fact, the *Univers israélite* noted, it was the Dreyfusards—with Péguy at their head—who were in the best religious and national tradition of France, while by implication it was the anti-Dreyfusards who, through their anti-Semitism, violated those traditions.[94]

By 1915 French Jews had come to realize that the *union sacrée* was not universally followed. While claiming that the anti-Semitic monotone of the likes of Drumont was becoming less popular, the *Univers israélite* called for the realization that "the enemies of Judaism are still with us."[95] Moreover, it vigorously protested the campaign of French anti-Semitic newspapers—particularly Drumont's *Libre parole* and the *Action française*—to identify Jews with Germans.[96] It also published an open letter to Cardinal de Cabrières, the bishop of Montpellier, who had declared his attachment to the *union sacrée*. If Catholics were adhering to the *union sacrée*, it boldly asked, why were those papers "supported by the Catholics and recommended by priests," repeatedly rupturing the national compact by systematically attacking an entire category of fellow citizens?[97] Furthermore, the *Archives israélites* demanded a speedier defamation process against libelous anti-Semitic attacks.[98]

The most vitriolic attacks were reserved for Russian Jewish immigrants, particularly after 1917, when White Russian *émigrés* made common cause with native French anti-Semites. French Jewish spokesmen branded the allegations against Russian Jews of cowardice and refusal to bear arms as defamation of all Jews. For the patriotism of the majority of Jewish immigrants had generated a *union sacrée* of immigrants and natives *within* the Jewish community. Replying to an article by a Russian general, Mouravieff-Amoursky, in *L'Eclaireur*, Rabbi Jules Bauer of Nice defended the bravery and patriotism of both Russian and French Jews.[99] The *Univers israélite* reprinted from *La Guerre sociale* a series of articles by Gustave Hervé protesting the treatment of Jews in Russia and describing the considerable participation of immigrant Jews in the war effort.[100]

It also documented the patriotism of the immigrant Jewish community by reprinting the proclamation circulated on August 3, 1914, by the immigrant Federation of Jewish Societies in areas of heavy immigrant settlement in Paris:

> Brothers! France the land of Liberty, Equality, and Fraternity. . . .
> France . . . which first of all nations recognized us Jews and gave us the
> rights of man and citizen; France, where we have found a refuge and a
> shelter, is in danger! . . . We, Jewish immigrants, what are we to do?
> While the whole of the French people rises as one man to the defense of
> the Fatherland, shall we stand by with our arms folded? No, if we are not
> yet Frenchmen in law, we are so in heart and soul, and our most sacred
> duty is to put ourselves at once at the disposal of that great and noble na-
> tion in order to participate in her defense.[101]

Similarly, the *Archives israélites* made public a patriotic letter addressed by a Russian Jewish volunteer to his wife shortly before his death in battle.[102]

When several members of the Municipal Council of Paris, among them Henri Galli and Charles Badini-Jourdin, who represented the fourth *arrondissement*, the center of immigrant Jews in Paris, demanded that subjects of allied countries—read Jews—residing in Paris be deported if they refused military service, native organizations reacted vigorously. The *Univers israélite* again printed a rebuttal by Hervé, for the words of a non-Jew were considered to carry more weight with the public than anything a Jew might say in self-defense. Many Jewish immigrants, Hervé argued, were unwilling to return to Russia to fight as long as Russia remained the home of anti-Semitism, and France had only recently allowed foreigners to join French regiments rather than the unattractive Foreign Legion. The paper concluded that it would settle its accounts with the gentlemen of the Municipal Council when it could freely write the history of the immigrant Jewish volunteers of Paris.[103]

The concern for documenting the service of Jews in the war was as much a response to anti-Semitism as a natural desire by Jews to memorialize their heroes. An eminently respectable Research Committee for Documents concerning the Israelites of France during the War, under the patronage of the Société des Etudes Juives, was established in 1916. Co-sponsored by the Central and Paris consistories, it boasted an impressive membership of academic figures, including Durkheim, its president, and Bergson. The Committee announced as its goal the collection and verification of the names of Jewish soldiers killed, wounded, decorated, or promoted during the war. For, it noted, while French Jews, like other Frenchmen, wished only to serve France in its struggle, "the love which they bear for their country does not command them to deny their Jewishness. . . . It is not without interest to know how Frenchmen of Jewish origin, who have not embraced another religion, conducted themselves in the war."[104] The results of this assemblage of data were issued in book form by Albert Manuel, treasurer of the Committee and secretary-general of the Paris Consistory as *1914–1918: Les Israélites dans l'armée française*, and published in 1920 and 1921.

Far more critical than domestic anti-Semitism was the question of Russian Jewry, which had become one of the major "Jewish issues" of the war. While French Jews initially reconciled themselves to the facile assumption that the victory of the Allies would automatically improve the status of the Jews living under Russian rule, it was difficult to ignore the pleas of Russian Jews, to which the immigrant community and Zionist leaders were giving much publicity.[105] Other factors as well impelled French Jews to action. The traditional sense of *noblesse oblige* which characterized the relation of the leaders of the Alliance Israélite to their less fortunate coreligionists of Eastern Europe and the newly found solidarity with immigrant Jews in France spurred native Jews to publicize and protest the situation of the Jews in Russia and to provide charitable aid. Moreover, the fact that Germany was reaping rewards in the propaganda war for the support of Jews in the war zone transformed criticism of the Russian government into a patriotic act designed to serve the best interests of the Entente. As the *Univers israélite* stated, "It is Russia's duty . . . to deprive Germany of any cause for vile accusations, and it is the concern of France and England to demand of their ally promises and acts which will not permit Germany to pose as the liberator of oppressed minorities in Russia."[106] Jewish leaders also portrayed the continued oppression of Jews by the czarist regime as an insult to all Jews and a mockery of the ideological principles for which the Allies were purportedly fighting.

Since it was awkward for the leadership of French Jewry to criticize the way an allied government treated its Jewish subjects, there was some resistance to providing special aid to Russian Jews. Chief Rabbi Alfred Lévy declared in an interview with the Paris correspondent of an American Jewish paper that French Jews had not responded actively until then to the appeal of Russian Jews because "we French Jews have to take into consideration the general situation of our country and act with prudence."[107] The Paris Consistory had previously denied authorization to a group of Jews to organize under its auspices a meeting to raise funds for Russian Jews. It noted that "circumstances make it difficult to initiate a special demonstration for a category of Israelites belonging to an allied power."[108]

In spite of these reservations, however, a Society for Aid to Jewish Victims of the War in Russia was established in February 1916, enlisting on its board of directors men and women from both the native and immigrant Jewish communities.[109] The Alliance Israélite Universelle also disbursed funds for aid to Jews in Russia.[110]

In addition to these immediate relief activities, French Jewish leaders concerned themselves with long-range strategy for the ultimate emancipation of Russian Jewry. As it became increasingly apparent that the map of Eastern and Southeastern Europe would be redrawn after the war and that new governments would be established, Jewish leaders saw that there would be an opportunity for presenting Jewish demands. After all, there was a precedent for making the issue of Jewish rights an international diplomatic question; as far back as 1878 the Congress of Berlin had imposed upon a hostile Romanian government the civic emancipation of the Jews there.[111] The issue of the status of Eastern European Jewry was bound to be raised, therefore, at the Peace Conference. Jewish leaders thus realized that through the Allied governments they could influence the shape of the solution to the Jewish question in the East. As André Spire—poet, civil servant, and Zionist—noted in 1917, by being militant, active and organized, "western Jews [would] give the governments of their countries the courage, the force to safeguard the execution of clauses protecting Jews which [would be] written in the future peace treaty."[112]

The Alliance Israélite Universelle relied on its tested pattern of private diplomacy to solve the problem of Russian Jewry, which was its primary special concern throughout the war.[113] The agenda of each of its sessions during the war, notes André Chouraqui, included a review of the state of the Jews in the Russian Empire and in Romania. Throughout the war the Alliance sent letters to the Ministry of Foreign Affairs, with which it enjoyed a close relationship, seeking French intervention to bring to an end the dire condition of the Jews in Russia.[114] Like all supporters of Russian Jewry, the Alliance played as its trump card the gratitude which a favorable policy would elicit for the Entente from the seven million Jews of Eastern Europe as well as the two million Russian Jews in the United States.[115] Furthermore, prominent members of the Alliance—the Baron Edmond de Rothschild, Sylvain Lévi, and Emile Durkheim— also relied on the private exercise of power, meeting quietly (and in vain) with Russian governmental figures in transit through Paris to persuade them of the necessity to improve the status of their Jewish subjects.[116] Even after the emancipation of the Jews in Russia on April 4, 1917, the Alliance, with an eye to the future Peace Conference, reiterated to the Minister of Foreign Affairs the importance of the emancipation of the Jews in Poland and Romania.[117] With their patriotism and integration ratified by their military and political services to France during the war, French Jews felt justified in assuming an activist political stance on specifically Jewish interests.

The Dissolution of the Jewish "Union Sacrée"

The temporary *union sacrée* within the Jewish community disintegrated, along with the national *union sacrée*, at the end of the war. Immigrant Jews no longer needed the protection of native Jewry. The overthrow of the czarist regime had resolved part of the Jewish question in the East.[118] However, the Jewish question in Poland and Romania remained an important issue at the Peace Conference, and the exact nature of the demands to be presented there proved a source of conflict between immigrant and native Jews. The former sympa-

thized with the demand for national minority rights for the Jews of
Eastern Europe; spokesmen for the latter did not.

The issue of national minority rights became a symbol for the
broader ideological challenge immigrant Jews would issue to their native brethren in the interwar years. To the Alliance Israélite emancipation meant civil and political equality. Any decision to accord
national minority status to the Jews of Eastern Europe would, in its
eyes, cast doubt on the tested solution of Western Jewry and provide
ammunition to anti-Semites, who had always claimed that the Jews
remained an eternally unassimilable people. During the Peace Conference the Alliance was, therefore, one of the most determined lob-
byists for civil emancipation and one of the most vigorous opponents
of national minority rights for Eastern European Jews.[119] Responding
to a request by Louis Marshall of the American Jewish Committee to
withdraw its memorandum opposing national minority rights, the Alliance refused to do so with the comment that support of national minority rights would "constitute a denial of its principles and its commitment to the moral and political emancipation of the Jews within
the national cadre of the countries they inhabited. By seeking national rights for the Jews of Eastern Europe," the text continued, "the
Alliance would be recognizing implicitly a Jewish nationality which
currently has no existence either in fact or in law."[120] The Alliance
accepted only as a temporary need the special educational, linguistic,
and cultural rights which were granted to Eastern European Jews in
the peace treaties. Such concessions were necessary so long as the
backward majority populations refused to accept Jews wholeheartedly
as fellow citizens.[121] Likewise, the Univers israélite, the quasi-official
organ of the consistorial circles, rejoiced that language stipulating
"national rights" was absent from the peace treaties.[122] Such opposition to Jewish nationalism—whether the nationalism implied in the
insistence on national minority rights in the Diaspora or the nationalism of the Zionist brand which had won international recognition at
the Conference table—could hardly be expected to attract the sympathy of Eastern European immigrant Jews in France or to maintain
the internal union sacrée of French Jewry.

With the demobilization, moreover, mutual collaboration in the
war effort ceased. Each community returned to its own major

concern—the rebuilding of its traditional institutions. The Central Consistory removed itself once again from the political arena to devote its attention and resources to local matters. After due consideration of a proposal, supported by the Chief Rabbi, that it protest the pogroms in Poland and Romania, the Consistory had decided that "it was not appropriate for the Union of Cultic Associations of France and Algeria, whose rationale was the exercise of the Israelite cult, to intervene officially on this matter."[123]

The war had severely damaged native French institutions. Membership in the local consistories had fallen off, and both the local associations and the Central Consistory found themselves in severe financial difficulties in a period of rapid inflation.[124] During the war many local associations had ceased paying their dues to the Central Consistory; moreover, in those communities ravaged by the war the Central Consistory had assumed the responsibility of paying the salaries of the local rabbi and other officials.[125] The synagogues of Thann and Seppois-le-Bas in Alsace had been destroyed, while those of Verdun, Pont-à-Mousson, Rheims, and Chalon had been seriously damaged.[126] With the cessation of hostilities these communities had to be reestablished, their synagogue buildings repaired, and their officials restored to their positions. In all communities rapid inflation dictated an upward adjustment of salaries.[127] Other native social and welfare institutions faced the task of restoring activities allowed to lapse during the war and recruiting members at a time when returning veterans were devoting themselves to their families and careers.[128] Moreover, the war became a generational barrier strengthening the self-conscious identity of postwar youth as a group in conflict with the values of its elders. It was this generation which was to challenge the political and ideological assumptions of native Jewish leadership in the interwar years.

Even the return of Alsace-Lorraine to French control, which was hailed by the French Jewish community,[129] entailed some difficulty for French Jewry. The separation of church and state, enacted while the area was under German control, did not apply to Alsace and Lorraine. The two provinces therefore remained governed by the system established under Napoleon I, which gave their local and departmental consistories greater power than that enjoyed by all other consis-

tories, including the Central Consistory. Gaining the cooperation of
these independent consistories was to be difficult. The Central Consistory noted privately that the prejudice against French Jewry, and
especially against the Ecole Rabbinique, which had been inculcated
in the Jews of Alsace during the German occupation, would have to
be combatted.[130] Similarly, Alsatian Jews, generally more traditional
in orientation than Paris Jewry, were suspicious of the latter's reputation for rampant assimilationism. Alsatian Jews, who had been the
source of both the lay and rabbinic leadership of French Jewry in the
nineteenth century, were proud of their local traditions and independence. Thus, the existence of a major Jewish community in Alsace
and Lorraine was to exacerbate the conflict between Paris and the
provinces.

Moreover, the Alsatian Jewish communities were impoverished.
The Jews of the two provinces had progressively abandoned the small
towns for the major centers of Strasbourg and Metz. Numerous synagogues were in a state of deterioration; others were abandoned with
the dissolution of the local Jewish communities. In the interwar
period alone no fewer than sixteen Jewish communities in the Department of the Moselle were to be officially dissolved.[131]

The most important factor governing the end of the era of tranquility for the French Jewish community, however, was the growth and
consolidation of the Eastern European immigrant Jewish settlement
in the years following the war. With their home communities impoverished by the combat and the postwar pogroms, thousands of Eastern European Jews fled to the West. While most had as their ultimate goal the United States, the American imposition of a
restrictionist immigration policy after 1921 stimulated numerous emigrants to end their westward journey in France. Settling in Paris and
other French cities, they provided the numbers to establish a complete network of independent communal and political institutions.
The new social institutions, the expanded Jewish press, the political
activity, and the new ideas introduced by the immigrants led to the
disruption of the *union sacrée* which had prevailed temporarily
among French Jewry during the war years. With the conclusion of
the war, the golden age of symbiosis came to an end.

3.
The Immigrant Challenge: Ethnicity and Economics

The Jewish immigrants—most of them from Eastern Europe—who settled in France in the years 1906 to 1939 disrupted the relative tranquility of native Jewry ideologically, institutionally, and socially: French Jewry had been moving toward cultural homogeneity; the immigrants introduced the diversified cultural patterns and concerns of Eastern European Jews. French Jewry had gradually achieved a consensus as to the nature of Jewish identity in France; the immigrants challenged that consensus and reestablished ethnicity as an openly acknowledged element of Jewish identity. French Jews maintained a narrowly defined range of institutions, with the consistorial system still in control; the immigrants founded a plethora of institutions, independent of the consistories and involved with issues other than the native-approved items of religion and philanthropy. Native Jewry was largely middle class; the immigrants were overwhelmingly working class and generally impoverished. And more disturbing still, a sizable sector of the immigrant population was drawn not to the respectable republican politics of native Jewry but to working class organizations and aggressively leftist political activity.

The Jewish population was concerned, as well it might have been, with its image. And the immigrants raised the spectre that the anti-Semitic portrait of the Jew might come true. If the successful integration of French Jewry were to be maintained, the immigrant challenge would have to be met by "taming" the newcomers and rapidly assimilating them into the prevailing style of French Jewry.

Jewish Immigration in the French Milieu

In the overall context of Jewish migration to the countries of the West, France played a relatively minor role. In the years 1881–1914,

when 1,974,000 Jews arrived in the United States and some 120,000
in Great Britain, France attracted only an estimated 30,000.[1] In the
1880s and 1890s, France was not the "golden land" that America was
and, unlike England, it was not on a direct transport route to the
U.S. Moreover, the eagerness with which native Jewish institutions
in France sought to ship immigrants overseas or repatriate them,
combined with their reluctance to provide sufficient charitable aid,
did nothing to enhance the reputation of France as a haven for East
European Jews.[2] Although Jewish immigrants from the East attracted
sporadic public attention throughout the last two decades of the nineteenth century and aroused consternation among native Jewry,[3] they
presented no cause for alarm. After the refugee crisis of the pogrom
years of 1881–82 had passed, their numbers were manageable and
their arrival gradual. At the turn of the century immigrant Jews in
France had only begun to assume the consciousness and institutional
framework of a community. It was not apparent to French Jews that
the immigrants would choose to settle permanently in France or that
they would challenge the values as well as the leadership of native
Jewry.

Jewish immigration to France was always dwarfed by that to the
U.S. However, in the first third of the twentieth century the number
of immigrants in France outstripped both Great Britain and Germany. Absolute numbers aside, the impact of immigration upon
French Jewry was heightened by the lateness of the process, the
smallness of the native Jewish community, and the sensitivity of
French society to the immigrant problem.

The challenge which East European Jews presented to French
Jewry thus became apparent primarily after 1905, when a massive
migration of Jews began. As a result of the failure of the Russian Revolution of 1905 and the closing of Great Britain to immigrants,[4] large
numbers of East European Jews proceeded to choose France as their
destination. French Jews quickly realized that immigration from the
East was assuming unprecedented proportions. In 1906 the Jewish
Comité de Bienfaisance of Paris estimated the number of recent Russian Jewish immigrants to Paris alone at 10,000 and noted bitterly
that "Israelite communities situated between Russia and our city

think to resolve the Russian Jewish question by facilitating the transit to Paris of all these unfortunates."[5] The local committee of the Alliance Israélite Universelle in Nancy also commented in 1907 upon the "prodigious recrudescence of emigration within the past year," which necessitated large expenditures to aid emigrants passing through Nancy.[6] While estimates as to the number of Jewish immigrants to France vary, all agree that the rate of immigration increased in the years 1905 to 1914, and then rose even higher following World War I.[7]

In the pre-war years, most Jewish immigrants came from Russia and Romania. An analysis of the indigent immigrants aided by the *Asile Israélite de Paris* in the years 1906 to 1911 reveals that fully 60 percent of them were originally from those two countries, with the rest divided among twenty-three other countires. A sizable proportion of the clientele of the *Asile* were from Central Europe, with 15 percent subjects of Austria-Hungary and 5 percent German citizens. In these pre-war years only 7 percent were from the Levant, of whom 70 percent listed Palestine as their country of origin.[8] Many of the foreign Jews were merely in transit. The most plausible estimates place the number of immigrants who settled in Paris at approximately 25,000, of whom 85 percent were from Central and Eastern Europe, the rest from the Balkans and the Levant.[9]

The war brought a halt to all immigration, but Jewish immigration was renewed after its end. When the United States all but closed its doors to Eastern European immigrants in 1924, France became an attractive destination for permanent settlement. Moreover, conditions in France and in Eastern European countries further stimulated immigration of Jews to France. Having suffered the decimation of a generation of young men, France actively welcomed immigrants to supplement its weakened labor force. The Ministry of Agriculture and the Ministry of Labor, which had administered two services to recruit foreign workers during World War I, continued such activity after the war and sent missions to Poland and Czechoslovakia to import labor. Private industrial and agricultural concerns were also engaged in the recruitment of foreign workers. It was not until 1932, when France began to suffer the full impact of the world-wide economic crisis, that the recruitment drive of foreign labor subsided.[10] Although Jews were not recruited as contract laborers, they benefited from the enhanced status of the foreign worker in France.

This is not to say that Frenchmen embraced foreigners whole-heartedly. Foreign laborers were necessary, but their contributions were considered in strictly economic terms. Moreover, most were not expected to settle permanently in France. Naturalization procedures were difficult and expensive, so that foreigners routinely lived a generation in France without acquiring French citizenship. In 1927 naturalization requirements were eased, but approximately one-fifth of all applications in 1928 and 1929 were summarily rejected.[11] Although immigrants generally arrived in France in their youth, even after 1927 about half of those naturalized were aged 40 or older.

In short, France did not consider herself a nation of immigrants. Throughout the entire Third Republic, French attitudes to immigrants were ambivalent at best. Anti-immigrant sentiment prevailed in the years before World War I, and Jewish immigrants were often singled out as importers of inferior moral standards and squalid living conditions in the new urban ghettos. In the municipal elections of 1907, for example, voters in the fourth *arrondissement*, the center of immigrant Jewish settlement in Paris, elected to office one Charles Badini-Jourdin, the candidate supported by Drumont's *Libre parole* and a member of the rightist League of French Patriots. Prominent on his campaign posters was a call for the "protection of national labor and of the French worker from foreign labor."[12] Badini-Jourdin remained in office through the First World War. Within the fourth *arrondissement* the representatives of culture also articulated the overtly anti-Jewish immigrant sentiment expressed by the voters of the area. In 1909 the journal *La Cité*, published by the Society of Historical and Archaeological Studies of the Fourth Arrondissement, reprinted as fact a scurrilously anti-Semitic article. The 10,000 foreign Jews in the arrondissement, it reported, "scarcely work, but plunder each other." Furthermore, they were immoral and dirty. "Fathers marry their daughters or brothers their sisters," noted the article in all seriousness. "In infected slums entire families swarm in . . . promiscuity." So detestable were the immigrant Jews that their "exotic quarter in the very heart of Paris has a veritable cut-throat look."[13] In 1911 the *Libre parole* took up the anti-immigrant argument, describing the fourth *arrondissement* as "a frightful ghetto in the center of Paris." Because of the intensity of the propaganda, the police feared attacks upon Jews in that quarter by the *Action Française*'s street gangs, the *Camelots du Roi*.[14]

While attitudes toward immigration improved after the war, when foreign labor became a necessity for the French economy, much ambivalence remained. Symptomatic of French avoidance of the implications of immigration is the fact that little sociological literature on immigration and acculturation was produced in France in the interwar years at a time when American sociologists, particularly those of the "Chicago school," concerned themselves with those very questions. The few academic studies of foreign workers in the 1920s, while not overtly anti-Semitic, reveal biases detrimental to the status of the Jewish immigrant.[15] It was agricultural workers and laborers in heavy industry, these studies suggested, who contributed the most to the French economy and were, moreover, the most likely to assimilate successfully. Since these workers were imported as contract laborers, they could be regulated with ease and sent home upon the termination of their contracts, should the economy warrant this step. Jewish immigrants, on the other hand, as noncontract urban immigrants, were viewed as competitors of French workers, contributing little to French economic growth. Furthermore, they bore the stigma of the city, that breeding ground for cosmopolitanism, political radicalism, and ethnic continuity. It was urban immigrants who remained most resistant to the treasured simple French virtues best incarnated in the peasant.[16]

Despite these French attitudes, in their home countries of Eastern Europe and the Levant, Jewish victims of the anti-Semitic persecution and economic deprivation which were fueled by growing nationalist sentiment, looked to France as a country offering both economic and sociopolitical opportunities. In the countries of the Levant, the schools of the Alliance Israélite had instilled in their Jewish pupils an appreciation of French language and culture, while in Eastern Europe France had long enjoyed a reputation as a haven for political refugees and as the home of the advanced ideals of the Revolution. Thus, the period between the two World Wars witnessed the immigration of some 150,000 Jews to France. Of those, three-fourths were from Eastern Europe, with Poland replacing Russia as the greatest reservoir of Jewish immigrants.[17] Of the rest, approximately two-thirds came from the Balkans and Asia Minor, with the remaining one-third divided between refugees from Germany and North African Jews.[18]

The 175,000–200,000 Jewish newcomers in the years 1906 to 1939 were but a small fraction—15 percent—of the total number of immigrants who flocked to France. According to French censuses of foreign residents in France, the years 1906 to 1935 witnessed the immigration of some 990,000 foreigners, primarily Italians, Poles, and Spaniards.[19]

There is a conspicuous divergence in the immigration pattern of Jewish and non-Jewish arrivals in France. The Jewish immigrants came with their families and with the intention of permanently settling in the country; many of the Italian, Polish, and Spanish workers arrived without their families and intended to stay in France only temporarily. However, in practice their temporary employment in France often assumed all the characteristics of permanent settlement.

Non-Jewish immigrants in France were concentrated on the Mediterranean coast and in the industrialized areas of the North and East. The overwhelming majority of Polish immigrants, for example, worked in the northern mines.[20] Not so the Jews. All through the periods of immigration and regardless of their country of origin, Jewish immigrants flocked overwhelmingly to Paris. Of the immigrant Jews who were naturalized from 1924 to 1935, fully 75 percent were concentrated in Paris and its suburbs, while the remainder lived primarily in such urban centers as Strasbourg, Metz, Nancy, Marseilles, Lyon, Lille, and Nice.[21] The percentage of Jewish immigrants settling in Paris gradually declined during the interwar period. While 81.9 percent of Jews naturalized in 1924 resided in greater Paris, in 1936 only 69.3 percent did.[22] In their pattern of settlement, immigrant Jews merely reflected the course toward urbanization on which they had been embarked in their countries of origin. Additionally their movement toward the cities was similar to that of native French Jewry, approximately two-thirds of whom resided in Paris in the years preceding World War II.[23]

In Paris several neighborhoods became for all intents and purposes immigrant Jewish ghettos. The quarter familiarly known in Yiddish as the *Pletzl*—a section of the third and fourth *arrondissements*, around the rue de Rivoli and Métro St. Paul—was the oldest area of modern Jewish settlement in Paris. First inhabited in the early nineteenth century by Jews from Alsace-Lorraine, the neighborhood had become by 1900 the home of Yiddish-speaking immigrants.[24] Its narrow streets displayed signs in Yiddish, harbored kosher butcher shops and Jewish restaurants, and gave shelter to the petty commerce of immigrant peddlers. In four local public schools in the fourth *arrondissement* there were so many Jewish children of Eastern European immigrant origin that the schools were closed on Saturday rather than the traditional Thursday.[25] Although Montmartre had also become a center for Russian Jews after 1882, its Jewish population was not so concentrated as in the *Pletzl*.[26]

The newest Eastern European immigrant Jewish neighborhood was Belleville, an area which included parts of the twentieth, eleventh, and nineteenth *arrondissements*. Belleville became an important Jewish quarter only after World War I, and its Jewish residents, who came to a large extent from urban centers of Eastern Europe, were more politically active than the earlier immigrants who had settled in the *Pletzl*.[27] In the interwar period Belleville was the largest immigrant Jewish quarter in Paris. Of the 2,634 children served by the welfare organization *La Colonie Scolaire* in the years 1927 through 1936, for example, two-thirds were residents of Belleville.[28]

Immigrant Jews from the Levant made one or two quarters in Paris their own. The first Sephardi immigrants resided in the eleventh *arrondissement*, in the quartier de la Roquette,[29] while immigrant Jews from Algeria, Morocco, and Tunisia lived not far from the *Pletzl*, on the other side of the rue de Rivoli.[30] Post-war immigrants settled also in Belleville, Montmartre, and Clignancourt.[31] For the most part Sephardi immigrants from the Levant and North Africa, who were fluent in French and familiar with French culture, chose not to associate with, and hoped to avoid identification with, the poorer and seemingly more foreign Jews from Eastern Europe.[32] Only the youth from the two immigrant Jewish communities began to make common cause in the interwar period.

The settlement of immigrant Jews in the provinces had barely begun before World War I. According to a 1939 report in the Yiddish daily *Parizer haynt*, a handful of immigrant Jews from Eastern Europe had settled in the provinces around the turn of the century and in 1911 had attempted to establish their own social institutions in Nice and Nancy.[33] A few immigrant Jews had also settled in Strasbourg immediately before the war.[34] There were, moreover, in the pre-war years large groups of foreign Jewish students in Nancy, Lille, and Toulouse, but such a population was transient and established only student associations.[35]

Not until after World War I did Jewish immigrants from Eastern Europe settle in large numbers in the provinces. A 1927 survey of local rabbis revealed an immigrant population of 400 families in Nancy, 500 in Metz, and an unspecified but larger number in Strasbourg.[36] Also, from 10 to 25 Eastern European immigrant Jewish families resided in Epinal, Sedan, Besançon, St.-Etienne, and Versailles.[37] Though most immigrant Jewish settlements were in the large centers of the East, some Polish Jews had settled in the North to provide goods for immigrant Polish miners, and a few worked as miners themselves. By 1927 the rabbis in the North estimated that both Lille and Valenciennes had an immigrant Jewish population of 200 families each and Lens of 60 families, while 300 Jewish families from Eastern Europe and the Levant resided in Rouen.[38] In 1933 Léon Berman, the Chief Rabbi of Lille, privately commented, "In sum, I have [in my jurisdiction] more Poles than Frenchmen, and I have become obliged to speak publicly in Yiddish."[39]

A survey conducted by the Communist Yiddish daily, *Naye presse*, in 1937 revealed the growth of the Eastern European immigrant Jewish population, particularly in the North and East. The largest centers were Strasbourg, Nancy, and Metz—Strasbourg with 2,000 immigrant Jewish families, Nancy and Metz with 600 families each.[40] Smaller immigrant Jewish populations, ranging from 50 to

200 families, were recorded for Lunéville, Saint-Quentin, Lens, Belfort, and Lyon.[41] By 1939, *Parizer haynt* estimated, there were some 8,000 Eastern European Jewish families living in 32 localities in the provinces, with the largest concentration in Strasbourg.[42]

While the bulk of Jewish immigrants from Eastern Europe who did not settle in Paris chose to reside in the North and East, those coming from the Levant, naturally enough, established themselves primarily in the South. The 1,300 immigrant Jewish families who were reported to be living in Marseilles in 1927 originated from Turkey, Greece, Syria, and Palestine (though some 100 families were from Russia and Romania). The Bordeaux immigrant settlement, which numbered approximately 100 families and 50 bachelors, was evenly split between Sephardim from the Levant and Ashkenazim from Eastern Europe. Smaller immigrant communities in Bayonne, Nîmes, and Avignon, however, were composed entirely of immigrants from the Levant.[43] In addition to the major Sephardi settlements in the Midi, there was a community in Lyon as well.[44]

Contributing to the cultural and social life of the immigrant Jewish communities, though not counted among their permanent residents, were the Jewish students from Eastern Europe who flocked to French universities to acquire the higher education denied them in their native lands. In 1923 they established the Jewish Student Association of France with branches in Lyon, Nancy, Paris, Toulouse, Caen, Rouen, Strasbourg, Bordeaux, Montpellier, and Chambéry. In 1928 the national membership of the Association totaled 1,700.[45] Unaffiliated students greatly swelled this figure; indeed, in Paris alone, an estimated 2,000 Eastern European Jewish students were at the universities in 1924.[46] The transient student population was thus an important element in immigrant Jewish centers, especially in the provinces.

The living conditions of the immigrants left much to be desired. Though some of the pre-war immigrant merchants in textiles, furniture, and metals were reported to be living in relative comfort by 1922,[47] most continued to live in poverty for an entire generation. Since the *Pletzl* was one of the oldest quarters of Paris, much of its housing was substandard. Describing the pre-war *Pletzl* for readers of the *Jewish Daily Forward* of New York, A. Frumkin commented that "the alleys are frightfully dirty, the houses mostly old ruins. . . . Without exaggeration one can find from twelve to fifteen persons living in two small rooms. . . . The largest and best room serves as the *atelier* [workroom]; one eats where one can and sleeps in a dark hole without windows."[48] According to a pre-war report, which focused on 962 persons earning their living as capmakers, their lodgings in the *Pletzl* had "neither air nor light, [but] narrow and dirty staircases, running water only on the ground floor, rare and hideous water closets—all the poor living conditions [which made] this quarter . . . one of the eventual homes of every epidemic that reaches the capital."[49] While there was one room for every two persons on the average, the report noted that "these rooms are small and poorly ventilated, facing either narrow streets or unsanitary little courtyards." Moreover, the average concealed such cases as a family of ten in three rooms, a family of six in two rooms, or a family of seven living in one room alone. The most fortunate bachelors lived in rented rooms, while the less fortunate boarded with families, often sleeping in the kitchen.[50] One of the early Yiddish papers in France, *Der Yid in Pariz*, also noted in 1914 that immigrant Jews lived in squalor and that prostitution, born of poverty, flourished.[51] The establishment by native Jewish women of a society for protection of immigrant girls against white slavery testified to the existence of that social problem.[52]

In the interwar period many immigrant Jews continued to live in unsanitary, overcrowded conditions. Of the children sent to summer camp by *La Colonie Scolaire* in the years 1927 through 1936, 1,568 lived in one-room apartments, 2,158 in two-room apartments, 325 in dwellings of three rooms, and only 46 in apartments of four rooms. The rest lived in hotel lodgings. This, in a sample where three-fourths of the families were composed of from five to twelve persons![53] Similar statistics are available from the *Colonie OSE* in Paris; 87.5 percent of its clientele lived in apartments of one or two rooms, or in a hotel room. Moreover, among the children it served, lice were a major problem.[54] When earlier immigrants moved out of the *Pletzl* into the suburbs of Paris in the 1920s and 1930s, the postwar immigrants took their place.[55] Slum conditions, thus, remained the norm for large numbers of immigrant Jews throughout the interwar period.

Occupations

While the size of the immigrant Jewish population increased substantially—approximately sevenfold—between 1906 and 1939, the professional distribution of that population did not change significantly. This is not to imply that social mobility was absent among the immigrants. Certainly, the earliest immigrant settlers and their children moved up the occupational ladder: from artisan to small, and later larger, entrepreneur; from peddler to established merchant; from petty commerce and industry into the liberal professions. However, the newer immigrants of the interwar period followed essentially the same occupations as their pre-war compatriots and filled the ranks so recently abandoned by the earlier immigrants. Within the major Jewish trades, there developed, however, a greater diversification of function, and several new trades grew to prominence.

From the earliest days of immigrant Jewish settlement in France, the most striking characteristic of the professional distribution within the Eastern European immigrant community was its heavy concentration of artisans. Although articles were written on the new Jewish proletariat in France, there was in fact no Jewish *industrial* proletariat. Jewish workers were found almost exclusively in the nonindustrialized artisan trades—a majority in the clothing trades.

An analysis of the occupations of 190 fathers of immigrant children enrolled in Jewish schools in Paris in the years 1907–1909 reveals the dominance of the clothing trade and the preponderance of artisans within the Jewish community.[56] Fully 64 percent of the fathers were employed in artisan trades as tailors, shoemakers, capmakers, leather workers, tinkers and locksmiths, furniture workers, printers, painters, and bakers.[57] Another 27 percent were engaged in commercial activities, though hardly on a large scale. The largest number of "merchants" were peddlers (*colporteurs*)—8 percent of the total sample—followed by small shopkeepers, clerks, jewelers, dealers in secondhand goods, grocers, a wholesaler, and a commercial representative. Most of those engaged in commerce, it should be noted, served the immigrant Jewish community rather than the larger French population. Only 2 percent of the sample were involved in the liberal professions, while 7 percent were employed in a variety of miscellaneous trades—including, in all likelihood, the only Jewish acrobat in Paris! The clothing industry in all its forms, both manufacture and sales, provided a livelihood for 58 percent of the sample, with 30 percent of the fathers employed as tailors. It should be added, moreover, that the distinction between manufacture and sales in the artisan trades, as well as between small entrepreneur and salaried worker, was often a fine one. Many self-employed artisans sold their own goods, and the small entrepreneur and his employees often worked together in the same shop. Because work permits had to be secured, and paid for, many immigrants worked at home rather than in regularly established shops. Most workers aspired to rise to the entrepreneurial level themselves.

The post-war immigration differed little in its occupational distribution from earlier immigrants.[58] A plurality of immigrants remained artisans. However, a growing proportion of immigrant Jews earned their living from commerce and the liberal professions. Whereas in the years preceding World War I more than 60 percent of immigrant Jews from Eastern Europe had worked in artisan trades, in the interwar period that number had fallen, according to the calculations of A. Menes, to 45 percent.[59] The number engaged in trade, on the other hand, had risen to 33 percent,[60] while those in the liberal professions were estimated at 7 to 8 percent.[61]

The clothing industry in all its forms continued to be the dominant source of livelihood for immigrant Jews from Eastern Europe. In a survey published in 1931 by *La Colonie Scolaire* 48 percent of their clients worked as artisans in various sectors of the clothing industry.[62] A 1938 study conducted by the *Colonie OSE* revealed that 56 percent of the total sample were employed in the clothing trade, 41 percent as tailors alone.[63] Other samples confirm that a substantial proportion of post-war immigrant workers sought employment in the clothing trade.[64]

Post-war Jewish immigrants were nevertheless prominent in a number of growing industries. The employment of Jewish immigrants in the metal trades, for example, was a post-war phenomenon. Of the applicants to the *Oeuvre d'Assistance par le Travail*, in the years 1923–1931, between 16 and 18 percent described themselves as skilled metallurgical workers.[65] In Menes's sample 4 percent of Eastern European immigrant Jews worked in the metal trades.[66] The furniture and carpentry trades had also expanded, employing 5 to 10 percent of immigrant Jews.[67] Responsible for the rapid development of the French handbag industry (*maroquinerie*), Jewish workers were also employed in that industry in large numbers. The surveys of *La Colonie Scolaire* and OSE listed handbag workers as 9 to 10 percent of their samples.[68] Finally, the percentage of unskilled laborers and workers without an occupation among the post-war immigrant population was substantial. Between 1923 and 1931, unskilled laborers constituted 13 percent of the applicants to the *Oeuvre d'Assistance*, while another 5 percent listed themselves as without profession.[69]

While women appear in few surveys, since the occupation of the male breadwinner alone was generally demanded, large numbers were gainfully employed. As early as 1911 a day-care center was established by the *Asile Israélite* for preschool children of working mothers (mostly widowed or abandoned), as well as a workshop to provide employment to young mothers.[70] In the 1930s, the need for adequate day care was widely recognized and the most popular Yiddish daily, *Parizer haynt*, called for the establishment of such institutions.[71] In a 1922 report Rabbi Metzger, who served a largely immigrant population in Montmartre, noted that it was common for women to help their husbands in their trade, working at their sides as artisans or merchants.[72] The conditions of work in the clothing industry in particular, where piece work was often done at home, facilitated the employment of women. Helping out in the store was also considered a normal undertaking for the wife anxious for her husband to succeed. Of the immigrants applying for a job at the *Oeuvre d'Assistance* a sizable minority—18 percent in 1926–1927 and 26 percent in 1931—were women.[73] It has to be remembered, however, that most women never left a formal record of their gainful employment since they probably engaged in work by lending a hand to their fathers or husbands.

Although most of the available statistics stem from Paris, the home of at least two-thirds of Eastern European immigrant Jews, there is no reason to assume that the distribution in the provinces was substantially different. Contemporary impressionistic accounts of immigrant Jews in the provinces describe them as small merchants, particularly in the public markets, tailors, capmakers, furniture makers, peddlers, shoemakers, carpenters, locksmiths, and clerks.[74] Only in the North are some Jewish immigrants mentioned as working in the mines and in the factories.

Statistical data on the Sephardi immigrants from the Levant are scanty. From available estimates, it appears that Levantine Jews were engaged in commerce to a greater extent than those from Eastern Europe. In his demographic study of Paris Jewry, Michel Roblin declares that between 40 and 50 percent of Jewish immigrants from the Levant earned their living in commerce as shopkeepers, haberdashers, proprietors of novelty stores, exporters, textile merchants, and dealers in Oriental rugs.[75] Menes places the percentage of Levantine Jews engaged in trade as high as 62 percent and the number in industry at only 19 percent, a far lower percentage than among immigrant Jews of Eastern European origin.[76] Roblin estimates that another 15 to 20 percent of the population were laborers, and 9 percent were liberal professionals.[77] A report on Sephardi immigrant Jews in the Midi notes that most of the Jews from Salonica and Turkey were merchants and shopkeepers, though there were some factory workers and artisans as well.[78]

To sum up: like most immigrant subgroups, immigrant Jews in France, whether from the Levant or from Eastern Europe, were not distributed evenly throughout the country's economy but were concentrated in a few industries and commercial enterprises. Living in immigrant neighborhoods, they used informal contacts with family

and friends to find employment. Because of that system of recruitment and because of their limited skills, they were concentrated in
the trades traditionally prominent among Eastern European Jews
wherever they settled—the garment and leather industries. [79]

Institutions

Although most immigrants voluntarily leave their native lands,
they invariably try to re-create those aspects of their former social,
religious, and cultural patterns of life which enable them to feel at
home in their new countries. Immigrants suffer a profound ambivalence. They are torn between, on the one hand, the demands of
adjustment to the new society and the urge to succeed in the new environment and, on the other, the desire to perpetuate facets of the
culture in which they were raised, despite the opposition of the host
society to their foreign culture.

The Jewish immigrants from Eastern Europe were no different.
Their Jewish identity was based as much on ethnic as on religious
distinction. Just as the Catholicism of Italian and Polish immigrants
was suffused with national elements, the Judaism of the Jewish newcomers was but one facet of an entire folk culture they imported with
them from the East. Even the purely religious expression of that
Judaism differed in style from the dignified westernized version which
official French Judaism had adopted. Because they spoke Yiddish and
were the bearers of a specifically Eastern European Jewish folk culture, because they were artisans or petty merchants, because they
wanted a *haimish* (unpretentiously homey and familiar) milieu, they
shunned the institutions of the bourgeois native Jewish community,
which they considered strange, and chose to set up their own. While
sporadic attempts were made, from the eve of World War I to 1939,
to bring immigrants into the native institutions or to unite the two
communities, fundamental cultural, social, and economic differences made the persistence of two distinct and separate Jewish
communities in France inevitable.

Some immigrant groups, however, assimilated more easily than others. Sephardi immigrants, for example, partly acculturated through the schools of the Alliance Israélite, tended to associate themselves with the institutions of the native Jewish community. Their only major separate organization was the *Association Cultuelle Orientale de Paris*, which was established in 1909 to meet religious and philanthropic needs and was in existence throughout the interwar period.[80] Though the Sephardim of the Levant had their own rabbi (N. Ovadia), their own school, and their own philanthropic organization (*Ozer Dalim*),[81] their institutions were affiliated with the Consistory and they did not sponsor the variety of independent institutions of the type supported by the Eastern European immigrants. Nor did they stress, as Eastern European immigrants did, the economic and cultural barriers between themselves and native French Jewry. For those reasons, our discussion of immigrant institutions, even when couched in general terms, actually focuses on the immigrants from Eastern Europe.

As a community jealous of its own customs, immigrant Jews tried to meet their religious needs independently of the established native French synagogue. Just as the Polish and Italian immigrants, though Catholic, felt uncomfortable in French Catholic churches,[82] so immigrant Jews, as a rule, avoided the stately consistorial synagogues and temples in favor of their own *shtiblach* (small synagogues); in the latter, religious services were conducted by immigrant rabbis and cantors according to the customs and rites of their native lands. Some immigrants of longer residence in France had already begun to accept French standards of fashion and sought to "remedy the proliferation of small groups. . . . which meet for the practice of our cult in locations which are too small, [and] where a lack of hygiene keeps many of our Paris coreligionists, and principally our children, from attending the services and religious courses which take place there."[83] Yet even they did not turn to the official Jewish institutions of Paris. Rather, in 1911 they established an association called *Agoudas Hakehillos*, engaged the services of Rabbi Herzog, an immigrant Russian, and proceeded to raise funds to build their own synagogue.[84] As a result of their efforts, the synagogue on the rue Pavée was dedicated in 1914.[85]

In addition to satisfying their immediate religious needs, the immigrants began to concern themselves with the education of the younger generation. They realized that to communicate *Yiddishkayt* (Jewishness in all its manifestations) to their children, they would have to consciously create a Jewish milieu in their schools rather than rely, as they had in Eastern Europe, on the general environment of the Jewish *shtetl*. [86] While some parents enrolled their children in the free courses of religious instruction administered by the Paris Consistory, [87] many established their own educational institutions. Thus, a group of prosperous Eastern European immigrant merchants and liberal professionals founded an *Association de l'Ecole de "Talmud Torah"* in 1911 to provide elementary knowledge of Hebrew and Jewish history to their children. According to the statutes of the Association, its teachers had to be "Russian or Polish Jews who have pursued their Hebrew studies in their own country." [88] This organization was merely one of several local educational groups established by immigrants to furnish their own style of Jewish education, be it religious or "progressive nationalist," to their children. [89]

The immigrants also established a wide variety of nonreligious institutions calculated to achieve two vital goals. One goal was (as in the religious institutions) the creation of a sense of congenial community and the preservation and celebration of the culture of their lands of origin. The other goal was to facilitate the adaptation of the Jewish immigrants to their new milieu. This goal was no less important: French society, after all, expected the rapid and complete assimilation of immigrants to what was deemed to be its superior culture.

First in importance among the immigrant social institutions were the *landsmanshaften*, mutual aid societies, organized most often by immigrants from the same town or locale and occasionally by members of the same trade. [90] While mutual aid societies were also established by non-Jewish immigrants from Poland, [91] they were far more common in the Jewish milieu. The earliest organizations date from the first period of mass emigration from Eastern Europe in the years following 1881, but of the 170 known to have existed in Paris in 1939, most were established by post-war Polish immigrants. [92] Besides serving as places for informal socializing, the *landsmanshaften* functioned as self-help organizations, providing the immigrant with sick benefits, small loans, and widows' pensions. Most importantly, membership in a society assured the immigrant of a proper burial—among friends, as it were—in the society's grave site. Although most societies were not organized for religious purposes, some employed a cantor and regularly held their own religious services.[93]

It was through the *landsmanshaften* that the earliest efforts at uniting the Eastern European immigrant community were conducted. Having lived in a highly structured Jewish community in Eastern Europe, immigrant Jews in France felt a need for a larger community beyond the confines of their small, barely solvent societies. This quest for the unification of a very fragmented immigrant population characterized the entire period from the years preceding World War I to the eve of World War II. The impact of anti-Semitism in the 1930s and the deteriorating economic and political conditions of those years only galvanized a pre-existing disposition.

It is no surprise, then, that the first attempt to unite the immigrant community through its societies took place as early as 1913. Interestingly, the initiative was undertaken by Zionist activists under the leadership of Dr. Alexander Marmorek, a noted biochemist. In 1912 he had called a preliminary meeting under the auspices of the Zionist group *Ateres-Zion* to found a federation and coordinate Jewish activity in France.[94] With Marmorek presiding, the Federation of Jewish Societies of Paris, composed of twenty-two immigrant Jewish societies, both *landsmanschaften* and charitable organizations, came into formal existence on April 10, 1913. Its office was located at the Zionist-oriented *Université Populaire Juive*.[95] The establishment of the Federation marked the recognition by immigrant Jews that Paris was not merely a transit point but, with the settlement of merchants, workers, and intellectuals, was becoming a real community.[96] The immigrant Jews who founded the Federation expressed the desire to liberate themselves from the degrading role of *schnorrers* (beggars) and sought, on an equal basis, "a closer collaboration between French Jews and immigrant Jews, principally on matters concerning institutions of charity and welfare."[97] As the founding commission of the Federation noted,

One can hope that the French Jews . . . will not be long in recognizing that the Jewish immigrant is a source of activity and precious good will, that he possesses by the force of circumstances—having suffered and struggled himself since his arrival in France—a more exact sense of the interests and needs of his coreligionists; that it would be unjust and prejudicial . . . to keep him constantly separated from all participation in the management of communal works; and that from the close collaboration of the French Jewish element and the immigrant Jewish element will result a renewal of life within French Judaism and a more just and effective distribution of Jewish charity and assistance.[98]

Moreover, the Federation proposed to "assume the defense of the interests of the immigrant Jewish population whenever threatened," rather than leave that defense to the native Jewish population.[99] Thus, even before World War I, Eastern European immigrants sought to declare their independence and their ability to determine their own needs and administer their own institutions.

Though most charitable organizations were controlled by the native Jewish community, the immigrants also founded welfare institutions of their own. Their oldest institution, the *Asile Israélite de Nuit*, which provided temporary lodging and meals for indigent immigrants, was established in 1900 at the initiative of immigrant Jews from Russia and Romania.[100] While it attracted the interest of Chief Rabbi Zadoc Kahn and occasional contributions from the Alliance Israélite and the Comité de Bienfaisance, it drew its support almost entirely from the immigrant community.[101] The *Asile* was not the only welfare organization established and funded by the immigrant community before World War I. The *Université Populaire Juive* set up a dispensary in the heart of the immigrant settlement in the fourth *arrondissement*,[102] and a popular soup kitchen, serving meals to the unemployed, was administered by the capmakers union in the same neighborhood from 1914 to 1921.[103]

In addition to creating their own welfare and educational institutions, the pre-war immigrants from Eastern Europe also began to transplant to French soil the Yiddish institutions which had served their cultural needs in Eastern Europe. Thirteen Yiddish newspapers appeared in print for the first time between 1906 and the outbreak of World War I.[104] Representing a wide range of interests, literary and political, they included two Zionist papers, six socialist, and one anarchosyndicalist. While their goal was to communicate and interpret news of both general and Jewish interest, each according to its own philosophy, the Yiddish papers strived both to strengthen Jewish culture and to aid the immigrant in his adaptation to French life. As one of the earliest papers, *Di Moderne tsayt*, declared in 1908, "From the fact that a Jewish people with a Jewish language exists, there rests upon us the obligation to use this language that it not become moldy."[105] At the same time the paper regularly published a Yiddish-French dictionary. Though most of the papers lasted but a few months, the political papers, which dealt with local events and appealed to a specific audience—workers involved in the nascent Jewish labor movement in Paris—survived for several years.[106] However, not until the 1920s was the Yiddish-speaking population of France large enough or wealthy enough to support a Yiddish press on a regular basis, especially since the Polish Yiddish press was easily available in France.[107]

Other cultural enterprises were imported along with the Yiddish press. Yiddish theater troops began to include Paris on their itineraries, and visiting Yiddish cultural celebrities and intellectuals performed and lectured for the immigrant community. The famous Yiddish writer Shalom Aleichem appeared in Paris several times, his last visit occurring in December 1913.[108] Chaim Weizmann, the Zionist leader, lectured on Zionism at the *Université Populaire Juive* in 1912, while the same year Abraham Cahan discussed, under the auspices of the Paris *Bund*, the development of the Jewish labor movement in America.[109] The Paris *Bund* also sponsored a literary evening in honor of the writer Abraham Raizin, with the participation of the novelist Sholem Asch, and a lecture on Shylock by Jacob Milch, the editor of *Tsukunft*.[110] Such cultural events were no rare occurrence. From the preserved publicity flyers it is evident that the Paris *Bund* alone sponsored no fewer than 13 lectures, theater performances, and concerts in 1912–1913.[111] The *Université Populaire Juive* also held regular lecture series.[112]

Not all cultural events were dependent upon visiting personalities. Though the immigrant community was relatively small and of recent origin, it supported a local Yiddish theater in Paris as early as 1907.[113] Indeed, the immigrant community of Paris counted among its members some resident intellectuals and political activists of its own. Personalities like Alexander Marmorek, Elie Eberlin, and Charles Rappaport (a prominent figure within the French Socialist Party) lectured frequently in Yiddish to immigrant audiences.[114] Besides furnishing entertainment or information on matters of general and Jewish interest, the lectures brought issues of international and local politics to the immigrant population. Furthermore, the courses and lectures sponsored by the *Université Populaire Juive* dealt with such practical matters as learning French, the legal status of aliens within France, and problems of naturalization.[115]

The Politicization of the Immigrant Jewish Community

The interwar period witnessed the further institutional development of the immigrant settlement as a community independent of native French Jewry. Organizations proliferated to meet the socioeconomic, political, and cultural needs of the rapidly growing immigrant population, which had become large enough and stable enough to support a full complement of institutions. Moreover, political divisions, significant even before World War I, became increasingly more so between the two wars. The majority of social and cultural organizations in operation in those years—whether devoted to furthering assimilation or busy with the strengthening of Yiddish culture—were either under the aegis of Jewish political parties or represented middle class interests hostile to the politics of the Left.

Typical of the politicization of the community was the situation of the Yiddish press in France, which after its decline during World War I, had again begun to flourish. While only about fifteen Polish-language periodicals served the larger, non-Jewish Polish settlement in France, an astounding 133 Yiddish periodicals were established between 1918 and 1939.[116] More importantly, a number of papers, assured of a sizable readership, appeared regularly throughout the years. Of the greatest significance were the two dailies, the anti-Communist and pro-Zionist *Parizer haynt* (1926–1939) and the Communist *Naye presse* (1934–1939); the latter succeeded the Communist biweekly *Arbeter shtime* (1923–1929), the weekly *Emes* (1930–1932), and the thrice-weekly *Der Morgen* (1933). Together the dailies were reported to have published between 15,000 and 18,000 copies.[117] There were a number of other politically partisan papers, including the Bundist semi-monthly *Morgenstern* (1929) and the weekly *Unzer shtime* (1935–1939), the anarchist *Arbeter fraynt* (1927–1929), and the *Poalei-Zion* weeklies *Arbeter vort* (1928–1936) and *Di Naye tsayt* (1936–1939).[118] Trade papers and nonpartisan papers devoted to literature also appeared.

The Yiddish cultural life of the interwar period was also dominated by political interests. While cultural associations (*kultur veraynen*) had been established in Paris, Nancy, Strasbourg, Lunéville, and Lille as nonpolitical organizations in the years 1919–1925, they gradually came under Communist domination.[119] The Paris *Kultur-Lige*, for example, was established in 1922 to provide "a corner for Jewish culture." It sponsored weekly lectures and discussions on a variety of literary and historical topics.[120] In the fall of 1925 Communists secured a majority on the administrative committee and proceeded to politicize the group. When a Bundist-sponsored resolution that the *Kultur-Lige* remain neutral and nonpartisan was rejected, the Bundists withdrew to form the *Medem Club*. The Communists retained control of the *Kultur-Lige* throughout the interwar period, using it as a forum for raising the class-consciousness of its members and urging them to affiliate with the Communist trade union movement, the C.G.T.U.[121] Under the aegis of the Jewish Communists of Paris the activity of the various cultural groups in Paris and the provinces was centralized, and the First National Congress of Jewish Cultural Organizations was held in January, 1927.[122]

Although the *Kultur-Lige* did not succeed in attracting as members the majority of the Yiddish-speaking masses, who remained in the nonpartisan *landsmanshaften*, it did sponsor a popular university, a choir, and a theater group (PIAT) for the expression of Yiddish culture.[123] Moreover, the *Kultur-Lige* attracted the collaboration of numerous Yiddish writers and poets, members of the Leftist Writers'

Group, who began settling in Paris in the late 1920s and who made
Paris a Yiddish literary center in the 1930s.[124] To be sure, their work
was scarcely influenced by their French milieu: theirs was rather an
expatriate literature, drawing its inspiration from the Jewish experience in Eastern Europe. Whatever the literary assessment, the presence of a host of creative talents in Paris greatly contributed to the
cultural life of the Yiddish-speaking immigrant community. Furthermore, it enabled the Paris community to host the Communist-spon-
sored International Culture Congress in September 1937.[125]

Other forms of cultural activity within the immigrant community
were similarly partisan in nature. Each group—the traditionally religious, the middle-class ethnic, the Zionist, the Bundist, and the
Communist—sought to perpetuate its own philosophy and its own
style of Jewishness, particularly among the younger generation.
Thus, there existed in Paris a network of nine or ten Yiddish supplementary schools under Communist auspices, established to provide a
class-conscious Jewish education and to draw the children of workers
away from the "religious chauvinist schools" conducted by the Jewish
bourgeoisie.[126] Also there were two Yiddish schools administered by
the Left *Poalei-Zion* group, two by the Federation of Jewish Societies,
and one by the Bundists, in addition to the sixteen traditional religious elementary Hebrew schools (*heders*).[127]

A similar diversity of educational institutions could be found in the
major centers of immigrant Jewish settlement in the provinces. In addition to secular schools, Jewish Communists, Bundists, and Zionists
conducted their own youth groups and clubs. The Bundist *Arbeter
Ring*, a social and cultural organization established in 1932, had
some 500 members, while the Communist "Friends of the *Naye
Presse*" enrolled 2,700 adherents by the end of the 1930s.[128] Communists and Bundists also sponsored their own libraries and popular
universities.[129]

Even the communal activity conducted by the purportedly neutral
Federation of Jewish Societies was not free of political significance.
Reorganized in the years 1924–1926, after its disappearance during
World War I, the politically neutral Federation drew its support from
the middle classes and from those craftsmen who were not involved

in the Jewish labor movement. During the 1930s, in particular, it was administered by persons sympathetic to Zionism and hostile to Communism. Not unfairly—though certainly scathingly—was it characterized by the Communist press as "petty bourgeois."

Starting with 12 societies, the Federation grew to 85 loosely affiliated *landsmanshaften* and charitable organizations by 1935.[130] Though it maintained some contact with societies in the provinces, its claim to be a national organization was largely a fiction. Its activity was overwhelmingly Paris-centered.[131] Moreover, by its nature, the Federation was dependent on its constituent groups for financial resources and membership. Hence, there were great fluctuations in the finances of the Federation, the popularity of its programs, and its active membership. All these handicaps notwithstanding, the Federation remained a viable alternative to the institutions of the Left.

Like the Communists and the Bundists, the Federation boasted a popular university, a library (established in 1933), and two Yiddish supplementary schools.[132] Since it had no ostensibly political goals, its cultural activity was limited to meeting the intellectual and practical needs of Jewish immigrants, both in cultural adaptation and in retention of their native culture. As the First Congress of the Federation declared in 1933, its goals included Jewish cultural activity, the teaching of Jewish history to adolescents and children in order to communicate Jewish spiritual values of the past and present, and "initiating the immigrant Jewish masses in the language, the history, and the culture of the French people."[133] The courses offered by the Popular University illustrate the nature of its program. Of the fourteen courses listed in 1931–1932 (seven in French and seven in Yiddish), four attempted to synthesize French and Jewish concerns (the French Revolution and the Jews, Israel in French literature, the Dreyfus Affair, the history of the Jews in France); four dealt with Jewish history and philosophy and Yiddish literature; three with general French history and literature and with current political matters; while three were devoted to such practical issues as the economic crisis and the Jews, and French laws regarding foreigners.[134]

Other agencies of the Federation reflected similar concerns. Among the welfare and philanthropic institutions affiliated with the

Federation was *La Colonie Scolaire,* established by middle class immigrants in 1926 and supported by contributions from *landsmanshaften.* It sent poor children to the seashore for the summer and administered a dispensary which provided free medicine and medical consultations for approximately 500 children per month, but its activity was not limited to physical welfare: It conducted a Yiddish supplementary school and children's clubs and sponsored lectures on hygiene for the immigrant community.[135] *La Colonie Scolaire,* also, "endeavored to create . . . a Jewish atmosphere" in its clubs, through the teaching of reading and writing in Yiddish, Jewish history, folklore, songs, and stories.[136]

While we have focused on Paris as the center of immigrant Jewish cultural and institutional developments, Jewish communities in the provinces followed a similar pattern. Their institutional life was both diversified and politicized. The 280 immigrant Jewish families in Lens, for example, supported two adult-education groups, a traditional religious school, a socialist-Zionist school, two Zionist groups, a culture and welfare association, two religious associations, a merchants' organization, and a Jewish Communist labor movement.[137] Similarly, Lille was endowed with an immigrant synagogue and library, a Yiddish and a Hebrew school, two Zionist groups, a merchants' association, and a Jewish Communist organization.[138] In addition to the usual spectrum of welfare and educational institutions, a large immigrant community like Strasbourg or Metz boasted local branches of the *Kultur-Lige,* a drama circle, a choir, and a sports club. Strasbourg was also the home of a Jewish lycée (yeshiva).[139] As was the case with the Federation in Paris, virtually all major communities in the provinces made some attempt to unite the various immigrant Jewish organizations into a more or less formal federation for the purpose of generating a sense of community and coordinating the activity of the constituent groups.

The proliferation of such institutions reflected the needs of a politically diversified, essentially first-generation immigrant community. Although the French milieu did not encourage such separatist efforts, all segments of the immigrant community hoped to perpetuate their own forms of Jewishness through their respective institutions. But their success among the younger generation was limited, for the forms of Jewishness cherished and propagated by immigrant parents were rooted in a sociopolitical and cultural experience alien to their children. For the latter, the assimilating power of French society was paramount. Moreover, only a minority of the children of immigrants received any type of Jewish education. Among an immigrant population of some 120,000, in 1939 only 760 children attended the 15 Yiddish supplementary schools then in existence in Paris, while an additional 753 students frequented traditional *heders*. A smaller number studied in consistorial schools.[140] As early as 1924 the Yiddish paper *Parizer bleter* found it necessary to insert pages in French, with the comment that "wherever Jews benefit from the rights accorded to citizens . . . the children born in the country no longer speak the language of their parents."[141] A contemporary Zionist report noted critically of Jewish immigrants in France that "their tendency towards assimilation is striking. . . . It is a fact that the young generation in this milieu is lost to Judaism."[142] Literary evidence poignantly highlights the dilemma described by journalists and Zionist activists. While all immigrants sought economic success for their children and recognized the need for acculturation, some were dismayed at the price to be paid for their dreams. As a financially successful immigrant whose children refused to be addressed in Yiddish lamented bitterly in a story by Yossel Tsucker, "It was for Yiddish that I longed. . . . I don't need an engineer [his son]. I don't want a dancer [his daughter]."[143]

While the public schools remained the primary instrument of acculturation for immigrant children, the process of assimilation of Jewish immigrants and their children in France was not determined by French institutions and attitudes alone. Both the Jewish labor movement and the institutions of the native Jewish community played a crucial role in the adaptation of immigrant Jews to France and became a staging ground for communal discord.

4.
The Jewish Labor Movement

The ethnic and economic differences between native and immigrant Jews in France found their sharpest expression in the Jewish labor movement, the most important creation of the Eastern European immigrant Jews in France. Though its original ideology derived from the particular situation of Eastern European Jews as an important ethnic minority in their respective countries of origin, the movement succeeded in adapting to the French milieu and remade itself to meet the economic and political needs of the immigrant labor force in France. Moreover it provided Yiddish-speaking workers with an alternative community both to native Jewish organizations and to middle-class immigrant institutions. Thanks to the Jewish labor movement, a considerable segment of the immigrant working class assimilated into French society through the medium of syndical activity and the politics of the Left. At the same time the movement's very existence embittered relations between native and immigrant Jewry and challenged the quietistic political stance of the organized Jewish community.

It is impossible to understand the nature of the Jewish labor movement in France without briefly dwelling on the antecedents of that movement in Eastern Europe. With the rise and growth of a substantial Jewish working class, primarily artisanal, in the cities and towns of the Jewish Pale of Settlement of Imperial Russia, conditions were ripe in the 1880s and 1890s for the maturation of a Jewish labor movement which would combine practical demands for urgent economic improvement with a revolutionary vision of a new system along the lines of socialist ideology. In 1897 the leaders of the local worker cells of Vilna, Warsaw, Minsk, and Vitebsk established a federation of Jewish workers which they called the General Jewish Workers' Union of Poland and Lithuania, familiarly known as the *Bund* (i.e., Union).[1] The movement—a true grass-roots awakening

of poverty-stricken Jewish workers who labored under abject conditions—enjoyed almost instant success. By 1900 the Bund had 5,600
members; three years later it had more than 30,000.[2]

The original leaders of the Bund were Russified Jewish intellectuals who had come to socialism through their contact with Russian
students in gymnasia and foreign universities. No wonder they espoused no specifically Jewish goals in the formative years of the
movement. A socialist revolution, they felt, would resolve the Jewish
question. Hence, practical grounds alone served as justification for
their agitation among the Jewish populace and for their founding of a
separate Jewish socialist party. They argued that Jewish workers were
isolated by their places of residence and of work as well as by their
language from members of the Russian proletariat. Hence, it was
necessary to conduct socialist propaganda among Jewish workers in
their own tongue and through labor institutions sensitive to their particular economic needs. Moreover, the Jewish proletariat had its own
class enemies within Jewish society—the Jewish bourgeoisie—against
whom it had to be organized separately. Finally, within the general
Russian socialist movement, a Jewish party could lobby to ensure the
abolition of the discriminatory measures under which Jews suffered
in the czarist empire and to press for the eventual bestowal of civil
equality upon all Jews.[3]

The contact of the intellectual leadership with the Jewish masses
and the development of a secondary level of leaders from among the
workers themselves led to an ideological transformation of the Bund's
justification of its own existence. While rejecting the "chauvinist nationalism" of the nascent Zionist movement, with which it competed
for support—both organizations arose in the same year, 1897—the
Bund began to stress the ethnic and cultural ties binding Jewish workers together. It even argued for the acceptance of Yiddish as the
recognized language of the Jewish masses. In political terms it demanded in 1903 of the Russian Social Democratic Party, with which
it was affiliated, independent federative status, recognition of the
Bund's right to organize all Jewish workers along ethnic lines, even in
areas where there existed functioning sections of the Russian party,
and support for cultural autonomy for Jews.[4]

The Bund's ideological stance was quasi-nationalist. Though it rejected the concept of a Jewish people transcending class antagonisms, it refused with equal consistency to accept the notion that to be a good socialist a Jew had to abandon his Jewish ethnicity and cultural roots and assimilate completely. Indeed, it considered the Jewish working class to be the only acceptable representative of Jewish ethnicity. Moreover, while characterizing as reactionary the traditional religious culture of the entire Jewish community, much of it in Hebrew, it promoted the validity of a secular Jewish folk culture in Yiddish as the legitimate expression of the Jewish working classes. Recognizing that the masses who adhered to the Bund were unwilling to sacrifice their folk culture and ethnicity in the name of a higher socialist universalism, its leaders thus incorporated an appeal to ethnic sentiment within their own program.[5] Cooperating with the Russian revolutionary movement in spite of the latter's reluctance to accept the Bund on its own terms, it saw itself as the Jewish branch of the international socialist movement.

Among the pre-war Jewish immigrants to France were workers and revolutionary activists who brought the Bundist ideology with them. By 1904 three earlier groups of Bundists had united to form "*Di Kempfer*," the central organization of Bundists in Paris.[6] Thus, while their hearts were in Russia and their activity focused on support for the Bund's home organization, they also were instrumental in laying the ground for a Jewish labor movement in France. Participating in this effort—though often bitter competitors of the Bundists—were Jewish anarchists, Jewish Mensheviks, Jewish Bolsheviks, and Jewish members of the Polish Socialist Party in exile, who had no commitment to Jewish culture of any kind but, because of shared origins, considered the ranks of Jewish workers in France as the natural constituency for their socialist and syndical activity.

There is a dispute as to which group was most influential. Zosa Szajkowski may be correct in suggesting that it was the anarcho-syndicalists who most strongly influenced the nascent Jewish labor movement in France. This is not surprising, considering the fact that the general French labor movement of the period was also dominated by anarcho-syndicalism.[7] Moreover, Jewish anarchists in France con-

centrated primarily on *local* syndical activity and were the first to
found a local Yiddish paper, *Der Agitator*, while Bundists and other
socialists concerned themselves above all with political issues in Russia. The Bundists, then, were only next in importance to the anarchists as founding fathers of the Jewish labor movement in France.
They, in turn, were followed by individual Jewish Bolsheviks and
Mensheviks and by a few socialist Zionists.[8]

Although several labor unions had already been established around
the turn of the century among those immigrant Jewish workers in
Paris who were concentrated in the Jewish trades of the garment industry, it was only with the upsurge of immigration in the years following 1905 that Jewish syndical activity became vigorous. Not only
did the immigrant Jewish working population increase, but a large
number of revolutionary activists, fleeing the 1905 political repression in Russia, settled in Paris and devoted themselves to labor organizing and socialist agitation while waiting for the political climate in
Russia to improve. In general, the new immigrants were more politicized and easier to organize than those who had emigrated earlier.
The Jewish capmakers' (*casquettiers*) union in particular, which became the center of Jewish syndical activity in Paris, was strengthened
by younger immigrants who struggled with the older and more moderate leadership in an effort to sharpen the class-consciousness of the
members and to engage in more militant conflicts with the employers. By 1911 committed young revolutionaries had taken over the
leadership of the union.[9] Similarly, new activists in the years between 1906 and the outbreak of World War I succeeded in organizing Jewish sections of labor unions among garment workers, furriers,
bakers, furniture makers, handbag workers, and shoe workers.[10] The
Jewish organizers were easily able to integrate the Jewish sections into
the existing French union structure. For French unions were small,
organized locally by trade from the bottom up rather than the top
down, and were only loosely federated into the national *Confédération Générale du Travail* (CGT).[11] The revolutionary rhetoric of the
French labor movement, despite its anarcho-syndicalist tone, was also
congenial to immigrant Jewish activists, who prided themselves on
belonging to the international revolutionary proletariat.

As in Russia, the separateness of the Jewish labor movement in France was initially due to practical necessity. Yiddish-language sections were set up in those trades which comprised large numbers of workers who spoke Yiddish among themselves and who understood little, if any, French. Here the similarity between the two scenes ends, however. In Russia, the Bund did eventually develop an ideological justification for a Jewish labor party with independent, federative status within the larger Russian movement; no such ideological development occurred in France. After all, Yiddish-speaking workers constituted a tiny minority of the French work force; as immigrants, separated from their folk roots, they were expected by all (their fellow workers included) to assimilate rather than preserve their uniqueness. The Bundists, the only group in France supporting the creation of separate Jewish unions to be federated with the French unions, argued for such separation, however, not in terms of cultural autonomy, but for such practical reasons as difference in language and the concentration of Jews in certain industries. The Bundists also suggested that it was necessary to organize Jewish workers without submerging them in French unions in order to prove to the French labor movement that Jews were not undermining the position of their French fellow workers.[12] Such a stance, to be sure, found support neither among other immigrant Jewish workers nor, more importantly, within the French labor movement. Only in the absence of a French union did the Jewish furriers, among whom Bundist influence was strong, establish an independent union in 1907; and in 1913 they merged with the German-language union, which agreed to maintain a Yiddish-language section.[13]

Even more extreme was the attitude of Jewish anarcho-syndicalists. Although they maintained their own Yiddish-speaking group, they went so far as to oppose the creation of Yiddish-language syndical sections, arguing that Jewish workers should be integrated within the general unions.[14] Such a position, however, was unacceptable as long as Jewish workers spoke French with difficulty.

In 1911 an Intersyndical Commission was established to unite the Yiddish-language syndical sections and to coordinate syndical and socialist propaganda among Jewish workers.[15] Bundists, Mensheviks,

and Bolsheviks worked hand in hand in the nonpartisan body, which
included delegates from the capmakers, furriers, handbag workers,
and garment workers.[16] The impetus for coordinating syndical activities among Jews was provided by sporadic anti-semitic outbursts in
1910 and 1911 in which syndical activists accused Jewish workers of
undermining the labor movement through unfair competition and attacked Rothschild as a Jew rather than a capitalist.[17] The establishment of the Commission marked the stabilization of the pre-war Jewish labor movement in France.

The anarcho-syndicalists, who still were dominant in the garment
unions, opposed the socialist tendencies of the Intersyndical Commission and particularly its involvement in political as well as economic matters. Given the traditional close ties of the Jewish labor
movement in Eastern Europe with political action and with a political party, however, it was natural for the Jewish labor movement in
France to be more politically oriented than the French labor movement: the latter had resolved in the 1906 Charter of Amiens to observe political neutrality and shun party politics, which diverted
workers from the true class struggle.[18] The revolution would be
achieved through the syndical organizations themselves.

The moving force on the Intersyndical Commission was a Bolshevik, A. Losovsky, the *de facto* secretary of the capmakers' union.[19] It
was Losovsky who was responsible for establishing and editing a Yiddish workers' paper, *Der Yiddisher Arbeter (L'Ouvrier Juif)*. At his
urging, the labor Commission of the Capmakers' union adopted (July
12, 1911) the following resolution, which sums up the ideological
position of the Jewish labor movement in France:

> Considering that there are thousands of capmaker workers in Paris who
> know only the Jewish language, and considering that . . . propaganda
> cannot be general or effective without a paper;
> Considering that no paper of this type [exists] in Paris and that as a result
> the workers can read only the bourgeois organs of Warsaw, London, etc.
> . . . the General Assembly approves the creation of a paper . . . [and]
> gives a mandate to its delegates to defend with the paper not only the in-
> terests of capmakers but also those of the entire working class.
> Finally, since there is only one common enemy, the *patronat*, the Asso-
> ciation expresses the wish that the paper not serve to isolate Jewish work-

ers from French workers but, on the contrary, to create and strengthen the bonds between the Jewish proletariat and the French proletariat and unite them in the struggle.
[The Association] decrees that this paper . . . be an organ of class struggle and international solidarity.
[The Association] will rise up against chauvinism and nationalism and every other bourgeois idea which can only build a barrier between the proletariat of different nationalities.[20]

Since the capmakers were the best organized of the Jewish workers, their approval eased the way for the Intersyndical Commission to accept responsibility for publishing the journal. With the publication of the first monthly issue in October of 1911, Losovsky also wrote to the Federation of Labor Unions of the Department of the Seine to secure its support for the paper's goal of "leading the Jewish working element to take a more active part in syndical action."[21] In its response the Federation of Labor Unions accepted the necessity of a Yiddish paper because of the language problems experienced by immigrant Jewish workers, the importance of the Jewish population in Paris, and the need to combat religious influences among Jewish workers.[22]

The Intersyndical Commission and the new Yiddish paper, thus, were accepted both by Jewish activists and by the leadership of the French labor movement as temporary measures necessary to bring the message of syndicalism to the Jewish workers. While remaining officially independent, the Intersyndical Commission cooperated with the French labor movement. Rejecting suggestions to establish a separate Jewish movement, the second Conference of Jewish Syndical Workers, convoked in Paris in December of 1912, again defined the task of the Intersyndical Commission and of *Der Yiddisher arbeter* as "conducting agitation and propaganda among Jewish workers in Paris on the basis of the class struggle and helping to lead the broad strata of the Jewish laboring masses . . . to the local syndical workers' movement."[23] While *Der Yiddisher arbeter* was touted at the conference as a free tribune, it was also announced that articles critical of the resolutions of the CGT would not be published, for the paper "was concerned to call the Jewish workers to carry out in their lives the decisions of the CGT [Confédération Générale du Travail]."[24] The CGT sought even closer cooperation of the Jewish labor movement. In 1914 it demanded of the Intersyndical Commission no longer to hold separate May Day demonstrations along with other immigrant groups but to join in demonstrations of the French proletariat.[25]

Jewish labor activists succeeded in strengthening Yiddish-language syndical sections before the outbreak of the war, particularly in Jewish trades.[26] Many of the employers in these trades were themselves immigrant Jews of an earlier era.[27] In their reminiscences labor activists spoke bitterly of the Jewish patrons who met "green" immigrants at the *Gare du Nord* and, under the guise of Jewish fellowship, hired them at wages well below the going rate.[28] Conducting strike actions against these Jewish employers, the Jewish unions sought to undermine the ethnic solidarity which the employers exploited in their own favor. The socialist Zionist paper *Der Yid in Pariz* reprinted an article from *L'Humanité* which noted that immigrant Jewish employers were exploiting their brothers and waging a vigorous campaign against the Jewish syndical sections.[29] During a 1913 strike the secretary of the Federation of Garment Workers declared that the directors of the Galéries Lafayette had successfully circulated the rumor among nonstriking French workers that triumphant Jewish unions planned to permit the employment of immigrant Jews alone. *Der Yiddisher arbeter* published similar stories.[30] At the same time the Jewish sections hoped to prove to French workers that the Jewish proletariat had no special ties with the immigrant Jewish patrons, despite their common origins and language, and hence would not undermine the position of French workers.[31]

Successful strikes were carried out in 1912 and 1913 by the capmakers and the ladies' garment workers against Jewish employers. The Jewish labor movement was therefore able to demonstrate its class solidarity with the French proletariat and its firm adherence to the principle of class conflict within the immigrant Jewish milieu. Collective bargaining agreements were very rare in this period, but the capmakers secured contracts with several Jewish manufacturers. The employers accepted the syndical wage, the principle of a union shop, and the arbitration of conflicts and agreed not to accept contracts from other houses being struck.[32] The success of the Jewish garment workers in their two-week strike against the Galéries Lafayette prompted favorable comment from *L'Humanité* about the impact of this example of international solidarity upon the French employers who were forced to yield to syndical demands.[33] A representative of the Garment Federation went so far as to characterize the triumphant foreign strikers as the best militants in France.[34]

However, as police reports on strikes in the garment industry indicate, the French Left—its political support of immigrants and admiration of their fervor notwithstanding—shared much of the larger society's ambivalence toward foreign workers. The French labor movement viewed with distaste the overt expression of immigrant ethnicity. Immigrant laborers deserved support as workers and real or potential allies within the French Left, not as members of an ethnic minority within France. In the garment industry tensions between Jewish immigrant and French workers often exploded during strike situations, revealing the resentment and misunderstanding with which French workers regarded their foreign mates. Immigrant Jews, informers reported, were disliked for being clannish and out for themselves, largely, it seems, because they conducted union and strike meetings in Yiddish. Occasionally, French workers even stalked out of immigrant-dominated strike meetings.[35]

The labor movement also bowed on occasion, particularly during World War I, to popular anti-Jewish immigrant sentiment in its propaganda efforts. Describing a 1916 strike in the couture industry, a police report noted that the union "has carefully refrained from speaking of the nationality of the strikers, who are 90% of them Russian or Polish Jews, the most detested of foreign workers."[36] Similarly, a few months later, the police declared that union leaders, "who recognize the little sympathy which the Parisian population feels for this type of workers—all Russian, Romanian, or Polish Jews—cannot conduct an energetic press or poster campaign."[37] It was not accidental, then, that *L'Humanité* omitted from its report on the strike any hint that the strikers were Jews.[38]

Yet the very activity of the Yiddish-speaking language sections in the years between 1911 and 1918 established the legitimacy of the

Jewish labor movement within the larger French movement. Despite
the friction between immigrant and French workers, the foundation
was laid for institutional cooperation between the two segments of the
labor force. And such prominent representatives of the French syndical movement as Jean Longuet and Marcel Sembat came to the
defense of immigrant Jewish workers, both from governmental persecution and from attacks from within the movement.

The Jewish labor movement failed, however, to maintain regular
activity in all the Jewish trades and to enlist the majority of Jewish artisans because of the high percentage of Jewish *façonniers* among the
immigrant population. *Façonniers* were home workers, who were
provided with raw material by an entrepreneur and who often sub-
contracted their work to other laborers. Immigrant Jews became
façonniers for several reasons. The ambitious ones could employ
others, starting with their wives and children, and entertain the prospect of becoming successful *patrons* themselves.[39] Until they
achieved that goal, they retained the illusion of being self-employed
and not simple workers. More importantly, the *façonniers* often were
able to elude regulations which required immigrant workers to obtain
a work permit (*carte de travail*). Difficult to organize, and often accepting lower wages than other workers, the *façonniers* remained the
bêtes noires of the French labor movement, which refused to consider
them real workers eligible for syndical membership.[40] Moreover,
the high percentage of *façonniers* among the immigrant workers—though *façonnerie* was by no means confined to the immigrant
milieu—helped to contribute to the anti-foreigner animus within the
French labor movement. The French representative at the International Congress of Needle Trades Unions held in Vienna in July
1913, for example, claimed that Jews now constituted a majority of
workers in the trade and that since the *façonnier* was their symbol,
most remained unorganized. He asked that no more foreign needle
workers come to France.[41]

For ideological and tactical reasons, then, the Intersyndical Commission, as well as the Jewish sections of individual unions, conducted a propaganda campaign against "the plague" of home labor.[42]
In 1914 the Jewish section of the garment workers' union supported a

bill proposed in the Chamber of Deputies to limit the wages of *façon-niers* to 75 percent of the shopworkers' scale, with the comment that "home work goes against our professional interests in general and our proletarian interests above all."[43] Not until the 1930s did the Jewish labor movement in France show willingness to accept *façonniers* as members of labor unions, though it recognized even earlier that they were exploited along with the simple workers. Nevertheless, since large numbers of immigrants were unable or unwilling to exchange the status of *façonnier* for that of worker, organizing efforts of Jewish labor militants met with only moderate success, and syndical activity in the immigrant Jewish milieu went from crisis to crisis, with the *façonniers* providing a ready source of strikebreakers.[44]

The War Years

Labor agitation continued in the Jewish trades, though on a reduced scale, throughout the war years. The Paris capmakers organized at least one strike in 1916[45] and no fewer than twenty-one strikes in which Jewish workers were involved erupted in the Paris garment industry, most of them between 1916 and 1918.[46] The furniture and handbag unions also remained active during the war.[47] However, the Intersyndical Commission did not meet until June 1916 and refrained from regular activity until 1917.[48] Tensions between French and Jewish workers seem to have become exacerbated during the war, and French syndical leaders warned foreign workers to remain calm or face arrest and expulsion.[49]

The new situation created by the war and pressure from allies in the French movement combined to curb overtly political activity among the political wing of the Jewish labor movement. The Paris Bund could muster little support for the war. In this the Bund shared the views of A. Losovsky and Y. Baer, who demanded of the Yiddish socialist paper *Di Yiddishe tribune* that their names be removed from its masthead because it had printed articles by French "social patriots."[50] The hostility of the Bundists to the Russian regime and their internationalist socialism translated itself into rejection of the wartime patriotism to which the French Socialist Party succumbed until 1917–1918. Only fear of forcible dissolution of the group by the government and concern that the Bund would encounter opposition within the French Socialist Party prevented the Bundists from openly engaging in antiwar political activity.[51] Indeed, a member of the Socialist Party, attending a Bund meeting to deliver a report on the Socialist Congress of London, had chastised the group:

> You too often forget . . . that we are in a state of war and consequently subject to military laws. Once again I adjure you to maintain order and inform you that if anything unfortunate were to happen to you, French socialists would consider themselves obligated to drop you. Do as we do; think only of the victory of the Allies. Afterward, you can seek your own way if you so desire.[52]

Therefore, the Executive Commission of the Bund urged its members not to read political newspapers during work, not to indulge in propaganda, and to avoid fights with anarchists.[53] It blamed its quiescence on the French Socialist Party.[54] Similar pressure to refrain from political activity was expressed to the Jewish members of the Garment Union of the Seine. When a meeting was held on March 12, 1916, to urge the union to adhere to a "Committee for the Resumption of International Relations," a French syndical leader rose to declare that foreigners "were not qualified to make such a decision, that they would be ungrateful to abuse the hospitality of France to the point of associating with a pacifist campaign which resembled treason."[55]

In such a climate most Jewish syndical and political activists turned their attention to specifically Jewish issues raised by the war. Under Bundist sponsorship they organized the Workers Fund to Aid Jewish War Victims and coordinated political activity to secure equal rights for the Jews of Eastern Europe. From October 1915 the Fund collected contributions and held theater benefits for Russian Jews.[56] Along with the Conference of Jewish Workers Organizations, established in December, 1916, it raised the Jewish question within the socialist and labor movements, calling upon the Congress of Syndicates of the Department of the Seine to express solidarity with the suffering Jewish workers of Russia and to protest the tyranny of the

Russian government toward its Jewish population.[57] The Jewish workers recognized, read the Fund's memorandum, that "the enfranchisement of the Jewish people could be achieved only through a common struggle in alliance with the democracies of the nations among which they lived, and they believed . . . that in that struggle they could count upon the support of the international proletariat."[58] Having received such support from the Russian, British, and American proletariat, they now turned with hope to the French workers' organizations.[59] The following spring the Conference of Jewish Workers' Organizations resolved to "draw the attention of local democratic circles, and in the first place, that of the workers, to the Jewish question; create a current of protests against the criminal intrigues of anti-Semitic governments, and influence the organized proletariat and the International to raise a campaign in favor of the Jews at the Peace Conference."[60]

In addition to lobbying on behalf of Russian Jewry, immigrant Jewish socialists in France engaged in self-defense as well. Mounting a campaign against the expulsion of alien noncombattants, the Jewish workers' movement in Paris set up a committee which published an appeal to the public and contacted socialist deputies for their support.[61] In response to anti-Semitic charges of Jewish cowardice, in June 1915 the Bund set up a Study Committee for the Preparation and Publication of Statistical Material on Jewish Volunteers in the French Armies. At the private meeting at which the Study Committee was founded it was clearly stated that its aim was to counteract rumors that the Jews were not doing their part in the war.[62] Following the suggestion of a famous Polish Jewish writer, I. L. Peretz, that the story of the Jewish experience in the war be told, the Study Committee published a bulletin in French and Yiddish calling for the collection of stories of Jewish heroism for "the honor of our race."[63]

Revival of the Movement

Because of the diversion of the attention of immigrant Jewish militants from pure syndical activity and because of the bitter split within the French Left, the Jewish labor movement had to be rebuilt and reshaped upon cessation of hostilities. The leadership of the movement had been decimated. As early as 1915, 185 members of the Paris Bund were reported to have departed for the U.S. in order to escape the mobilization orders they feared would soon be imposed upon the subjects of allied governments.[64] With the outbreak of the Russian Revolution, a number of Jewish militants, among them the dynamic Losovsky, returned home to contribute their talents to its cause, thus leaving the leadership of the movement even more impoverished.

The situation was exacerbated by post-war internecine quarrels over whether to affiliate with the Communist Party. In this regard the Jewish labor movement in France shared the agony of the larger French movement, which split in 1921 when the reformist majority within the CGT expelled the leftists from its ranks. The latter established the revolutionary *Confédération Générale du Travail Unitaire* (CGTU), which soon affiliated with the international Communist Labor movement.[65] Similarly, the *Yiddishe Arbeter Organizatsie*, established in 1919, fell victim in 1921 to tensions between revolutionary and reformist members.[66] Its demise was accelerated by the expulsion from France of its most radical leaders, who had been kept under police surveillance.[67] Unlike the majority of French union members, who remained within the reformist CGT, however, most Jewish activists chose the revolutionary path of the Communist labor movement.

While the Bund was the most important organized party within the pre-war Intersyndical Commission and prevailed among Jewish leftists during the war, the Communist party dominated the Jewish labor movement and all political activity on the Left within the immigrant Jewish milieu following the end of World War I and throughout the period which culminated in the outbreak of World War II. This dominance imposed relative unity on the Jewish labor movement and enabled the Jewish Communists to become the largest organized bloc within the interwar immigrant Jewish community, although they never came to enlist the majority of that population. Non-Communist workers who wished to participate in Jewish syndical activity had to join the Communist labor unions. The Jewish labor movement, virtually in its entirety, opted for affiliation with the Communist trade union movement, the CGTU, not only because of the widespread conviction of Eastern European immigrants that Communism represented the progressive wave of the future but also because the CGTU addressed itself specifically to the cause of immigrant workers.

Although non-Communist members of unions affiliated with the CGTU protested Communist "dictatorial control" and "red hooliganism" and sought greater political independence for the Jewish syndical sections,[68] there were no non-Communist Jewish unions in the major Jewish trades. Although the socialist CGT represented the majority of organized French workers,[69] only bakers and immigrant printers maintained affiliation with the CGT.[70] The Bundists organized an association entitled Friends of Foreign Workers with the participation of members of the SFIO and the CGT, which sought a protective statute for foreign workers and combatted xenophobic propaganda, but, on the local syndical level, they offered the foreign worker no viable alternative to participation in Communist-controlled Yiddish-language sections.[71]

As early as 1921 the labor congress of the garment industry had proposed the reestablishment of foreign-language sections. These were designed to facilitate the organization of immigrant laborers and prevent their use as strikebreakers, to help them understand French workers, and to discourage the arrival of foreign workers when no jobs were available.[72] Sympathy was expressed for the newly arrived immigrant Jews, who "ate and slept in the same room, on straw mattresses . . . and knowing no French, were ignorant of the customary wages and could not find work elsewhere."[73]

It was not until 1923, however, that the CGTU reestablished the Yiddish Intersyndical Commission, part of a general program regarding foreign workers the CGTU had adopted at its Second Congress, held in Bourges in November of 1923. The Congress approved the creation of a *Bureau de Main-d'Oeuvre Etrangère* (MOE) and of new intersyndical committees on the local and regional levels which had been set up during the year in order to incorporate foreign workers into the French labor movement.[74] To win the support of the foreign workers, each CGTU Congress from 1925 to 1933 passed a resolution in favor of equality of rights for immigrant workers and called for the extirpation of xenophobia within the ranks of French workers.[75] Moreover, the CGTU was willing to breach the law and allow foreign workers to serve on syndical councils, commenting, "Shall we pay heed to this bourgeois legality to forbid . . . in our own house the administration of unions by foreign workers?"[76]

The Yiddish Intersyndical Commission was merely one of six foreign-language commissions founded by the CGTU in 1923 and expanded to twelve in 1926.[77] The Party, too, established foreign-language subsections. As *Cahiers du Bolchevisme* reported in 1926, the creation of language sections within the Party (and, by extension, within the Communist-affiliated labor union movement) was motivated by the desire "to extend our influence over masses whom we could not otherwise reach."[78] As in the pre-war period, the establishment of foreign-language sections thus represented a response to practical necessity, not a theoretical legitimization of ethnic separatism.

Theoretically, each language section in the unions as well as in the Party was to have no independent decision-making power but was to be under the direct supervision of the appropriate syndical or Party unit at each level—local, regional, and national.[79] In practice, the language sections, particularly at the syndical level, exercised a great measure of independence. For example, at the Fifth Congress of Labor Unions of the Seine, convoked during January and February of 1925, the complaint was voiced by the Bureau of MOE of the Region of the Seine that the Jewish representative never came to meetings and that the Jews had failed to contact the Bureau though it was known that they published a paper and were engaged in syndical activity.[80] Similar complaints about "uncontrolled ethnic sections" in the Jewish trades persisted into the 1930s. "Our factions in all [the Jewish Communist] organizations . . . are not controlled and directed by the Party committees," noted a publication of the Central Section of the MOE in 1930.[81] Party resolutions of 1929 and 1930 warned that "we must see to it that the language sections and the labor groups do not in any case fill the role of organisms independent of the Party."[82] Likewise, in 1931 and 1932 Communist publications reiterated the need for direct control of the language sections by the appropriate Party organ and the immediate supervision of the Central Section of the MOI (*Main-d'Oeuvre Immigrée*, the new title for the former MOE) by a member of the Political Bureau of the Communist Party.[83] A member of the syndical council was to represent the party in each syndical language section while the latter was to send one member to the Syndical Council. On the local and regional level, each Intersyndical Committee, which represented its particular ethnic sections in the area, was to send a delegate to the local or regional Commission of the MOI.[84]

The Paris region, the center of Jewish syndical activity, drew especially heavy criticism. Thus it was noted that the foreign-language sections there were not only free of the control of the regional party structure but presented the danger of factionalism.[85] In brief, the complex centralized pattern of foreign-language sections within the CGTU and the expected ultimate control of those sections by the Party's Bureau of MOI appear to have remained in theory only. In practice, immigrant activists within the Jewish labor movement were permitted relative flexibility to respond to the particular needs of their special constituency, although they certainly would not act in opposition to official CGTU policy.

In the interwar years Yiddish-language sections existed in the ladies' and men's garment labor unions, the handbag, shoe, raincoat, capmaking, hosiery and leather industries, and among butchers, restaurant waiters, printers, bakers, and furniture workers.[86] The success or failure of the Yiddish-language sections was closely connected with the general economic and political conditions. Since the unions offered little protection against unemployment, they tended to disintegrate in periods of economic crisis. And economic crises occurred rather frequently throughout the 1920s and 1930s, especially in 1926, the spring of 1928, 1930–1931, and almost continually after 1932 when the Depression struck France.[87] Moreover, as a result of the Depression, restrictive legislation was imposed upon immigrant workers, artisans, and merchants, beginning with the law of August

10, 1932, which limited the ratio of foreign workers to be employed in any industry or trade to 10 percent of the total. Since Jewish economic distribution, as we have seen, was skewed, the impact of this decree upon the Jewish trades was particularly severe, and the number of immigrant *façonniers* increased substantially as workers attempted to evade the provisions of the decree and its successors in 1934 and 1935.[88] The ups and downs of Jewish syndical activity, then, was cyclical, following the course of the French economy.

Although the opposition of the Communist Party and of the Yiddish Intersyndical Commission to the government's policy of blaming the crisis upon the foreign workers was attractive to immigrant Jews,[89] the inability of the CGTU to defend the masses of immigrant workers from government repression limited that appeal. The insecure economic and political position of the immigrant workers, fearful of expulsion and of other forms of reprisal, prevented many Jewish immigrants from joining the Jewish syndical sections and especially the Party. Thus, it was estimated that only 100 foreign Jews were actually members of the CP in 1930–1931 and only 300 belonged to Jewish syndical sections, though the number of sympathizers was much higher.[90]

As the Jewish labor movement began responding to the rapid rise in the number of *façonniers* after 1932, however, it attracted more workers to its ranks. In 1933 the Communist paper *Der Morgen* articulated a new policy toward *façonniers:* Those who employed no more than one helper were to be eligible for membership in a union, because they were exploited like workers and, as unorganized laborers, were serving to depress the general wage scale.[91] A campaign to organize the *façonniers* and to "draw them close to their class brothers" was thereupon undertaken by the Yiddish-language sections.[92] Beginning in 1934, numerous strikes in the hosiery and garment industries successfully mobilized both workers and *façonniers*.[93] Furthermore, self-employed artisans and small entrepreneurs began to organize themselves independently into associations and to cooperate with workers' unions in a common struggle against the larger entrepreneurs and the *grandes maisons*.[94] By early 1936, according to the figures of Zosa Szajkowski, there were 2,123 organized workers and 2,476 organized *façonniers* within the Jewish labor movement.[95]

It was the electoral triumph of Blum's Popular Front and the sitdown strikes of June 1936 which galvanized the Jewish labor movement. In a burst of enthusiasm, immigrant Jews who had feared to join the unions enrolled *en masse*, and the number of organized Jewish workers in Paris leaped to 11,830 following the heady June days while the number of organized *façonniers* rose to 4,253.[96] In the spring of 1937, the *Naye presse* claimed that there were 13,000 organized Jewish workers in the Paris region.[97]

This triumph of Jewish syndical organization, which paralleled the extraordinary gains in membership in the French movement as a whole,[98] was short-lived. In response to the continued economic crisis and the rising xenophobia, even among workers, in 1937 the French CP shifted its policy toward immigrant workers, declaring opposition to further immigration of foreign workers and adopting the slogan *C'est complet* (It's full). As part of this new policy the CP abolished the foreign-language sections within the Party,[99] though the language sections appear to have continued to function at the syndical level. Almost immediately the new Party policy was reflected in the pages of the *Naye presse*, which published articles opposing immigration because of the high level of unemployment in France and because of the resistance of new immigrants to joining the unions.[100] Although the Jewish unions continued to protest the agitation against foreigners already resident in France, the new emphasis of Communist policy did not pass unnoticed.

The new attitude of the CGTU, the persistent economic crisis, and the repressive governmental legislation against foreigners, which was extended in 1938, combined to reduce incentives for union membership among immigrant workers. By 1939 the number of organized Jewish workers had declined precipitously. According to *Unzer shtime*, in early 1939 the Ladies' Garment Union, which had numbered 2,500 at its peak in 1936, had a membership of only 200. Similarly, the number of organized hosiery workers had fallen from 700 in 1936 to 63 in 1939.[101] Though as a Bundist organ *Unzer shtime* can be suspected of partisanship, the 1939 report in the *Naye presse* of the annual meeting of the Yiddish Intersyndical Commission suggests that the Jewish labor movement was in a state of disarray. Rather than glorifying in the successful strike actions and propaganda activity of the unions, as in 1936 and 1937, the report affirmed the need for stronger organization of Jewish workers.[102] As a capmaker declared early in 1939, in a remark which characterizes the mood prevalent among Jewish workers, "When we capmakers evaluate what is left from the June achievements, we must with sorrow state that we have suffered a complete loss."[103]

The Jewish Labor Movement as an Agent of Assimilation

The stated goal of the Jewish labor movement was the syndical organization of immigrant Jewish workers and the dissemination in the immigrant milieu of socialist and Communist principles. Just as the pre-war socialist paper *Der Yiddisher arbeter* had proclaimed its hope to unite the French and Jewish proletariat in a common struggle against the bourgeois oppressors, so the Communist *Arbeter shtime* announced as the purpose of the Intersyndical Commission "to lead the Jewish workers into a common front with the French workers in the struggle for the revolution."[104] The legitimacy of radical labor in France enabled the highly politicized Jewish labor movement to flourish on French soil more easily than in Britain or the United States.

In pursuing their goal of integrating Jewish and French workers, Jewish militants established an institutional structure and conducted an ideological campaign which served to prevent the identification of the immigrant Jewish worker with the larger Jewish community, both immigrant and native, and to facilitate his assimilation into the French working class. Toward the end of World War I, Jewish socialists opposed cooperation with Zionists and middle-class immigrants in the effort to secure rights for the Jews of Eastern Europe. At the Conference of Jewish Workers' Organizations for Equal Rights for Jews, convoked at the initiative of the capmakers' union in December 1916 and January 1917, speakers attacked the Zionists and objected to the notion of a *union sacrée* within the Jewish community on the grounds that it would undermine the class consciousness of the workers. The Conference also adopted a measure which condemned the "irresponsible propaganda conducted by nationalist and chauvinist Jewish groups."[105] This attitude was typical of Jewish politics on the Left in the interwar period as well. Thus, Jewish Communists called upon their followers to shun institutions administered by their class enemies: "Will a [class-] conscious working man enroll his child in the summer colonies organized by bourgeois clerical committees?" rhetorically queried a brochure of a Communist educational society.[106] In similar fashion, the *Naye presse* admonished its readers not to send their children to the religious schools administered by the Jewish bourgeoisie, who took advantage of the desire of workers to educate their children. Education under middle-class auspices, stated the Communist paper, resulted in the estrangement of children from their working-class parents. Moreover, the proper goal of a Jewish education was not merely the learning of Yiddish but the inculcation of class-consciousness.[107] Contact with class enemies could only dissipate working-class energy and commitment to the revolutionary struggle which alone could resolve the Jewish question.

Although a policy of cooperation with middle-class Jewish institutions was initiated by Jewish Communists during the Popular Front period, it represented merely a temporary stratagem, designed to respond to the socioeconomic and political needs of the mid-1930s. Even at the height of the Popular Front, the Paris Bund, which boycotted the Jewish Popular Front, published a statement attacking "the *klal-yisrael* (Jewish unity) politics on the Jewish street." It refused to cooperate with the Federation of Jewish Societies in the fight against anti-Semitism because it was the Federation, as the representative of the Jewish upper bourgeoisie, that remained the enemy of the Jewish masses. The Bund further denounced the *klal-yisrael* atmosphere, which was predicated on the concept that adherence to a specific political party was not important. Since anti-Semitism was a product of fascism, the true battle was to be waged against the capitalists, not in cooperation with them.[108]

The *Poalei-Zion*, the smallest of the Jewish parties of the Left, also

pursued a policy of noncooperation. It did so even though, imbued
with Zionist ideology, it was most concerned with the Jewish content
of its program. Its First National Conference in 1928 resolved to
boycott a project which cut across class lines to establish a unified
kehilla (communal structure) in Metz. Instead it proposed the founding of a united workers' organization to serve the interests of the
working-class elements within the Jewish community.[109]

To minimize the ties of ethnicity across class lines, the Jewish
labor movement attempted to meet not only the economic and political demands of the immigrant Jewish worker, but his social and cultural needs as well. As the major immigrant social institution, the
landsmanshaften therefore remained the primary target of all Jewish
leftists—Communists, Bundists, and socialist Zionists alike. Bundists
proclaimed that "it should be a disgrace for each worker to belong to
bourgeois burial societies" and exhorted their followers to get "out of
the societies, which are concerned only with the dead and with
graves."[110] The *Poalei-Zion* paper, too, discussed the need for coordinated and intense cultural activity so that Jewish workers would
have no reason to join bourgeois societies.[111] Likewise, the Communist Intersyndical Commission listed prominently on its agenda ways
to "lure Jewish workers away from the societies."[112] In the 1930s the
struggle against the societies loomed as a major task of the Intersyndical Commission. The struggle could not be won, commented one
correspondent to the *Naye presse*, until proletarian organizations provided burials for members and their families, for it was the death
benefits and the sense of security which they afforded that motivated
the membership of immigrant workers in bourgeois societies.[113]

Although the political parties appear not to have favored the practical, if nonideological, suggestion that they furnish death benefits to
their members (as the Jewish Left in America did), they consciously
set out to compete in terms of activity and benefits with the societies.
To reach the "masses of workers . . . mired in the societies," the Intersyndical Commission determined to establish unemployment and
strike funds, provide medical and legal aid, and improve its day-to-
day activity.[114] Similarly, the Communist press called for bringing
bourgeois philanthropy to justice and for establishing worker-

controlled welfare funds.[115] According to its Bundist founders, the
Arbeter Ring was established to free unemployed workers from dependence upon bourgeois charity.[116] Similar motives led Jewish
Communists and members of *Poalei Zion* as well to set up their own
unemployment committees.[117]

Jewish labor activists thus hoped to create so extensive a network of
social, cultural, and political institutions that the immigrant worker
would not need to have any contact with bourgeois organizations.
Jewish Communists, as we have noted, provided a wide range of educational, social, and cultural services for their constituents. The *Arbeter Ring*, too (which offered its members medical care, legal aid,
adult education in both French and Yiddish, a sports club, and a
youth group, and sponsored vacation colonies and a workers' restaurant) openly declared worker self-sufficiency to be its goal.[118]

No need and no justification, then, for the class-conscious immigrant Jew to venture beyond the borders of the working-class community. Youth groups, sports clubs, dances, lectures were all available under the auspices of the Jewish labor movement. The
politicization of the sociocultural life of immigrant Jewry in France
resulted in the creation of an independent immigrant working-class
community. Although the boundary lines of the working-class community were not sharply defined, particularly in the years when the
reigning Popular Front mentality stimulated temporary cooperation
with the middle classes, the most loyal members of that community
experienced in their political institutions a process of assimilation
which led them into the native French Left.

From its early days the Jewish labor movement had sought, after
all, to integrate its members into the international socialist movement. As the major Jewish party in pre-World War I France, the
Bund participated in joint actions with the SFIO and the League of
Rights of Man as with the members of the Russian Social Democratic Party and the Polish Socialist Party in France. Even the response to matters of specific Jewish concern, such as the notorious
Beilis trial of 1911–1913, was coordinated with other revolutionary
groups in order to point up how working-class solidarity cut across
national lines and in order to indicate that the oppression of the Jews

was but another manifestation of reactionary excesses to which only socialism provided a solution.[119]

In keeping with its internationalist outlook, the Jewish labor movement also called upon Jewish workers to reciprocate and to demonstrate with the Russian Social Democratic Party "to show solidarity with our brothers struggling in Russia," or to celebrate the destruction of the Paris Commune along with the rest of international socialism, or to commemorate the tenth anniversary of the Irkutsk protest.[120] At such demonstrations and May Day celebrations the politicized Jewish workers were brought into contact with their French and their Russian and Polish emigré counterparts. Moreover, they were introduced to the leading representatives of the international socialist movement, including Paul Lafargue, Jean Jaurès, and Kameniev.

In the interwar period the various sectors of the Jewish labor movement continued to coordinate their activity with the major parties they were allied with. Typical of such activity was the French Bund's co-sponsorship of a protest meeting against pogroms and anti-Semitism in Poland (in which representatives of the SFIO, Italian Socialist Party, and Polish workers in the CGT participated) and of a discussion in August 1933 on the situation of the International Workers' Movement at which Heinrich Erlich, Victor Alter, Paul-Henri Spaak, and Pietro Nenni were among the featured speakers.[121] As Raphael Ryba, active in the Bund in France in the 1930s, has observed, "Thanks to our close contact with the Socialist Party we took part in all its actions, demonstrations, and even electoral campaigns, although formally we were not a section of the SFIO. . . . We made every effort to popularize the Socialist Party in the Jewish milieu."[122]

Just as the Bund drew its supporters into the French socialist milieu, the Jewish Communists in their turn brought their followers, if not into the Party itself, then at least into the larger circle of Communist sympathizers who could be mustered for electoral campaigns and protest demonstrations.[123] Thus, Jewish Communists marched en masse in May Day demonstrations, were active in the effort to send volunteers to Spain, and cooperated despite linguistic difficulties with nonimmigrant branches of the CP.[124] The minute book of an unemployment committee of Yiddish-speaking workers noted, for example, "a closer connection between Jewish and French unemployed comrades" and added that the "French Unemployment Committee [of the CP] states that first of all our activity must be conducted in unison, that both committees must together undertake a variety of actions."[125] French workers within the Jewish trades were also invited to meetings of the Jewish sections of the unions, in which Jewish workers were increasingly urged by the Communist leadership to conduct their business in French.[126] Thus, on the local level, the Jewish worker and his family were brought into contact with their French counterparts. Virtually all informants confirmed in interviews that their primary contacts, outside their own Jewish labor milieu, occurred within the French labor movement. They neither had nor desired relations with native French Jews.[127]

Though rooted in the Jewish milieu of Eastern Europe, Jewish Communists did not sentimentalize that milieu. Rather, through the ideology of the Communist Party, they provided a critique of, and a solution for, the suffering of Jews as a minority group. Besides speaking to the daily economic problems of immigrant Jewish workers, Communist ideology promised that the building of a Communist society would ultimately bring to an end the persecution of the Jews. And in the time before that society came about, as Annie Kriegel, the historian of the French CP, has perceptively suggested, party membership offered immigrant Jews a means to escape their minority status as Jews. By defining themselves in political terms, they were able "to *choose* [to belong] to a minority of a social and political character rather than being *condemned* by birth to that fundamentally odd minority which is the Jewish minority."[128] While the French CP paid no particular attention to the special case of the Jews as victims of persecution, it did exalt all victims of capitalism and fascism, thus furnishing psychological sustenance to the immigrant Jewish workers. Communist ideology enabled Jews to find meaning in their status as objects of discrimination within the pantheon of the oppressed. By identifying with, and furnishing aid to other victims, such as the Spanish workers during the Civil War, Jewish Communists transcended the sense of isolation often experienced by persecuted Jews.

While concerned with anti-Semitism and committed to the propagation of Yiddish, the Jewish Communists taught Yiddish without *Yiddishkayt* (Jewishness). Their program, which lacked any specifically Jewish content, essentially used Yiddish as a means of evoking working-class loyalties engendered originally in Eastern Europe and as a means of strengthening class consciousness. It was, therefore, a one-generation phenomenon, dependent upon the personal experience and memory of Jewish life in Eastern Europe. In fact, the French-born children of Yiddish-speaking parents moved with ease into the general branches of the French labor movement. During the years of its ascendancy, however, the Jewish labor movement vociferously attacked the social and political assumptions of native French Jewry. It denied the existence of a Jewish community and of common Jewish interests across class lines. It rejected religion as the basis for Jewish identity. Offering an ideological analysis of the Jewish question, it decried the politics of neutrality and quietism in favor of organized and public Jewish politics. More than any other element within immigrant Jewry, the Left crystallized the conflict between native and immigrant Jews.

5.
Immigrants and Natives, 1906–1933

In every country in which East European Jews settled, they clashed with the native Jewish community to which they turned for aid. In France the conflict between native and immigrant Jews was exacerbated by the timing of Jewish immigration. East European Jewish immigration to France came late; the majority of immigrants chose France as their ultimate destination only in the interwar period. The constant influx of new immigrants tended to retard the integration process and keep visible a foreign Jewish population in France's major cities. In the 1930s, facing the dual problems of a contracting economy and expanding xenophobia, native Jews became ever more insistent that the pace of immigrant acculturation be quickened and that immigrants defer to native political leadership to forestall anti-Semitic incidents. While the Jewish communities of the United States and Great Britain had several relatively quiet decades in which to integrate their immigrant populations, French Jews had to deal with highly politicized newcomers in particularly difficult times—first in the aftermath of the Dreyfus Affair, then when the rise of Nazism and of domestic anti-Semitism was challenging their sense of security. Moreover, the absence of any notion of cultural pluralism in the French polity confirmed in French Jewry, even in the economically secure years following World War I, their sense of the urgency of assimilating the immigrants to their own model of Jewish communal behavior.

Despite their differences in social class, politics, and ethnicity, immigrant and native Jews were bound together in a complex web. Although native and immigrant Jews often viewed themselves as belonging to two separate communities and maintained their own religious, philanthropic, and cultural institutions, their communities were not mutually exclusive. While French Jewish survivors of both native and immigrant origin have tended to emphasize the social barriers which had existed between the two groups until after World War II, there was, in fact, more social contact than is generally supposed. Marriage between the groups, a good indicator of the breakdown of social barriers, was not infrequent. A sampling of the marriage records of all the major Paris temples for the years 1906–1925 reveals that an average of 14 percent of marriages joined East European immigrant and native together,[1] while another 4 percent linked Levantine and North African immigrants with natives.

Most contacts between the two communities, however, were institutional, shaped by factors both external and internal to the two communities. The fact that the non-Jewish world made little distinction among various classes of Jews and considered all Jews mutually responsible for each other's behavior made it necessary for settled Jewish communities to care for their less fortunate coreligionists, if only to prevent the social problems of immigrant Jews from becoming a matter of public interest and concern. Moreover, a tradition of Jewish philanthropy had raised expectations of services to be rendered among both the recipients of philanthropic largesse and their benefactors. New immigrants, in particular, came to depend upon native Jewish institutions for aid. That dependence elicited in the leadership of the native community a spirit of paternalism *vis-à-vis* their immigrant clientele.

The paternalistic attitude was reinforced by the clash of social classes and of the mentalities of immigrant and native Jews respectively. Proud of their status as French citizens, at home in French culture, and disdainful of immigrant Jewish manners, customs, and of what they viewed as lack of culture, the native Jews were unable to accept their immigrant coreligionists as they were. Nor could they envisage them as potential contributors of new intellectual and cultural resources to the French Jewish community. The natives perceived it as their responsibility to remake immigrant Jews in their own image and to use their institutions as agents of assimilation. For they believed that only their form of adaptation to France—as French nationals of the Jewish faith—was consonant with the reality of French social and political principles.

Thus, from the early period of mass immigration of Eastern European Jews to France in the wake of the Revolution of 1905 until World War II, the dominant attitude of native Jewish leaders to their immigrant coreligionists was condescension, be it benevolent or angry. Pierre Abraham wrote of his parents' generation that "one considers with vaguely pitying repugnance the unfortunate immigrant Jews of Eastern Europe. One prides himself on being several generations ahead of them, [for] they were not yet 'assimilated.' " [2] In an article of 1906 which called for more than tolerance "for our unfortunate brethren," a correspondent for L'Univers israélite confirms Abraham's reminiscence: "Their mentality seems to us to be insufficiently adapted to ours. But we forget that we did not require less than a century to attain the assimilation of which we are proud and which was made impossible for them in their country of origin. Whatever faults they have are the fruit of servitude." [3] Thus, the very argument which the proponents of emancipation advanced, back in the period of the Revolution, in order to explain away the inferior level of French Jews was now adopted by the Jewish heirs of emancipation with regard to their immigrant coreligionists who arrived in France a century and a quarter after the Revolution.

The same spirit continued to permeate the pages of L'Univers israélite in the interwar period as well. A review of Jacob Lévy's novel Les Pollaks smugly suggested that "we should give credit to these Jewish masses who aspire to a better life but whom persecution and suffering . . . have imbued with a special mentality of the type found among slaves. . . . Let them see in us the example of what they must become to be adapted to liberty." [4] No wonder the development of independent institutions by the immigrants was taken as a sign of their failure at the task of assimilation. "If . . . living among us, they tend only to stick together"—so proclaimed the 1926 General Assembly of the Paris Consistory in a veiled threat to exclude immigrants altogether—"we will not be able to overlook the essentially national character of our Association." [5] To be sure, this harsh judgment was not entirely justified even from the native French Jewish point of view. It was the continued arrival of fresh immigrants into France throughout the interwar period that prolonged and magnified the visibility of the unassimilated immigrant Jewish population and obscured from native Jewry the longer-settled immigrants' considerable adaptation to French manners and language.

The pronounced ethnicity of the immigrants and their propagation of Jewishness, as distinct from Judaism, as the basis for assertion of identity were summarily rejected as inappropriate to the French scene. France, native Jews recognized full well, tolerated no ethnic particularism. "These new arrivals," bemoaned Baron Edmond de Rothschild at the 1913 General Assembly of the Paris Consistory, "do not understand French customs . . . , they remain among themselves, retain their primitive language, speak and write in jargon."[6] Similarly, in 1925, Jules Meyer, a prominent native Jew affiliated with native institutions, reacted with equal distaste to the evidence of immigrant ethnicity: "The walls of Paris must no longer be covered with Hebrew characters; Paris must cease being flooded with Yiddish newspapers, books, films, and plays."[7]

Yiddish, the badge of immigrant ethnicity, was viewed at times with contempt and at times with alarm. Sagely, moderate voices within French Jewry commented that the natural process of assimilation would, within one generation, solve the problem of the use of Yiddish by immigrant Jews. Indeed, in 1913 an article in L'Univers israélite attacked the scorn in which Yiddish was held even though it had developed a rich literature; pragmatically, the article suggested that Yiddish be employed by native Jewish institutions to facilitate the adaptation of immigrant Jews to French life.[8] Similarly, half a generation later another article was published to calm the fears of native Jews confronted with the massive post-war immigration. The visibility of Yiddish was only a temporary phenomenon, it suggested, and the appearance of Yiddish newspapers in Paris merely paralleled the existence of a foreign-language press for other immigrant groups.[9]

However, in periods in which anti-Semitic incidents proliferated, fear prevailed over moderation. Though Yiddish symbolized the alien status of the immigrant Jew alone, the anti-Semites persisted in linking the latter with the native Jew. Hence, Yiddish came to be considered a factor endangering the native Jew's status. Because Yiddish is a Germanic dialect, the Paris Consistory even demanded, during World War I, an end to Yiddish sermons in the new and indepen-

dent immigrant synagogue on the rue Pavée. As the representatives of
the Pavée synagogue were informed, "current circumstances make
the use of Judeo-German [sic] dangerous. . . . The Consistory . . .
would be held responsible because, according to public opinion, it
represents the entire [Jewish] community of Paris."[10] When the immigrant leaders protested that Yiddish was the language of six million
subjects of Russia, France's ally in war, and when they pointed to the
150 (Yiddish-speaking) soldiers which their synagogue had furnished
to France, such self-defense was characterized by the consistorial
leaders as aggressive. "War imposes obligation," the immigrant
leaders were told. "French must be used [in order to] prevent a hostile campaign," they were advised, notwithstanding the fact that their
rabbi, Rabbi Herzog, spoke only Yiddish and English.[11]

The immigrants, of course, sought to perpetuate their own customs and ideologies not merely as a matter of practical necessity or
convenience but because they considered the native Jewish community to be an abject example of the deleterious effects of thoughtless
assimilation. In 1913, Nathan Frank, an immigrant jounalist, commented of native Jewry, "We consider them to be fools, and they
consider us to lack honor."[12] Immigrant Jews found the *Univers
israélite* to be lifeless and wanting in *Yiddishkayt*, much like the native community as a whole, and considered the Alliance Israélite a
vehicle for spreading French culture under the banner of Jewish
philanthropy.[13] The fact that immigrants in need were treated by the
Alliance and the Paris Comité de Bienfaisance as children and
beggars (*shnorrers*) was thoroughly resented.

More than twenty years later, the immigrant perception of the native Jewish community remained strikingly similar. Writing now for
Parizer haynt, Nathan Frank noted, after a generation of experience
with native Jewry,

Even while adapting [to the French milieu] we remain ourselves, and it is
precisely that which troubles the [native Jews]. . . . We want to adapt in
a manner in which that adaptation will harm neither our national interests nor our cultural aspirations. We know that that is possible. But the
leaders of French Judaism want to assimilate us while leaving us only a
bit of Jewish religion.[14]

Israel Jefroykin, president of the Federation of Jewish Societies, aptly summarized this view in 1935: "The immigrant Jew sees himself as the bearer of authentic Jewish culture and sees the native Jews as neither here nor there."[15] The social, cultural, and ideological differences separating the two communities, as well as their differing assessments as to what was permissible within French society, thus shaped the nature of the relations of native and immigrant Jews in the period after Dreyfus and before Vichy.

Meeting Immigrant Needs

Confronted with the immigrant masses, native Jewish leaders believed their most urgent tasks were to coordinate aid and meet the immigrants' needs without seriously depleting the resources of their institutions or jeopardizing the social and political situation of their own constituency. When these goals conflicted, their own interests took precedence.

The Comité de Bienfaisance of Paris Jewry, run by the same personalities who were active in consistorial affairs, bore the brunt of the burden of immigrant aid before World War I. Its quarters on the rue Rodier (in the ninth arrondissement) were besieged by poor immigrants from Russia and Romania, who were provided with food, clothing, and loans.[16] Between 1905 and 1913 the Comité de Bienfaisance paid out 450,207 francs in charity and made available another 348,135 francs in loans.[17]

As early as 1906 the Comité began to seek ways to free itself of its burden, for it found the immigrants difficult to deal with. Occasionally, those denied aid would refuse to exit gracefully, and the police had to be summoned no fewer than twelve times between January 1906 and September 1907 to eject or arrest recalcitrant applicants.[18]

With regards to foreign Jews already in Paris, the Comité resolved in 1906 "to continue the distribution of aid with the same benevolence and impartiality as in the past."[19] However, in the spring of that year it sent a circular to provincial and foreign communities,

urging them not to channel immigrant Jews to Paris, "for these indigents can find neither resources nor work in the capital and . . .
the Comité finds it necessary to send them back to the border, [a
request] which, moreover, many of them make of [us] . . . after dis-
covering that they cannot find here the means of subsistence which
they had hoped to find."[20] At the same time the Comité sent letters
to Jewish organizations affirming its unwillingness to assume the fiscal responsibility of transporting immigrants on their way. For the
Comité defined itself as an institution "of local assistance . . . not
established to encourage the emigration of foreign Israelites passing
through Paris or residing there. . . . It can no longer serve as an intermediary to other institutions for transports to America."[21]

Lamenting its growing deficits and the large number of new arrivals in the years preceding World War I, the Comité further tight-
ened its regulations. In 1913 it accepted a report on foreign Jews in
Paris which declared, "In principle the Comité is in agreement to attempt to check immigration and to demand of new arrivals a waiting
period before giving them aid. . . . The Comité also agrees to the
publication of a notification in Russia to warn the Israelites that they
will find neither work nor aid in Paris."[22] Concerned first and foremost with protecting itself and the interests of the native Jewish community in France, the Comité de Bienfaisance could see no alternative to sharply discouraging immigration and shifting the burden to
other localities. Such activity often met with resistance, and in the
summer of 1913 the Comité resolved to limit further instances of repatriation after receiving from the *Deutsche Zentralstelle für Jüdische
Wanderarmenfürsorge* a request "no longer to send poor [immigrant
Jews] to Germany," coupled with a threat to send them back to
Paris.[23]

By 1914 the Comité de Bienfaisance was seriously discussing a proposal to "bring the matter [of immigration] to the competent authorities to ask for a measure to prevent the free entry of foreigners into
France."[24] Although the Council of the Comité de Bienfaisance
decided to leave matters as they were because fiscal disaster was not
imminent,[25] it is clear that the well-established leaders of the Comité
were prepared to intervene politically against the immediate interests

of Eastern European Jews. The tradition of France as a haven for the oppressed notwithstanding, French Jewish leaders were willing to subordinate that ideal to their primary institutional loyalties. Although their posture may appear excessively short-sighted and narrowly focused, it is representative of a continuing tension in Jewish history between the rational decision to defend local communal interests and the idealistic response of incurring sacrifices to help persecuted brethren in time of crisis.[26]

However, the behavior of French Jews contrasts startlingly with that of their British and American counterparts. In both English-speaking countries the native Jewish leadership, despite their earlier opposition to immigration, and their contempt for the low cultural level of the immigrants, vigorously combatted attempts to restrict the full flow of newcomers. Prominent leaders of the American Jewish Committee, of the Union of American Hebrew Congregations, and of B'nai B'rith met repeatedly with government officials to protest the rigid enforcement of the ban on "assisted immigrants" or those likely to become public charges, to prevent the adoption of literacy tests, and to argue against a quota system.[27] Large segments of the Jewish community in England marshalled their forces against the Aliens Act of 1905. Indeed, fighting the Aliens Act became the central issue of Jewish political activity and served to legitimize the notion of specific Jewish political interests for much of British Jewry.[28]

And what of the Jews of France? They remained concerned only with the philanthropic aspects of immigrant aid. The problems which confronted Paris and other transit points and centers of immigrant settlement in France stimulated proposals for national coordination of aid to immigrants. In October 1905 the president of the Jewish community of Nancy had proposed, without success, the establishment of a National Relief Fund, to which all the communities on the route to Paris would contribute.[29] The following spring the local committee of the Alliance Israélite Universelle in Nancy complained to the organization's headquarters in Paris that some method had to be found to relieve it of its financial difficulties, for not a sou remained in the treasury. It urged the Alliance to advise its group in Strasbourg not to send any more emigrants. Strasbourg had been forwarding daily "caravans of refugees which were sent there by other local committees of the Alliance."[30]

Nancy's committee offered further suggestions the following year. It proposed that the Alliance centralize aid and arrange to pay the transporation costs of emigrants from border communities like Strasbourg and Belfort. For as it happened, most emigrants arrived without funds to continue their journey. Local charitable organizations in the provinces, including those of communities not visited by emigrants, would then contribute to the Paris headquarters according to their resources.[31] Thus, the responsibility of aiding emigrants in transit would be shared on a national basis.

Because the problems raised by immigration were not limited to local Jewish institutions, they attracted the attention of the French rabbinate, which saw itself as a national force. In 1913 Rabbi Maurice Liber made a proposal. In a report to the Association of French Rabbis he suggested nationwide coordination of charitable efforts and division of fiscal responsibilities, as well as careful screening of candidates worthy of aid, as a solution to the pressing problem of caring for the emigrants.[32] That problem, incidentally, enabled the rabbinate to stake a claim to the moral leadership of French Jewry and to its independence of lay control. For the separation of the church and state had spelled out restrictions on the rabbis' freedom of action. Liber's report indicates the concern of the rabbinate over the disruptive effects of immigrant aid upon French Jewish institutions and the recognition that "no central philanthropic institutions [exist] which could take the initiative" to resolve the problem. Moreover, the report reflects the fears harbored by the leadership of the native French Jewish community. According to Liber, should Jewish aid prove insufficient and should the emigrants fall into the hands of municipal charity or the police, "the result could be scandal which would compromise the honor . . . of Judaism." More importantly, he noted that his program had excellent prospects for being implemented. The support of the Paris Comité de Bienfaisance could be counted upon, since, after all, "it was to its interests to screen [the emigrants] at the border and to disperse them in the provinces to prevent the establishment in the capital of a modern ghetto with its plagues of alcoholism, tuberculosis, and prostitution."[33] The anxious tone of the report prompted the *Univers israélite* to comment that "it is important to bear constantly in mind that the goal of the prospective organization is to come to the aid of the poor and of the immigrants and not to get rid of them."[34]

Localism prevailed over coordination. Only the threat of the Alliance's committee in Nancy to disband had forced the parent organization to provide temporary financial relief in 1908; it did not result in the formation of an official national fund.[35] Liber's plan, too, seems not to have been fully implemented. Although a Central Office of Israelite Philanthropy was founded in 1914 by figures prominent in consistorial circles and in the Paris Comité de Bienfaisance, it was limited to collective fund raising and moreover had no opportunity to establish itself before the outbreak of World War I.[36] With the separation of charitable organizations from the consistorial associations, resources for charitable purposes had become limited, for they could not be transferred, even in time of crisis, from consistorial treasuries. Furthermore, Liber was correct in asserting that there existed no central institution—not even, apparently, the Alliance—with sufficient authority to coordinate aid and to command donations from localities not immediately faced with impoverished emigrants.

The reluctant native Jewish leaders nevertheless provided numerous forms of aid in addition to the food and clothing available to the most needy at their local charitable bureaus. The *Fondation de Rothschild* opened its doors to immigrant orphans, who became the majority of its clientele.[37] Similarly, immigrants constituted approximately 30 percent of the patients of the hospital administered by the *Fondation* in the years preceding World War I and as many as 70 percent in the interwar period.[38]

Outright charity was not the only form of aid offered to new immigrants. As early as 1906 native Jews founded *L'Atelier* to provide temporary work and job training for unemployed immigrants.[39] Under the presidency of Baron James de Rothschild and later of David Weill, *L'Atelier* was clearly designed by its bourgeois sponsors as an organization of social pacification as well as social welfare. In a fund-raising appeal, its administrators boasted that their training and placement service "keeps [their clientele] from enlarging the mass of *déclassés* who congest the populous centers and succeeds, on the contrary, in transforming them into self-supporting laborers who rapidly assimilate the ideas and customs of our country."[40]

For many Russian Jews, the legal assistance offered by the Consistory determined their relations with the native Jewish community. For example, Russian law recognized neither civil marriage nor divorce; therefore the Consistory was obliged to become the arbiter of the marital status of Russian Jews residing in France. Before the separation of church and state the Russian government had conferred legal recognition upon marriages and divorces performed for its subjects by French rabbis, who were, after all, state functionaries. In fact, the decision of the Consistory of Paris to establish a *Beth Din* (Jewish court) in Paris was motivated by the pressing problem of the civil status of foreign Jews. Article Five of the Consistorial Ordinance stipulated that the *Beth Din* "would be concerned with the deliverance . . . of certificates of civil status demanded by certain foreign countries of their nationals domiciled in France."[41] However, after the separation of church and state, Russian Jews in France were left in limbo as the Russian government refused to recognize the proceedings of French rabbis because they were no longer state officials, while according to French law, as determined by the *Cour de Cassation* on May 29, 1905, the civil status of foreigners was determined by the marriage and divorce laws of their home country.[42]

The legal situation of Russian Jews was of great concern to native Jewish leaders in their role as protectors of their immigrant coreligionists. They were particularly worried about such social problems as wife abandonment and common-law and clandestine marriages which followed inevitably from the inability of immigrant Jews to change their personal status. An editorial in *L'Univers israélite* protested the situation of immigrant women from Russia who were totally dependent upon their husbands for a divorce.[43] Furthermore, the paper devoted a series of six articles to the general problem of divorce for Russian Jews living in France.[44]

After several years of legal uncertainty, in 1912 the Paris and Central Consistories became determined to acquire once again legal recognition of marriages and divorces conducted under the auspices of French rabbis and thus "take in hand the defense of a great number of foreign coreligionists."[45] Early attempts to secure the aid of the Russian consul in Paris in representing the case of the consistories to the Russian government were unsuccessful.[46] Conveniently, however, Emile Deutsch de la Meurthe, industrialist and member of the Paris Consistory, was able to volunteer his son-in-law, Pierre de Gunzbourg, scion of a family of Russian Jewish financiers who spent much time in France, to conduct negotiations with the Russian government. He contacted the Chief Rabbi of St. Petersburg and the director of nonorthodox cults in Russia, and secured a promise from the Russian government to forward instructions to its Consul General in Paris. According to these instructions either the Chief Rabbi of France or all consistorial rabbis would be granted the legal powers they had enjoyed before the separation of church and state and would wield the same authority as rabbis of the Russian Empire.[47] This solution would "endow the actions [of French rabbis] with all the absolute and practical import which their Russian coreligionists could expect of them."[48] Thereupon, the Central Consistory also resolved to act on this decision and, perhaps, claim partial responsibility for the anticipated change in the status of the French rabbinate. On March 26, 1912, therefore the Central Consistory decided that

> the Chief Rabbi of the Central Consistory would, through the mediation of the Chief Rabbi of St. Petersburg, make an official contact with the Russian government in his own name as well as in the name of the Central Consistory and its affiliated associations, in order that [consistorial] rabbis obtain the qualification of Imperial rabbi with the resulting power to marry Russian Israelites validly in France, pronounce their divorce, and in general, conduct all acts concerning civil status.[49]

The initiatives undertaken by the two consistories appear to have been successful. According to a note sent later that year from the Russian Consul General in Paris to the Advocate of the *Cour d'Appel* of Paris, consistorial rabbis had power, in the eyes of Russian law, to perform marriages and divorces.[50]

Immigrant Jews in France were grateful for the existence of the *Beth Din*. As *Der Yid in Pariz* commented in 1913, "Without it, the

Russian-Polish Jewish community would have no civil status."[51] However, this happy situation was soon disrupted. With the cooperation of the Russian consul in Paris, a French anticlerical deputy of Jewish origin, Alfred Naquet, campaigned against the French government's acceptance of the acts of the *Beth Din*. When the *Beth Din* lost a case regarding a divorce it had granted, the Consistory, much to the distress of immigrant Jewry, decided to close this source of unfavorable publicity.[52] As a compromise, the *Beth Din* was reorganized rather than abolished, for the Religious Section of the Paris Consistory had expressed the fear that "the suppression of the *Beth Din* would be unfavorably interpreted by our coreligionists of foreign origin," and that "certain communities abroad [would be] tempted to consider this measure as a grievous indicator of the indifference of French Israelites in the matter of faith."[53] Whereas the former *Beth Din* had included an immigrant rabbi and had been concerned primarily with the legal problems of immigrant Jews, the reorganized version was composed solely of consistorial rabbis, who would deal with a wide variety of religious questions.[54] Thus, the Consistory reasserted its exclusive control over religious affairs affecting immigrants and downgraded the importance of the immigrants' legal problems.

During the war, however, the contribution of the immigrants to the military effort and the unjust attacks upon them by French anti-Semites roused the native Jewish community to action. A new feeling of unprecedented solidarity inspired native Jews to come with great sympathy to the political and financial aid of immigrant Jews. The *Univers israélite*, for example, despite opposition of the native Jews to the public use of Yiddish, protested the war censor's ban on its use in correspondence. Surely, it claimed, a censor familiar with that language could be found, since the use of Yiddish was so widespread.[55] Furthermore, native charitable institutions undertook new activities for the benefit of immigrants in need. A number of prominent French Jews organized a fund-raising concert, the proceeds of which were to aid disabled soldiers and widows of Jewish volunteers. Their publicity noted that "immigrant Jews in France have no natural protector. It seemed to us that French Jews had contracted a debt toward

their coreligionists, who had spontaneously devoted themselves to
their Fatherland. It is to pay a part of that debt that this concert is
designed."[56] The *Oeuvre des Orphelins Israélites de la Guerre*,
founded in October 1915 and headed by the Baron Edmond de
Rothschild, also provided charitable aid to war widows and orphans
of the immigrant community in conjunction with the Comité de
Bienfaisance of Parisian Jewry. In addition, the consistorial schools,
now in operation seven days a week, served two meals a day to their
students and occasional meals to indigent parents. During the war
242 schoolchildren were evacuated to the countryside.[57]

Under the leadership of Sylvain Lévi, of Rabbis Dreyfuss and Israël
Lévi, and of the philo-Semitic socialist deputy Marius Moutet, a
special meeting was held in May of 1916 to organize legal assistance
for Russian Jews residing in Paris. Both Durkheim and Lévi expressed
the wish that French and immigrant Jews draw closer together.[58]
Durkheim even became the head of the committee established to effect the rapprochement of the two communities.[59] In Lyon a charitable organization was established to care for all coreligionists, regardless of origin, and the local consistory founded a special fund for
Russian Jewish prisoners of war.[60] Finally, the Union Scolaire, an
association concerned with the assimilation of immigrant Jews within
France, provided employment for immigrant women, who sewed and
knit warm clothing for combatants and for the wounded.[61]

The president of the Alliance Israélite Universelle, Narcisse Leven,
went so far as to contact Louis Marshall of the American Jewish
Committee to alert him to the acute need of unemployed Russian
Jews in Paris and of Russian Jewish students in France and Switzerland, for whom local aid might prove insufficient.[62] Moreover,
the Alliance intervened politically on behalf of Ottoman Jews living
in France. In contacts with the Minister of Foreign Affairs it stressed
that many of these Ottoman Jews, though legally classified as "enemy
nationals," were former students of Alliance schools, in which "they
learned to know and love France, [and] that about 2,500 of them
. . . had enlisted in the French army." The organization sought,
and secured, on their behalf the right of continued residence in
France on the same terms as those granted to *Christian* Ottoman citi-

zens.[63] When faced with discrimination, Ottoman Jewish immigrants naturally turned to the Alliance to obtain redress of their grievances.[64] It should be noted, however, that sympathy for Russian Jewish immigrants, citizens of an allied country, was more widespread than for Ottoman Jewish immigrants, who were "enemy nationals." As late as the spring of 1915 the Paris Comité de Bienfaisance denied all aid to Ottoman Jews. By 1918, however, both the French Consul and the Paris Prefect of Police were declaring the solicitude of the French government to Israelites of the Levant and expressing their gratitude to Rozanès, president of the Association Orientale de Paris, for his calming influence on the members of the Association.[65]

Although long the recipients of the largesse of their native brethren, immigrant Jews rose in status and importance due to the war situation. Before, they had been the poor beneficiaries of grudgingly offered aid; now they were contributing to the war effort. And they had become participants in their own right in the charitable undertakings of the French Jewish community on behalf of war victims. Thus, immigrant and native Jewish women together established the *Aide fraternelle au soldat.* Fittingly, the president of the organization was Mme. Alfred Lévy, wife of the Chief Rabbi of France; its secretary was Mlle. Rosette Polack of the immigrant sector.[66] Likewise, the benefit concert for war widows, though organized by native Jews, included on its committee several members of the immigrant community.[67] Most social and charitable institutions remained either completely native or completely immigrant in composition. Nevertheless, at least temporarily, the immigrant Jews had now taken the first steps toward integration.[68] For all members of that community, immigrant and native alike, shared a common cause in the war.

After World War I, the native Jewish community continued to be more responsive to the legal and philanthropic needs of the rapidly expanding immigrant community, even though active collaboration between immigrants and natives had ceased and political differences over the situation of Jews in Eastern Europe had surfaced. The native Jewish community was aware of, and took part in, the new socioeconomic climate in France, spurred by the recognition that the war had transformed immigration into a boon for a France starved for man-power. Toleration of immigrants was therefore temporarily replaced by a more activist approach. The newly formed *Comité de Protection des Emigrants israélites*, established in 1920 to provide legal aid for Jewish immigrants, thus planned an appeal to the Minister of the In-terior and to the Prefect of Police to secure their "intervention on behalf of Israelite emigrants whose establishment in France is useful to the rebuilding of the country and whose expulsion would injure the prestige of France abroad."[69] At the same time the *Comité de Protection* expressed its willingness to heed the recommendations of high authorities that the immigrants not concentrate in Paris and to investigate possibilities for settlement in the liberated territories.[70] Such an approach, it need hardly be pointed out, was far different from the Comité de Bienfaisance's consideration on the eve of World War I of seeking governmental restriction of immigration.

Given the new political climate Chief Rabbi Israël Lévi had little difficulty in securing the financial collaboration of the Alliance Israélite, the international Jewish Colonization Association (ICA), the Paris Comité de Bienfaisance, and the *Société de secours aux juifs russes* for the expanded program of the *Comité de Protection:* provid-ing information to new arrivals as to available welfare facilities, inter-vening with French and foreign consular authorities on behalf of worthy immigrants, and concerning itself with the needs of those seeking repatriation.[71]

The organization which succeeded the *Comité de Protection* in 1927, the *Comité Central d'Assistance aux Emigrants Juifs* (CCAEJ), founded at the initiative of Chief Rabbi Lévi, continued the legal ac-tivity of its predecessor. From its offices in Lille, Marseilles, Stras-bourg, Metz, and Paris, it conducted searches for relatives, and coop-erated with the *Comité d'Assistance par le Travail* to find employment for immigrants in industry and agriculture.[72] The CCAEJ claimed good relations with the French government and with foreign consulates and aided 34,574 immigrants between 1927 and 1936, as the economic crisis in France worsened. It nevertheless received a growing number of negative replies from the Ministries of the Interior, Labor, and Foreign Affairs to which it appealed a total of 6,897 times on behalf of its clientele. In particular, papers for permanent residence became very difficult to acquire. Moreover, as a result of a xenophobic campaign conducted against it by the paper *L'Ami du Peuple*, the CCAEJ had to suspend its activity temporarily in 1930 and resumed it, with less success, the next year.[73]

While the CCAEJ valiantly pursued its activity, it was unable to secure adequate financial support from French Jewry. Though the Comité de Bienfaisance, the Alliance Israélite, and the Federation of Jewish Societies made significant contributions, between 70 and 80 percent of the CCAEJ's budget came from the international organization, HIAS-HICEM.[74] Along with its government, French Jewry began to look with less favor upon immigrants, who came to be seen as illegitimate competitors for the limited positions available in the French economy and as potentially dangerous revolutionaries as well. The Comité de Bienfaisance proposed as a solution to immigrant unemployment during the recession of 1926–1927 the subsidizing of immigrant journeys to the Belgian and Swiss borders.[75] Rabbi Maurice Liber was reported to have chided an immigrant worker at a meeting, "Don't you realize that you are taking the place of a French worker?"[76] His point of view was widely shared in native Jewish circles. By 1931 the Comité de Bienfaisance was pointing out that the high level of unemployment in France made it impossible to justify the arrival of new immigrants.[77] While offering moral aid to the German Jewish refugees who fled to France in 1933, the Comité de Bienfaisance added that "aid to refugees . . . must at no time tend to create, for the benefit of refugees, possibilities to engage in commerce or labor on French soil. The administrators must, in effect, prevent all unfortunate consequences to French merchants and laborers, themselves [undergoing] serious difficulties and unemployment."[78]

The hesitation which the Comité de Bienfaisance expressed toward Jewish refugees from France's traditional enemy was extended to other immigrants as well. An administrative report noted in 1935 that "none of us must forget that the Comité is called the Comité de Bienfaisance Israélite *de Paris*, and that Paris is in France."[79] The following year it was unanimously decided that, when needs were equal, preference should be given to those of French origin.[80] Furthermore, the political activity of immigrants became a criterion as to their eligibility for aid. One administrator's account of his refusing aid to a young foreign applicant "who had not done his military service in France and had taken part in the political demonstrations of February 6, 1934" received enthusiastic approval, with the comment that such criteria "should be applied in all cases of this nature."[81] As xenophobia and anti-Semitism increased in France the Comité de Bienfaisance resolved to deny aid also to "those indigents [who] go to cafés where they . . . ostentatiously read Hebrew [i.e., Yiddish] newspapers, [an act] which is likely to provoke or develop anti-Semitism."[82]

Agents of Assimilation

As crucial as charitable aid and legal assistance were for the well-being of the immigrants, they were considered inadequate by native Jewry for the achievement of its primary goal: the successful assimilation of the immigrants. Assimilation was considered desirable for the immigrants themselves as a means to uplift them from their state of cultural inferiority and confer upon them the only form of identity appropriate to modern Jews. It was also seen as necessary to safeguard the security of the Jewish community in France and retain the tolerance of the French polity for its Jewish citizens. Thus the attitude of native French Jews toward the socialization of the immigrants was born of the union of self-interest and the realistic appraisal of the French situation. As early as 1907 a writer for *L'Univers israélite* proposed as a major reason for the establishment of an employment bureau for immigrant Jews the need "to prevent [the foreign population] from becoming a danger to ourselves."[83]

The concern of the native Jewish population over the possible repercussions from the settlement of large numbers of immigrant Jews was no paranoid reaction; it reflected an undeniable reality. In 1910, for example, an anti-Semitic campaign was conducted by the paper *La Liberté*, which accused the immigrant Jewish community in Paris of spreading conjunctivitis and of being a general social nuisance. In response the Paris Comité de Bienfaisance, which had found no evidence of a conjunctivitis epidemic, still encouraged its clients to move from the *Pletzl* to more hygienie quarters.[84]

Even the most liberal elements within French society rejected the concept of cultural pluralism. They viewed the residential concentration, albeit voluntary, of an ethnic group in a close-knit neighborhood and the public recognition of that reality as a violation of the liberal principles of France. This was in sharp contrast to the situation in England. There the early Friday and Saturday closing of government schools in which immigrant Jewish students predominated met with no public outcry. Moreover, certain state schools with high Jewish enrollments were tacitly recognized as "Jewish schools." Jewish religious instruction was given in the schools, and an effort was made to hire Jewish teachers and, if possible, a Jewish headmaster.[85]

In France, however, the situation was far different. While a law of March 28, 1882, mandated the appointment of a foreign language teacher wherever a large proportion of foreign children of the same nationality attended school,[86] this law was never applied to Yiddish-speaking immigrant Jewish children. On the contrary, in 1907 both the socialist paper *L'Humanité* and the League of the Rights of Man attacked the existence of four public schools in Paris, the great majority of whose students were immigrant Jews. Although the schools were not confessional, as they had been prior to the laicization of public education in the 1880s, classes did not meet on Saturday out of deference to the customs of their students. Furthermore, a committee of Jewish women provided kosher food at no cost to the children. *L'Humanité* found the voluntary segregation of these students reprehensible:

> Separated from their neighborhood pals, these children retain their customs and their language; they form a closed caste and later . . . in the large Parisian city they will form a very distinct society scarcely penetrable by the customs of modern life. . . . The separation of races must cease to exist; the schools of confessional tendencies, which constitute a challenge to lay education, must disappear. How can we be surprised at racial hatred when . . . the administration itself favors the particularist development of these races instead of seeking to facilitate their fusion, even from childhood.[87]

L'Humanité called for the distribution of immigrant children, even against their will it seems, among other public schools and for an end to the special aid provided by the Jewish community.[88] The League of the Rights of Man also entered the fray, complaining to the Minister of Public Instruction that the toleration of these four schools violated the religious neutrality of the state.[89] While the Minister of Public Instruction defended the existence of the schools and noted the ease with which immigrant children studying together learned French and assimilated French customs,[90] the opposition of two major liberal groups signaled a consensus of Left and Right as to the necessity for the complete and rapid assimilation of immigrant groups. In spite of their support for the four schools and their wry criticism of liberal reforms which "harm those very persons to whom one thinks to render services,"[91] native Jewish leaders could not ignore the sentiment expressed in those complaints.

Even after World War I French public opinion, anti-Semitic and not, continued to express concern with the failure of the Jews to assimilate. A long article by Georges Batault, published in 1921 in the *Mercure de France*, when the furor over the *Protocols of the Elders of Zion* was at its height, suggested that the assimilationist position was untenable because the Jewish religion could not be separated from the Jewish nation. He contended, moreover, that most Jews were simply unwilling to sever their ties with fellow Jews and assimilate.[92] Anti-Semitic books less judicious in tone than Batault's article proliferated in the interwar period, and a Jewish periodical noted that the French press constantly attributed crime to the foreigners and most especially to Jews.[93]

Anti-Semitic incursions on immigrant neighborhoods were also common. From their inception, the *Camelots du Roi* of the *Action Française* saw the *Pletzel* as a fertile area for their political hooliganism. In 1925 and 1926 anti-Semitic demonstrations, involving 2,000 to 3,000 workers, took place in Belleville, the newest immigrant quarter of Paris, and elicited from Jacques Biélinky, an assimilated Russian Jewish correspondent for *L'Univers israélite*, the comment that it was the new immigrants "who in their life-style, their excitement in the street, their Yiddish . . . strongly disturb the French population."[94] In response to Biélinky's article an anonymous reader added that Jewish organizations "must make disappear these crowds of foreign Jews of diverse languages which sound disagreeable to French ears. Moreover, these foreigners must make an effort to cast off the former man."[95] Only by transforming immigrant Jews into French citizens, it was argued, would the anti-Semitic incidents, which soon extended to the native Jewish population as well, be prevented.[96]

Native Jewry, therefore, sought to use its institutions as vehicles for the assimilation of Jewish immigrants into French life. The educational facilities administered by the Paris Consistory, and in particular its three parochial elementary schools, were heavily frequented by the children of immigrants. In fact, the Inspection Committee of the Paris Consistory reported that the 594 students enrolled in 1907 in the three elementary schools (and the 989 enrolled in 1912) were almost exclusively foreigners, as were the majority of the 3,000 students taking religious instruction in the supplementary schools of the consistory in the years preceding the First World War.[97] A similar situation prevailed among the thousand students who attended the parochial schools after World War I.[98] While immigrant parents chose to send their children to consistorial schools at least partly in order to provide them with a religiously observant atmosphere, the Paris Consistory, in its fund-raising appeal for the schools, chose to stress their assimilatory functions rather than their religious nature: "They succeed in transforming into useful citizens children who, without them, could become a charge to society and a matter of shame for their brethren by origin. *It is less to a confessional institution than to a social institution that we ask of each one to pledge his support.*"[99] The publication of the results of examinations given the students in these schools was even proposed as a means of showing the public "the educational impact of our schools on students of diverse origins."[100] In its deliberations the Paris Comité des Ecoles noted that the foreign students in the consistorial schools were better disciplined and more successful in their studies than their brethren in the public schools. "That fact alone," the spokesman concluded, "would suffice to show the need for our groups [*which are*] more favorable for the assimilation of the foreign Jewish population."[101] It was to educate and exercise influence on immigrant children that consistorial parochial schools, though reduced in number, were maintained until World War II, despite the lack of interest expressed by native Jewish parents in parochial education for their own children.

On a smaller scale, the *Ecole Rabbinique* served a function similar to that of the consistorial parochial schools. The immigrant students who pursued their studies there rapidly acquired French culture and were assimilated into the French rabbinate. While rabbinical students were expected to be—or at least about to become—French citizens, in fact, a significant minority of rabbinical students were foreign immigrants both before and after World War I. In 1932 it was noted that only one of four graduating rabbinical students was a French citizen, and in 1937 six of fifteen rabbinical students were foreign.[102]

In a like manner the religious courses offered after school several times a week and in a number of *lycées* under consistorial auspices were designed to facilitate assimilation while communicating the essentials of Jewish religious instruction."[103] As a 1908 report on religious education conducted at the rue des Tournelles temple in the fourth *arrondissement* concluded, "It is . . . only through religious instruction that a healthy influence can be exercised on these young minds. . . . It is thus that these uprooted [children], so brusquely transported to a society totally different from their own, will be able, thanks to the effect of moral and religious instruction, to adapt more easily to their new life."[104] The courses offered by the Consistory, unlike those administered by the immigrants themselves, were conducted in French, and French manners and modes of thought were considered an incalculable benefit of instruction by native teachers and rabbis. Throughout the period from 1906 to 1939 immigrant children frequented consistorial courses. Despite the establishment of immigrant-controlled schools after World War I, in 1932 *Parizer haynt* noted that it was through the Consistory's courses that most immigrants had their sole contact with the native institution.[105] The Consistory reciprocally cited the devotion of the poor immigrant community.[106] To meet the needs of an expanded immigrant population, courses were offered in new areas of immigrant settlement such as Belleville, and in the Paris suburbs as well.[107] To recruit immigrant children advertisements were placed in *Parizer haynt* and parents' meetings were held in Belleville and Montmartre.[108] For native Jewish leaders the rationale for funding these courses remained the same in the years of the post-war immigration as in the earlier period. As the 1926 report of the Paris Consistory candidly commented, "new elements abound, numerous children for whom it was suitable that education be given under our auspices [*chez nous*] in order to begin the task of assimilation. . . . Hearing only our language spoken, these children will quickly adapt to our manners and customs."[109]

At the same time concern was expressed by both the lay and the rabbinic leadership of French Jewry that the assimilation of the immigrants occur under the aegis of Jewish religious institutions in order to prevent the abandonment of Judaism by immigrants easily absorbed into French society. Of the 769 Jews converted to Catholicism in Paris between 1915 and 1934, 43 percent were of foreign birth.[110] It was axiomatic to consistorial circles that it was possible, without conflict, to be both a good Frenchman and a good Jew. Hence their desire to undertake themselves the assimilation of the immigrants so that they would not be lost to French Judaism. As the 1927 General Assembly of the Paris Consistory noted,

> Too many foreign Jews are inclined to believe that to be really French, it is necessary to abandon any religious practice which might make them conspicuous. Too many people are ready to aver that progress consists in standardizing souls as one standardizes machines, the American way! You [members of the Consistory] are not at all of that type. For . . . religious practice remains the only real way to preserve the Jewish family cell and to struggle against the disappearance of Judaism through the dissolving of Jews into the milieu which surrounds them.[111]

According to the definition of native Jewish leaders, the assimilation of the immigrants thus entailed their cultural transformation, combined with their attraction into the orbit of native French Jewry. A narrow path had to be steered between immigrant adherence to a foreign form of Judaism and immigrant assimilation entirely out of Judaism.

In addition to the courses of religious education provided for children, native Jewish leaders established and supported institutions designed to instruct adult immigrants in the language and customs of their adopted country. The *Université Populaire Juive*, though established by immigrant Zionist sympathizers, received favorable publicity in the pages of *L'Univers israélite* for its French classes and lectures which "turn these foreigners into excellent patriots."[112] The Paris Consistory went so far as to subsidize on a regular basis the courses offered by the *Université*.[113] Such efforts were intensified after World War I in order to deal with the larger immigrant population. In 1922 the Paris Consistory placed its facilities at the disposition of the Alliance Israélite, which organized French courses for immigrants.[114] Such prominent personalities within the native community as Sylvain Lévi, Chief Rabbi Israël Lévi, Dr. Léon Zadoc-Kahn, Léon Blum, and Colonel Alfred Dreyfus—an incongruous grouping—served on the Honorary Committee of the *Acceuil Fraternel Israélite*, an association established in 1926 and dedicated to the "civic development and instruction of Israelite immigrants."[115] Offering free French courses and judicial aid in securing naturalization, identity cards, and work permits, it conducted its publicity in Yiddish in order to reach those not drawn to the *Foyer Français*, an association for all types of immigrants.[116]

Most ambitious of the associations whose goal was the assimilation of the immigrants was the *Union Scolaire*, an organization of Jewish graduates of Paris schools, which shifted its focus to immigrant absorption when it experienced a decline following World War I. With its French courses, lectures, "*soirées artistiques*," the *Union Scolaire*, which absorbed the *Acceuil Fraternel Israélite* in 1931, came to embody the most insensitive appeal of native Jewry to their immigrant coreligionists. Anti-Zionist and smugly assimilationist, the *Union Scolaire* boasted that "such is the perfection of Jewish assimilation in our country that . . . [we] had to restore the meaning of Judaism for young Frenchmen who appeared ignorant of it and now propose to add the reverse operation . . . teaching French to young Jews ignorant of it."[117] In the same declaration of purpose, the *Union Scolaire* grimly added: "Our foreign brethren are the guests of France. . . . they must not even let it appear that they forget it."[118] While excluding foreigners from its committee, the *Union Scolaire* established its locale next to the Federation of Jewish Societies to attract the attention of the immigrants.[119]

Although some immigrants did take advantage of the French courses, *Union Scolaire's* repeated attacks on *Parizer haynt* for encouraging "noisy agitation" and its characterization of the culture of immigrant Jewry as "thinking, speaking, and writing in a German *patois*" alienated the vast majority of those it sought to reach.[120] The Union's conviction that "France will never tolerate ethnic or national particularism" implied that immigrant Jews must instantly renounce their self-conception and culture.[121] Furthermore, the few young immigrants who frequented the Union Scolaire had little opportunity to meet young native Jews there, for the latter shunned the institution and its immigrant clientele.[122]

Recognizing the need for learning French and becoming familiar with French customs, immigrant Jews availed themselves of the free practical instruction offered by native Jewish institutions. However, they understood the motives of native Jewry quite well and rejected the ideology which accompanied the French lessons. As *Parizer haynt* noted,

> The leaders of the Union Scolaire are persuaded that they will succeed in raising the young immigrant Jew according to their model: revive in him a feeling for the Jewish religion and kill in him national consciousness. . . . But we are all suspended like fruits on the national tree, on the branches of our national consciousness, and we will always struggle against those who want to rob us of it.[123]

Who Shall Rule?

The paternalism the native Jewish community showed the newcomers was most blatant in the repeated conflicts of immigrant and native leaders over what might be described as issues of community control. Even at their most benevolent, the leaders of native Jewry were unwilling to accept immigrants as partners in the governing of communal institutions over which they themselves had so long wielded exclusive control. In fact, when consistorial leaders in Paris spoke of "the Community," they were referring to the Paris Consistory and its membership. This attitude, naturally enough, strengthened the Jewish immigrants' resolve to establish their own institutions. The desire of native French Jews to refashion the immigrants and then draw upon these newly perfected and right-thinking coreligionists to swell the ranks of their own institutions was thus thwarted by their rigid insistence on determining virtually alone the proper agenda of Jewish life in France.

While the local consistorial associations established after the separation of church and state for the most part admitted foreigners to membership on their councils, no consistory permitted more than one-fourth of its council to be composed of foreign members. Moreover, a residency requirement, usually of ten consecutive years in the department and of five years' membership in the local consistory, severely limited the number of foreigners eligible for election.[124] Some consistories, among them those of Chalons-sur-Marne and Le Havre, banned noncitizens entirely from election to the administrative council.[125] In fact, even in the most populous immigrant community of Paris, no foreigner had served on the council of the Consistory by 1919, when the eligibility of foreigners was repealed so that all twenty council members of the Paris Consistory might serve on the Central Consistory, to which foreigners were not admitted.[126] Never was it suggested that the statutes of the Central Consistory be accommodated to those of the Paris Consistory in the matter of foreign members.

The natural desire of immigrants to select their own religious leaders was rebuffed by the consistorial circles. It was not until after the separation of church and state, when immigrants became free to choose whether or not to affiliate with the consistory, that consistorial leaders were motivated to try to meet their needs and keep them under the consistorial aegis. Thus, in 1911 religious immigrants were pacified by the inclusion on the Butchers and Mikveh commission of the Paris Consistory of one member each from two competing immigrant groups, both of which claimed to be the sole legitimate representative of the Russo-Polish population in Paris. However, the largest immigrant group alone, the *Agoudas Hakehillos*, had asked for five representatives.[127] Furthermore, the Consistory made it clear that "in no case may these new members be considered as delegates of their compatriots."[128] Their recognition as delegates would have presumed the *right* of immigrant representation on consistorial commissions, when in fact it was a favor granted by the Consistory.

The Paris Consistory, moreover, refused to permit an immigrant rabbi to serve in any of its temples. Although consistorial leaders sought to prevent the *Agoudas Hakehillos* from establishing a synagogue in the *Pletzl* which would compete with their own Tournelles temple and promised the president of that immigrant association that services there would be celebrated according to Eastern European Orthodox custom, they balked at his demand that Rabbi Herzog be appointed to the temple. Rabbi Israël Lévi declared that the Consistory "would never accept the designation of a foreign rabbi" and added obliquely that "preaching in a foreign tongue would not fail to have repercussions for the totality of Israelites."[129] Similarly, the Paris Consistory rejected a proposal of the Sephardi *Association Orientale de Paris* that a Turkish rabbi, already approved by Turkish authorities to perform marriages and divorces for Ottoman citizens residing in France, be added to the *Beth-Din* of the Paris Consistory. As the minutes phrased it, the Consistory had "to abstain from any involvement with the acts of a rabbi over whom it exercises no control whatsoever" and had further resolved that the rabbis of the Consistorial Association "could in no manner lend their support to the rabbis of the *Association Orientale*."[130]

While immigrant cantors had been permitted in exceptional cases to practice in immigrant neighborhoods, in 1913 the Paris Consistory's dissatisfaction with one M. Koenig of the St. Isaure temple in Montmartre led to a reconsideration even of that concession. Consistorial leaders agonized over Koenig's dismissal because they feared to alienate the immigrant population who attended the temple.[131] However, the desire of the immigrant population for an officiant "of their

own mentality" could not be fulfilled, according to consistorial
leaders, because

> functionaries *of that mentality* are really functionaries who care little
> about discipline. . . . The question which arises is the following: Must
> they [the immigrants] be given a functionary who will satisfy them as
> regards the chants and melodies of their country but who will really not
> be, we won't say French, but *au courant* of our customs or even of the
> French language, and therefore not of our mentality. [The matter is
> especially important since] in Montmartre it's a question of molding, of
> educating . . . this population.[132]

What was really at issue was the ability of consistorial leaders to control their officiants and to demand ideological and cultural confor-
mity of them. To prevent the appointment of an independent officiant, the commission of the St. Isaure temple was denied the right
to appoint Koenig's successor.[133] This unwillingness of consistorial
leaders to tolerate diversity and to welcome the infusion of new perspectives along with new blood only encouraged immigrant Jews to
seek independence and take advantage, as we have seen, of the separation of church and state and establish their own religious institutions.

How the consistorial leaders would have treated their immigrant
coreligionists had there been no separation is suggested by an incident which occurred in Metz, a major center of Lorraine Jewry,
where the separation of church and state was not effected. In 1932
the departmental Consistory of the Moselle, seeking to prevent the
danger of "religious autonomism" and "to bring a little order into the
spiritual life of the post-war Eastern European immigrants to Metz,"
had welded the small immigrant religious associations, which it had
previously authorized, into one organization called *Knesset Israel.* To
serve the needs of the group and, admittedly, "to prevent the existence of oratories evading its surveillance," the Consistory had
opened three auxiliary synagogues.[134] All the Polish immigrant
groups save one joined the new association. The holdout, *Linas
Hazedek*, persisted in providing independent services for the members
of the society despite the repeated remonstrances of consistorial authorities. The President of the Moselle Consistory therefore appealed to

the departmental prefect to enforce the law against the renegade society. For, he noted, "Such obstinacy, which sets a bad example for certain unruly elements, demands severe sanctions."[135] To aid the authorities in carrying out their duty, Eugène Weill, the president of the local Metz Consistory, phoned the police in advance of the major Jewish holidays in the fall to advise them that *Linas Hazedek* was planning to hold illegal religious services. Served with injunctions, the president of the society refused to comply and was brought to trial.[136] Although he was later acquitted (his lawyer claimed that the services celebrated by *Linas Hazedek*, with sixty people in attendance, were private rather than public)[137] the incident shows how far consistorial authorities were willing to go in order to exercise control over the local immigrant Jewish population.

New Approaches

The growth and institutional development of the immigrant community in the years following World War I, the proof of patriotism which immigrants had given during the war, and the obvious failure of attempts by Jewish organizations to attract the support of the immigrant population led consistorial circles to consider new tactics. Were the immigrant population to remain independent of, and antagonistic toward, consistorial circles, then those circles would no longer be able to speak in the name of the Jews of France or direct their political and cultural activity. As the immigrant community grew in size and self-confidence, the consistorial circles found their authority questioned and sought to effect a *rapprochement* between immigrant and native Jewry. While their goal remained the retention of power and influence, the methods adopted to achieve that goal had changed.

Native Jewish leaders began to turn to those immigrant Jews, middle class and upwardly mobile, who already had contacts with their institutions. Instead of summarily rejecting the request of congregations composed largely of immigrants that their officiants likewise be of immigrant origin, the Paris Consistory, for example, agreed to allow the Administrative Commission of the St. Isaure temple to choose an officiant of Polish nationality as long as he was not imported from abroad but was already resident in France.[138]

If immigrant Jews were to become loyal to native institutions, then a token number of prominent immigrants would have to be coopted into native institutions. This became the most favored tactic. In 1925 a director of the Comité de Bienfaisance of Paris suggested that "persons of foreign nationality should be admitted as administrators of the Comité given that the majority of our poor are foreigners and that we have among our subscribers and donors a rather large number of foreigners."[139] It was also noted in the same period that appointing a distinguished immigrant delegate would avert the immigrants' antagonism toward the Comité.[140] Since the leadership of the Comité was oligarchic and self-perpetuating, it was natural that it should seek to designate the representatives of immigrant Jewry appropriate to serve on its administrative board. In 1926 the Comité decided to invite a few immigrant Jewish notables—particularly Messrs. Rosenthal, Naiditch, and Salem—of both the Eastern European and Sephardi immigrant communities to a meeting with the specified goal of attracting a larger number of donors from those populations.[141]

While the Comité de Bienfaisance was pondering the selection of immigrant delegates, the Central Consistory and the Paris Consistory were adopting similar tactics. At the initiative of the French rabbinate, which at the 1926 meeting of its Association expressed concern about improving relations with immigrant Jews, the Central Consistory decided to establish a commission to study the problem. In addition, it resolved to send the text of the Rabbinical Association to the presidents of all local consistories with the purpose of sensitizing them to the issue.[142] Moreover, the accompanying circular proposed for consideration the admission to local consistorial councils of "a certain number of foreigners . . . on condition that they be part of the community for at least five years."[143] In response the Lille Consistory sought permission to modify its statutes in order to allow foreigners to serve on its council.[144] It was not until 1939, however, that the Central Consistory itself modified its statutes to permit it "to convoke to its meetings foreign representatives of cultic associations which are not part of the Union."[145]

The Paris Consistory, too, undertook to bring a select number of immigrant personalities into its administration. It was struck by the "shocking disproportion" between the increasing Jewish population of Paris and the membership of the Paris Consistory, which stood at approximately 5,000 in the mid-1920s,[146] and by the financial opportunities that growing population offered. With an eye to increasing its membership, the Paris Consistory decided to coopt on an exceptional basis several persons "who by their origin or their special competence know . . . the immediate needs of new immigrants."[147] Of the four men so appointed, three—Baron Alfred de Gunzbourg, Isaac Naiditch, and Maître Salem—were of foreign origin. Although the stated purpose of their appointment was the Consistory's "conscious[ness] of its obligations,"[148] it is clear that it intended their cooptation to buttress the legitimacy of the institution in the eyes of immigrant Jews, to resolve the Consistory's financial problems, and to unify the Jewish population of Paris under its own aegis. As the Baron Robert de Rothschild declared in his speech to the Paris Consistory, "the Consistory was guided in its decision by the authority enjoyed by each of these new collaborators among certain elements of the Jewish population . . . which we wish to bring close to our Association and for whom we seek incorporation in the great Parisian community" (i.e., the Consistory).[149] As the *Univers israélite* added, immigrant Jews made extensive use of the religious facilities of the community and "it was unjust and imprudent to keep them completely apart from the direction of the community."[150]

In 1930 the Paris Consistory repealed the 1919 decision banning foreigners from serving on its council and declared that since "it is more equitable that foreign members of our Association be represented in the Consistory by foreigners," immigrants resident in Paris for ten years and members of the Consistory for at least five years would be eligible to be candidates for the council.[151] When one member of the Paris Consistory, Alfred Bechman, chose not to stand for reelection because he was offended that immigrant Jews, who enjoyed no political rights in France, not only could vote but would be eligible to serve on the council, he was answered publicly by William Oualid, a prominent jurist of Algerian birth, who was associated with the Consistory. The Consistory, Oualid pointed out, was a religious organization. "How, then, could a coreligionist—moreover, one who had chosen to live in France—be denied the right to have his say in a religious matter merely because he was born on the other side of the frontier?"[152] A liberal on the question of immigration, Oualid also publicly defended immigrant Jews against charges that they might form a national minority in France. "Polish or Russian Jews," he declared, "have broken their ties with their countries of origin and aspire only to education, to assimilation, and to naturalization which will efface for them a religious and ethnic inequality from which they have only too often suffered."[153] The *Univers israélite* also joined in the task of reconciliation, promising that it would try not to publish derogatory stories about foreigners because it sought "to unite the diverse elements of the Israelite population."[154]

Besides bringing select immigrant Jews into the Paris Consistory, its leaders also supported, and collaborated with, those immigrant associations whose aims and influence were considered consonant with the values of the consistorial circles. Thus, the Paris Consistory expressed considerable interest, for example, in the Ohel-Jacob Association, established in 1926 by such middle-class and wealthy Russian Jewish émigrés as Baron Alfred de Gunzbourg and Henry Sliosberg, former president of the Jewish community of Petrograd. Sliosberg's desire was to organize and eventually bring into the consistory those immigrant Jews who still kept their distance from the native Jewish institution.[155] *Ohel-Jacob* presented itself to the Paris Consistory as the organization best suited "to adapt these groups [of immigrants] to French civilization . . . [and to serve as] a liaison between them . . . and French Judaism." Its religious instruction, moreover, would protect immigrant Jewry from the propaganda of atheism, communism, and [Christian] proselytism which takes place in its midst.[156] To facilitate its activity, the Chief Rabbi of France expressed his approval of the new organization and the Paris Consistory conferred a special status upon the *Ohel-Jacob* rabbi, Rabbi Aisenstadt, as a collaborator in the great task of uniting the disparate elements of Parisian Jewry, although he could not, as a foreigner, serve as a regular member of the Paris rabbinate.[157]

The Consistory expressed its willingness to provide to *Ohel-Jacob* suitable facilities for religious services but hesitated to fund its educational program, which served 350 children, because its classes were conducted in Yiddish. While *Ohel-Jacob*'s administrators pointedly noted that communists and Christian propagandists made use of Yiddish for their own purposes and added that instruction in Yiddish would be only a temporary measure as immigrant youth quickly adopted French as their primary language, consistorial leaders insisted that the courses offered by *Ohel-Jacob* must be conducted in French if consistorial aid were to be forthcoming.[158] Furthermore, even in expressing its support and willingness to provide material aid to *Ohel-Jacob*, the Consistory insisted, this in 1928, that its relation with the association not be considered a collaboration—which implied equality—for "it could not open its doors to a population with which it was not familiar and whose tendencies still had not taken clear shape."[159] However, it agreed to serve as financial patron to the organization in its religious and educational activities aimed at adapting Russian immigrants to their new French environment, with the understanding that it would have a say in the administration of new religious facilities constructed by *Ohel-Jacob*. Though anxious to effect a *rapprochement* between immigrant and native Jewry, consistorial leaders insisted that such a *rapprochement* occur on their own terms.

Until confronted by the political and economic situation of 1933–39, native Jewish notables continued to see the management of the immigrants as the most important item on their agenda. As Adolphe Caen, president of the *Union Scolaire*, declared in 1931 to fellow members of the Paris Consistory, "Since the Dreyfus Affair, the consistories have not been faced by a question so important for French Judaism as that of the foreigners."[160] The first hesitant steps taken by the Consistory had not yet eradicated the visible ethnicity of the immigrants or their Jewish national spirit, which had inspired such articles in the French press as "Do Jewish Nationalists Seek the

Rebirth of Anti-Semitism?"[161] Consistorial leaders were therefore concerned with expanding their program of *rapprochement*.

Caen's proposals reveal his ultimate goal: to enable the Consistory to exercise its influence over various segments of the immigrant community. For the school-age population he suggested the creation of new schools and courses of religious instruction and "the control of those organized by other associations—like *Ohel-Jacob*—while obtaining from these associations [assurances] that their courses would be taught in French and . . . inspected by consistorial rabbis." For youth, he stressed the support of groups on the model of *Union Scolaire*, which attempted to bring native and immigrant youth together. Only these groups could draw immigrants away from their own youth groups, which proclaimed the dangerous (to Caen) doctrine of Jewish peoplehood and supported exclusively leftist politics. Finally, religious services could be used to reach immigrant adults. As Caen noted, the Consistory should facilitate "the organization of religious services by special foreign associations while gaining assurances that authority could be exercised by the Consistory over their rabbis or officiants and that consistorial rabbis could, on certain solemn religious occasions, be sent to them 'on mission.' "[162]

The secretariat of the Paris Consistory, which declared in a confidential memo that it hoped to remedy the situation of having present "in Paris a considerable number of Jews of very diverse origins [and] of poorly defined tendencies over whom we have no hold,"[163] supported Caen's approach. Indeed, Israël Lévi, the Chief Rabbi of France, confirmed the existence of the problem. In a reply to the Paris Prefect of Police's request in 1929 that he discourage public street demonstrations by Jews, he confessed his helplessness and lamented that "for the past two or three years there are in our Paris groups turbulent elements, little known to us . . . who escape somewhat from our authority."[164] It was therefore vital, in the eyes of consistorial leaders, "that all of those [immigrants] who have retained connection with Judaism be incorporated in the community and strengthen its organism without changing its nature." Toward that goal the Consistory proposed drawing upon its prestige and power and taking advantage of what was seen as a lack of organization in immigrant circles to encourage the immigrants to rely on the leadership and authority of the Consistory. Official approval and support could be expected from French authorities, "for if we succeed in turning our foreign coreligionists into good French Jews, we will be giving good citizens as well to France."[165]

The strategy of the Consistory was to become involved in all areas of Jewish life. As the report of its secretariat stated, "nothing in the Jewish life of Paris must remain foreign to us. We must know, watch over and, if possible, guide every aspect of Paris Jewish organizations, whatever their importance and whatever their character." Such an approach represented a break with the strictly religious definition of the limits of consistorial activity as mandated by the ideology of emancipation. Consistorial responsibility was to extend, for example, even to the "pernicious and inferior Yiddish theater," attendance at which was to be discouraged. Such a shift in policy, however, did not represent a shift in ideology. Realizing that immigrant Jews defined their Jewishness as a combination of the religious and the national, the Paris Consistory assumed as its task the responsibility to take an interest in nonreligious activities in order "with solicitude" to lead immigrant Jews to "make the necessary disassociation" between the religious and the national.[166]

To accomplish its goal the Paris Consistory favored the establishment in the immigrant neighborhoods of Paris and its suburbs of "small communities, *autonomous* but placed under our control," to which Yiddish-speaking consistorial rabbis could be delegated. These communities would be permitted to organize religious services according to the rite of the majority of their members. In addition, religious instruction, exclusively in French—the Consistory refused to yield on that point—would be offered, as would courses of adult education in which "the history of French Judaism and notably of the emancipation would occupy a preponderant position."[167] All educational activities would be supervised by an administrative committee on which the collaboration of Jewish intellectuals of foreign origin would be sought as a useful device to attract immigrants. To counteract the harmful effects of the Yiddish theater and of meetings of "dangerous political tendencies," it was proposed to organize a mo-

bile team of lecturers, actors, and musicians who would lure immigrants from less constructive activities and perform for them in
evening programs in their neighborhoods while dispensing publicity
for the Consistory. Written propaganda in French and Yiddish would
supplement the activity of the entertainment corps.

Such an ambitious program indicates a transformation in tactics of
the native leadership (though not in their attitudes toward immigrant
culture). Instead of waiting for the immigrants to assimilate, consistorial circles determined to involve themselves actively in the process.
Whereas in the years prior to World War I, consistorial rabbis would
not deign to appear, much less speak Yiddish, at immigrant functions, in the early 1930s they were envisioned as missionaries to bring
the message of French Judaism—*Religion et Patrie*—to the immigrant masses.[168] Whereas the Consistory had held itself aloof from
all activities except its own religious functions, it now sought to meet
the immigrants on their own ground and adapt them to the reality of
French life. For that purpose it was willing to cooperate with immigrant personalities who had already given proof of their successful
adaptation to France.

The success of the new enterprise of the consistorial circles depended upon a reciprocal willingness on the part of immigrant Jewish
leaders to cooperate with native Jewish institutions. The Jewish labor
movement naturally shunned all contact with bourgeois native Jewry
and was considered as well beyond the pale by consistorial circles.
Worried by the competition of the Jewish Left and seeking ways to
augment its prestige and financial resources, the Federation of Jewish
Societies, composed primarily of middle-class immigrants, was the institution most receptive to consistorial overtures. Beginning in 1930 it
included on its cultural commission such native Jews as Adolphe
Caen, William Oualid, Pierre Dreyfus, treasurer of the *Acceuil Fraternel Israélite* and son of Captain Dreyfus, and the writer Pierre
Paraf, with the hope of establishing "an effective liaison with the
milieu of French Judaism."[169] Despite criticism from *Parizer haynt*
that it was forgetting its duty to honor Yiddish,[170] the Federation retained the native luminaries on its commission. Similarly, the *Asiles
de Nuit et de Jour* added several native Jewish philanthropists,

members of the Comité de Bienfaisance, to their board of administrators.[171] Furthermore, the president of the Federation, Israel Jefroykin, the editor of *Parizer haynt*, and the Sephardi Rabbi Ovadia
agreed to cooperate with the Comité de Bienfaisance to facilitate its
fund-raising efforts in immigrant circles.[172] The middle-class Yiddish
press as a whole welcomed such contact despite its reservations about
native Jewish attitudes.

On the grass-roots level, however, consistorial initiatives met with
disappointment. Evaluating the efforts at *rapprochement* of immigrant and native Jews, Jacques Biélinky, who moved in both
worlds, saw the proselytizing efforts of the Consistory to "substitute
[itself] for the small religious associations created by the immigrants,
associations which seemed to seek to fortify the particularism and
isolation of the foreign groups," as partly successful in certain areas
and completely negative in others.[173] Immigrant Jews continued to
prefer to donate charity through organizations they administered,
rather than through the Comité de Bienfaisance.[174] They continued
to prefer their own social, cultural, and religious institutions and, as
we have seen, were unwilling to renounce their values and ideologies
in the name of assimilation. And, as *Parizer haynt* noted, as long as
native Jews remained shy of foreigners, *rapprochement* could occur
only on an institutional level.[175]

The initial efforts at unifying the native and immigrant Jewish populations were only moderately successful for several reasons. Most
importantly, the goals of *rapprochement* were profoundly different for
the two groups involved. The consistorial circles had no intention of
sharing power and prestige with the immigrant leaders but welcomed
rapprochement as a means of recruiting new troops for their own
command. They could ignore neither the indifference of the masses
of native Jews nor the fact that it was the children of immigrants who
filled consistorial courses of religious instruction and provided students for the *Ecole Rabbinique* as well. As was stated at the 1928
General Assembly of the Paris Consistory, "Happily we have an important group of immigrants who have educational needs. . . . I say
happily for [without them] we could rightly fear the complete disappearance of our Association in the near future."[176]

Immigrant Jewish leaders recognized full well that while native Jewry had the capital, they had the masses to contribute to the community.[177] Convinced that native Jewry was unsure of itself and was concerned about the spread of anti-Semitism, immigrant spokesmen sought "attention to our mentality in the united French Jewish family which we want to build."[178] Immigrant leaders thus expected to share on an equal basis in the direction of the community.

Consistorial circles, however, developed no respect for the Jewish culture and prevalent ideologies of the immigrant Jews. While lamenting the indifference of vast numbers of native Jews, they refused to attribute that indifference to the failure of their own approach to assimilation. Without a reappraisal of immigrant Jewish culture, the policy of *rapprochement* proved fragile indeed. Under the turbulent social and political conditions of the mid and late 1930s, as we shall see, mutual misunderstanding and real ideological differences could not yield easily to the lure of *rapprochement*. Yet, despite the failure of the new tactics, the encounter of native and immigrant Jews in France introduced new cultural elements—not the least of them Zionism—into the interwar French Jewish community.

6.
The Infiltration of Zionism

As the major supporters of Zionist activity, immigrant Jews wielded a powerful tool to strengthen Jewish cultural life and self-perception in France. As one native French Jew noted in 1935, "Virtually all Jewish movement, all the essential stimulus of Jewish activity, particularly . . . of Zionist tendency are due to these newly arrived French Jews of foreign origin. It is to them that we Jews resident in France for generations owe our being led to these properly Jewish activities to which we had become unaccustomed."[1] This assessment may appear paradoxical, for the Zionist movement itself often despaired of French Jewry and lamented its profound assimilation. Focusing on public opposition to Zionism and on the failure of Zionist organizing campaigns, historians of French Jewry, too, have dismissed Zionism as a force within French Jewish life prior to the Holocaust. Yet the indirect impact of Zionism, particularly in the 1930s, should not be underestimated. It would be impossible to understand the transformation of French Jewry without taking account of the infiltration of Zionism into the French Jewish community.

Even in the absence of a thriving Zionist organization in France, elements of Zionist ideology penetrated into the world view of major segments of French Jewry. Zionism attracted the support of famous men of letters like Edmond Fleg and André Spire, who came to represent in their much respected persons the fusion of French sentiment and support for Zionism. Zionist influence can be discerned in what was termed the cultural renaissance of French Jewry. Moreover, Zionism provided an alternative to the assimilationist model which had been the norm for Jews in post-emancipation France and which did not appeal to immigrant Jews from Eastern Europe.

The relative weakness of organized Zionism in France stems from a variety of factors, not all of them limited to France. In all Western countries the comfortably assimilated Jewish circles viewed Zionism as antithetical to their position as citizens and potentially dangerous to their very well-being.[2] French Jews of old stock merely shared the outlook of their upper-class coreligionists of England, the U.S., and Germany. Moreover, as we have noted, the ideology of assimilation had scarcely been challenged in France until the interwar period, when the immigrant community grew sizably larger.

Mass support for Zionism came from Jews whose cultural matrix was of Eastern European origin. As members of a new community, which had to cope with the special socioeconomic and cultural problems of the recent immigrant, Eastern European immigrants in France had neither the energy nor the surplus funds to devote to an idealistic movement of no immediate benefit to themselves. Moreover, the Jewish labor movement, imbued with anti-Zionist socialist ideology, considered Zionism a regressive nationalist movement which undermined class consciousness. Still, the Zionist movement in France drew upon immigrant Jews, primarily small merchants, professionals, and intellectuals (and later workers) for its active support. Zionist leaders in the immigrant community included in the years before World War I a well-known expatriate doctor, Max Nordau, and a biologist, Alexander Marmorek. After the war Marc Jarblum, a lawyer, B. Iudcovici, the owner of a printing establishment, Léon Filderman, a physician, Hillel Zlatopolsky, a merchant, and Isaac Naiditch, an industrialist, joined the leadership.

The association of Zionism with immigrant activists accounts in part for the virulent and prolonged opposition of native French Jewry to the movement. Native hostility to Zionism, dating from its earliest days and peaking in the years immediately after World War I, dissipated only gradually. While Zionist societies were established in Paris as early as the 1890s, it was not until the 1930s, when the fate of much of Central and Eastern European Jewry was in question, that Zionism began to overcome its association with immigrants and leave its imprint upon French Jewry. Despite its rejection of the ideological and political implications of Zionism, French Jewry was changed by it.

Attitude of French Jewry toward Zionism

From its first appearance, the native Jewish leadership saw Zionism as a movement which flew in the face of the development of Jewish history. One columnist in *L'Univers israélite* claimed, echoing the views of the prominent French Jewish historian Théodore Reinach, "The history of Judaism is the history of a progressive denationalization. . . . Where they [the Jews] live, there is their fatherland. . . . Let us be Jews above all, and faithful to the spirit of Judaism. But the spirit of Judaism, as it is reflected in its history, is the condemnation of Zionism."[3] The thesis that Jewish influence in history depended ultimately upon the dispersion of the Jews throughout the world—the "mission doctrine" as it had come to be known—was invoked to provide teleological ammunition against Zionist ideology.[4]

Anti-Zionist articles predominated in the pages of the major organs of the native community throughout the pre-war period, but less hostile articles began to make their appearance in the last years before World War I. This was, as we have noted, a period of security for French Jewry, and the apparent failure of Zionism had mitigated its threatening aspects. Some contributors to the French Jewish press were even able to evaluate sympathetically the contributions of the movement to Jewish life. Zionism, it was said, was becoming mere philanthrophy.[5] Indeed, in 1913 a young Romanian-born graduate of the *Ecole Rabbinique* suggested that the rebirth of Zionist activity might be beneficial to French Jewish life. Certainly, being a Zionist was not incompatible with being a good Frenchman. And Zionism could appeal to those "coreligionists" whom the synagogue no longer attracted. Finally, Zionism and Judaism shared a "common scourge, complete assimilation," and a common concern, the survival of the Jews.[6] Both the Jew and the Zionist had an equal interest in the diffusion of the Hebrew language, the one for prayer, the other for daily living and culture. Both were the heirs of the Jewish religious tradition. Moreover, Herzl himself had often stated that a return to Judaism was necessary before one could return to Judea. For these reasons the young rabbi, who bridged the immigrant and native communities, wished "much, much success to Zionist propaganda."[7]

Although they were ideologically opposed to Zionism, neither the Alliance Israélite Universelle nor the Central Consistory considered it sufficiently powerful as a movement to be treated as a serious adversary in the pre–World War I period. Public neutrality and indifference were judged the best methods for dealing with the Zionist nuisance. The situation changed, however, with the increased visibility of Zionism during the war, when Zionist meetings proliferated and drew large audiences. It was during the war that Zionism became an international diplomatic question—an unanticipated success that inspired a renewal of hostility toward the nationalist movement by native French Jewry.

French Zionists succeeded in linking Zionism with French patriotism and French national interests. As early as June of 1915 a Zionist lecturer could state that Zionism had become particularly important in view of the French claim to Syria.[8] A Franco-Zionist League was established in April 1915 by a small group of immigrant Jews to gain support in France for the Zionist movement.[9] It soon brought together in a committee of patronage an impressive number of Jews and non-Jews prominent in literary circles, the academic world, and politics. Among the members of the committee were the writers Edmond Fleg and André Spire (sympathetic to Zionism, though not continually active in the movement, since the days of the Dreyfus Affair), Gustave Kahn, F. A. Hérold, Wilfred Monod, Marius Moutet, Paul Passy (professor at the Sorbonne), Nahum Slousch, and Emmanuel Weill.[10]

The Franco-Zionist League enjoyed only a brief existence. However, after the publication of the Balfour Declaration it was renewed under the name of the League of the Friends of Zionism and its activity expanded under the leadership of André Spire. As secretary-general of the League and a member of André Tardieu's Information and Press Service, Spire was able to appeal to French interests, both in private conversations with government ministers and in public debate, to counteract the anti-Zionism of the leadership of native

French Jewry. In response to an anti-Zionist article by Joseph Reinach in *Le Figaro* of April 8, 1917, he wrote,

> In combatting Zionism our Jewish elite scarcely perceives that its egoism
> and incomprehension make it fail in its clearest obligation as Frenchmen.
> . . . When the Jews receive from the Peace Congress the instrument of
> their regeneration, do . . . our French Jews want France to be absent
> from the concert of their [the Jews'] blessings? [11]

Spire thus turned on their head anti-Zionist accusations of lack of patriotism on the part of Zionists! And Spire was successful in his efforts. As Stephen Pichon wrote to Tardieu on January 26, 1918,
"French Israelites are for the most part barely sympathetic to any organization tending to create a Jewish nationality. The government
does not allow itself to be guided by them." [12]

The support of F. A. Hérold, the vice-president of the League of
the Rights of Man, followed by the endorsement of Zionist goals by
that organization, was of critical importance in popularizing Zionism
among the French public. Individual Zionist leaders also recruited
well-placed French supporters to aid their cause. Marc Jarblum, the
energetic leader of the small *Poalei-Zion* group which existed in Paris
at the time, met with socialist ministers in the government to prop-
agandize for Zionism. [13] Enric Braunstein, a committee member of
the Franco-Zionist League and Zionist activist, succeeded in bringing Albert de Monzie, Marius Moutet, Jean Longuet, and Charles
Gide to Zionism. In an era when French socialists were loyal
members of the government, the support even of socialists served to
legitimize Zionism and to make it an issue of universal justice for the
French public, Gentile and Jewish alike.

As immigrants from Eastern Europe the Zionists were able to
present themselves to a concerned Jewish public as the spokesmen for
and interpreters of the interests of their brethren who remained in the
East. Speaking in French before an audience of two hundred at one
of the numerous Zionist meetings which took place during the war,
Enric Braunstein appealed to his listeners, "Group yourselves, Jews
of France, around us, the intellectuals who seek a place in the sun

for those who suffer. . . . Certainly, we realize that a goodly number of Jews do not desire to return to Palestine, but let us work for those who do, and who are the large majority."[14] This line of argument enjoyed success and inspired the Chief Rabbi of France, Alfred Lévy, to write a letter to a French periodical that French Jews

> understand that these persecuted coreligionists [of Eastern Europe] have but one desire, to recover a fatherland in that land of Palestine to which so many religious memories bind them. French Israelites seek for their unfortunate coreligionists the realization of that desire and hope that our dear France, the home *par excellence* of liberty and justice, will aid in that realization.[15]

Zionist propaganda also made effective use of the active participation of Jews as combattants in the Allied armies and argued that its own program was in accordance with the ideology of national self-determination espoused by the Allies. If every national group could demand the redress of its national grievances, then the Jewish people would not rest until its national demands were satisfied by European diplomacy. A broadside announcing a Zionist meeting of January 20, 1916, sponsored by the Zionist Committee of the Fourth *Arrondissement*, stated,

> You, too, you are giving your children to this horrible war. Political circumstances compel you to spill your blood for the causes of others, for the national ideal of any people whatsoever, except that of the Jewish people. That unhappy state must not remain without political result, without bringing a homeland to the Jews.[16]

Well before the promulgation of the Balfour Declaration, at numerous well-attended public meetings, Zionist orators called for Jewish unity, a *union sacrée* of Jews in France, to present national demands at the Peace Conference.[17] "We will not allow the peace to be signed," Braunstein declared, "until we have obtained our beautiful Palestine."[18] The rhetoric of wartime propaganda was thus put to good use by Zionist spokesmen.

Zionism was taken so seriously as a political force by the French government that police agents regularly attended and filed detailed reports on Zionist functions and investigated Zionist groups from

1915 to 1923.[19] One major conclusion of the intelligence reports was that Zionism exhibited Germanophile tendencies. Nahum Sokolow, for one, was attacked as a dangerous Germanophile, and the use of a Judeo-German dialect (i.e., Yiddish) was cited as proof of pro-German sympathies.[20] It was also claimed that French Zionists, though not themselves Germanophiles, maintained contact with German and Austrian Zionists, using Max Nordau as intermediary. Members of the "Zionist government constituted in Palestine" were said to be almost all Germans or Germanophiles.[21]

Despite this assessment, Zionism made headway during the war years. In order to take best advantage of the opportunities which the climate of wartime France afforded for publicizing the Zionist cause, French Zionists established a network of local organizations in Paris. Zionist sections were set up in six *arrondissements* with heavy immigrant Jewish settlement.[22] From 1915 to 1919 these local sections and the Zionist Central Committee sponsored more than fifty large Zionist meetings in Paris.[23] Attendance at these meetings, as reported by police agents, was often in the range of 500 to 1,000 people, with an occasional event, particularly following the Balfour Declaration, drawing as many as 1,500.[24] During this period a Zionist student group composed of immigrant youth studying in French universities was renewed,[25] and a Yiddish paper "under the influence of socialist Zionists" appeared for several months in 1916 under the stewardship of Marc Jarblum.[26]

Though Paris was the site of the Peace Conference, the French Zionists were too insignificant in numbers and influence to figure in the delicate lobbying and maneuvering. True, André Spire, as we shall see, played a role in the proceedings, but he did so as an individual—a prominent French Jew, a man of letters, a civil servant—not as a delegated representative of French Zionism. Enric Braunstein complained that Spire had accepted the invitation to speak before the Peace Conference without even seeking the consent of the Executive Committee of the French Zionist Federation. For the rest, the international leadership of the movement found their way to Paris when the occasion called for their presence, and French Zionists bitterly expressed their sense of exclusion as they saw themselves dis-

placed by major Zionist leaders coming and going between Paris and
London.

The Peace Conference

It was international Zionist activity, centered in Paris during the
Peace Conference rather than local Zionist meetings, which attracted
most of the attention of the leadership of native French Jewry and
aroused their consternation and active opposition. For the inclusion
of the Balfour Declaration in the post-war treaties and the recognition
of national minority rights for the Jewish masses of Eastern Europe
threatened the claim to leadership and the self-definition of the circles of the Consistory and the Alliance Israélite. Both issues presumed a nationalist definition of Jews, which was anathema to native
leadership. In both matters the Zionists naively hoped to present a
united Jewish front to the diplomats in whose hands the decision lay.
However, the notables of the Consistory and the Alliance, along with
their English confrères of the British Joint Foreign Committee, conducted their own diplomacy and actively combatted the nationalist
definition of the Jewish problem both in Eastern Europe and in Palestine.[27] The bitterness engendered by this conflict intensified the
hostility of the spokesmen for native French Jewry toward Zionism.

Since it defined itself as a worldwide defense organization which
had been lobbying in behalf of the extension of civil rights to Jews of
all countries, the Alliance was loath to follow the leadership of Eastern European Jews, its clients. As we have seen, its leaders could not
accept the legitimacy of national minority rights for Jews as an alternative model of emancipation for the multinational states of Eastern
Europe. During the discussion of the Minority Rights treaties in the
spring of 1919 they remained steadfast in their opposition to the
inclusion of minority rights in the treaties with the newly constituted
countries of Eastern Europe,[28] and published their own program
calling for civic emancipation without national minority rights.[29]
Because the issue of minority rights for Jews was pushed vigorously by
individual Zionists and by the Zionist organized and led Committee

of Jewish Delegations at the Peace Conference, the opposition which the issue itself raised among the leadership of French Jewry intermingled with antipathy for Zionists, who were its most prominent spokesmen. Although the Committee of Jewish Delegations was not sufficiently well organized to publish its memorandum on national minority rights for Jews until June 9, 1919, after the treaties had already been drawn up, its leaders, with Leo Motzkin at their head, had been attempting to win support for their position among the representatives of Western Jewry. Relations between the two groups were less than cordial. In a letter which summed up his experiences with the Western European Jewish leaders, Motzkin wrote,

> Now for your question whether the French and English representatives *refused* to sign our memorandum to the Peace Conference. . . . After the refusal by the members of the Joint Committee and the *Alliance Israélite* to walk hand in hand with us, on account of the expression "national claims," it would have been absurd for us to directly ask these organizations to sign our memorandum. . . . They also knew what stress we laid upon the whole of Jewry proceeding with uniformity. Were it not for this uniformity, we should never have made the concessions we did when we formulated our claims. These concessions we made although we considered ourselves as the only legitimate representatives of Judaism and although we represent the great majority of same. We cannot understand how these gentlemen can now state that they knew nothing whatever of the memo presented by us to the Peace Conference.[30]

The conflict between the Committee of Jewish Delegations and the established leadership of French Jewry was one of opposing self-definitions, ideologies, and claims to leadership of world Jewry—conflicts which could not easily be resolved. Just as these conflicts found expression in the issue of national minority rights, so they were reflected even more blatantly in the controversy over the Zionist claims to Palestine at the Peace Conference.

After the promulgation of the Balfour Declaration it became clear that the powers of the Entente were prepared to support Zionist claims to Palestine.[31] Like the British Jewish notables, the leaders of French Judaism found the Balfour Declaration offensive, for it undermined their public and private position that civic emancipation and national integration in the lands of their birth represented the sole acceptable and workable solution to the Jewish question. It also, they felt, fanned the flames of anti-Semitism by confirming its basic tenet that Jews were, and would always remain, a nation apart.[32] In so doing, it raised the spectre of dual loyalty, threatening the standard of French Jewry, its devoted patriotism.

French Jewish leaders circulated their anti-Zionist views privately and saw to it that, in André Spire's words, "two notorious anti-Zionists were installed in the Quai d'Orsay" to head a Service of Study and Information.[33] Although French Jewish notables preferred to maintain a low profile, the discussion of Zionism at the Peace Conference called for the presentation of their point of view. Baron Edmond de Rothschild, who opposed what he saw as the fanatic nationalism of the Zionists, proposed that Sylvain Lévi, professor of Sanskrit at the Collège de France, assume that task. As a prominent member of the Alliance Israélite, veteran of a trip to Palestine, and protegé of Rothschild, Sylvain Lévi was then selected by the French Foreign Ministry, along with André Spire, to speak on behalf of French Jewry before the Supreme Council of the Allies at the Peace Conference. Behind the scenes Lévi had already discouraged the French government from allowing other than a written representation to the Conference from French Zionists or the League of the Friends of Zionism. "You would be in the position of shocking the deepest sentiments of French Judaism were you to give Zionism a more considerable role," Lévi advised. "That which is called French Zionism is essentially a group of foreign Jews residing in France as a cadre of Jewish . . . dilettantes whom it would be compromising to take seriously." Lévi promoted instead the "emancipationist and assimilationist tradition" of the Alliance and native French Jewry, which he labeled France's own.[34] As Rothschild's representative, Lévi had serious objections to Zionism. The report which he presented on February 27, 1919, to the Council of Ten as a neutral observer on the potential for Zionist colonization in Palestine was calculated to undermine the Zionist case. Lévi's speech proffered sympathy to the Zionist movement as long as it respected the rights of Jews who did not define themselves from a nationalist perspective. It praised Zionist accomplishments in instilling a sense of personal dignity in the

Jewish masses of Eastern Europe, in introducing them to the modern concept of nationalism so essential to advanced political development, and in mitigating the threat of Yiddish, which could be exploited by Germany for its own profit.[35] Although he had some good words for Zionism, he also cautioned the Council against accepting inflated Zionist expectations of success. Palestine, he pointed out, could not support a large population, and Jews, particularly those from Eastern Europe, had little practice in developing the moderation and discipline necessary for self-government. Finally, he raised the issue of dual nationality, which Western Jews found particularly disturbing.[36] The Zionist spokesmen present, among them Chaim Weizmann and Nahum Sokolow, as well as the French Zionist movement as a whole, considered Lévi's patronizing remarks a betrayal of his supposed sympathy for Zionism. The Zionists were particularly disturbed that the French press had picked up Lévi's speech but not Weizmann's or Sokolow's and that Lévi had been described as a Zionist spokesman.[37]

French Zionists realized that the native Jewish Establishment had commenced a serious offensive against Zionist influence in French circles, both Jewish and non-Jewish. Sylvain Lévi's report was not merely a personal statement but was conceived and edited under the deliberately anti-Zionist influence of the Alliance.

The Zionist perception after World War I that the Jewish notables had abandoned their purported neutrality for an all-out attack on Zionism is borne out by the confidential records of the Central Consistory and the Alliance and by the files of the Ministry of Foreign Affairs. In response to the discussion of Zionism at the Peace Conference the Permanent Section of the Central Consistory decided that it was necessary to take a stand on the issue of Zionism. At the next session debate centered on the wisdom of issuing a statement which "would be a declaration of war against Zionism."[38] Paradoxically, the Consistory leaders were concerned less with the possible repercussions in the Jewish world than with the possibility that such a statement might be against the interests of the French government. To prevent such an unhappy result, they decided to submit the declaration, which would be drawn up by Chief Rabbi Israël Lévi, to a

member of the French government for advice and approval.[39] A
week later the declaration on Zionism was adopted by the Permanent
Section and approved by the Central Consistory.[40] The text of the
declaration opened with the expressed desire of French Israelites that
the benefits of emancipation be assured to all groups within the Jewish population. In a conciliatory tone it noted their joy at the potential economic, cultural, and religious developments to be expected
from the Jewish foyer already in existence in Palestine, (established, it
was claimed, thanks to the activity of French Jewish individuals and
organizations). However, French Israelites felt

> that it was a humane obligation to warn their coreligionists of Eastern
> Europe . . . that the economic and social conditions of that country
> [Palestine] would not permit for a long period the settlement of more than
> a few thousand immigrants. . . . They feel constrained to add that if
> . . . the establishment of a Jewish state is at issue, they cannot associate
> themselves with demands which misread the very course of history, which
> tends to eliminate the concept of states founded on religion, a concept
> against which Enlightened Judaism has not ceased to protest for more
> than a century and which will surely result in drawing the suspicion of
> their fellow citizens on the millions of Jews of Eastern Europe who will
> remain in their country of origin.[41]

The major objections to Zionism on practical and ideological
grounds thus found expression in the Consistory's statement.

However, the declaration was never made public. For Chief Rabbi
Lévi reported that the Minister of Foreign Affairs, with whom he had
met, preferred that such a statement not be published. As a result of
Lévi's report the Permanent Section decided that for the time being
circumstances did not appear favorable to the declaration. The text,
however, would be placed in the archives of the Central Consistory
for publication when deemed necessary. Moreover, the Chief Rabbi
promised that he would communicate to all French rabbis "the standard of conduct inspired by the sentiments of the Central Consistory
which they ought to follow relative to Zionism."[42] Such a standard
of conduct clearly was not one of benevolent neutrality regarding Zionism, no matter what the public stance of the Central Consistory.
And, even in public, the French rabbinate felt free to express its pop-

ular anti-Zionism, with Chief Rabbi Lévi taking the opportunity of his Yom Kippur eve sermon in 1920 to raise objections to Zionism both in principle and in practice.[43] Indeed, Rabbi Lévi was described in a note to Philippe Berthelot as being "horrified at all who profess Zionism from Spire to Sokolow to Slousch. . . . He follows basically the politics of the Reinachs. . . . It's reactionary Jewish politics dependent upon the plutocrats."[44] The "neutrality" toward Zionism adopted by French Judaism did not preclude discussing the factual difficulties of achieving the Zionist goal and ideological objections to Zionism. Rabbi Maurice Liber, for example, was particularly vociferous in expressing his opposition to Zionism throughout the interwar period. *Parizer leben* mockingly reported Rabbi Liber's participation as an anti-Zionist spokesman in a lecture series at the *Ecole des Etudes Sociales* at the Sorbonne. ("Who spoke against Zionism? Naturally, a Jew.")[45]

Similarly, the Alliance Israélite, while pursuing a policy of proclaimed public neutrality,[46] acted in private to undermine Zionist influence. In June 1918 the Central Committee of the Alliance had determined to discuss the question of the "new sympathetic attitude" of the *Univers israélite* toward Zionism, and the secretary of the Alliance warned the editor of the periodical, S. Lehmann, of the impending deliberation, soliciting a defensive and conciliatory letter in response. Lehmann claimed that he remained opposed to political Zionism, which he found irreconcilable with French patriotism, but had allowed the publication of articles on religious Zionism, as espoused by a semi-convert, Aimé Pallière, because they were not incompatible with patriotism. Moreover, the change in the attitude of the governments of the Entente toward Palestine was worthy of comment. He also noted that an ideological movement which offered consolation and comfort to millions of persecuted Jews had to be viewed with sympathy. Finally, he had hoped, through a conciliatory attitude, to forestall the publication of a new Zionist journal, which could become an element of division within the community. Such a possibility had been raised by a group of French coreligionists and Palestinophiles, who had sought space for their views several months before in the *Univers israélite*.[47] Clearly, the Alliance's communication to the journal merited such a detailed reply because it was seen as a threat to suspend the Alliance's subsidy.

In the Alliance's own organ, *Paix et droit*, articles detailing the dangers and impracticalities of Zionism continued unabated, though the Alliance claimed that such articles were not polemical.[48] Prominent figures in the Alliance, among them its new president, Sylvain Lévi, also continued to lecture publicly on the dangers of Zionism.[49]

Private communications to members of the Alliance who had solicited advice regarding affiliation with Zionist institutions made it clear that the leadership of the organization promoted the idea of a basic incompatibility between being a member of the Alliance and a participant, however minimal, in any Zionist activity. Thus, when Simon Salomon, a member of the Central Committee of the Alliance and of the Consistory of the Lorraine, asked if he could add his name to the publicity lists of the Keren Hayesod, a fund sponsored by the Zionist Organization, and still remain on the Central Committee, he was advised that "we can only urge you vigorously not to join the committee of Keren Hayesod."[50] Several months later he was also discouraged from any collaboration in the activity of another Zionist fund, the Keren Kayemeth Le-Yisrael.[51] Even within consistorial circles voices were raised to indicate that the Alliance was carrying its anti-Zionism too far. Chief Rabbi Lévi, for one, suggested that the Alliance cooperate more fully in the moral and material reconstruction of Palestine.[52] Yet such cooperation was precluded, as the leadership of the Alliance recognized full well, by the competitive nature of the relationship of Zionists and the Alliance in Palestine as well as by their differing diagnoses of the Jewish question. The demands which the Alliance would make of Zionism— abandonment of political propaganda in countries where Jews had been granted the rights of citizenship and noninterference with the activities of the Alliance in Palestine—could not have been realized without the Zionists' surrender of their most fundamental claims.[53] Because of their opposition to Jewish nationalism, in their contacts with French governmental figures Alliance leaders repeatedly disparaged Zionism and discouraged consultation with Zionist personalities. Zionism, they claimed, provided no solution to the Jewish problem. Since the Alliance rejected as unfounded the concept of a Jewish nation, it would make no concession to Zionism, even if asked to do so by the French authorities. As Jacques Bigart declared, "French Jews are Jewish Frenchmen. . . . They belong to the French people and accept national solidarity only with the French nation."[54]

Although organized Zionist activity had declined in France after the adoption of the Treaty of San Remo in June of 1920, Zionist leaders did not abandon their efforts. In particular, the appeal to French Jewry on a philanthropic basis to aid the struggling Jewish enterprise in Palestine continued to enjoy success.[55] The Keren Hayesod could point to the suffering of the Jews of Eastern Europe, who were the victims of pogroms and unceasing persecution in the years immediately following World War I, to suggest that their salvation lay in emigration to Palestine, whose Jewish National Home had now been recognized by the League of Nations. Moreover, as prominent a member of the Jewish Establishment as Dr. Léon Zadoc-Kahn, son of the universally beloved former Chief Rabbi of France, had assumed the presidency of the Keren Hayesod.[56] Although French Jews tended not to join Zionist groups or subscribe to Zionism's nationalist ideology, at least some of them were susceptible to Zionist appeals to their sense of solidarity with their fellow Jews. Zionism made sense to them as a movement for the Jews of Eastern Europe, and the emotional attraction of Palestine, atavistic though it might have been, had not been entirely extinguished among French Jewry.

To the leaders of French Jewry it became apparent that the Zionist movement should not be allowed to exploit these sentiments unimpeded. Such a situation, if unchallenged, could ultimately undermine the loyalty of French Jewry to established Jewish institutions and leadership. Rather, the non-Zionist leadership decided to confront the Zionists on their own turf and to depoliticize the philanthropic sentiment and emotional response which they had elicited. Thus, in August 1922, Rabbi Maurice Liber's anonymous lead article in L'Univers israélite, entitled "Is Collaboration with the Zionists Possible?" suggested that French Jews who were not Zionists by conviction should not contribute to Zionist causes, even to so pur-

portedly a neutral one as Keren Hayesod, as long as Zionism retained
its partisan nationalist basis which was unacceptable to much of
Diaspora Jewry. Those non-Zionists who were interested in the Jewish home—not, of course, the Jewish national home—should work
on its behalf through either new or veteran non-Zionist organizations.[57] The Jewish National Home thus was acceptable only if de-
nationalized.

Acting upon Rabbi Liber's advice, the following year the Association of French Rabbis, meeting in Strasbourg, in virtual unanimity
adopted a resolution which called for "the creation of a society which
would favor the participation of French Judaism in its entirety in the
renaissance of Jewish Palestine.[58]

While recalling

> the religious and historical ties which connected Palestine to Judaism,
> and proclaiming that Jewish colonization of the Holy Land always was,
> and is today more than ever, an obligation [mitzvah] of the greatest im-
> portance . . . the French rabbinate considers that the national and politi-
> cal doctrines of Zionism, of which they recognize the moral and ideal
> value for millions of their brethren, cannot be reconciled with the princi-
> ples of French Judaism and with the conception which the latter has
> always had of its duties vis-à-vis world Judaism.[59]

Two years later, to implement the resolution, the French rabbinate
established the Oeuvre Palestinienne.[60] Heralding its creation with
the announcement that for the first time the totality of "Israelites" of
one Western country had been won to the cause of the rebirth of
Eretz-Israel, Rabbi Liber, its spokesman, argued that such a body was
necessary because Zionist funds were controlled by persons inimical
to the Jewish religion. Unanimity had been achieved by the French
rabbinate, he claimed, precisely because "Zionism had been left
aside." Therefore, he continued, the French rabbinate could recom-
mend to French Jews neither the Keren Kayemeth nor the Keren
Hayesod, "which were Zionist funds."[61]

Aimé Pallière, a semi-convert to Judaism, noted that the objection
to Zionism on religious grounds was contrived: "It is rather singular,
that French Judaism, whose religious life is so anemic that many of
its communities are threatened with total disappearance, should be

alone in raising an objection of this nature."[62] French Zionists based in Paris understood, and rejected, the motives behind the creation of the Oeuvre Palestinienne but welcomed at first the financial support it could bring from new sources to the development of Palestine. Alsatian Zionists, however, feared that the new body would only sow dissension where Zionism had set down roots and weaken the effectiveness of both Keren Hayesod and Keren Kayemeth. A 1927 confidential report on French Zionism to the Zionist Organization Executive indicated that the Oeuvre Palestinienne had, in fact, had adverse effects on Keren Kayemeth fund raising in the provinces.[63]

The policy which had been adopted in the case of the Oeuvre Palestinienne—active opposition to the Zionist nationalist *Weltanschauung* combined with adoption of concerns which the Zionists had arrogated unto themselves—became standard for the French Jewish leadership in its relation with Zionism. Gradually, however, the needs of European Jewry in the years following the rise of Nazism impelled the leadership to shift from a righteous and fearful anti-Zionism to a neutral and hesitant non-Zionism.[64]

On the face of it, this pro-Palestine yet non-Zionist attitude had its parallel in the U.S. at the time, and Zionist leadership definitely perceived its potential practical benefits for the cause. However, when the Jewish Agency was expanded in 1929 to include non-Zionists in its membership, the Consistory and the Alliance Israélite, their collaboration actively solicited by the Zionist Organization, once more declined to associate themselves with the Zionist movement.[65] The Consistory fell back on its traditional rationale for noninvolvement in causes which did not elicit its active sympathy—that its statutes did not permit its participation in a political organization like the Jewish Agency.[66] Sylvain Lévi, speaking for the Alliance Israélite, haughtily noted that the Zionist Organization had erred in asking the Alliance to represent French Jewry on the Jewish Agency, for the Alliance "is and claims to remain the Alliance Israélite *Universelle,* and we do not intend to renounce the honor of speaking and acting in the name of all Jewry."[67] The Alliance retained its perception of the Zionist Organization as its primary competitor in international Jewish affairs.

From Hostility to Accommodation

In spite of this official policy, individuals within Establishment circles (with Chief Rabbi Israël Lévi at their head) did feel it necessary to cooperate with the Zionist Organization in selecting French representatives to the Jewish Agency. As a recognized Judaic scholar, Lévi had already served on the Board of Governors of the Hebrew University.[68] In response to his recent inquiry of the French government's attitude toward the participation of French Jews in the Jewish Agency, Lévi had received a positive and enthusiastic reply.[69] Through the Oeuvre Palestinienne he volunteered to select the French delegates. In fact, he proposed to exercise a monopoly on delegate selection, and protested vehemently against the Zionists' plan to consult with other organizations. For the Oeuvre Palestinienne, he contended, was the only non-Zionist and pro-Palestine organization in France "which represented all the elements of French Judaism . . . and included members of the Central Consistory, the Alliance, the Keren Hayesod, Israelite notables from Paris, the provinces, and Algeria, Ashkenazim and Sephardim."[70] However, Lévi had overlooked, as the native Establishment was wont to do, the importance of immigrant Jews of East European origin, for whom the Zionist Organization had chosen Léon Blum, a "Zionist sympathizer" of long-standing, as representative.[71] The only concession which Leo Motzkin, who was in charge of establishing the enlarged Jewish Agency, was prepared to offer to Lévi was that Blum would not be designated by the Federation of Jewish Societies, whose importance Lévi had denigrated, but by the League of the Friends of Labor Palestine, a newly established organization designed to attract both Jewish and non-Jewish socialists to support the Zionist enterprise in Palestine. Motzkin also reassured Lévi that the Zionists had never expected the Oeuvre Palestinienne to sponsor Blum, "given his political tendencies and connections."[72] A third delegate had been reserved for the Jews of Alsace.

Although Zionist relations with the Consistory and the Alliance remained difficult,[73] from 1929 on, prominent French Jews of native as well as immigrant origin served on the council of the Jewish Agency. Among them were Henry Lévy, industrialist, public servant, vice-president of the Consistory of the Lower Rhine, and president of the Strasbourg section of the Alliance Israélite; Israël Jefroykin, the president of the Federation of Jewish Societies, which had adhered officially to the Jewish Agency; and Robert Bollack, a native French Jew who was active in the Keren Hayesod.[74]

Gradually, involvement in Zionist activity during the 1930s no longer led to the censure of French rabbis nor prevented laymen from serving in positions of communal leadership, particularly in Alsace. Thus in 1931 Grand Rabbi Aisenstadt became vice president of the Central Commission of the Keren Keyemeth, while Gustave Lévy, a Zionist, was elected to the Metz Consistory.[75] In addition, Emile Frank, the secretary-general of the Metz Consistory was extremely active in the work of Keren Hayesod.[76] When the Regional Union of Zionists of Eastern France held its congress in Metz in 1934, its members were welcomed formally by the president of the Jewish community of Metz.[77]

Philanthropic Zionism required no personal commitment even to the concept that the Jews were a nation in exile—much less to actual settlement in Palestine; support for it had therefore become respectable. As early as 1930, the Alliance·Israélite responded vigorously, if only verbally, to the publication of the British Passfield White Paper on Palestine.[78] Despite its neutrality on the issue of Zionism, the Alliance declared that it "could not remain indifferent to this measure taken with regard to a movement which has aroused in the hearts of our coreligionists so many idealistic aspirations and comforting hopes."[79] The nature of events in Europe as well as in Palestine had made Zionism a practical necessity in international Jewish political considerations. With the deepening world economic crisis and the spread of fascism in Central and Eastern Europe, the promise of a liberal, "emancipation-in-place" solution to the problems of the Jewish masses of Germany and Eastern Europe had turned to ashes even for the most optimistic of French Jews. The rise of xenophobia in France and in other countries of the West in response to the economic crisis had effectively terminated their role as havens for immigrants. Jewish settlement in Palestine, on the other hand, was continuing and had reached close to 400,000 souls by 1937.[80]

This new reality had converted Zionism from Utopia to lifeline. The leadership of French Jewry, and in particular the rabbinate, took note of the new reality and adjusted its public stance accordingly. In a well-publicized sermon, Jacob Kaplan, the future Chief Rabbi of France, declared that French Jews must support Zionism. While objections had been acceptable forty years earlier, Zionism was now aimed at, and would benefit, not French Jews but refugees. French Jews need not fear that their loyalty to France would be questioned, for "we have given sufficient proof of our patriotism" and the Jewish National Home has won support among non-Jewish Frenchmen. In keeping with the religious basis of the traditional self-definition of French Jewry, the type of Zionism Rabbi Kaplan specifically promoted was Torah (religious) Zionism.[81] Moreover, a number of French rabbis actively involved themselves in Zionist politics, appealing publicly to their coreligionists to vote the Mizrahi (Religious Zionist) list in the 1939 elections to the Twenty-First Zionist Congress.[82] By 1939 a number of French Jewish notables—Robert de Rothschild, Isaiah Schwartz (the Chief Rabbi of France), and Julien Weill (the Chief Rabbi of Paris)—were willing as well to criticize publicly, though in mild terms, the 1939 British White Paper on Palestine.[83]

The Infiltration of Zionists

Although the number of dues-paying Zionists in France remained small—never more than 10,135[84]—the impact of Zionism on French Jewish life was not negligible. The influence of an ideological movement must be sought not only in membership lists but in the transformation of its ideas and its concerns into common cultural currency. While Zionist nationalism did not succeed in displacing the ideology of assimilation which had flourished among French Jewry since the time of Napoleon I, its promotion of Jewish pride, of the legitimacy of Jewish ethnicity, of Jewish and Hebrew cultural creativity, and of the pioneering ethos in Palestine made significant inroads, particularly among Jewish youth, in interwar France. In Alsace-Lorraine, Zionism generated much support. The Alsatian Zionists maintained their own Regional Union independent of the immigrant-dominated and Paris-based Zionist organization of France.[85] Many prominent critics of French Jewish life attributed to Zionism the "Jewish revival" they discerned in France.[86] Even the consistorial circles, no Zionists they, did not remain insensitive to the changes in French Jewish life which had followed World War I, and they attributed to Zionism a decisive role in the new developments. Thus, a 1931 report of the Paris Consistory noted that

> factors of a moral or political nature, such as the Balfour Declaration, the renaissance of the national idea, etc. have instilled in Jewish life in the Paris community aspects which, unexpected though they may be, are no less significant of rather profound movements which must be followed attentively in order to be able one day to channel them and make them contribute to the development of the community. Zionism and, with it, a kind of "ethnic, ethical, aesthetic" Judaism, in any case a Judaism independent of religion, have made, and continue to make, under our very eyes, progress which we ought not dispute but from which we can, we must profit.[87]

Though some claims by Zionists of their own influence upon French Jewry may be unsubstantiated, the grudging respect accorded them by neutral, or hostile, observers can only confirm more partisan reports. Rabbi Mathieu Wolf, a contributor to L'Univers israélite, commented that

> Zionism, by its return to Hebraism, that is, to something comprehensive enough to exclude no aspect of Judaism—neither its religious and literary aspect, nor its ethnic and national aspect—has been able to provoke in the most divergent milieux and among the adherents of all religions, sympathy for the place of Israel, and the word "Jew" has naturally benefited from this sympathy.[88]

Zionism was thus perceived as a movement which instilled pride in Jews and respect for Jews among Gentiles.

The Zionist message found a variety of suitable means of expression during the interwar period. Despite the fact that the Zionist Federation of France was in an almost perpetual state of reorganization, a number of Zionist periodicals were published: *L'Echo sioniste* (1906–1922); *Le Juif* (Strasbourg, 1919–1921); *La Nouvelle aurore* (1922–1926); *La Terre retrouvée* (1928–1939), the monthly publication of the Keren Kayemeth; and *Palestine—Nouvelle Revue Juive*, the periodical of the pro-Zionist organization France-Palestine.[89] A number of other periodicals in French, though not officially associated with organized Zionism, looked kindly upon the Zionist movement and accorded it extensive press coverage.[90] Within the immigrant community, the daily *Parizer haynt*, the Yiddish paper with the largest circulation in France, was recognized as a vigorous supporter of Zionism.[91] As a Zionist report of 1935 commented, with a touch of hyperbole, "The Jewish press in France is devoted to us; there are no anti-Zionist papers."[92] Even *L'Univers israélite*, the Consistory publication, had begun to reflect the accommodation of the native Establishment with Zionism.[93] While the two papers published by the French-born children of immigrants, *Samedi* and *Affirmation*, retained an independent and critical stance toward Zionist leadership, both reflected an acceptance of the basic premises of Zionist ideology and a recognition of Zionism as the most important movement in the Jewish world.[94]

The Jewish media were only one form of communication which Zionists utilized and which reflected Zionist influence. They also sponsored an array of cultural events which widened the scope of Jewish activity in France. Zionist films were shown and lectures and debates on Zionism organized.[95] Ten Zionist youth groups, which reflected the entire ideological spectrum from Revisionists on the Right to Hashomer Hazair on the Left, flourished in Paris in the late 1930s.[96] *Maccabi*, the Zionist Sports Club in Paris, alone boasted 450 members.[97] In the eastern provinces Strasbourg supported four Zionist youth groups.[98] Local Zionist groups in Strasbourg, Nancy, Thionville, Mulhouse, and Belfort sponsored courses in Zionism, Jewish history, and Hebrew.[99]

Jewish educational activities were of particular concern to Zionists, who saw them as a vehicle for propagating a healthy (hence pro-

Zionist) Jewish consciousness. Hebrew education, they felt, should be in Zionist hands, or it would be conducted, with Zionist funding, against Zionist goals.[100] However, the Consistory circles resisted Zionist participation in communal Jewish education.[101] And the Zionists did not succeed in establishing an autonomous educational network in France.

To promote the legitimacy of Zionism and to win adherents to the cause among both Jews and non-Jews in France, the Zionists quietly sponsored the Committee "France-Palestine," which was established in 1925 as the successor to the League of the Friends of Zionism.[102] Under the presidency of Justin Godart (senator, former Minister of Labor, and great philo-Semite) and the stewardship of Henri Hertz, its secretary-general, France-Palestine collected an impressive roster of prominent political figures to serve on its board, among them Louis Barthou, Aristide Briand, Jules Cambon, Edouard Herriot, Paul Painlevé, Raymond Poincaré, Albert de Monzie, Albert Thomas, and Léon Blum.[103] Through demonstrations and lectures, through the founding of a Franco-Palestine Chamber of Commerce, through support of the Hebrew University, and through its publication *Palestine*, France-Palestine popularized Zionism in France and contributed the aura of non-Jewish respectability to a cause which many native French Jews associated with hardly respectable immigrant Jewry.[104]

Involvement in communal activities, in particular in the synagogues, the *landsmanshaften*, and traditionalist Orthodox circles of native French Jewry, was a primary tactic for the dissemination of Zionist influence. Proposed as the main task of the Zionist Federation of France as early as 1919,[105] it was again promoted as a strategy by Hillel Zlatopolsky in 1928, at a meeting of the Directing Committee of the Federation: "To have influence and serve Zionism, the members of the Zionist Federation of France, in that capacity, should participate in every manifestation of Jewish activity here, from the Consistory to the sports clubs."[106] The tactic was followed with some success. As a Zionist report of 1935 commented:

Our representatives sit on the administrative commissions as well as in the consistories, and the collaboration of . . . Jewish bodies with us is often

less a question of *good will* on *their* part than of *tactical* ability on *ours*.
. . . This is an instrument which we should learn to play; and to do that,
to substitute for the Herzlian slogan of conquest of the communities that
of *attraction* of the communities *into our zone* of activity.[107]

Toward that end, the Zionists had succeeded in securing the recognition of the Keren Kayemeth as a legitimate institution for charitable
contributions made upon being called up to the Torah during religious services. Likewise, they saw in their participation in religious
observances an opportunity to reach those Jews who did not normally
attend Zionist functions.[108] Zionist activity then was predicated on
infiltrating established institutions and using them for purposes not
always envisioned by their founders.

The success of the strategy depended upon the personal leadership
capacity and enthusiasm of individual Zionist activists. Neither qual-
ity was lacking in their ranks. Within the Eastern European immigrant community, Marc Jarblum, the head of *Poalei-Zion* in
France, served during the late 1930s as president of the Federation of
Jewish Societies. Its previous president, though not a shekel-paying
Zionist, had been Israël Jefroykin, whose pro-Zionist sympathies can
be inferred from his activity as chairman of the special Keren Hayesod Committee for Eastern European Jews and as representative of
immigrant Jews in France to the Jewish Agency.[109] A number of
other Zionists devoted themselves to the Federation and succeeded in
creating there an atmosphere congenial to Zionist interests.[110]

Perhaps the most effective Zionist infiltrator into native French
Jewish circles was the ubiquitous semi-convert to Judaism, Aimé
Pallière.[111] A regular contributor to the columns of *L'Univers
israélite*, occasional preacher at the Reform *Union Libérale* temple,
and active participant on the Jewish lecture circuit, he used every opportunity to promote his view that Zionism was an integral part of
Judaism and the most significant phenomenon of modern Jewish experience.[112] His most important sphere of influence was the *Union
Universelle de la Jeunesse Juive* (UUJJ—World Union of Jewish
Youth), a youth organization with headquarters in France and local
affiliates in North Africa, the Levant, the Balkans, and Italy. Al-

though the Union, which was founded in 1923, claimed to be non-Zionist, Pallière confided that "the secret aim of its organizers was to win over to Zionism the elements of Jewish youth who remained outside the movement."[113] While refraining from demanding adherence to the Zionist Organization as a criterion for membership, in 1926 the UUJJ adopted as part of its program collaboration through all possible means in the restoration of Jewish Palestine and the "reconquest" of Hebrew as a living language of Israel.[114] Pallière argued that the non-Zionist autonomy of the UUJJ enhanced its effectiveness as a vehicle for Zionist ideas: "You can certainly consider that a *Union Universelle* whose program is regarded as dangerous by assimilated Jewry is destined to serve the interests of Zionism much more completely than would simple adherence in principle to the Zionist Organization."[115] Jacques Castel, active in French Zionist circles, stated in agreement with Pallière's analysis, "In our opinion, it is better that the UUJJ not transform itself into a Zionist youth group . . . for in that way it would lose its influence and prestige in non-Zionist Jewish milieux, where its activity is very useful for us."[116] Pallière was not alone in bringing Zionism into the top echelons of the UUJJ. A number of other Zionists, including Hillel Zlatopolsky, Yvonne Netter, and Nathan Hermann, served on its Central Committee.[117] Thus, while retaining its independence, the UUJJ served from 1926 until its decline in 1934–35 as a platform for the dissemination of Zionism.

The Consistory circles, too, were not immune to Zionist infiltration. Isaac Naiditch, leader of the General Zionist wing, took advantage of the desire of the Consistory circles to broaden their appeal among immigrant Jewry during the struggle for leadership in the 1930s and was elected a member of the Paris Consistory.[118] Later, he served as president of the French section of the Brith Ivrith Olamith, an organization dedicated to the propagation of Hebrew language and literature, along with non-Zionist Consistory rabbis Julien Weill, Maurice Liber, and Meïr Jaïs.[119] Zionists were also particularly prevalent among the members of the Consistories of Alsace and Lorraine.[120] Thus, rather than relying solely upon the activity of their own partisan organizations, French Zionists made effective use of the existing structures of the Jewish community to communicate their message.

Though the vast majority of Jews in France chose not to define themselves as Zionists in the years 1906 to 1939—and many remained inimical to Zionism—French Zionists and the Zionist ideology were central to the development of new ideological perspectives among French Jewry. The stage upon which the struggle to define those ideological perspectives was conducted was the Jewish youth movements which proliferated in France in the interwar period.

Workers' Cooperative, Syndicat des Casquettiers, Paris 1912
Central Archives for the History of the Jewish People

Shalom Aleichem reading from his work to a Paris audience, 1913
Central Zionist Archives

Fédération des Sociétés Juives de Paris

~~CO~~MITÉ des VOLONTAIRES JUIFS

Aux juifs immigrés

Au moment où la France entière est debout pour défendre ~~son~~ territoire, asile sacré des libertés humaines;

~~A~~u moment où les juifs de France font vaillamment leur de~~voir~~ patriotique,

LES JUIFS IMMIGRÈS demandent d'une seule voix à être ad~~mis à~~ l'honneur de participer aux luttes de l'armée française.

~~P~~lus de 4000 engagements ont été déja contractés dans nos bureaux.

~~Que~~ ceux d'entre nous, qui sont prêts au sacrifice de leur vie, et qui ne ~~se~~ ~~sont~~ pas encore fait inscrire dans le corps des volontaires juifs s'empressent ~~de le~~ faire dans l'une des permanences suivantes :

~~Univ~~ersité populaire Juive 8, Rue de Jarente אין אינווערטיטע פֿאָפולער א רוע דע זשאראנט

~~Asso~~ciation des Etudiants Israélites 3, Rue du Puits de l'Ermite אין אידישען סטודענטען פֿערצין
3 רוע די פר דע לערמיט

~~Bel~~levilloise 21; Rue Boyer ~~ב~~עלווילין בעלעווילין 21 רוע בֿיאיע

~~En~~ outre

~~Grou~~pe de volontaires juifs d'origine russo-roumaine 6, Rue Eugène Süe אין אייך צווײ דעם מאמארט
6 רוע יוזען סיע

~~au~~ groupe des juifs ottomans 68, Rue Sedaine de 10 h. à 12 - 9, rue Cadetde 16 h. à 18 h.

אידין קומען זיד אייייאיירייריין אין אידישען באטאלי

Poster urging immigrant Jews to volunteer for army service, 1914
Central Zionist Archives

A street scene in the "Pletzl," the heart of the immigrant Jewish quarter in Paris (1922)
YIVO Institute for Jewish Research

Marc Jarblum, labor Zionist activist, at a French workers' conference, 1921
Central Zionist Archives

Drawing of André Spire, poet, civil servant, Zionist
Archives of the Jewish Theological Seminary of America

Léo Cohn, refugee scout leader, addressing the Eclaireurs Israélites de France
Centre de Documentation Juive Contemporaine, Paris

Léon Blum and Marc Jarblum
Central Zionist Archives

7.
Toward a New Pluralism: the Youth Movements

The Proliferation of Youth Groups

In the network of Jewish youth movements which came into being in the years which followed World War I, the most active and concerned representatives of the post-war generation of French Jewry attempted to forge a unified Jewish community and to redefine the nature of Jewish identity in France. In the process they mounted a serious challenge to the ideology of assimilation which had dominated French Jewry since the mid-nineteenth century.

The development of youth movements in the West is a phenomenon of this century, though the earliest groups were established in the latter half of the last one.[1] The movements reflect a growing tendency on the part of young people to define themselves as a separate entity with needs and aspirations different from those of the older generation. The extension of education to the masses and the concomitant postponement of the assumption of adult responsibilities were major factors in the definition of youth as a distinct phase of life and in the flowering of youth movements.

Youth movements found fertile soil in Germany, where they had first appeared.[2] The *Wandervogel*, in particular, have captured the imagination of historians, who see in their anti-bourgeois and *völkisch* ideology tendencies which later facilitated the acceptance of Nazism. However, youth movements were not restricted to Germany. Scouting movements, for example, began as a product of Anglo-Saxon societies before growing to international dimensions. In France during the interwar period a host of political, religious, social-action, and scouting groups—which supplemented the more traditional and increasingly passé charitable and social groups— flourished.[3] These youth groups provided more than opportunities for social diversion. In post-World War I France—where the conflict of generations was exacerbated by the sense of a peace lost—they provided a testing ground for independence, an opportunity for social action to transform society, and a sense of community.[4]

In whatever society they lived, Jewish youth shared the general impulse toward special organizations. However, the specific problems of Jewish identity and activity in their respective lands helped to shape the contents and concerns of these organizations. Jewish youth movements in Germany, for example, responding to German anti-Semitism and nationalism and to the sterile nature of established German Judaism, were virtually all animated by a Zionist spirit.[5] For Jewish youth rebelled not only against the older generation who wielded power in society as a whole but also against the older generation of Jews who determined the structure and content of Jewish communal life.

Unlike the major German Jewish youth movements, the Jewish youth groups which took root in France and which exercised the greatest influence on the interwar generation were not sponsored by Zionists and did not call for *aliya* to Palestine as the ultimate goal of their ideologies. Rather, they were groups which struggled to redefine and reinvigorate a Franco-Judaism which they saw as moribund. Perhaps naively, they sought, through the medium of popular education and creation of an alternate community, to find a way to balance the duality of their Frenchness and their Jewishness.

Like their French counterparts, Jewish youth groups in France represented a wide variety of social and political tendencies. The groups which had existed prior to World War I, primarily the native *Union de la Jeunesse Israélite* and the immigrant *Association des Jeunes Juifs*, were essentially social in nature. Though the Association, which met at the *Université Populaire Juive*, sponsored a library and offered its immigrant members free legal and medical consultations as well as an occasional lecture on self-defense or the situation of the Jews in Russia, its major activities were games, excursions, and evenings of entertainment.[6] Within the immigrant community after World War I partisan political groups, as we have seen, sponsored their own youth groups, which propagated their respective ideologies through the means of social events, sports activities, and discussions. Thus, one could find sports clubs and youth groups under the patronage of Zionists, Bundists, and Jewish Communists.[7] LICA, the International League against Antisemitism, was extremely popular among Jewish youth, especially in the 1930s, when the need to combat anti-Semitism and promote self-defense became ever more apparent.[8]

For the most part, the Jewish political youth groups did not concern themselves with defining a new mode of Jewish identity in France. Rather, they pursued the political policy and the Jewish self-definition determined by the adult organization. In the case of the Jewish Communists and Bundists, that Jewish definition, secular and ethnic in nature and based on the culture and life-style of Jews in Eastern Europe, was becoming increasingly irrelevant to the French-speaking children of immigrant parents, who were bereft of the Eastern European experience.[9] For LICA as well as the other political groups, the political ideology of the organization and its combat against anti-Semitism predominated over any specifically Jewish cultural content.

From the perspective of Jewish cultural development, the political groups, however, were not the most important Jewish youth groups formed in France after World War I. Of greater impact were three nonpolitical associations—*Chema Israël*, the *Union Universelle de la Jeunesse Juive* (UUJJ), and the *Eclaireurs Israélites*, the Jewish scout movement—which were all committed to the survival of Jews as an entity. Through educational and community activities, they strove to revitalize Jewish life in France and to unify the disparate elements of French Jewry. In doing so, they undermined the ideology of assimilation and developed new bases for Jewish identification and a critique of the place of Jewish culture—religious, historical, and ethnic—within French society.

Why did the ideology of assimilation, which had dominated French Jewish life for a century, encounter its first serious challenge in the youth movements of the interwar years? Clearly, the tendency of such movements to be critical of the older generation—indeed to crystallize and institutionalize youthful rebelliousness—is one factor.

For young Jews who had grown up with assimilation as something to be taken for granted, it was natural to lay the blame for the unresolved Jewish question directly upon the ideology of assimilation, so widely espoused by the older generation of native Jewry. Assimilation even to the point of conversion had been tried and had failed. The post-assimilation, native-born young felt that their own alienation from the sources of authentic Jewishness had been a high price to pay for integration into a society willing to accept them only with reservations. As for the children of immigrants, they also believed that their own integration into French society had to follow a pattern different from what they saw as the bankrupt assimilationist model.

Chema Israël

The most traditional and conservative of the new groups was Chema Israël, essentially a religious and educational association, established in 1919 by native young adults under the auspices of the French rabbinate.[10] It was the war which had led the founders of the association back to Judaism. In their appeal to Jewish youth, they stressed the impact upon themselves of the most shattering experience of their generation: "We are those who, matured by the ordeals of war, have become aware of the necessity of returning closer and closer to Judaism."[11] As members of the war generation, they recognized the inadequacy of their preparation for Jewish life, and they expressed a need to provide a more intensive Jewish education for themselves and their peers and to deepen their Jewish commitment.

Following the model of the adult community, the founders of Chema Israël accepted a purely religious definition of the Jewish community in France. However, they included a wide variety of educational functions within the purview of the religious. Besides their well-attended weekly lectures on aspects of Jewish doctrine, ritual, and prayer, from the first they conducted courses in spoken as well as Biblical Hebrew and in Jewish history and literature.[12] Occasional lectures were devoted to topics which could hardly be characterized as religious—such as Shalom Aleichem's place in Yiddish literature and Zionism as seen by a Palestinian Zionist.[13] Yet the basic aim of Chema Israël remained the expansion of Jewish knowledge and experience primarily on a religious basis.

To supplement its educational activities, Chema Israël took tentative steps toward providing an alternative setting to the family and the adult community for the celebration of religious occasions. At first, only minor holidays like Purim and Chanukah were celebrated together. Later, the association sponsored its own *seder* on the first evening of Passover, though the observance was customarily a familial one, and built its own *sukkah* (booth) for the festival of *Sukkoth* (Tabernacles).[14] Both activities were designed to respond to the needs of assimilated young Jews, "who could not celebrate [the *seder*] in their homes," much less find a convenient *sukkah*.[15]

Within two years of its establishment in Paris, Chema Israël began to expand into the provinces to promote "the revival of tradition in all of France."[16] At its height the organization had fourteen branches in the provinces.[17]

In spite of this proliferation of sections, however, Chema Israël began a period of decline in the late 1920s. The association had always appealed to a limited clientele, primarily to native Jewish youth who had at least a minimal interest in Judaism as the basis of their Jewish identity. Although the problem of bringing together immigrant and native youth was broached within the organization, it was not accorded major consideration.[18] Moreover, programming for the organization included few sessions specifically related to Eastern European Jewish culture.[19] Like the institutions of the adult community, Chema Israël tended to focus on the immigrant Jew as the object of philanthropic concern. Thus, the organization did establish a society called "Enfant Israélite Protégé" (Protected Israelite Child) to provide a Jewish education to the children of immigrant working-class Jews.[20] Although youth of immigrant origin served on several committees, they remained a small fraction of Chema Israël.[21] Jewish youth of immigrant origin looked elsewhere for organizations more suited to their Jewish needs.

By the late 1920s Chema Israël was challenged by other Jewish youth organizations—particularly the UUJJ—which adopted a

broader definition of Jewish identity and activity and a more critical
stance toward the institutions of the adult native community than was
congenial to Chema Israël, which had been founded under the aegis
of the French rabbinate and was subsidized by the Central Consistory.[22]

In reaction, Chema Israël defined itself ever more narrowly as a
"movement of religious education and propaganda within the cadre
of the community," unwilling, therefore, to "participate in demonstrations [organized by other youth groups] whose goal and attitude
vis-à-vis religion and the community did not conform to this definition."[23] In particular, as the UUJJ recognized, they were objecting to
the pro-Palestine activities of that group.[24] Although permitting individual sections to take part in demonstrations which were nonpartisan
in nature and did not endanger the welfare of Judaism, the final authority was left to the rabbi of the local community.[25] This restriction
on the autonomy of the groups, combined with the growing appeal of
youth groups which attempted to attract nonreligious as well as religious youth, led to the decline of Chema Israël. In 1931 it was
noted that attendance at lectures had progressively diminished.[26] Soliciting aid in 1932 and 1933, the leaders of Chema Israël complained that they had been forced to reduce the level of activity of the
organization to the extent that Chema Israël was threatened with ex-
tinction.[27] Indeed, Chema Israël appears to have curtailed its activity
beginning in 1934.[28]

The UUJJ

While Chema Israël was declining in popularity and support, the
Union Universelle de la Jeunesse Juive was expanding its mem-
bership and developing a program new in the history of French
Jewry. Established first in Salonica in 1921, the organization was
transferred to Paris in 1923 when its two Sephardi founders, Charles
Néhama and Jacques Matalon, emigrated to the French capital.[29]
Although it was an international organization with sections in North
Africa, Italy, and Palestine, its center remained Paris, and its activity

was conducted in French. The UUJJ experienced rapid growth, expanding to ten sections in 1926 and to twenty-three in 1928, though the majority remained outside of France.[30] The Paris section alone claimed 600 members in 1928 and close to 1,000 a year later.[31] It is no wonder, then, that Zionist observers described it as "the most important and most popular Jewish association in Paris."[32]

The UUJJ introduced an innovation to French Jewish life—its willingness to abandon the traditional exclusively religious definition of French Jewish identity and to challenge assimilationism as a threat to Jewish survival in France. The organization opened its doors to all Jews who chose to identify themselves as such. As was proclaimed at the first annual conference of the Regional Committee of the UUJJ for France:

> It is the unity of the Jewish people which constitutes our doctrine. . . . It is capable of uniting . . . in the same federation all young Jews of the present time, for many are the manifestations of the life of a people. Religion, with its vast spiritual patrimony, embodies the most noble expression [of that life]. But religion is an individual matter. There always were, there always will be, among any people, religious persons and persons who are less religious or not religious at all, and consequently, Jews who do not evidence religious sentiment, however regrettable their state of non-belief may seem to those who have faith, they are none the less the children of the Jewish people of the same status as the believers.[33]

Similarly, Aimé Pallière, guiding spirit of the UUJJ, reiterated that the organization would "exclude no child of Israel who comes to her, whatever the difficulties he evinces in personal belief and practice. The UUJJ will defend against all exclusiveness and all sectarianism the youth who tell us they have no faith but who feel themselves Jews and wish to affirm themselves as such."[34] Thus, without espousing the Zionist program, the UUJJ restored to Judaism the unity of religious and ethnic elements which had been sundered, at least in theory, during the period of emancipation.[35]

Only one Jewish tendency was to be definitely excluded from the organization, and that was "the tendency toward assimilation, conceived as destructive of the ethnic particularity of Israel."[36] The 1926 statutes of the UUJJ did not define the assimilation which was to be

shunned. However, as primary ideologue of the organization, Pallière came to base his definition of assimilation upon the dual nature
of Judaism which the UUJJ recognized: peoplehood and religion.
The denial of Jewish peoplehood and the rejection of the Jewish
religion constituted assimilation.[37] In contrast to the ideology of
emancipation propounded for generations by the leadership of native
French Jewry, either facet of the duality was an acceptable form of
Jewish identity.

Since the leaders of the UUJJ recognized the vague nature of their
all-inclusive definition of Judaism and of their opposition to assimilation, they attempted to develop a positive program of Jewish content. Although originally adopting a position of neutrality toward Zionism,[38] in 1926 the Congress of the UUJJ passed a resolution which
pledged "its active support to the effort of reconstituting Jewish Palestine."[39] While the UUJJ refrained from formal affiliation with the
Zionist Organization, for fear of alienating those members unprepared to declare themselves Zionists, its pro-Palestine stand and activity, particularly on behalf of the *Keren Kayemeth L'Israel* (Jewish National Fund), became integral to the organization.[40]

In addition to its pro-Zionist stance, the UUJJ promoted Jewish education, broadly defined, as the primary weapon in the combat
against assimilation. As a lecturer at the organization noted, Jewish
education in France was so superficial that it precluded the development of a Jewish renaissance. The cultural formation of French Jews
was purely and exclusively French.[41] To rectify the situation, UUJJ
statutes called for the study of the "literary, social, political, and
religious history of Israel."[42] Each section was called upon to organize courses and lectures in Jewish history and literature. And each
member was exhorted to learn Hebrew, the "national language" and
official, though scarcely used, language of the UUJJ.[43] Hebrew was
promoted as the symbol of Jewish unity and solidarity; while the
study of Jewish history assumed one role traditionally performed
among French Jewry by religion—to enable the Jew to feel a sense of
belonging to a defined collectivity.[44]

However, the UUJJ did not limit its goals to the educational. It
defined itself as a defense organization, concerned with protecting the

rights of Jewish youth wherever they were endangered.[45] Thus, it called for a World Congress of Jewish Youth to struggle against anti-Semitism and for minority rights, to study the position of Jewish youth in the Soviet Union, and to explore possibilities for colonization outside of Palestine.[46] In addition, it communicated its protest against laws of *numerus clausus* (Jewish quotas) to the Prime Minister of Hungary and to the Ambassador of Poland in Paris and vehemently protested the ban on the teaching of Hebrew in the USSR.[47] Finally, like many other youth groups of the time, it expressed its desire to work toward the *rapprochement* of all peoples and for universal peace, in accordance with the program of the League of Nations.[48] Without espousing a partisan political platform, it thus sought to respond to the general political concerns of Jewish youth in France.

Besides introducing a new variety in the goals, activities, and self-definition of a Jewish youth organization, the UUJJ took advantage of, and promoted, a new self-consciousness and pride among French Jewish youth. As Raymond-Raoul Lambert, a prominent young native French Jew, secretary to Herriot, noted in the pages of *Chalom*, the organ of the UUJJ: "It is the sign of a new era that Jewish youth has become aware of the forces it represents. . . . One expresses the need to affirm himself a Semite, and the word 'Jew' no longer bears the pejorative connotation that made the pale adjective 'Israelite' preferable."[49] Another correspondent mocked those Jews who attempted to Gallicize their names, accusing them of cowardice and shame and of attempting to be more French than the French.[50] The crusade against assimilation, upon which the UUJJ had based its program, thus signaled a conscious pride in being a Jew.

THE CONFLICT WITH NATIVE JEWISH LEADERSHIP

The ideology of the UUJJ—in particular its rejection of religion as the sole basis of Jewish identity and its pro-Zionism—inevitably brought the association into conflict with consistory circles and with the French rabbinate. Indeed, Pallière complained that the organization had failed to establish sections in the provinces because of the opposition of the rabbis. In the provinces, he noted, "nothing can be done without the rabbis and nothing with them."[51]

In 1928 the tension between the UUJJ and the other Jewish institutions surfaced in the pages of the French Jewish press. An attempted *rapprochement* with Chema Israël was scuttled when its Congress rejected a resolution, proposed by an Alsatian representative, to participate, as the UUJJ was doing, in the reconstruction of Jewish Palestine.[52] The proposal inspired at the Congress a vehement protest against Zionism by the formidable Rabbi Liber and, among UUJJ leaders writing in *Chalom*, a vigorous attack on Chema Israël for its intolerance.[53]

On the eve of the second UUJJ Congress, an anonymous rabbinic contributor to *L'Univers israélite* summarized the reasons for his opposition to the UUJJ. The organization, he claimed, had placed itself "outside the French Jewish community and the religious and civic principles which it recognizes." True, it had thus succeeded in rallying to itself those elements of French Judaism which were not yet assimilated. But those elements were poorly educated and undisciplined and had introduced their harmful ideas into the UUJJ. In particular, they had led the organization to support Jewish nationalism, which could not be reconciled with French patriotism. Finallly, he asserted, a Jewish renaissance in France could not be based upon anti-assimilationism. Only religious Judaism could preserve Jews in a modern society.[54] The leadership of the native French Jewish community was unprepared to accept the ideological as well as the ethnic transformation of French Jewry which the UUJJ portended. And it found most offensive the alien, immigrant origin of much of the organization's leadership.

The conflict was exacerbated when the UUJJ responded to the hostility it encountered from the French rabbinate not by seeking compromise but by asserting its autonomy and attacking the rabbinate. As an opening thrust, it was alleged that the Chief Rabbi of Paris, at the insistence of certain members of the Paris Consistory, notably Adolphe Caen, the head of the assimilationist Union Scolaire, had forbidden the rabbis of Paris to collaborate with *Chalom*.[55] Then, the second UUJJ Congress, meeting in Strasbourg, adopted the following resolution:

The Congress of the UUJJ states . . . that a part of the French rabbinate manifests with regard to the Union a hostility which tends to undermine its effort.

It reaffirms that the UUJJ will not cease, in the person of its leaders, to express the greatest deference with regard to religion and that its general goals and its educational program will contain nothing which does not reflect the pure doctrine of Judaism.

It rejects with no less energy all accusations leveled against the Union regarding the question of nationalism, considering that its leaders must inculcate in their disciples feelings of loyal attachment to the various countries of which they are citizens and for whose well-being and prosperity they must labor.

Consequently, it expresses its grievous indignation to see several of the spiritual leaders of Israel, upon whom in particular should fall the role of encouraging and guiding the movement of renaissance, disowning their mission and failing to bring to youth the moral support which their effort merits.

. . . . It addresses its gratitude to those members of the rabbinate who have shown it their kindness and have lent their support.

. . . . and expresses once more the resolute will of the Union to react vigorously against the current decadence of Judaism and to acquire, without the rabbis should they be opposed, the entire patrimony of Israel.[56]

Although the UUJJ described its resolution not as an act of war, but as an attempt to encourage the rabbinate to assume its natural position of religious leadership and to collaborate with the Jewish youth movement,[57] its charges against the rabbinate widened the breach between the movement and the consistory circles. It was soon noted in the pages of *Chalom* that the official circles of Judaism were totally opposed to the youth movement, primarily, it was thought, because of its stand on Zionism. Official Jewish circles, it was contended, accepted an areligious Judaism as long as it was anti-Zionist.[58] While leaders of the UUJJ hoped for recognition by the consistory circles of the services which the movement provided to Jewish youth and hence to the entire Jewish community, and continued to aspire to a liaison with the Consistory-sponsored Chema Israel (both organizations, after all, were working in the same vine-

yards toward the same goal) the consistory circles expressed no interest in accepting the UUJJ as a partner in the Jewish community.[59] Its
autonomy, its ideological pluralism, and the visibility of immigrants
among its leadership remained abhorrent to the older generation of
native French Jewry. For that generation retained equal commit-
ments to the uniquely religious nature of Jewish identity, upon which
its integration into French society had been based, and to its
cherished former supremacy over all organized Jewish life in France.

The UUJJ did not long flourish on French soil. Its history was
marked by a fluctuation of activity and interest on the part of its
members. When its leaders gradually departed from the organization
for a variety of personal reasons in the mid-1930s, the organization
foundered. Moreover, a split occurred within the movement when
Pallière, as editor-in-chief of *Chalom*, rejected the growing militancy
of young immigrant spokesmen, led by Wladimir Rabinovitch (Rabi),
who proposed a vigorous campaign against anti-Semitism and encouraged independent political action.[60] The growing religious in-
trospection and suspicion of secular Jewish nationalism which Pallière increasingly expressed paled beside the activism of such political
organizations as LICA, which were actively involved in combatting
anti-Semitism.[61] Under the leadership of its most important native
French collaborators, the UUJJ retreated from the implications of
Jewish cultural nationalism and lost much of its immigrant following.

The successes of the movement, however, had been notable. It
had integrated members of the native, East European immigrant,
and Sephardi immigrant communities, with the latter serving as me-
diators between the two former groups. It had questioned the ideological assumptions of French Jewry and had provided a tentative alternative model for Jewish identity. Finally, it had questioned the
assertion that assimilation to French culture, which had in practice
necessitated the abandonment of Jewish culture as a central element
in the cultural formation of most French Jews, was an unmixed
blessing. While never advocating the abandonment of French culture, for the first time in the history of modern French Jewry the

UUJJ preached the necessity of biculturalism. If French Jewry were
to survive as a vigorous entity, particularly in a secular age, then according to the UUJJ, French Judaism had to release itself from the
restrictive definition of church imposed upon it during the process of
emancipation. Representatives of the youth of interwar French Jewry
had rejected the ideology of assimilation. Moreover, the UUJJ's rejection of assimilation was articulated as well by the Sephardi intellectuals who moved in the organization's orbit and from 1933
through 1936 published the *Cahiers juifs* in Paris and Alexandria. As
Maxime Piha wrote in its pages, "There is a tragedy of assimilation:
that is to try with all one's strength to become what one can never
be."[62]

The Jewish Scout Movement

Ultimately the most significant and successful of the youth movements was the Eclaireurs Israélites de France, the Jewish scout movement, which developed ideological tendencies similar to those of the
UUJJ.[63] However, unlike the latter organization, the founders of the
Eclaireurs sprang from the ranks of the native community and maintained, throughout the interwar years, a close, if occasionally
strained, liaison with prominent adult members of that community.

The first Jewish scout troop was founded in Paris in February 1923
at the initiative of Robert Gamzon, the 17-year-old grandson of the
former Chief Rabbi of France, Albert Lévy, and the son of an immigrant engineer from Eastern Europe.[64] By 1924 the movement of
Eclaireurs Israélites de France had been established under the patronage of a Central Committee composed of wealthy members of
the native Parisian community. Its purpose was to provide a scouting
experience for young French Jews, immigrants and natives, within a
Jewish milieu. The goal, in Gamzon's words, was to shape "French
scouts of the Israelite religion."[65] Its original goals, then, were in no
way radical in the eyes of the leadership of French Jewry. Rather, the
movement set out to fill a void in the lives of adolescent members of

the community, who might otherwise have been drawn to Catholic or free-thinking troops.[66] The Eclaireurs were to incarnate the identity and ease of simultaneously serving Judaism and France.

During its first decade, however, the Jewish scout movement evolved in ways which sorely tried its Central Committee of patrons. Under the influence of Edmond Fleg, an intellectual who never abandoned the responsibility of leadership, and of the young scout leaders, who were sensitive to the currents of anti-Semitism in contemporary Europe and open to the message of cultural Zionism, the Eclaireurs Israélites gradually developed a program based on a pluralistic concept of Judaism. In doing so, they formulated a critique of modern French Judaism. It was Fleg, invited to serve as president of the movement, who first suggested that traditional religious observance not be required as a criterion for membership in scout troops; rather, according to his conception, "all youths who declare themselves to be Jews, including Zionists and even free-thinkers, should be accepted in a Jewish scout movement."[67] Moreover, Fleg added, in an appeal to the traditionalists of the Central Committee, such a policy would provide an opportunity for the *rapprochement* of nonobservant Jews with traditional Judaism. Although Fleg declined the post of president when the Central Committee remained antagonistic to his vision of the movement, he was an important force within the Eclaireurs Israélites and instrumental in establishing a federation with local Zionist scout groups and with the UUJJ, which had independently established several scout groups.[68] By 1927 the Eclaireurs Israélites were prepared to hold a joint camp, ultimately successful, with a Zionist scout group, the *Chomerim*, for as Gamzon argued, "the EIF has nothing to fear from a rapprochement with other troops, equally Jewish, but professing more or less different opinions."[69]

While the movement expanded rapidly—from ten members in 1923, to 250 in 1927, 600 in 1929 and 1,200 in 1930—[70] and extended its Jewish educational and cultural functions, the debate as to its ideological nature continued between the young leaders of the Directing Committee and the older advisers of the Central Committee. Not unexpectedly, the most vigorous opponent of change was

Rabbi Maurice Liber, who contended, in opposition to the lay intellectual Edmond Fleg, that "a Judaism without religion does not exist,"[71] and proposed that a purely national Judaism be excluded from the purview of the Eclaireurs.[72] Despite Liber's antagonism, the trend toward diversity continued, with the support of Fleg and Aimé Pallière. In 1928, for example, Zionist insignia were included among brevets available to be chosen by local troops.[73]

As the Jewish program of the movement, both religious and national-cultural, was strengthened, criticism became more vocal. In 1930 the young leaders were informed by their patrons that there had been some criticism in prominent circles that the National Council of Troop Leaders had exhibited a "too Jewish tendency." Both Fleg and Gamzon took the opportunity to insist, at the meeting with the Central Committee, on the changed nature of the movement: "The youth leaders recognize," Gamzon stated, "that the movement has evolved, since its origin, in a much more Jewish direction. In general, religious practices are more widely observed, though the Directing Committee exerts no pressure on the particular spiritual direction of the troops. . . . Orthodox Jews from Alsace have become tolerant of Zionist leaders, while the latter, for their part, understand the strictest religious observances."[74] The contact of different forms of Jewish expression was considered mutually beneficial.

The debate regarding the nature of the movement was exacerbated when the National Council of the Eclaireurs, meeting at Moosch in Alsace in 1932, resolved that the "EIF tends henceforth to a conception of Judaism including at the same time both the religious ideal and the Zionist ideal."[75] In horror, the Central Committee refused to ratify the vote and openly articulated their sentiment that it was they who should direct the movement, and not the troop leaders of the younger generation. Liber even threatened to resign from the organization should Zionism become an integral part of the movement.[76]

The debate soon assumed the form of a generational conflict as to the nature of Judaism, of French Jewish assimilation, and the position of Jews in French society. Zionism, the troop leaders argued, was a legitimate part of Judaism and attractive to the young as a

concrete ideal easier to comprehend than the religious ideal.[77] Moreover, they contended, it was time that young French Jews be taught
the Hebrew language and literature and be raised with a more pervasive Jewish culture. This was necessary because it could not be denied that French history and literature were profoundly imbued with
Christianity, as was the environment in which Jewish scouts lived.[78]
When young French Jews had recaptured their originality as Jews,
which the present adult generation had lost, they would be of greater
service to France.[79] Although the Central Committee had opposed
the alliance with the Zionists, the troop leaders had found the contact with them beneficial, effective, and mutually supportive. If Zionism were rejected, many troops, in North Africa, Alsace, and even
in Paris, would in fact disaffiliate from the movement.[80]

To the members of the Central Committee, the analysis of the
scout leaders expressed a repudiation of French Jewish patterns of assimilation. French Jews had always overlooked, or denied, the Christian basis of much of French culture. They preferred to evaluate
French culture as the product primarily of the revolutionary-national
consciousness, equally the heritage of all citizens of the *patrie*. The
native Jewish elite of the Central Committee now argued that it was
completely assimilated Jews, like Henri Bergson, who had made the
greatest contribution to France, rather than Jews steeped in traditional Jewish culture.[81] Moreover, Rabbi Liber went so far as to claim
that there was no Jewish culture and no original Jewish literature except for the Bible. He also lent the weight of his rabbinic authority to
the contention that one could not be both French and Zionist.[82] Finally, fears were expressed that the new posture of the Jewish scouts
was potentially harmful since it could be misunderstood by Gentiles
as a form of ethnic particularism unacceptable to French society.[83]

While attempting to be conciliatory in manner and reiterating the
loyalty of all Jewish scouts to France, Gamzon asserted the independence of the movement from its patrons. He declared that the
Eclaireurs Israélites had to be defined by the scout leaders, particularly since the Central Committee was not representative of the
movement: "It represents only one tendency, that of Parisian Judaism, while it should, by rights, contain members of the Zionist as-

sociations, since there are Zionist scout leaders in the movement."[84] Judaism as defined and practiced by native Parisian Jewry was rejected, he exclaimed, by Jewish youth. "If a great number of young people are attracted by Zionism," he noted, "it is because they see in it a living Judaism in contrast to the dead Judaism which Western Judaism has become."[85]

When the new honorary president of the Eclaireurs Israélites, General Rheims, proposed an anti-Zionist resolution which specified as the unique goals of the movement "the practice of scoutism and the love of France," his proposal was rejected by the youth leadership. For it was based, they felt, on inadequate information as to the nature and purpose of the movement.[86] However, a compromise was reached when the scout leaders and the Central Committee agreed to leave the goals of the movement as those defined by Fleg in 1926 and 1927—open to all young Jews, but without specific mention of the Zionist ideal.[87]

In the ranks of the movement its Jewish activity, including cultural Zionism, was to continue even more vigorously than before. The acceptance of a "common minimum" of Jewish observance in scouting activities, in particular *Kashruth* and respect for the Sabbath, had been voted in 1932.[88] Scout leaders were expected to take intensive courses in Hebrew, Jewish history, and liturgy in order to direct the education of their troops; and the scouts themselves earned badges in Judaica, celebrated Jewish festivals in their encampments, sang Hebrew songs, reenacted major events in Jewish history, and enthusiastically learned Hasidic and Zionist folk dances.[89]

With the advent of young German Jewish refugees, who had been greatly influenced by the active Zionist youth movement in Germany, to positions of leadership in the movement, its Jewish program was further enriched. The most notable of the young German refugees was Léo Cohn, who introduced a lively neo-Hasidic fervor to the Eclaireurs, who dubbed his brand of Judaism "Léo-Hasidisme."[90] The Eclaireurs began to adopt some of the pioneering (*halutz*) values which had characterized the Zionist movement in Germany and in 1934 initiated a *Simha et Avoda* (Joy and Labor) program to encourage a balance between intellectual and manual

labor.[91] Toward that end the Eclaireurs established carpentry work-
shops in Paris and an agricultural training school in Saumur.[92]
Moreover, support for Zionism was openly stated as one of their
goals: "For some Jews, serving Judaism necessitates their leaving for
Palestine in order to create a Jewish Home," declared the scout manual. "The task for us, who are called upon for the most part to
remain in the Diaspora, is to facilitate their undertaking by helping
them with all our means."[93] In addition, as the Eclaireurs became
more concerned with anti-Semitism, they broke with the political
quietism of the native adult leadership. Although the scout leaders
determined that the Eclaireurs Israélites would remain politically
neutral as a movement, they vigorously asserted their right as Jews to
protest against each and every manifestation of anti-Semitism and
successfully proposed that the Eclaireurs aid, though not join, the International League against Anti-Semitism (LICA), the bane of the
adult native Jewish elite.[94] Finally, in 1936, Edmond Fleg, who had
done so much to stimulate the active Jewish commitment of the
movement and to define its pluralism—that is, its acceptance of
diverse forms of Jewish identity—became its president.

The last manual prepared by the Eclaireurs Israélites before the
onset of World War II reaffirmed the adherence of the movement to
diversity within the Jewish community and to the compatibility of
French and Jewish cultures. All types of Jews were eligible to be
scouts, "for in all times there were different currents within the Jewish fold."[95] Yet one problem remained, the perennial one of finding
an acceptable mode of integrating the French and Jewish facets of
their identity. The national Eclaireurs de France had refused to accept the Jewish Scouts as an affiliate (though it accepted Catholic
troops) because the former were considered too sectarian.[96] Jewish
scouts were expected to affiliate with free-thinking troops. That rejection suggested a painful truth to Jewish youth groups—that French
society in theory and in practice did not consider the assertion of Jewish religious identity completely parallel to the expression of Catholic
interests and would neither favor nor help the development of an ethnic Jewish identity. France had welcomed immigrant groups, but
always on the condition that they recognize the superiority and exclu-

siveness of French culture and adopt it as their own. Jewish scouts then made use of the argument that their peculiar situation resembled that of French provincials. "There is no contradiction between the fact of loving France and loving Judaism, any more than there is when a Corsican loves both France and Corsica," declared their scout manual.[97] The analogy was ingenious but strained, for Judaism (which the scouts defined not as a creed alone but as a religio-ethnic culture) was neither a geographic nor a cultural component of the French nation. However, the provincial parallel seemed to young French Jews the only acceptable way of describing their position as Jews within the French socio-political tradition. Since that tradition was rigid in structure, like the UUJJ, the Eclaireurs Israélites simply *added* an ethno-cultural component, essentially secular in definition, to the basic religious component of Jewish identity.

In spite of its development of an ideology which criticized the nature of French Jewish assimilation, espoused support for Zionism, and promoted Jewish pluralism, the Eclaireurs Israélites retained the patronage of the leadership of the native Jewish community. In 1934 the secretary-general of the Paris Consistory, Albert Manuel, joined the Central Committee.[98] Further, in 1937 the Consistory included the Eclaireurs on the list of organizations to which donations could be made during religious services in Consistory temples.[99] The Eclaireurs continued to be the recipients of the philanthropic largesse of prominent individuals as well, in particular of Mme. Jacqueline Rothschild, who in 1936 donated a building to serve as the center of the organization.[100]

There were several reasons for this mutually beneficial coexistence. In the first place, most of the major leaders of the movement originated from within the native community. Therefore, they were never seen as completely alien, but were tolerated, in spite of their sometimes exasperating and outrageous ideas, as "our youth." Furthermore, as the native adult leadership recognized, among immigrant youth the Eclaireurs served as an acculturating force, bringing immigrant youth into contact with native youth and into the native Jewish community, teaching French songs along with the Hebrew. Although there was little mixing of immigrant and native youth in local troops, which were organized by neighborhoods, in the scout camps there was considerable contact between youths of different ethnic origins and social classes.[101] The Eclaireurs could be considered a countervailing force to the totally alien (and mostly leftist) youth movements of the Yiddish-speaking community. Since their leaders were, for the most part, natives, the Eclaireurs were far more acceptable than the UUJJ. As Robert Gamzon noted, referring to the Consistory circles, "they have understood that our influence has not been harmful among immigrant Jews and that from this point of view, as well as from our impact on youth in general, we can render service."[102] Clearly the native adult community believed that the positive aspects of the organization—the pedigree of its leadership, its religious program, its proclaimed political neutrality, and its professed loyalty to French values—outweighed the negative factors of its pluralism.

The Eclaireurs Israélites had redefined the nature of Jewish assimilation into French society without being ostracized by the major institutions of the native adult community. While recognizing the primacy of the religious element of Judaism, it strove to develop a consciousness of the manifold varieties of Jewish identity. It began the delicate task of bringing together the different ethnic and social elements of French Jewry. It accepted the burden of vigorously fighting anti-Semitism. Moreover, rejecting the facile identification of French and Jewish cultures, though never their love for France, the Eclaireurs Israélites proclaimed that French Jews served France best by maintaining their self-respect and authenticity, and by developing their unique natural qualities and historic ideals as Jews, which they might then contribute to France. The fact that they sought to serve France as Jews, rather than as individual citizens of the Jewish faith, itself implies a renunciation of the ideology of emancipation. The terms of Jewish integration into French society, defined early in the nineteenth century, were being modified by the most aware component of interwar young Jewish Frenchmen. But that modification remained unacceptable for the host society in a period of growing xenophobia and cultural chauvinism within France.

8.
The Futile Struggle for Leadership: Jewish Politics in the 1930s

La solidarité juive est le "slogan" le plus mensonger qui soit.
—*Wladimir Rabinovitch (Rabi)*
Samedi, *June 11, 1939*

The Centrality of Anti-Semitism

While native and immigrant youth were making common cause and laying the foundations for a unified community, native and immigrant adults were pulled apart by the political pressures of the years 1933–1939. The inherently conflicting goals and world views of the two communities were revealed ever more clearly as the rise of Nazism in Germany and the resurgence of xenophobia and anti-Semitism in France drew very different responses from native and immigrant circles. While various segments of each community—from consistorial leaders to immigrant Jewish communists—called for a united front to combat anti-Semitism, the drive for unity ultimately stumbled because of the lack of consensus as to the nature of French anti-Semitism, the best way to fight it, and the legitimacy of collective Jewish political action.

Anti-Semitism thus became the key factor in the struggle for leadership in France's Jewish community of the 1930s. Fear of it and of its consequences shaped the relations of the Consistory and immigrant groups and likewise was invoked by immigrant Jewish communists to justify their willingness to form a coalition with bourgeois elements in the Jewish community. Yet the inability to find within either the immigrant or native communities leadership and strategy acceptable to broad strata of the Jewish population led to a progressive fragmentation of French Jewry by the end of the critical decade of the 1930s.

French anti-Semitism accelerated and changed its tone during that decade. The French Right had a long tradition of anti-Semitism, for

the Jews were associated, not entirely unjustly, with the republicanism and capitalism detested by the monarchist and Catholic foes of
the Republic.[1] Early French socialists, too, had attacked the Jew as
symbol of capitalism and exploiter of worker and peasant. The Right,
however, had made political and cultural anti-Semitism (as popularized by Drumont) its own by the time of the Dreyfus Affair. The
alien status of the Jew in the eyes of those who favored an organic,
noncapitalist, Christian society remained a common theme. Even
more frequent in the 1920s was the renewed emphasis upon the Jew
as subverter of French tradition and culture. As Bolshevik or as radical artist or intellectual of foreign origin, the Jew appeared as a
scourge upon France. In its xenophobic campaign against immigration, François Coty's *L'Ami du peuple,* a paper popular with the
lower middle classes, branded the Jews as a major source of decadent
art, communism, foreign labor competition, and financial domination (through "la finance judéo-germano-américaine").[2] Furthermore, a racism which appears to bear a direct German influence became a new component of French anti-Semitism of the 1930s. The
Jewish-Masonic conspiracy cited by the Catholic Right was supplemented by a radical "Jewish peril."[3] Moreover, the triumph of Nazism inspired a shift in emphasis from unfocused xenophobia to anti-
Semitism.[4]

    As the right-wing leagues grew in strength during the 1930s, the
sheer quantity of anti-Semitic propaganda kept pace. The *Action
française* and *Libre parole* were joined by a host of anti-Semitic,
anti-democratic periodicals, published in Paris and the provinces,
including Darquier de Pellepoix's *La France enchaînée,* Jean-Charles
Legrand's *Le Défi,* Jacques Doriot's *La Liberté et l'émancipation nationale,* Jean Boissel's *Le Réveil du peuple,* Louis Pemjean's *Le
Grand occident,* and Colonel Guillaume's *Choc,* along with propaganda published by Henri Petit's *Centre de documentation et de la
propagande.*[5] Not only was German-language Nazi propaganda
widely distributed in Alsace, but much of it was actually foreign-
funded, particularly through the efforts of Otto Abetz, a German agent
who moved in the best French social circles.[6] A spate of anti-Semitic
books also appeared during the period, even by such serious literary

figures as Louis-Ferdinand Céline, whose scurrilous *Bagatelles pour un massacre* was published in 1937. Céline repeated the familiar litany of Jewish control of the press and responsibility for the Bolshevik revolution and called for a pogrom.[7] Other literary figures who were drawn to fascism—among them Drieu La Rochelle and Robert Brasillach—propagated a fascist aesthetic which casually attacked Jews as symbols of the city, of the bourgeoisie, and of industrialization.[8] Two popular writers, the Tharaud brothers, who had long taken an interest in the exotic qualities of Eastern European Jews, became increasingly anti-Semitic during the 1930s. Much to the consternation of Jewish spokesmen, they had numerous defenders in intellectual circles.[9] As the traditional anti-German hostility of the French Right yielded to neo-pacifism and fear of social revolution, even the respectable right-wing press, such as *Le Temps* and *Le Matin*, heaped scorn upon the pro-war parties, "among whom the Jews were considered to figure prominently."[10]

In a period of economic and political crisis, anti-Semitic propaganda made headway in *petit-bourgeois* circles and even among the working class.[11] In 1934 a Jewish communist unemployment committee in Belleville decided to print a tract in French to alert French workers to the proliferation of anti-Semitic incidents.[12] Throughout the thirties attacks on Jews occurred sporadically in the fourth *arrondissement* and in Belleville and Jewish businesses were attacked in Alsace-Lorraine.[13]

The most important political scandal of the 1930s, the Stavisky Affair of 1933–1934, confirmed for many the traditional anti-Semitic stereotype of the Jews. A foreigner of Jewish origin, Stavisky was a financial swindler with extensive governmental connections. The revelations about his deals led to the antiparliamentary riots of February 6, 1934 and provided much grist for the *Action Française*'s propaganda mills.[14] In the political arena anti-Semitism found further expression in the Chamber of Deputies, particularly with Xavier Vallat's outburst following the appointment of Léon Blum as France's first Jewish premier in 1936, and in the General Council of the Department of the Seine, where Darquier de Pellepoix, the publisher of *La France enchaînée*, served.[15] Anti-Semitism thus achieved in the 1930s a visibility and respectability unprecedented since the days of the Dreyfus Affair. And, as in that earlier period, it was difficult to find a nonpolitical way to combat what was essentially a political phenomenon.

Assessments of Anti-Semitism

Throughout the 1930s the leadership of native French Jewry continued to see anti-Semitism as an aberration imported from Germany and fueled by the economic and political crises of the period. Occasional early efforts of *L'Univers israélite* to suggest vigilance in the wake of the Nazi triumph because anti-Semitism was contagious met with a subscriber's reaction that such insinuations were "shocking" and "an insult to our fellow citizens."[16] Refusing to recognize the rootedness within France of anti-liberal and nationalist forces which tended to define even native Jews as aliens, native leadership stressed France's liberal traditions and love of justice as the ultimate guarantee against anti-Semitic excesses. As Alfred Berl of the Alliance Israélite declared in *Paix et droit*, the Alliance's monthly periodical, "it seems hardly plausible that France would desert her traditional doctrine of justice, humanity, and peace."[17] Such an attitude was not unique to French Jews, but was shared by most French liberals, who thought, as Jacques Maritain did, that "the anti-Semitic mania here scarcely goes beyond the cadres of an exalted *petit-bourgeois* ideology" and found the anti-Semitic propaganda of their day "artificial."[18] This widely held point of view, a product of the ideology of the emancipation, contributed to shaping a mentality among native Jewry which militated against their assuming an active part in the struggle against anti-Semitism.

Among the leadership of native Jewry, the more traditional Jews of Alsace alone appear to have questioned the ideology of emancipation in the light of the striking popularity of the new anti-Semitism. In a sad and bitter article *La Tribune juive* of Strasbourg stated that contemporary events proved that emancipation had not been sincerely granted to the Jews, while the price of emancipation was "an assimi-

lation so profound that survival of Western Jewry . . . [could] be
traced only to immigration from Eastern Europe." It noted with
irony that the most assimilated Jews were now the victims of anti-
Semitism.[19] Even the intentions of French society were doubted, as
the paper questioned whether French intellectuals would respond
favorably to a new Dreyfus Affair and attacked the silence of the
French press in the face of the 1934 pogrom in Constantine,
Algeria.[20] Having revised its attitude toward assimilation, the Alsatian
Jewish press used the existence of anti-Semitism to attract alienated
Jewish youth back to the fold. Why cultivate another's garden, asked
La Tribune juive, when one's contributions would ultimately be re-
jected as foreign?[21] Choose Jewish life freely, it advised in 1939,
before persecution cruelly reminds you of your Judaism.[22]

The native Jewish establishment centered in Paris refrained from
the soul-searching undertaken by Alsatian Jews. Instead, consistorial
circles in Paris found it most comforting to attribute the spread of
anti-Semitism in France to the presence of unassimilated immigrant
Jews who offended the sensibilities of native Frenchmen. As early as
1931 the Union Scolaire proposed that the sources of French anti-
Semitism lay in the national and religious particularism as well as the
social defects of Jewish immigrants.[23] This attitude, which spelled
the defeat of the Consistory's policy of cooptation, reached its culmination in a vehement address delivered to heavy applause by the
Baron Robert de Rothschild, president of the Paris Consistory, in
May 1935 at the General Assembly of that body. The political activity of immigrant Jews, Rothschild admonished, was increasing the
danger of anti-Semitism:

> With the crisis which rages in France . . . is born a xenophobia which
> degenerates too easily into antisemitism. We who . . . are charged to
> defend the interests of the Israelite Community, we warn our coreligion-
> ists, recently immigrated and still insufficiently familiar with the French
> mentality and customs, against this danger. It is vital that the foreign ele-
> ments assimilate as soon as possible to the French elements. Until they
> adapt, until they are naturalized and have completed their military service
> . . . no one forbids them to have their own ideas and preferences, but let
> them abstain . . . from all political manifestations. One does not discuss
> the regime of a country whose hospitality one seeks.[24]

There is evidence in the Yiddish press that Rothschild's speech was even sharper than the version printed by the Consistory, for three Yiddish papers of vastly different political tendencies all reported Rothschild to have declared, "Immigrants and guests must know how to behave and must not be too critical . . . and if they don't like it here, let them leave."[25]

If the consistorial circles viewed the political activities of immigrant Jews as the source of anti-Semitism, they did not seek to deny entirely their ties with the immigrants. This position was too moderate for a small group of highly assimilated, upper-middle-class, and politically conservative native Jews, many of whom were associated with the reform congregation, the Union Libérale. In May of 1934, following the wave of xenophobia unleashed by the Stavisky Affair and the massive demonstrations in February of right-wing leagues and the communists, the *Union Patriotique des Français Israélites* was constituted to oppose the *Ligue Internationale contre l'Antisemitisme* (LICA) which, according to the new Union, used the struggle against anti-Semitism as a pretext for conducting propaganda in favor of social revolution.[26] Carefully distinguishing native from immigrant Jews, the Union allowed only the former to join its ranks and attacked the latter for mixing into French politics.[27] Moreover, it denied the existence of a "Jewish question" in France and proudly proclaimed that "the sacred interest of our fatherland . . . remains our only ideal."[28] Though the Union remained a marginal group, its extreme formulation of the ideology of assimilation exerted pressure from the right on consistorial circles.

The consistorial circles, indeed, shared with the Union Patriotique an unwillingness to view anti-Semitism in political terms. They still adhered to the ban on Jewish politics imposed by the ideology of emancipation and felt that past experience confirmed such a ban as most appropriate to their situation. Defense against anti-Semitism clearly could not imply a struggle against fascism.

For some young native Jews, however, and for the vast majority of immigrant Jews and their offspring, combatting anti-Semitism necessitated political action. Their quarrel with the consistorial circles and with the right-wing Union Patriotique was thus both philosophical

and tactical: philosophical in their acceptance of the legitimacy of
Jews' organizing and acting politically to defend themselves; tactical
in their espousing the techniques of mass politics. LICA, founded in
1928 by Bernard Lecache, son of Eastern European immigrants and
a former communist, attracted the support of both native and immigrant youth with its activist approach and mass demonstrations
against all manifestations of anti-Semitism, whether in France or
abroad. It is significant in this regard that LICA received prominent
coverage in *Kadimah*, a French-language periodical published in
Mulhouse by a group of young native Jews, socially concerned and
sympathetic to Zionism, under the direction of Rabbi René Hirschler.[29]

LICA activists rejected as a myth the attribution of anti-Semitism
to the activity of immigrant Jews. It was axiomatic to them that anti-
Semitism was an expression of the parties of the Right and hence had
to be combatted politically. "Judaism would not be torn apart," noted
Georges Zérapha of LICA, "by taking a political form."[30] The key to
LICA's success was this identification of the struggle against anti-
Semitism with the universalist goal of combatting fascism.[31] As
Lecache proclaimed in a propaganda pamphlet, by fighting anti-
Semitism one fought for all the oppressed and for peace as well.[32]
Lecache was thus able to tie his nonsectarian organization to one of
the major themes of French politics of the Left in the 1930s and to
appeal to young Jews who might otherwise have considered defense
against anti-Semitism as too particularistic for their sensibilities.

Within the immigrant community itself, the Jewish Left, with the
communists very much in the forefront, enjoyed a similar success in
organizing the struggle, for the communists were able to provide a
theory which would both explain the causes of anti-Semitism and link
its abolition to the triumph of universal justice. As a 1933 Jewish
communist pamphlet declared simply, "All national bourgeois movements ride the anti-Semitic horse."[33] France, therefore, was not immune to anti-Semitism. Only the revolutionary movement could
keep it from infecting the French working class. Like LICA, the Jewish communists were able to integrate the question of anti-Semitism
into the general scheme of French politics.

The middle-class Jewish immigrants, whose views were reflected by *Parizer haynt* and the Federation of Jewish Societies, did not consider France as ripe for anti-semitism as the communists did and resisted partisan political analyses. It was hard to take French anti-Semitism seriously, noted one correspondent for *Parizer haynt* in 1933. True, by 1934 the same writer was calling for vigilance against anti-Semitic groups but he, and others, continued to stress the difference between France—where even in the days of the Dreyfus Affair defenders had arisen from among the French people—and Germany, where no voice was raised to defend the Jews.[34] Needless to say, middle-class immigrant Jews also differed with consistorial circles in rejecting the notion that their own presence in France was responsible for anti-Semitism. Lack of tact on the part of immigrants, a writer for *Parizer haynt* noted after Rothschild's inflammatory speech, could hardly be blamed for precipitating anti-Semitism in France.[35]

While refraining from accepting a partisan explanation of, and cure for, anti-Semitism, middle-class immigrant spokesmen, unlike the established leaders of native Jewry, accepted the legitimacy of Jewish political interests. When twenty-three Jews were killed on August 4, 1934 in Constantine, Algeria, *Parizer haynt* called upon the Consistory to go beyond strictly religious questions and end its policy of silence.[36] Articles called for abandoning political neutrality to vote against all candidates who exhibited anti-Semitic tendencies.[37] In September 1936 the Federation participated in the International Conference against Racism and Anti-Semitism convened by LICA and declared that "it has always considered that its first duty was to combat anti-Semitism by every means possible . . . and it will join with anyone in order to do so."[38]

The Immigrant Response

These differing political attitudes and assessments of anti-Semitism were at the root of the subsequent differences in strategy espoused by the various segments of French Jewry to deal with the influence of

Nazism and with indigenous expressions of anti-Semitism. The divisions between immigrant and native Jews, and within the two communities as well, became so significant and visible, as the political tensions of the 1930s increased, that the consistorial circles lost the last vestiges of their exclusive authority over the Jewish community and their claim to be the sole legitimate spokesmen for it.

Within the immigrant community there was little unanimity on how to deal with the major issues of specific concern to French Jewry: anti-Semitism, the refugee problem, and, for immigrants, their own deteriorating legal and economic situation. True, all organized groups within the community agreed that action was necessary, but the form that action should take was in dispute. Moreover, the major forces—the Federation and the Jewish communists—both sought to take command and unite the immigrant community under their own leadership.

The Federation saw itself as the natural leader of the noncommunist majority within the immigrant community. Although its member-societies were federated in a rather loose framework and its program controlled by a small group of activists who served as its officers, the Federation could claim to speak for more than eighty societies and it had established contact with consistorial circles as early as 1930. Despite Israël Jefroykin's criticism in 1932 of the system of "notables" in French Jewish life, the Federation continued throughout the 1930s to espouse a policy of cooperation with native Jewry.[39] While this policy enabled it to claim the status of a partner in French Jewish activities, the Federation lost support in the immigrant community after Rothschild's 1935 speech made it clear that in any coalition with the organizations of native Jewry immigrant Jews were at best expected to be the junior, and very much silent, partner. The Federation did, in fact, send a formal protest to the Consistory, seeking clarification of the incident; nevertheless, its president Jefroykin urged that the Rothschild speech not be allowed to stand in the way of Jewish unity in a period of danger.[40] While, as we shall see, the Jewish Popular Front was pursuing an activist program in 1935–1936, the Federation appeared to remain subservient to the quietistic consistorial circles in its insistence that unity with native Jewry was the best approach to solving Jewish problems in France.

This should by no means obscure the fact that in earlier years, before it saw its authority undermined by the Jewish Popular Front movement, the Federation did exert leadership over immigrant French Jewry in both international and domestic matters. In 1932 the Federation was the only non-Zionist Jewish organization in France which sent representatives to Geneva to participate in the planning conference for the World Jewish Congress, a Zionist-sponsored effort to unite world Jewry for defense purposes.[41] Jefroykin became the vice-president for Yiddish-speaking immigrants on the French Provisional Executive Committee for the Congress.[42] By supporting and actively publicizing the Congress in numerous mass meetings,[43] the Federation affirmed its support for the concept of a Jewish people transcending national boundaries, and for the need for mutual support on an international level to counter the economic and political oppression of Central and Eastern European Jews. Such an affirmation remained anathema to the leadership of native Jewry.[44]

With Hitler's rise to power, the Federation joined the Union Universelle de la Jeunesse Juive in organizing a protest meeting on April 5, 1933, in which Justin Godart, Paul Painlevé, Victor Basch, and Jean Longuet participated, and a second mass meeting on May 16.[45] Furthermore, the Federation actively supported the boycott of German goods initiated by immigrant war veterans and LICA in April 1933 and participated in 1935 in the creation of a unified Committee for the Boycott of German Products and Services.[46] The Federation was also the first Jewish organization to establish a relief committee for German refugees, though its lack of funds forced it to merge with the native-dominated Comité National de Secours.

With respect to domestic issues affecting immigrant Jews, the Federation assumed responsibility for combatting the new anti-foreign decrees, legislated in 1934, according to which the proportion of foreign workers in various sectors of the French economy was to be sharply restricted. Depending upon the geographical location of the industry and the composition of its labor force, the ceiling upon foreign workers varied from two to twenty percent; lower ceilings were to be applied a year after the decree went into effect. In the trades most popular among immigrant Jews—in particular, the garment and leather industries—Jews constituted a larger percentage of the work force in urban centers than was now legally permissible.[47] Six hundred delegates of Jewish professional associations met together under the auspices of the Federation in December 1934 to collect information on the situation in each trade and to formulate strategies for achieving the retraction of the decrees. In an attempt to take charge and to indicate that constructive action was feasible, the Federation announced to the assembled delegates that it had already achieved unspecified positive results from its two memoranda sent to the government and its meeting with Marius Moutet, with whom its leaders maintained cordial relations. It was important, according to the Federation's leaders and the correspondent for *Parizer haynt*, that the antiforeigner decrees not become a partisan question. In other words, they hoped to prevent communist exploitation of the issue by proposing a struggle against the decrees across the entire political spectrum.[48] And they welcomed as politically constructive the expression of support from such prominent associates of consistorial circles as Raymond-Raoul Lambert and William Oualid and the latter's proposals for immigrant–native cooperation to defend the interests of all Jews in France.[49]

The Federation's claim to be the spearhead of an organized immigrant Jewish community in France was challenged by the establishment in 1934 of the Jewish Popular Front (*Mouvement Populaire Juif*). Since the Federation's efforts first to consolidate Jewish activity in Paris under its own banners and then to organize Jews in the provinces had involved few people at the grass-roots level, it was vulnerable to the challenge.[50] Indeed, with its intimate connection to the reality of French politics in the mid-1930s, the Jewish Popular Front Movement was able to present itself as a more effective means for Jews to organize and combat anti-Semitism.

As late as March 1934, the Jewish communist press was still proclaiming that the only way to fight fascism and anti-Semitism was to join with French workers within the CGTU rather than with fellow

Jewish victims.[51] Anti-Semitism, it declared, marched hand in hand both with Zionism and with the religious circles of the Consistory.[52] Likewise, LICA was attacked as a politically neutral society, led by ineffectual intellectuals and democrats; the Federation was dismissed with great frequency as a tool of the reactionary Jewish bourgeoisie and of the Consistory.[53] With the French Communist Party's adoption in June of 1934 of a united front policy to combat fascism, the Jewish communists also became receptive to the idea of a popular front on the Jewish street—an idea first suggested in February by "Trotskyites and anarchists" and rejected by the Communist Intersyndical Commission.[54]

At first the popular front program was designed to unite only the Jewish working-class parties. The Coordinating Committee for the United Front, which was composed of the Jewish subsection of the CP, the Bundist *Medem Farband*, and the Left *Poalei-Zion* first proclaimed the existence of a United Labor Front on the Jewish street to combat fascism and anti-Semitism and to secure equal political and syndical rights with French workers on July 28, 1934.[55] As a workers' movement the early United Front declared its opposition both to the Federation and "the Zionist reaction."[56] Because of its anti-Zionist stance, the socialist *Poalei-Zion-Hitachdouth* of Paris refused to affiliate with the new movement.[57]

The United Front rapidly acquired popular support. A meeting called at its initiative in August 1934 was reportedly attended by more than 1,000 persons, and 160 sections were established in each of the Paris *arrondissements* and suburban areas which had a heavy concentration of Jews.[58] By combining a program against anti-Semitism, fascism, and the xenophobia of the anti-foreign decrees with a call for unity with French workers, the United Front offered the hope that specifically Jewish problems could be solved within the framework of French politics of the Left.

In the spring of 1935 the French CP advocated unity at the base, or complete merger, with the SFIO and later that year proposed a program which welcomed progressive bourgeois elements as partners in the battle against fascism and refrained from attacks on the capitalist regime of the Third Republic. Reflecting the CP's new approach, in June of 1935 the Jewish Communist press dropped its attack on middle-class elements within the immigrant Jewish community and suggested enlarging the United Front to embrace the *petite-bourgeoisie*. Among the goals of the proposed Popular Front were the defense of Jewish rights, the support of foreign workers, the organization and coordination of Jewish philanthropic activities, and the establishment of a democratic system within the Jewish community.[59] In short, the Popular Front presumed to fulfill the major nonreligious functions supplied by a communal structure. The struggle against the present capitalist regime had no part in the program of the Jewish Popular Front just as it was absent from the larger French Popular Front.[60]

There was also a marked shift on the religious aspects of Jewish life. Realizing the continuing and nostalgic attachment of immigrant Jews to traditional customs and religious holidays, the *Naye presse* changed its official attitude toward Jewish religion. Whereas it had printed no fewer than three articles attacking Passover and rabbinical exploitation in April 1935 (the most picturesque of them paradoxically entitled "Passover, a Holiday for Slaves"[61]) from late 1935 through 1939 it refrained from antireligious propaganda and printed such articles as "A Happy Passover—the *Seder* in the Jewish Quarters" and "Passover, the Holiday of Liberation."[62] In the fall of 1936 it even appealed to religious Jews "to join us in the struggle."[63] Tactical adjustment in the political sphere was even less difficult. Given the great popularity which the boycott of German goods enjoyed among the Jewish masses of all classes, the *Naye presse* abandoned its previous opposition to the boycott.[64]

In its plan to bring much of the immigrant Jewish community into a unified Popular Front, the Jewish communists appealed to the Federation and its member-societies to affiliate with the new movement. Organizing in July 1935 a new Popular Committee for a Protest Movement against Pogroms in Germany, the Popular Front succeeded in drawing more than 100 delegates from Jewish organizations, including representatives of the Federation, to a conference devoted to combatting Nazism.[65] With effusive publicity in the *Naye presse*, Popular Front enthusiasts thus were able to use the coordina-

tion of a campaign against Nazism as a springboard for introducing
and strengthening the enlarged Popular Front within the immigrant
community. The popularity of such an issue among all elements of
that community could, after all, hardly be contested, and it was difficult for the Federation to refuse to attend such a meeting, which
was arranged in a spirit of nonpartisan coalition politics. The
bourgeois *Parizer haynt* was placed in the awkward position of con-
gratulating the communists for "recogniz[ing that] the Federation is a
democratic institution and the voice of the Jewish masses in Paris."[66]

The proposed Declaration of Principles of the Popular Front,
drawn up by a coalition committee and published in September of
1935, was calculated to assuage the fears of middle-class circles reluctant to cooperate with communists. While uniting "all workers and
democratic forces on the Jewish street [to] defend the interests of the
Jewish folk-masses everywhere; [to] struggle against all attacks on their
existence, against anti-Semitism, and against all forces in the Jewish
as in the non-Jewish environment which plan to undermine democratic freedoms and lead to xenophobia and chauvinism," it promised
that "all organizations included in the people's movement will take
care to respect each other and avoid every disloyal form of discussion."[67]

In spite of this declaration, after two months of cooperation with
the communists and participation in protest meetings against Nazism, the Central Committee of the Federation, under Jefroykin's
leadership, voted on September 20, 1935, not to join the Popular
Front. Since it was composed of groups of many political tendencies
and was itself "a non-political and neutral organization," the Committee argued, it could not affiliate with what remained essentially a
political movement. It would, however, participate with the Popular
Front in protest and defense actions against anti-Semitism and would
allow its member-societies to join individually should they so desire.[68] The decision was a controversial one and provoked acrimonious debates on September 24 and October 1, 1935 in the larger fed-
eral council of the Federation. While the majority ratified the
Central Committee's negative decision in a 52–16 vote, a minority
faction, led by Marc Jarblum, urged that the Federation join the

Popular Front and thus play a role in shaping its decisions. Whereas the majority report contended that it would be dangerous for immigrant aliens to be politically partisan, the minority argued that political neutrality was a luxury at a time when it was clear that victory of the Right would usher in anti-Semitism.[69]

The negative decision of the Federation notwithstanding, a broadened Popular Front was officially proclaimed on October 8, 1935, by 154 delegates of 60 Jewish organizations. The Popular Front succeeded in uniting the Jewish workers' parties, LICA, the Jewish veterans' association, organizations of merchants and artisans, and a few of the Federation's member societies.[70] Interestingly, it was the Bundist *Medem Farband* which removed itself from the Popular Front. It declared that it could not affiliate with the movement unless a clear commitment to struggle against the capitalist regime, against the reactionary Federation, and against Zionism were included in the movement's platform and unless the Front agreed to drop from its ranks all those who supported the Zionist Transfer Agreement.[71] The willingness of the communists to accept the existence of a community of Jews which included the middle as well as the working class was attacked as the adoption of a nationalist, *klal-yisrael* position which the Jewish Left had always repudiated. The Bund thus mirrored the position of the SFIO vis-à-vis the CP in the general Popular Front. However, this is where the parallel ends. Whereas the SFIO ultimately agreed to a united front with the communists, the Bund was too weak to be able to join the communist-dominated Jewish Popular Front without losing its raison d'être and its hard-core following. Yet, by choosing to remain an independent opposition force, despite its role in the still existent Coordinating Committee of Jewish labor parties, the Bund relegated itself to a marginal role in the immigrant community during the Popular Front era.

The defection of the Bund was symptomatic of the tensions within the Popular Front movement. By taking an anti-Zionist position during the 1935–1936 disturbances in Palestine and by insinuating that the Zionists were making secret deals with the Nazis (on the Transfer Agreement), the Jewish communists alienated their socialist Zionist partners within the Popular Front.[72] Repeated and vicious attacks on everything Zionist—so Jarblum protested in the new *Poalei-Zion* paper *Naye tsayt*—violated the spirit of the Popular Front.[73] Responding to the *Poalei-Zion* demand that the Communists cease their attacks, the Jewish subsection of the CP divorced itself from the Palestine Communist Party's appeal "to arm the Arabs and disarm the Jews," but nonetheless reserved the right to express its opposition to Zionism at large. For, so it claimed, the mutual tolerance of the Popular Front allowed each party the freedom of its own convictions.[74]

Although the Left *Poalei-Zion* remained within the Popular Front, the half-hearted apology of the Jewish communists and the communist domination of the Front inspired Jarblum to call for a democratically organized popular community structure (*kehilla*) in every city and a national union of such local communal units for the purpose of self-defense and the promotion of Jewish education and culture. Lacking a large popular base, the *Poalei-Zion* joined with the leadership of the Federation and *Parizer haynt* in reviving the idea that the Federation should serve as the rallying point for organizing, clearly in opposition to the Popular Front, a unified immigrant Jewish community in France and that it actively recruit new member societies.[75] In the long run, thus, the communists remained the sole major immigrant group wholeheartedly supporting the Popular Front.

In spite of these tensions, the Popular Front mentality seems to have prevailed among immigrant Jewry. Popular Front committees were established in Metz, Nancy, Strasbourg, and Lyon as well as Paris.[76] Through the *Centre de Liaison pour un Statut Juridique*, a leftist lobby, the Popular Front led a widely heralded campaign to assure legal protection for foreign artisans.[77] Moreover, the residents of the *Pletzl* rejected *Parizer haynt*'s heated campaign in favor of Edmond Bloch, a right-wing candidate and member of the *Union Patriotique des Israélites Français* who had friendly contacts with anti-Semitic politicians. They elected overwhelmingly his communist opponent in the second round of the 1936 elections. In Belleville, too, the communist candidate drew the largest number of votes.[78] The anticommunism espoused by *Parizer haynt* in an effort to give the lie to anti-Semitic charges that all Jews were communists thus appears to have been out of touch with the sentiment of the majority of immigrant Jews. So popular did the Jewish Popular Front appear to observers that the Central Consistory announced in August 1936 that it would participate informally in the conference of the movement to be held later that month.[79] *Parizer haynt*, too, could not ignore the movement's achievements, which it listed in modest terms as conducting efforts (along with the *Centre de Liaison pour un Statut Juridique*) to secure a juridical statute for foreigners, cooperating with LICA in its activities, and participating in the World Congress for Peace in Brussels.[80] Whatever the case, one would not go wrong in assuming that the "secret" of the Jewish Popular Front's appeal and success lay outside the perpetual bickerings on the Jewish domestic scene. In a period in which a Popular Front Government, headed coincidentally by France's first Jewish premier, ruled France and in which the country's political Right seemed more and more intractable to Jewish problems, there simply was no effective alternative to a Jewish counterpart of the Popular Front.

The success of the Jewish Popular Front was as short-lived as that of its larger general French model. When the CP became increasingly nationalist and dissolved its foreign-language subsections, it precipitated the downfall of the Popular Front on the Jewish street. Upon the disappearance of the Jewish subsection, *Poalei-Zion* and the *Medem Farband* announced the breakup of the Jewish Popular Front, since the Jewish communists were no longer an independent Jewish organization.[81] Although the Jewish communists maintained that their representatives would continue to serve the Jewish Popular Front with the mandate of the Paris region of the CP,[82] the Front never regained its former vitality. The fall of Blum's second government in June of 1937 confirmed the demise of Popular Front efforts.

On the Jewish street, the former members of the Popular Front as well as their opponents turned from cooperation to competition, each trying to strengthen its own position within the immigrant community and assume a position of uncontested leadership. While the Federation stepped up its campaign to organize immigrant Jews in the spring of 1937, the Jewish communists called for the unification of all Jewish societies on a new basis.[83] They invited the Federation to join in this venture, but refused to participate in the Federation's own National Conference, held on April 24, 1937, on the grounds that the Conference was undemocratic and required affiliation with the Federation.[84] Thus, two unity campaigns were conducted simultaneously, with the brickbats and attacks emanating from both sides.

Continuing their appeal to the lower middle classes and riding the crest of the International Yiddish Cultural Congress planned for September 1937, the Jewish communists and the Jewish Intersyndical Commission established the *Tsentrale fun Arbeter un Folksorganizatsies* (the Central Committee for Labor and Popular Organizations) in June of 1937[85] and throughout the fall and winter declared their willingness to include all except the reactionary forces within the Jewish community in the new association.[86] On April 24, 1938, they convoked their own unity conference to create a central union of all Jewish democratic and popular organizations in France.[87] Though invited, the Federation refused to submit to the leadership of communists "who destroyed Jewish unity in the name of unity."[88] Instead, the Federation stepped up its independent activities on behalf of foreign immigrants, calling a conference to deal with the new decrees and sending a delegation to the Minister of the Interior and to the Minister of Labor to plead that Jewish immigrants merited special treatment and to ask that, as political refugees, their naturalization be facilitated.[89] Despite the opposition of the Federation, some individual societies affiliated with that body joined the new *Farband fun Yiddishe Gezelshaften* (*Union des Sociétés Juives*) which was born of the conference and which counted 82 member societies.[90] On its part, LICA, too, attempted in 1938 to unite immigrant Jewry in its own *Farband fun di Yiddishe Gezelshaften far der Aktsie fun der LICA* (*Union des Sociétés Juives autour de LICA*). This other *Farband* claimed 91 member societies, many of which were former adherents of the Federation or the communist Union.[91] With the major groups within the immigrant community vying for leadership, the immigrant community was left as fragmented after its unity campaigns as before.[92]

The Native Response

If immigrant Jews were fragmented in the struggle against anti-Semitism and the defense of their rights to remain and work in France, they were nevertheless united in their commitment to political activism on the issues that affected their lives. Mass demonstrations and protest meetings, self-defense against anti-Semitic gangs in Jewish neighborhoods, and left-leaning politics were part of the accepted political legacy of a large segment of Eastern European immigrant Jews. As we have seen, these patterns of action were not part of the historical experience of native French Jewry. The consistorial circles whose authority as spokesmen for French Jewry was undermined by the activity of the various coalitions within the immigrant community rejected the immigrants' tactics and attempted to discourage their use while reasserting their own leadership. In doing so, they alienated both the masses of immigrants and their own youth.

For the consistorial circles, quiet and discreet diplomacy and restrained pronouncements of the kind which they had traditionally relied upon remained even in the 1930s the sole acceptable form of political activity. The native Jewish press avoided taking stands on general political issues or even reporting them. When it did comment on matters of political interest, it was quick to add, "Nous ne faisons pas de politique ici."[93] While both the Paris Consistory and the Central Consistory issued politely phrased anti-Nazi statements,[94] they did not take the lead in organizing protest meetings. Moreover, at a conference of French Jewish organizations concerned with the rise of Hitlerism, held on June 6, 1933, the Paris Consistory was the sole body to abstain from voting on a proposal to collaborate in disseminating anti-Nazi propaganda. Like the American Jewish Committee in the U.S. and the Board of Deputies in England, it also rejected the boycott movement supported by the masses of French Jewry.[95] As Rabbi Liber wrote in his pseudonymous column in L'Univers israélite, "It is not a bad thing that the leaders have been pressured by the public; the movement is thereby more spontaneous and will be . . . more profound."[96] As far as protests were concerned, abdication of leadership became a virtue. Furthermore, consistorial leaders fell back upon an ever more narrow definition of the kinds of activity permitted them. In an effort to justify consistorial in-activity on behalf of German refugees, a spokesman actually declared that "as a consistory, all non-cultic initiative is forbidden to it."[97] This rationale masked a deep reluctance to become involved in con-troversial activity in a period of political upheaval. In earlier and more secure times, as we have already seen, the consistories did take upon themselves the defense of Jewish equality.

The theory of passive leadership, combined with the quiet style of protest that was favored in practice by the consistories, convinced im-migrant Jews and LICA personalities that they must assume leader-ship on their own. The failure of consistorial figures to respond quickly and publicly to the bloody pogrom in Constantine led *Parizer haynt* to bemoan their lack of leadership and to demand that the Consistory abandon its policy of silence and come to the defense of its own Algerian constituents.[98] It was not until more than a month had elapsed, however, that the Chief Rabbi of Paris, Julien Weill, appealed to French justice during his *Rosh Hashanah* sermon and not until the winter that the Central Consistory resolved—in pri-vate—that one of its members would transmit a note about the po-groms to the vice-president of the *Conseil d'Etat.*[99] The major public protest against the pogrom was organized—in August—not by the Consistory but by LICA.[100]

More, themselves reluctant to embark on aggressive political ac-tion, consistorial circles sought to limit political activity in France by other Jewish groups through pretense of leadership on the main is-sues. As early as April 1933, Alliance leaders convoked a meeting designed to bring the Federation and an immigrant sponsored refugee defense committee under their wing. As a police report noted, "The intentions of the Alliance, in full agreement with the Central Consis-tory, would be to lead the Jewish groups to renounce all demon-strations capable of troubling public order"[101] At the same time both Grand Rabbi Israel Lévi and Grand Rabbi Julien Weill appealed to Jews not to participate in anti-Nazi street demonstrations.[102] These early efforts failed, and the initiatives of the Federation, LICA, im-migrant war veterans, and the Jewish Popular Front in defense efforts against anti-Semitism compelled consistorial circles to make further responses to the issue. By 1936 the native Jewish press ran articles decrying the excesses of the anti-Semitic press and calling for the formation of Jewish defense organizations.[103] At the February 21, 1935, meeting of the Permanent Section of the Central Consistory, Rabbi Maurice Liber had already proposed the creation of an Advisory Committee of French Judaism with the comment that such a committee was "necessary so that an official organization could speak out, if such be the case, in the name of French Judaism and to prevent the intemperate conduct of organizations which have no mandate."[104]

To implement Liber's proposal, discussions were initiated with representatives of the Alliance Israélite. A report was then accepted in June of 1935 by the Central Consistory[105] urging the establishment of a Committee for the Study and Defense of the Moral and Social Interests of French Judaism, to be composed of appointees of the Central Consistory, the Alliance, the Consistories of the Rhine and Moselle, and the Federation. As the elaboration of the project continued, disillusion with immigration organizations and with efforts at rapprochement led to the elimination of the Federation from the project. The *Centre de Défense et de Vigilance*, which was finally established in January 1936, comprised three delegates from the Central Consistory and three from the Alliance.[106] With the announcement of the formation of the committee, consistorial spokesmen appealed to French Jews to leave political decisions to the new committee and to refrain from "individual, irresponsible steps."[107] Yet the new committee was essentially a study committee, devoted to publishing a mimeographed bulletin which reported news of interest to French Jewry.[108] It undertook no protest actions or political activities of its own. It did send a delegate to LICA's 1936 International Conference against Racism and Anti-Semitism; the latter, however, called for a careful differentiation between racism and fascism and declared, "In France, except for a fraction of the extreme right, there is no longer any anti-Semitism."[109] Understandably, the Committee did not succeed in convincing other Jewish organizations in France to cease their political activity.

The response of consistorial circles to the refugee problem provides a case study of the political theory and leadership style of the native Jewish establishment. France received the greatest number of German Jewish refugees of any European country, with some 26,000 arriving in 1933 alone.[110] However, government officials felt that France could not integrate the refugees into the French economy during this period of economic crisis. French public opinion toward German Jewish refugees, many of whom were intellectuals, was described as "scarcely warm" because of popular concern about unemployment. Moreover, after the initial wave of Nazi anti-Jewish measures had passed, police reports reveal widespread skepticism that German Jews were actually forced to flee their homeland. After all, there were no real pogroms in Germany.[111] The economic crisis and the skepticism regarding Nazi intentions led the French government to adopt severe measures, including refusal to extend temporary transit visas and the expulsion or imprisonment of stateless refugees.[112] Moreover, the French were completely unreceptive to the permanent settlement of German refugees, and declared that new refugees seeking even temporary residence as of December 31, 1936, had to prove they were victims of political persecution.[113] On March 23, 1938, the government announced that aliens illegally settled in France (including an estimated 18,000 Jews) were to be given the choice of settling on the land as farmers or leaving the country.[114] Still another Decree Law, purporting to make the practice of expulsion more humane, ultimately worked against the refugees. It barred their entry into France unless they showed proof of their ability to emigrate overseas and it imposed automatic prison terms of one month to three years upon foreigners who failed to leave the country after the expiration of their residence permits.[115] Only in 1939 was the condition of the refugees alleviated, thanks to the creation by Foreign Minister Bonnet of the *Comité Interconfessionel pour les réfugiés* and to the upswing in the economy which stimulated the demand for labor.

The refugees were thus in need of charitable aid and of political support. The two must be clearly distinguished in terms of the native Jewish response. As for the former, native Jewish circles, along with immigrant groups, mobilized their resources to provide food and shelter for their homeless coreligionists. They were instrumental in establishing the *Comité d'acceuil et d'aide aux victimes de l'antisemitisme en Allemagne* in March 1933[116] and in uniting that committee with immigrant-sponsored relief associations to form the nonsectarian *Comité National de Secours*, which was controlled by native Jews and administered by the Baron Robert de Rothschild. Affiliated with the *Comité National* was the *Fédération de Comités de Secours de l'Est de la France*, which itself coordinated relief agencies in fifty communities.[117] The *Comité National* was founded and administered by Jews, but a number of prominent French politicians, among them Paul Painlevé and Justin Godart, were recruited to confirm its nonsectarian status, for native Jews felt most comfortable and legitimate working through the channels of nonsectarian committees. By October 1933 the Comité had registered 9,241 refugees (50 percent of them German, 40 percent Polish, and 10 percent stateless) and was spending 600,000 francs a month.[118]

Although the giving of charitable assistance was a nonpolitical act, the *Comité National* was plagued by dissension in its two years of existence. Immigrants charged that refugees of Eastern European origin were treated with less consideration than native German refugees.[119] The communist press, in particular, accused the Comité of mistreating its clients and of suppressing legitimate political activity. Well might the Jewish communists have complained, for the Comité reacted with hostility toward refugees suspected of communist activity. In November 1933, for example, Raymond-Raoul Lambert, administrator of the Comité, in an urgent and confidential letter called for police intervention to remove two young communist agitators from the Comité's quarters and expel them from France.[120] In 1934 André Spire angrily resigned from the board of the *Comité National* because "they worked without heart and without soul."[121]

Moreover, the establishment of the *Comité National* did not relieve the Consistories of criticism. In June of 1933, it was noted in an article defending the Central Consistory that "people are astonished . . . that the Consistory has not done more for the German emigrés."[122] The justification for this inactivity was the by now familiar rationale that the Consistory was a body devoted to purely religious matters. Thus, even in matters of relief, the Consistory held aloof, defining its religious function so strictly as to exclude the donation of charitable aid. The justification was neither understood nor accepted by the immigrant Jewish community.

Furthermore, the consistorial personalities involved in the *Comité National* actively opposed political activity on behalf of German refugees. In this they differed little from their coreligionists in the U.S., who did not challenge America's restrictive immigration policy on behalf of the German refugees. When Pierre Dreyfus, the son of Alfred, proposed at a preliminary meeting that the future *Comité National* coordinate political as well as philanthropic efforts, his proposal was summarily rejected by the delegates of the Alliance and the Consistory.[123] Consistorial circles were simply unwilling to challenge French policy, though they used their contacts to plead for leniency toward refugees who had entered France illegally.[124] Spokesmen for the native community rather complacently accepted the need for France to regulate the number and employment of the refugees it admitted because of the economic crisis. They feared the effect of large-scale Jewish immigration on French opinion: "The French remain individualists," Raymond-Raoul Lambert wrote, "and all that the immigrants have to do for quite legitimate resistance to be felt is appear to stick together and act according to imported customs."[125] With this attitude toward the immigration of Jewish refugees, it is no surprise that native Jewish organizations encouraged emigration from France (though they had reservations about expulsion) and supported the French effort to persuade the League of Nations to assume responsibility for the refugees.[126]

As individuals some native Jews did participate in the *Comité pour la défense des droits des israélites en Europe centrale et orientale*, which had avowedly political aims. However, of the 43 officers and prominent members listed by the *Comité de Défense*, only four moved in consistorial circles, and one of those, Dr. Léon Zadoc-Kahn, was an avowed Zionist sympathizer. Moreover, the non-sectarian Committee, which included the names of 19 prominent non-Jews, primarily politicians, on its list, was run by Boris Gourevitch and Pierre Dreyfus, both beyond the perimeter of consistorial circles.[127]

The Committee saw an opportunity to link the solution of the refugee problem to French foreign policy interests. Thus, in a private letter of November 29, 1933, to the Minister of Labor, Justin Godart, the secretary of the Committee declared that its goal was "to gather together all the moral, political, and economic forces of the Jews of England, the United States, Central and Eastern Europe for the support of French foreign policy";[128] their support would be won through favorable action toward Jewish refugees. However, in the 1930s Jewish support was no longer the valuable commodity it had been during World War I.

Between 1933 and 1936 the Committee wrote letters and sent delegations to such high government officials as the representative of the French government to the League of Nations, the vice-president of the *Conseil d'Etat*, the High Commissioner of the French Republic in Syria and Lebanon, and the Ministers of Labor and the Interior.[129] In these contacts it argued against the mass expulsion of Jewish refugees from France, basing its claims on economic grounds. The German refugees, it was stated, had established industries which already employed between 8,000 and 10,000 French workers. Therefore, an equal number of refugees should be allotted identity cards and work permits.[130] When this appeal was repeatedly rejected by governmental officials who claimed that most newly established refugee industries competed with French firms for the same labor, the Committee shifted its attack. It declared that the unregulated expulsion of refugees was hypocritical and harmful to the image of France: "The very nations which struggle against the expansion of the racist plague prevent the entry of victims of racism or expel these victims under the slightest pretext."[131] Because of this attitude, wealthy Jewish refugees specializing in commerce, who "could bring to France the clientèle which they possessed in Western Europe" were shunning France.[132] In spite of these appeals the expulsions continued.

Again appealing to France's self-interest, the Committee urged that Jewish refugees be allowed to settle as farmers in the south of France and in Syria and Lebanon, where they would aid the French cause. Should these approaches be followed, it was suggested, France would win the support and gratitude of the 17 million Jews of the world. Although this last proposal was under consideration for a while, by the end of 1935 it was ultimately rejected because of hostility in the colonies and the decision to allow no more immigration to France.[133]

Although its concern for the refugees was real, the Committee did not allow this concern to exceed the limits of its political vision. It did not argue for the permanent settlement of all Jewish refugees in France but only of the "desirable elements." It did not oppose, until March 1936, the forced emigration of refugees, but only their unregulated and coercive expulsion. The Committee therefore proposed that "the Minister of the Interior establish relations with the large Jewish charitable institutions which are all disposed to facilitate the exodus from France of Jewish refugees on condition that the expulsions cease, and that these measures be replaced by preliminary accords with those Jewish institutions which have taken upon themselves the search for visas and the financial means for the departure of those elements recognized as undesirable."[134]

Despite the Committee's moderation and phrasing of its aims in terms of French interests, both the Alliance and the *Comité National de Secours* dissociated themselves from the Committee's political lobbying for changes in France's refugee policy. In a meeting of the Committee, Georges Leven of the Alliance emphasized that "the Alliance Israélite Universelle was not at all interested in the problem of refugees and had taken no position in this question."[135] When the *Comité National* was attacked for refusing to combat the expulsion of refugees and to support their settlement in agricultural colonies in the south of France, Jacques Helbronner, the vice-president of the *Comité National*, came to its defense: "The Comité . . . as well as the successive French governments, have done all that was humanly possible for the refugees, in spite of the most difficult circumstances." The remaining refugees, he claimed, included "many nonentities of no use in any human group." Agricultural colonies of refugees were dangerous, for they would "provoke the susceptibilities of the population." Both the Alliance and the *Comité National* hoped that the League of Nations would relieve them of the refugee problem.[136] Furthermore, when in February 1938 Philippe Serre, the Under-

secretary of State for Immigration and Foreigners, invited Jews active
in refugee work to join a government advisory committee, consistorial figures, who originally hoped to be the only representatives of
French Jewry on the committee, resisted in particular the inclusion
of members of the *Comité pour la défense des Israélites* (referred to as
the Comité Gourevitch or Gourevitch-Dreyfus). As Raymond-Raoul
Lambert, then secretary-general of the *Comité d'assistance aux
réfugiés d'Allemagne*, (C.A.R.) which had succeeded the *Comité National de Secours*, wrote in a letter to Robert Schumann, adjunct
secretary-general of the Paris Consistory, there was no need to include the Comité Gourevitch, "which is *pro-Jewish*"—apparently a
detriment—"and represents nothing." [137]

As unpopular as the Consistory's approach to the refugee problem
was, consistorial reactions to Nazism and consistorial flirtations with
right-wing organizations which loudly proclaimed their patriotism
were more significant in militating against the mass acceptance of
consistorial leadership which the formation of the *Centre de Défense
et de Vigilance* had been calculated to attract. In response to the is-
suance of the Nuremberg laws, the Central Consistory published a
statement more moderate than that of the League of the Rights of
Man and couched in the most universalistic language, which deem-
phasized the singling out of the Jews as victims:

> German racism confuses in its hatred all religions, all moralities which
> aspire to bring men together in a common ideal of peace, of justice, and
> of love. In persecuting today the children of Israel . . . it prepares itself
> to persecute in the same way . . . all noble and pious souls.
>
> In the name of French Israelites, patriotically faithful to the generous
> Nation which emancipated their fathers, the Central Consistory is obliged
> to condemn the outrage committed in the midst of the twentieth century
> against the sacred principles of divine law and of human conscience. [138]

There was little evidence of empathy with German Jewry. Rather,
the statement could have been written by any group of liberal French
humanists. Moreover, issuing the statement represented the extent of
consistorial reaction. The Consistory sponsored no protest meetings
and devoted none of its closed sessions to consideration of other

responses to Nazi anti-Semitism. Failing to deal resolutely with issues of major concern to both native and immigrant Jews, the consistorial circles in effect abdicated their position of leadership.

By focusing on proving the patriotism of French Jews, moreover, consistorial circles alienated all segments of immigrant Jewry and the progressive elements within native Jewry. Expressions of patriotism, as we have seen, had always been considered the most acceptable form of political activity by native Jewry, even when the uninhibited exhibition of patriotism became identified almost exclusively with the Right. During the 1930s, when anti-Semites labeled all Jews as Bolsheviks, when the Stavisky Affair suggested that Jews were sordid wheelers and dealers, and when a Jewish socialist governed France in its first Popular Front government, the upper and middle classes, who ruled the consistories and whose class sympathies lay with the parties of order rather than with the revolutionary Left, felt constrained to make it clear where their allegiance lay.

Upon Blum's appointment as premier, the native Jewish community felt itself particularly vulnerable to attack. Since Blum was a socialist, his triumph fed the myth of the Jewish conspiracy against established order. Indeed, Blum's appointment inspired vitriolic attacks upon him as a Jew. In the Chamber of Deputies Xavier Vallat, a right-wing deputy destined to serve during World War II as Vichy's Commissioner for Jewish Questions, deplored the day when "for the first time this old Gallo-Roman country would be governed . . . by a Jew."[139] The press of the Right conducted a massive campaign along the same lines. "It is as a Jew that one must see, conceive, hear, fight, and destroy this Blum" wrote Charles Maurras. "This man is anything but French."[140] Blum was also criticized for having too many (three) Jews in his government; it was charged that the Jews were taking over France. Because of this political situation, it has been reported by several sources that the Chief Rabbi of Paris himself tried to persuade Blum to resign from office so as not to expose the Jewish community to further attack.[141]

In the same vein, from 1934 through 1936 the Paris and Central Consistories permitted Colonel de la Rocque and his *Croix de feu*, a right-wing league, to participate in memorial services to the Jewish war dead held at the temple of the rue de la Victoire. Furthermore, Rabbi Jacob Kaplan of the Victoire temple also spoke at the inauguration of the women's section of the *Croix de feu*.[142] Despite de la Rocque's repeated protestations that he was not an anti-Semite,[143] immigrant Jews and native Jewish youth found his declarations unconvincing. Marc Jarblum and *Parizer haynt* pointed out that de la Rocque's bands were actively involved in anti-Semitic agitation in Algeria and Tunisia and quietly involved in France.[144] The young editors of the new journal *Samedi* agreed that de la Rocque's declaration of sympathy for the Jews "did not prevent . . . his troops from disavowing [his statement] and . . . from engaging in militant anti-Semitism."[145] Even Raymond-Raoul Lambert uttered cautious criticism in *L'Univers israélite*.[146] Comparing Rabbi Zadoc Kahn with contemporary leadership, to the detriment of the latter, a LICA partisan declared that he would prefer "that the official Judaism of our miserable time act [as Kahn did] . . . by joining in our protests rather than delegating a rabbi to bless the pennants of the Croix de feu."[147] Léon Blum, on the other hand, saw a similarity between the attitudes of the Jews of his time and the time of the Dreyfus Affair:

> The rich Jews, the Jews of the middle bourgeoisie, the Jewish functionaries feared the struggle undertaken for Dreyfus exactly as they fear today the struggle undertaken against fascism. . . . They imagined that the anti-Semitic passion would be turned aside by their cowardly neutrality. . . . They understood no better than they understand today that no precaution . . . would delude the adversary and that they remained the victims offered to triumphant anti-dreyfusism or fascism.[148]

The outrage expressed in virtually all nonconsistorial Jewish publications led to repeated protests by the Federation against the Consistory in the name of the entire immigrant community. Inviting the *Croix de feu* to participate in Jewish ceremonies, noted the Federation, was a political act which implied criticism of the present French regime.[149]

Criticism intensified when it was learned that Rabbi Kaplan was to speak, along with Edmond Bloch of the *Union Patriotique des Français Israélites*, at a meeting "to save French civilization" called by Jean Goy, the right-wing veterans' leader who had been favorably impressed by Hitler in an interview with him. Even the normally re-strained anticommunist *Parizer haynt* proclaimed, "Getting together with a band of anti-Semites and fascists, the best of Hitler's friends, to fight a supposed danger . . . is doing dirty work."[150] So hostile and widespread had the criticism become that Rabbi Kaplan declared that he had participated at the meeting only after having been specifically ordered to do so by the Consistory, which had authority over its member rabbis; he argued that he had permitted the *Croix de feu* cer-emonies in his synagogue for the same reason.[151] In response to the criticism, the Consistory cancelled Kaplan's appearance.[152] Thus, 1937 was the last year that the *Croix de feu* took part in Jewish me-morial services.

While the implacable hostility of the vast majority of French Jewry halted the consistorial circles' flirtation, under the guise of patriotism, with right-wing elements in French politics, this policy had clearly reflected the desire of the established leadership of native French Jewry to divorce themselves from immigrant Jews and their politics and to proclaim themselves to be de la Rocque's acceptable, patriotic, and nonrevolutionary "good Jews." It was the logical conclusion to their conviction that unassimilated immigrant Jews were the primary cause of anti-Semitism in France. In this, they shared the xenopho-bia of their countrymen. By tilting to the Right, they attempted to prove their own assimilation, secure protective political support, and ensure, as it were, that the French Right would not succumb to the anti-Semitism that did not differentiate between "good" and "bad" Jews.

The policy quickly earned the scorn of immigrant and native youth alike, who easily perceived that consistorial leaders were acting on false assumptions. In October 1933 *Chalom*, the organ of the UUJJ, noted that assimilation was used by certain native Jews as a code-word for right-wing patriotism and pointedly declared that extreme assimilation and super-patriotism had done the German Jews no good.[153] The young native Jews who edited *Kadimah* also compared the Jewish members of the rightist *Francistes* with those misguided Jews who had supported Hitler.[154] And *Samedi* editorialized that in-viting anti-Semitic groups like the *Croix de feu* to religious ceremonies with the intention of thereby accomplishing a patriotic act was "at the least, useless." It was democratic and leftist governments—not the Right—which provided Jews with greater security and protection against anti-Semitism.[155] The consistorial definition of legitimate Jewish political behavior was thus seen as hypocritical and self-serving and out of touch with the political realities of the period. The Consistory's tilt to the Right resulted, in effect, in a reversal of its previous policy of rapprochement with immigrant Jewry and in undermining the native-immigrant unity campaign championed by the Federation and *Parizer haynt*. While continuing to call for unity, consistorial leaders followed a policy of laying all blame for the failure to achieve unity at the feet of the immigrants and demanding immigrant submission to consistorial rule.[156] This policy only succeeded in undermining consistorial authority within the larger Jewish community.

Munich and After

The year which preceded the outbreak of World War II witnessed the progressive political isolation of all segments of French Jewry and a concomitant growth of pessimism within the Jewish community. Anti-Semitic agitation reached its peak in the "fin Septembre" of the Munich negotiations when anti-Semitic bands, charging that Jews were inciting the government to go to war for their own selfish ends, led attacks on individual Jews in immigrant neighborhoods and on Jewish businesses, particularly in Alsace-Lorraine.[157] The spread of a brand of anti-Semitism fanned by war panic was noted even within the labor movement.[158]

Finding no effective means of combating the diffusion of anti-Semitism, French Jews of all persuasions fell back on the trite anti-defamation formula of yesteryear. The Jewish press kept refuting anti-Semitic charges as though they could be deflected with rational argument and hailing Jewish patriotism and war service as if that information really was relevant.[159] Consistorial circles renewed their efforts to prove their patriotism by indicating that they would always place larger French interests above specific Jewish needs. In November 1938, the Chief Rabbi of Paris, Julien Weill, was quoted in an interview printed in the rightist and pro-Munich paper *Le Matin* as refusing to make "the least contribution" to the problem of saving German Jews, for the problem "largely exceeded the competence" of a spiritual leader. As Weill concluded, "It is not for us, at this time, to take an initiative which could in any way disturb the approaches currently under way towards a Franco-German initiative."[160] According to his secretary, Rabbi Henri Schilli, Weill was misquoted and sought to issue a statement to correct the error, but he was forbidden to do so by lay leaders in the Paris Consistory who were pleased by the "patriotic" impression made by the *Matin* interview.[161] The denial of Jewish solidarity was expected to win over French anti-Semites.

While the native Jewish establishment was indulging in its own form of political neutrality, LICA and its activities won increasing support and widespread coverage from the organ of middle-class immigrant Jewry, *Parizer haynt*. At the same time the Bundist *Unzer shtime* continued to assert that only the unity of the working-class movement could prevent war and destroy anti-Semitism.[162] During the September crisis, both LICA and the Federation issued appeals to the immigrant Jewish population urging restraint and calm in the face of anti-Semitic provocations and expressing their solidarity with France.[163] In its own appeal the communist-led Union of Jewish Societies assured immigrant Jews that "these incitements are in vain; the people of France are not taken in by such gross maneuvers."[164] Israël Jefroykin of the Federation went so far as to suggest that even naturalized immigrant Jews maintain a low profile, as in the Middle Ages, and shun activism in both political and economic affairs.[165] Across the political spectrum, then, French Jews judged the political climate dangerous to any initiative except the nonactivity long urged by consistorial circles.

The mood of frustration shared by French Jewry led to expressions of disillusion with the non-Jewish world and with Jewish leadership on the part of several segments of French Jewish opinion.[166] While the Paris Consistory used the opportunity of a protest statement against the *Krystalnacht* in Germany in order to express its gratitude to France,[167] the young editors of *Samedi* angrily accused the French government of being the only democratic government to have remained silent, perhaps, it intimated, at the request of certain French Jewish circles.[168] In response to the Munich pact, they wondered whether peace had been saved ultimately at the expense of the Jews.[169] Looking inward, the young native Jewish contributors to the new paper *Affirmation* called for cultural revival and self-defense on an international basis and urged fellow Jews to "count only on ourselves."[170] Such a statement was not a rejection of outside aid but a chastened realization that that aid might not be forthcoming. Ever the Young Turk, Wladimir Rabinovich declared that the anti-Semitism unleashed by the Munich crisis proved that there was no solution to the Jewish problem other than Zionism.[171]

While spurned by the Jewish communists, the new pessimism within the immigrant community made its appearance in the pages of *Parizer haynt*. A. Kremer described the despair evoked by the spread of "the anti-Semitic poison" in France, and Israël Jefroykin voiced his uncertainty as to whether French liberalism would prevail.[172] Nathan Frank added that the traditional panacea of native French Jewry—assimilation—was "a sinking ship in the middle of the sea."[173]

Both *Samedi* and *Affirmation*, the periodicals of the younger generation, also lamented the absence of the heroic Jewish leadership which the times demanded.[174] Julien Weill's *Matin* interview, in particular, provoked angry editorials and an open letter of protest from the Coordinating Committee of Jewish Youth of Strasbourg. Speaking for 600 immigrant and native youth, the latter group expressed its profound disappointment with leaders who transformed inaction and silence into doctrine. Jewish youth, it declared, was convinced that one's dignity as a Frenchman could not be bought at the expense of one's dignity as a Jew.[175]

Although appeals for unity were issued on all sides, the tenor of the Jewish responses to the political situation of 1938–1939 remained fragmented and essentially passive. The quietism and superpatriotism of the consistorial circles had proven morally bankrupt and had been publicly challenged. But the activism of immigrant Jews and of the younger generation of French Jewry, though in opposition to consistorial circles, had also proven largely ineffective, limited as it was to verbal pyrotechnics.

Only the beginning of World War II released French Jews from the paralysis of the politics of the 1930s. Immigrant and native Jews alike welcomed the opportunity to provide real proof once more of their patriotism in a combined defense of Jewish and French interests.[176] Even the *Naye presse* broke with the policy of the French Communist Party and, after some hesitation, expressed wholehearted support for the war against Hitler and called upon immigrant Jews to volunteer for military service.[177] With the fall of France in June 1940 and the introduction of anti-Jewish measures by the German occupation in the North and the Vichy regime in the South, French Jews, both native and immigrant, were to face a test for which their prior experience had not prepared them. Out of defeat a new French Jewry was to emerge.

Conclusion

The social, cultural, and ideological changes which occurred within the pre-war French Jewish community raise fundamental questions about the limits of Jewish identity in France. The ideology of emancipation, which had shaped the institutional, political, and cultural expression of nineteenth-century French Jewry, was challenged by a broader conception of Jewish identity, which included the ethnic and cultural elements formerly discarded as the price of emancipation. Fostered by the folk culture imported from Eastern Europe, by the dissemination of Zionist ideas, and by the impact of anti-Semitism, this new concept of Jewish identity took into account that many French Jews retained a strong sense of Jewishness despite their lack of religious belief. A multidimensional definition of Jewish identity thus appealed especially to those young French Jews for whom religious observances were inadequate for the expression of their Jewishness. It also appealed to Jewish intellectuals seeking new sources of inspiration and new forms for creativity. While philanthropic and political concern for Jews of other lands could be expressed according to the ideology of emancipation only in terms of *noblesse oblige* toward less fortunate coreligionists, the new shape of Jewish identity legitimized international ties of solidarity with foreign Jews as natural empathy with brethren.

The challenge to the ideology of emancipation was a minority phenomenon among native French Jewry, and perhaps a temporary phenomenon even within the immigrant Jewish community. However, it is significant for the understanding of French Jewry, for it pointed the way to possible new forms of creative Jewish life in France and underscored the impact of Eastern European Jewish immigration upon Western Jewry. It also raises questions about the nature of the French polity. By offering a new perspective, the study of the sociopolitical evolution of a minority group and its self-perception reveals as much about the larger society with which it interacts as it does about the smaller group's internal developments.

The ethnic and cultural efflorescence of French Jewry, which many observers described with some surprise as a Jewish renaissance, came into conflict not only with the ideology which had prevailed among late-nineteenth-century French Jewry but also with social and political norms which prevailed in France itself. The rejection of a purely religious definition of Jewish identity implied the acceptance by French society of some type of cultural pluralism. There was no indication, however, that any segment of French society was moving toward the toleration of cultural pluralism, which had been rejected by that generating force of Jewish emancipation, the French Enlightenment. In fact, the French Right was becoming increasingly xenophobic and saw even the religiously defined Jew as hopelessly alien. So pervasive was this view that between the Dreyfus Affair and the downfall of the Third Republic a number of politically conservative Jews converted with great fanfare to Catholicism, convinced that only as Catholics could they be truly and completely French. Thus, the new trends within French Jewry had to contend with the overwhelming assimilatory force of French cultural hegemony, especially in the absence of pluralism as a cultural norm.

Even the United States, which boasted of the diversity of its population and advertised itself as a nation of immigrants, stressed the ideal of the melting pot rather than true cultural pluralism. And France was not the United States. While accepting thousands of immigrants as a necessity, France did not glory in the diverse provenance of its inhabitants and demanded of its foreign-born population the surrender of its customs to the all-embracing Gallic culture. In adopting the ideology of emancipation and making it their own, native French Jews thus correctly perceived and themselves absorbed the dominant national sentiment in France. Because they believed in the ideology of emancipation and asserted that its congruence with French social and political axioms ultimately benefited Jewish interests, native French Jews fiercely resisted the challenge of new forms of Jewish identity and of political action. They felt that they alone of the Jews resident in France understood the French situation.

Excepting the Jewish Left, which evinced little concern about Jewish communal survival in France, young Jewish leaders of both native and immigrant origin appear in the years before World War II to have abandoned the ideology of emancipation. Instead, they moved in the direction of accommodating an ethno-cultural Jewish identity with the reality of French social and political norms. Through their contact with the folk culture of Eastern European Jews and with popularized Zionist ideas, they became aware in the 1930s that assimilation had entailed for French Jewry the abnegation of a large part of Jewish culture. However, they did not wholly reject assimilation. Rather, they sought to redefine it and to correct what they perceived as an imbalance in the education of young French Jews. They hoped thereby to move hesitantly toward a tenuous biculturalism, adding to French Jews' dominant French culture an acquaintance with Jewish history and literature, folk songs and dances, and modern Hebrew. In one respect, their break with the dominant ideology of French Jewry was not a radical one. Continuing the traditional claim that there was no conflict between French and Jewish interests and that French-Jewish symbiosis was possible and mutually beneficial, the younger generation of French Jewish leaders asserted that their own expanded definition of Jewishness in no way impeded their love of and loyalty to France.

However, the outspoken leaders of the younger generation were unwilling to deny—as they felt consistorial circles tended ever more frequently to do—the existence of specifically Jewish political interests. Rather, they assumed responsibility for defining and defending Jewish interests, even in the face of both public apathy and antipathy. The challenges of the 1930s revealed to these young French Jews the bankruptcy and irrelevancy for their own time of the ideology of emancipation, with its strictly religious definition of Judaism. In their eyes the discredited ideology was responsible for the abject political quietism which characterized the native French Jewish establishment. The ideology of emancipation had proved functional for French Jewry in the nineteenth century, when a triumphant liberalism could be relied upon as a defender of the equality of French Jewry. However, the erosion of liberal forces in the last years of the

Third Republic left a Jewish community, which cautiously defined itself as "politically neutral," vulnerable to right-wing elements. For the forces of the Right had always seen as a fiction the elimination by French Jews of their ethnic particularity or the description of that particularity as but another French provincial tradition.

The social, political, and ideological ferment of the years between the Dreyfus Affair and World War II belie the illusion, often fostered by both Eastern European and Zionist observers, that Western European Jewry simply stagnated after achieving its emancipation. French Jewry gives evidence of change, diversity, and vigorous attempts to find appropriate socio-cultural and political forms of self-expression within the limits established by the conditions of the declining Third Republic. Its tragedy lies more in the nature of those limits than in its political blindness. For none of the different political courses of action proposed by various segments of French Jewry could mitigate the vulnerability of the Jewish community.

The new trends discerned in French Jewry in the first four decades of the twentieth century were cut short by the Holocaust, which claimed 30 percent of the prewar community. Among its victims were large numbers of the emerging leadership of the younger generation. In particular, because the Vichy regime was willing to sacrifice noncitizens first, the community of Eastern European immigrants and their offspring was decimated; the ideologies generated and fed by the immigrant population withered. While the acculturation of the immigrant community would have progressively reduced the appeal of movements rooted in Eastern European rather than French soil, the attempts to adapt immigrant culture to the French environment were denied the test of time.

Yet the meeting of immigrant and French Jews in the years between Dreyfus and Vichy was not without long-term consequences. The experience of that confrontation prepared French Jewry to integrate into its midst, with far more generosity than it had shown to earlier immigrants, the 300,000 North African Jews, who were to make France's Jewish community in the 1960s and 1970s the largest in Western Europe.

Appendixes

Appendix A

Professions of 190 fathers of immigrant children enrolled in Jewish primary schools, 1907–1909.

Artisans	*Number*	*Percent*
Tailors	57	30.0%
Shoemakers	24	12.6
Capmakers	13	6.8
Leather workers	6	3.2
Tinkers and locksmiths	4	2.1
Mechanics	3	1.6
Miscellaneous (carpenters, butchers, printers, bakers, painters)	14	7.4
	121	63.7%

Commerce		
Peddlers	15	7.9%
Shopkeepers	14	7.4
Clerks, employees	9	4.7
Second-hand dealers	3	1.6
Grocers	3	1.6
Jewelers	4	2.1
Miscellaneous (wholesalers, travel agents, commercial representatives)	4	2.1
	52	27.4%

Liberal Professions		
Teachers, librarians, cantors, pharmacists	4	2.1%

Miscellaneous		
Sculptors, acrobats, concierges, laundry workers, day laborers, chauffeurs, bus drivers, waiters, movers	13	6.8%
	190	100.0%

Appendix B

Excerpts from original and final versions of the "Appel des Israélites Français aux Israélites des Pays Neutres," 1915

ORIGINAL DRAFT

Rappelez-vous ce qu'a couté au Judaïsme l'année 1870. Aux doctrines d'émancipation et de fraternité que la Révolution Française avait propagées, l'Allemagne victorieuse prétendit substituer une doctrine de haine et de brutalité; ses Universités élaborèrent, au nom d'une science frelatée, une théorie des races qui aboutit à l'antisémitisme: l'Allemand, seul héritier authentique du sang aryen, devait à toute force en preserver la pureté; le Juif etait l'intrus séculaire qu'il fallait exclure à tout prix. De son foyer natal l'antisémitisme s'élança sur le monde: à l'Est, où il rencontrait une bureaucratie impregnée de l'esprit germanique, il réussit d'abord à s'implanter; mais l'émancipation de nos frères de Russie, victimes dans le passé d'une bureaucratie impregnée d'esprit germanique, est liée à la victoire des grandes puissances libérales d'Occident, unies à la Russie pour la défense du droit. . . .

ACIP, B 100 (1915)

FINAL VERSION

Rappelez-vous ce qu'a couté au judaïsme l'année 1870. Aux doctrines d'émancipation et de fraternité que la Révolution française avait propagées, l'Allemagne victorieuse prétendit substituer une doctrine de haine et de brutalité; ses universités élaborèrent, au nom d'une science frelatée, une théorie des races qui aboutit à l'antisémitisme; l'Allemand, seul heritier authentique du sang aryen, devait à toute force en préserver la pureté; le juif était l'intrus séculaire qu'il fallait exclure à tout prix. De son foyer natal, l'antisémitisme s'élança sur le monde: a l'ouest, il succomba; à l'est, il réussit d'abord à s'implanter, mais déjà des symptomes rassurants font entrevoir des temps nouveaux; la victoire des grandes puissances libérales d'Occident, unies à la Russie pour la défense du droit, ne pourra manquer d'achever l'émancipation de nos frères de Russie. . . .

L'Univers israélite,
October 8, 1915, p. 116.

Appendix C

Fund raising letter of Comité Français d'Information et d'Action auprès des Juifs des Pays Neutres, January 1916

Monsieur,

Le Comité qui vient des se constituer sous le titre ci-dessus se propose de lutter contre la propagande allemande auprès des juifs des pays neutres. L'Allemagne a créé, dès le début de la guerre, une vaste et solide organisation destinée à agir sur les juifs neutres. Nous avons pu constater les résultats de cette savante préparation. En Suisse, en Hollande, en Scandinavie, et surtout aux Etats-Unis, des nouvelles tendancieuses ont éveillé et entretenu parmi les israélites des préventions et des malveillances. Nous avons le devoir de combattre ces menées. Notre réponse est facile. Nous n'avous qu'à rappeler ce que les juifs doivent à la France, qui a été l'initiatrice de l'émancipation des israélites dans le monde entier, tandis que l'Allemagne a le mérite d'avoir créé l'anti-sémitisme à prétentions scientifiques.

Notre action sera diverse comme celle de nos adversaires: nous aurons recours surtout à la presse quotidienne; des brochures courtes et claires appuieront nos efforts; nous grouperons toutes les bonnes volontés et toutes les sympathies pour faire connaître la vérité et pour dementir les erreurs et les mensonges répandus sur notre cause.

Notre oeuvre n'a rien de confessionel, elle ne vise qu'à servir l'intérêt national. Nous adressons à tous les Français, sans distinction de confession ou d'opinion, pour assurer à notre activité les ressources matérielles nécessaires. Seuls de puissants moyens peuvent nous permettre d'obtenir des résultats rapides et efficaces. Nous comptons sur votre coutumière générosité pour le succès de notre entreprise.

Veuillez agréer, Monsieur, l'assurance de notre haute considération.

Le trésorier   Le président

AIU, France I D 3

Appendix D

Le Comité Ouvrier Juif pour aider les Juifs éprouvés de la guerre 15 Rue Ferdinand Duval, Paris IV me.

Au Congrès des Syndicats du département de la Seine.

Camarades,

Le comité sus-mentionné dont l'action quotidienne a pour but le groupement des éléments ouvriers juifs de Paris autour de l'oeuvre d' assistance et de solidarité vers les Juifs des pays éprouvés par la guerre, s'est constitué en Octobre 1915. Y participent la plupart des organisations politiques, professionelles et mutuelles des ouvriers juifs de Paris, tels que le "Bound" (organisation socialiste des ouvriers juifs de Russie et de Pologne), l'organisation des ouvriers juifs socialistes-territorialistes, le syndicat des ouvriers casquettiers, la société ouvrière de mutualité, etc.

Vous n'ignorez certes pas la situation dans laquelle se trouvent les Juifs dans quelques-uns des pays belligérants, et tout particulièrement celle des Juifs de Russie. Durant des 21 mois de guerre, la population juive de Russie pâtit sous un coup permanent de "pogromes" qui continuent à sévir. Les représentants du régime de corruption, d'oppression et de (. . .) qui ont (. . .) la Russie jusqu'à l'abîme, ont considéré toujours les 6 millions de Juifs de Russie comme gage de leur propre existence. Cette population, privée des droits humains les plus élémentaires, a été toujours le bouc émissaire, sur laquelle le gouvernement criminel faisait retomber ses propres fautes et l'accusait de tous le malheurs qui arrivaient sur les peuples de Russie.

Pendant toute la période, décennale de la contrerévolution, le gouvernement reactionnaire n'a cessé de créer des nouvelles restrictions, de répandre des calomnies abjectes, dont le fameux procès Beylis a été l'expression rententissante. Actuellement, pendant la guerre, toute la population juive a été rendue responsable de tous les désastres militaires, de toutes les trahisons des Miassoiedoff, des Grigorioff, des Soukhomlineff, des toutes les souffrances qu'épreuvent, grace à l'incapacité administrative, tous les peuples de Russie.

Et tout cela persiste, malgré que ce peuple est représenté sur les champs de bataille de Russie par un demi-million de ses enfants, malgré la situation tragique de cette population qui, forcée par la fameuse loi de la zône de séjour d'habiter principalement les régions limitrophes de Russie, a été la première victime de cette guerre et a été ruinée, chassée et exterminée presque complètement.

Un vaste mouvement d'assistance et de solidarité en faveur de ces éprouvés s'est formé parmi les Juifs et les autres peuples, tant de Russie que d'autres pays, tout particulièrement dans les Etats-Unis d'Amérique dont le président M. Wilson a organisé récemment une journée pour les éprouvés juifs, qui, par son grand succès matériel, a démontré les sympathies unanimes de la nation américaine vers ce peuple martyr.

Mais il peut constater que toute oeuvre philanthropique perd son efficacité là ou la situation sinistre n'est due tant aux effets directs de la guerre elle-même qu'aux persécutions et cruautés d'un regime politique arbitraire. C'est pourquoi les ouvriers juifs de Russie même et de ceux des autres pays, considèrent ce mouvement de solidarité vers ses frères éprouvés non comme un simple acte de philanthropie, mais comme un geste de protestation et de lutte contre ce regime abject auquel on doit la plupart de ces terribles souffrances.

Ils considèrent que l'affranchissement du peuple juif ne peut être conquis que par une lutte commune avec les démocraties des nations parmi lesquelles ils demeurent, et croient fermément que dans cette lutte ils peuvent compter sur l'appui du prolétariat international. Ils croient que c'est surtout le devoir de la classe ouvrière des pays alliés à la Russie d'élever leur voix contre la mise hors la loi d'un peuple de 6 millions d'âmes. Et en effet, les élus de la classe ouvrière de Russie ne laissent passer à la Douma aucune occasion pour flétrir le gouvernement coupable de menées antisémitiques. Le prolétariat des Etats-Unis, par la voix de son Parti Socialiste et sa Fédération de Travail, a, lui aussi, exprimé ses sympathies à la lutte des ouvriers juifs pour l'affranchissement de tout le peuple juif de Russie.

Les ouvriers anglais, dans leur récent congrès de Bristol, n'ont pas manqué aussi de protester contre ces persécutions.

Nous voulons espérer que les organisations ouvrières de France feront elles aussi l'acte de solidarité internationale vers ce peuple martyr mis littéralement hors la loi.

Nous considérons comme notre devoir de vous présenter ce bref exposé et nous espérons que vous vous prononcerez d'une voix à votre congrès d'une façon equitable et dictée par votre conscience prolétarienne.

Le Comité

Paris, Mai 1916.

Archives Nationales F⁷ 13.943

Appendix E

Proposed Declaration on Zionism by Central Consistory (1919)

Le Consistoire Central des Israélites de France, au moment ou les revendications dites "sionistes" sont portées devant la Conférence de la Paix, croit devoir faire la déclaration suivante:

Les Israélites français se sont toujours intéressés au sort de leurs coreligionnaires dans les pays ou la condition de ceux-ci n'a pas encore été réglée selon les exigences de l'humanité et de la justice. Leur voeu le plus cher, c'est que le bienfait de l'émanicpation que la France a été la première à accorder aux Juifs en 1791 soit assurée de façon nonseulement théorique, mais effective et définitive à tous les groupes de population juive que subissent encore dans le monde un régime d'exception incompatible avec l'idéal proclamé par toutes les Puissances de l'Entente et par les promoteurs de la future Ligue des Nations.

Mais, considérant qu'une forte tendance entraîne un grand nombre de Juifs, principalement des régions de l'Europe orientale ou ils vivent en agglomérations compactes, à essayer de constituer en Palestine, antique patrie d'Israël, autour d'un noyau de colonies agricoles déjà prospères, un grand foyer de vie juive ou la religion, la langue et la culture hébraïque pourraient se développer sans entraves, et un lieu d'asile pour ceux qui auraient à souffrir encore des préjugés de race et de religion et des explosions du fanatisme;

Considérant, en outre, que ces aspirations, qui ne doivent en aucune manière porter atteinte aux droits des Juifs indissolublement attachés à leurs patries respectives et les droits des populations palestiniennes non-juives ont rencontré la faveur et la sympathie des gouvernements des grandes puissances et en particulier de la France;

Se réjouiront des effets qui seront tentés en vue du développement economique, culturel et religieux du foyer juif déjà existant en Palestine—grace à l'action d'organisations et d'Israélites français—sous la tutelle politique et avec l'appui de la Ligue des Nations;

Ils estiment toutefois que c'est un devoir d'humanité de prévenir leurs coreligionnaires de l'Europe orientale impatients d'émigrer en Palestine que les conditions economiques et sociales de ce pays ne permettront de longtemps encore qu'à quelques milliers de nouveaux venus de s'y établir;

Ils ajoutent qu'ils seront heureux d'offrir leur concours pour que l'ex-

périence réussisse dans l'intérêt des victimes des persécutions et pour le
développement religieux du Judaïsme.

Mais ils se croient tenus de déclarer que, si comme certains le prétendent,
il s'agit de la constitution d'un état juif, ils ne peuvent s'associer à des revendications méconnaissant le cours même de l'histoire qui tend à éliminer la
conception d'etats fondés sur la religion—conception contre laquelle le
Judaïsme éclairé n'a cessé de protester depuis plus d'un siècle—et qui aura
pour seul effet assuré de désigner à la suspicion de leurs concitoyens les
millions de Juifs de l'Europe orientale qui resteront dans leur pays d'origine.

AIU France II D 6 bis

Notes

1. The Legacy

1. Hannah Arendt was among the most vociferous critics of French Jewry. See, in particular, her *The Origins of Totalitarianism*, pp. 117–18. She has been followed by such historians of French Jewry as Michael Marrus, in *The Politics of Assimilation*. David Weinberg, *A Community in Crisis: Paris Jewry in the 1930s*, while critical, is less judgmental. Contemporary observers, like Léon Blum, also took French Jewry to task. See his *Souvenirs sur l'Affaire* (Paris, 1937), p. 97.

2. For a recent major study of French Jewry in the eighteenth century, see Arthur Hertzberg, *The French Enlightenment and the Jews*. Earlier studies of French Jewry during the Revolution include Baruch Hagani, *L'émancipation des juifs*; Léon Kahn, *Les juifs de Paris pendant la révolution*; Eugène Sraer, *Les juifs en France et l'égalité des droits civiques*; Boruch Szyster, *La révolution française et les juifs*. A useful collection of articles on French Jewry in this period is Zosa Szajkowski's *Jews and the French Revolutions of 1789, 1830, and 1848*. Finally, the primary sources concerning the emancipation of the Jews have been collected in *La révolution française et l'émancipation des juifs*, 8 vols. Of the estimated 40,000 Jews in France on the eve of the Revolution, some 25,000 were Ashkenazim who lived in the provinces of Alsace-Lorraine. Michel Roblin, *Les Juifs de Paris: Démographie-Economie-Culture*, pp. 35–41; Hertzberg, pp. 321–22. There was a small community of about 500 Jews in Paris, composed of Portuguese Sephardim, Jews of Avignon, and immigrants from Alsace-Lorraine. Roblin, pp. 42–48; Kahn, p. 10. The rest of the Jews in France were divided between the Jews of the Papal Territories and the Portuguese Jews of Bordeaux and Bayonne, who had come to France as Marranos beginning in the mid-sixteenth century. Roblin, pp. 36–37; Hertzberg, pp. 15–28.

3. See, in particular, Salo Baron, "Ghetto and Emancipation," pp. 515–26 and "Newer Approaches to Jewish Emancipation," pp. 56–81. See also Selma Stern-Taübler, "The Jew in Transition from Ghetto to Emancipation," pp. 102–19.

4. For an analysis of French opinion in the years 1789–91, see Hertzberg, *French Enlightenment*, pp. 350–68 and *La révolution française et l'émancipation des juifs*, vols. 6 and 8.

5. The former attitude characterizes the writing of virtually all proponents of emancipation, including Adolphe Thiéry, Honoré Mirabeau, Clermont-Tonnerre and the Jews Zalkind-Hourwitz and Isaiah Berr Bing. See Hertzberg, *French Enlightenment*, 328–38, 360–61 and *La révolution française et l'émancipation des juifs*, vols. 1, 2, 4, 7, and 8. The Abbé Grégoire was the most prominent of the French proponents of emancipation who hoped for the ultimate conversion of the Jews. See Hertzberg, pp. 264–67; 335–38 and *La révolution française et l'émancipation des juifs*, vol. 3. In his influential tract *Über die bürgerliche Verbesserung der Juden*, 2 vols. (Berlin & Stettin, 1783), Christian Dohm had also articulated hopes for the conversion of the Jews and had introduced the term amelioration into the vocabulary

of Jewish emancipation. See Ismar Schorsch, *Jewish Reactions to German Anti-Semitism, 1870–1914*, pp. 1–3.

6. Hertzberg, *French Enlightenment*, p. 334; Adolphe Thiéry, *Dissertation sur cette question: est-il des moyens de rendre les juifs plus heureux et plus utiles en France* (Paris, 1788). Acculturated Jews who had been educated in the spirit of the Englightenment shared similar views. See Michel Berr, *Appel à la justice des nations et des rois*, p. 40.

7. Thiéry, *Dissertation*, p. 2.

8. National Assembly, December 23, 1789 in *Réimpression de l'Ancien Moniteur (Gazette Nationale ou le Moniteur Universel)* (Paris, 1859), 2:456.

9. For a comprehensive account of Napoleon and the Jews, see Robert Anchel, *Napoléon et les juifs* and Baruch Mevorach, *Napoleon utekufato* [Napoleon and his Era] (Jerusalem, 1968).

10. Diogène Tama, *Transactions of the Paris Sanhedrim*, p. 181.

11. *Ibid.*, pp. 194–96. See, in particular, Jewish responses as to the role of the rabbi in the modern period. For an analysis of the Napoleonic Sanhedrin, see Mevorach, *Napoleon*, pp. 88–101.

12. "The love of the country is in the heart of Jews a sentiment so natural, so powerful, so consonant to their religious opinions, that a French Jew considers himself, in England as among strangers, although he may be among Jews. . . ." *Ibid.*, p. 182.

13. See Anchel, *Napoleon et les juifs*, pp. 285–335 and Achille-Edmond Halphen, *Receuil des lois, décrets, ordonnances, avis du Conseil d'Etat, arrêtés, et règlements concernant les israélites depuis la révolution de 1789* (Paris, 1851), pp. 44–48.

14. For an analysis and the provisions of the Law for the Organization of Cults of December 10, 1806, see Phyllis Albert, "Le rôle des consistoires israélites vers le milieu du xixe siècle," pp. 232–33; Halphen, *Receuil*, pp. 37–44; and Tama, *Transactions*, pp. 285–92. Albert summarized the functions of the consistories as defined in the legislation as promoting the regeneration of the Jews, administering the Jewish communities, and exercising a police role (p. 232). Paradoxically, the establishment of the consistorial system and the passage of discriminatory legislation served, in reality, to perpetuate Jewish group distinctiveness rather than foster assimilation.

15. Uriel Tal, *Christians and Jews in Germany*, pp. 18–19 and Phyllis Cohen Albert, "Ethnicity and Jewish Solidarity in Nineteenth Century France," In the *Alexander Altmann Festschrift*, 1977.

16. On the triumph of the religious definition of French Jewry, see Zosa Szajkowski, "Secular vs. Religious Jewish Life in France," pp. 107–27 and Patrick Girard, *Les Juifs de France de 1789 à 1860*, pp. 133–48.

17. For the distinctions between behavioral and structural assimilation, see Milton Gordon, *Assimilation in American Life*, pp. 65–73.

18. Théodore Reinach, *Histoire des israélites depuis la ruine de leur indépendance nationale jusqu'à nos jours*, p. 306. Cited in Marrus, *Politics of Assimilation*, p. 94. Marrus describes the evolution of a Franco-Jewish ideology which stressed the affinity of Judaism and French culture and the importance of France within the totality of modern Jewish history (pp. 88–92, 100–116). However, he does not emphasize the impact of the emancipation experience upon the development of that ideology.

19. Sermon by Felix Meyer, rabbi at Valenciennes, in Benjamin Mossé, ed., *La Révolution française et le rabbinat français*, p. 175.

20. For a discussion of this factor in the attitude of liberal Germans to the Jewish question in the nineteenth century, see Tal, *Christians and Jews*, pp. 49–58.

21. On the decision of the state to assume responsibility for rabbinical salaries, see Jules Bauer, *L'Ecole Rabbinique de France, 1830–1930* (Paris, n.d.). For the abolition of the Jewish oath, see Halphen, *Receuil*, pp. 329–32.

22. For the limited defense activities of the consistories, see Albert, "Ethnicity . . ." For the best study of German Jewish defense organizations, see Schorsch, *Jewish Reactions*.

23. For a history of the Alliance, see André Chouraqui, *Cent ans d'histoire: L'Alliance Israélite Universelle et la renaissance juive contemporaine 1860–1960*. For the Alliance's reluctance to defend Jewish rights in France, see pp. 140–41 and Marrus, *Politics of Assimilation*, pp. 238–39. See also Joan Gardner Roland, *The Alliance Israélite Universelle and French Foreign Policy in North Africa, 1860–1918* (Columbia University diss., 1965).

24. Jules Isaac's autobiography, for example, relates his happy relationship with the children of the local prefect and his close friendships with non-Jewish students at his *lycée* during the 1880s and 1890s. See Jules Isaac, *Expériences de ma vie*, 1:20, 43, 64–66. Such experiences were not uncommon. Georges Wormser informed me that anti-Semitism was neither visceral nor violent except in Algeria and among the followers of Drumont. He recalled fist fights in his *lycée* during the Dreyfus Affair, "but more in fun than in passion. My 'anti-Semitic' comrades of those days later became friends of mine." My interview, October 27, 1972. Of course, many German Jews could supply similar testimony. Perception and objective reality do not necessarily coincide.

25. Marrus, *Politics of Assimilation*, pp. 99, 125, 147.

26. Mossé, *La Révolution française*, p. 12.

27. The French Jewish community included large numbers of artisans, mostly foreign-born, and small tradesman who lived on the verge of poverty. An examination of funeral statistics of the Consistory of Paris in the decade before World War I reveals, for example, that 46 percent of all funerals were without charge. In this period, however, most of the poor were immigrants. ACIP, *Exercice 1913*, pp. 43–44. For a study of the extent of Jewish poverty in France in the nineteenth century, see Zosa Szajkowski, *Poverty and Social Welfare among French Jews (1800–1880)*.

28. Marrus, *Politics of Assimilation*, pp. 126–37.

29. For the political ideology of the French Right, see René Rémond,*La droite en France: De 1815 à nos jours* and J. S. McLelland, ed., *The French Right from de Maistre to Maurras*.

30. For an analysis of French political life during the Third Republic, see Stanley Hoffmann, "Paradoxes of the French Political Community," pp. 1–18.

31. The Church was one of those forces which sought to destroy the Republic and the social system which was the product of the Revolution. See Adrien Dansette, *Religious History of Modern France*, 2:32–33. For the similar situation of Jews in Germany during the Kulturkampf, see Tal, *Christians and Jews*, pp. 93–107.

32. "Le budget du culte à la chambre," *Archives israélites*, March 19, 1885, p. 91.

33. Marrus, *Politics of Assimilation*, pp. 240–42. For a detailed analysis of Jewish responses to the Dreyfus Affair, see pp. 196–242. On the committee, see Marrus, "Le Comité de Défence contre l'antisemitisme," *Michael*, 4 (Tel-Aviv, 1976):163–75.

34. Mossé, *La Révolution française*, pp. 58–59.

35. Eugen Weber, *The Nationalist Revival in France, 1905–1914*, p. 7.

36. Among them Marcel Proust, Paul Claudel, Jacques Lacretelle, Georges Duhamel, Montherlant, Georges Bernanos, Romain Rolland, Anatole France, Robert Martin du Gard, Emile Zola, Charles Péguy, and a score of minor writers. In this discussion, in addition to my own reading I am drawing upon the work of Denise Goitein, *Jewish Themes in Selected French Works between the Two World Wars* (Columbia Univ. Dissertation, 1967); Charles Lehrmann, *The Jewish Element in French Literature*, trans. by George Klin (Rutherford, N.J.: Fairleigh Dickinson University Press, 1971); Jacques Petit, *Bernanos, Bloy, Claudel, Péguy: quatre écrivains catholiques face à Israël* (Paris, 1972); Earle Stanley Randall, *The Jewish Character in the French Novel, 1870–1914* (Menasha, Wisc., 1941); Pierre Pierrard, *Juifs et catholiques français* (Paris, 1970).

37. Marcel Proust, *A la Recherche du Temps Perdu*, (Paris, 1914–1922), 1:237.

38. Cited in Goitein, *Jewish Themes*, pp. 24–25. For similar attitudes on the part of other French writers, see Petit, *Bernanos, Bloy . . .* p. 56; Randall, *Jewish Character*, p. 203.

39. Petit, *ibid. passim*.

40. Lehrmann, *Jewish Element*, p. 207; Randall, *Jewish Character*, p. 205.

41. Petit, *Bernanos, Bloy . . .* pp. 100–101. Cf. also Maurice Barrès, *The Uprooted*, 2: pp. 70–71, cited in Robert Soucy, *Fascism in France: The Case of Maurice Barrès*, pp. 132–33.

42. Edouard Drumont, *La France juive*, 2:49.

43. Pierre Sorlin, *La Croix et les juifs, passim* and Drumont, *France juive* 1:30.

44. Soucy, *Fascism in France*, p. 2.

45. Maurice Barrès, *Scènes et doctrines du nationalisme*, 1:67–68.

46. Cf. his reference to Dreyfus, *Scènes . . .* , 1:161.

47. "Le programme de Nancy," in *Scènes*, 2:161.

48. Cited in Henri Clouard, *La Cocarde*, p. 30.

49. *La Cocarde*, Dec. 28, 1894, cited in William Buthman, *The Rise of Integral Nationalism in France*, p. 218.

50. For a description of the status of metics in ancient Athens, see Buthman, *ibid.*, pp. 219–20, and Michael Curtis, *Three against the Third Republic*, pp. 206–7, 217.

51. Barrès, *Scènes*, 2:234.

52. *Le Figaro*, July 31, 1893, p. 1. Cited in Soucy, *Fascism in France*, p. 235.

53. Barrès, *Scènes*, 2:161.

54. For a discussion of Fourier's and Proudhon's anti-Semitism, see Edmond Silberner, *Western Socialism and the Jewish Question*, pp. 13–28 and 67–77.

55. George Lichtheim, "Socialism and the Jews," p. 316.

56. Victor M. Glasberg, "Intent and Consequences: The 'Jewish Question' in the French Socialist Movement of the Late 19th Century," pp. 61–71.

57. Cited in Harvey Goldberg, "Jean Jaurès and the Jewish Question: The Evolution of a Position," *Jewish Social Studies*, 20, no. 2 (April 1958):1.

58. *Ibid.*

59. Cf. Gustave Rouanet's reflections on socialist misreading of Drumont, cited in Glasberg, "Intent and Consequences," p. 63 and Robert Byrnes, *Antisemitism in Modern France*.

60. Goldberg, "Jean Jaurès," p. 74.

61. John M. Sherwood, *Georges Mandel and the Third Republic*, p. 11.

62. Barrès, *Scènes*, 2:161, 182–83. See also Henri Delassus, *La question juive*.

63. Romain Rolland, *Jean Christophe*, Book II, pp. 385–86.

64. Drumont, 1:376–77, 408.

65. *The Uprooted*, 2:71, cited in Soucy, *Fascism in France*, p. 133.

66. Charles Maurras, *Romanticism and Revolution* (Paris, 1922), cited in J. S. McClelland, ed., *The French Right from de Maistre to Maurras*, p. 241.

67. Goitein, *Jewish Themes*, p. 69.

68. Rolland, *Jean Christophe*, Book III, pp. 387–88.

69. Pierrard, *Juifs et catholiques*, pp. 225–26.

70. *Notre Jeunesse* (Paris, 1910), p. 101.

71. Péguy argued that the modern world had increased both their dispersion and their anxiety and found that "les Juifs sont plus malheureux que les autres. . . . C'est pas facile d'être Juif." *Notre Jeunesse*, pp. 216–17, 221, and 209–10.

72. *Ibid.*, p. 102.

73. *Ibid.*, p. 121.

74. *Ibid.*, p. 104.

75. Rolland, *Jean Christophe*, Book II, pp. 383–85.

76. For an evaluation of *Du Mariage*, see Louise Dalby, *Leon Blum: Evolution of a Socialist*, pp. 114–15.

77. On Mandel's anticlericalism, see Sherwood, *Georges Mandel*, pp. 6–8.

78. See, for example, the reaction of the Catholic press in Sorlin, *La Croix*, pp. 82–85, 211, 217. On Sorel's attitude, see Silberner, *Western Socialism*, p. 96.

79. Peter Gay has argued, with reference to Wilhelmian Germany, that Jews were no more drawn to modernist movements and radical cultural criticism than any other group. However, he has not explained why they were perceived as standing in the forefront of modernism. See his article, "Encounter with Modernism: German Jews in German Culture, 1888–1914," pp. 23–65.

80. On Sorel's attack on the role of Jewish intellectuals, see Silberner, *Western Socialism*, p. 96; Rolland, *Jean Christophe*, Book II, p. 384.

81. For a recent analysis of Durkheim's social theory, see Dominick La Capra, *Emile Durkheim: Sociologist and Philosopher*. For a different point of view, see John Murray Cuddihy's *Ordeal of Civility* (New York, 1975), which argues that the universalist theories of Sigmund Freud and other nineteenth-century Jewish thinkers were a specifically Jewish response to the rational Protestant pattern of modernization

and hence an assault upon bourgeois society. Significantly, he pays little attention to Durkheim, who cannot be subsumed in his thesis. Gay argues that Jewish artists and intellectuals in Germany were also well integrated in the larger cultural milieu.

82. John B. Wolf, "The Elan Vital of France: A Problem in Historical Perspective," in Edward Mead Earle, ed. *Modern France*, p. 27. See also John E. Sawyer's essay, "Strains in the Social Structure of Modern France," in *ibid.*, pp. 293–312.

83. Sawyer, *"Strains,"* p. 302 and David S. Landes, "French Business and the Businessman: A Social and Cultural Analysis," in Earle, *ibid.*, pp. 334–53.

84. Agathon, *Les Jeunes gens d'aujourd'hui*, p. iv.

85. *American Jewish Yearbook*, 15:287.

86. "De l'organisation administrative du Judaïsme français," (1931), JTS, France, Box 19, 01924, No. 432; Phyllis Albert, "Le rôle des consistoires israelites. . . . ," pp. 232–33, 235–38, 241–42. For a full history of the development of the consistorial system in the nineteenth century, see Albert, *The Modernization of French Jewry: Consistory and Community in the Nineteenth Century*.

87. Albert, "Le rôle," pp. 247–49.

88. Zosa Szajkowski, "The Effect of the 1905 Separation of Church and State on the Jewish Communities in France," [Yiddish], *Davka*, 5, No. 21 (October–December 1954):386–87.

89. A rabbinical conference was held in 1856 to introduce such reforms as the use of an organ during religious services and confirmation ceremonies for boys and girls. See W. Gunther Plaut, *The Growth of Reform Judaism* (New York: World Union for Progressive Judaism, 1965), pp. 60–63. For the earlier protest of Jews in Metz, see Plaut, *The Rise of Reform Judaism* (New York: World Union for Progressive Judaism, 1963), pp. 44–47. For an overview of the abortive efforts at reform, see Patrick Girard, *Les Juifs en France de 1789 à 1860* (Paris, 1976), pp. 211–44, and Zosa Szajkowski, "The Conflicts of Orthodoxy and Reform," pp. 253–92.

90. On the minyanim, see Phyllis Albert, *Modernization of French Jewry*, pp. 197–229.

91. See Marrus, *Politics of Assimilation*, pp. 36–43 for a detailed account of the stratification of the Jewish community.

92. For a study of the growing concentration of Jews within the urban centers of Alsace and the decline in the Jewish population of Alsace because of emigration to the interior of France, see E. Schnurmann, *La population juive en Alsace*, pp. 7–10. Szajkowski notes that between 1871 and 1910, the Jewish population of Alsace-Lorraine declined by 10,329 and points to the tendency of French Jews to concentrate in larger towns. See Zosa Szajkowski, "The Growth of the Jewish Community in France," pp. 309, 314.

93. Consistory census, Archives Nationales, F^{19} 11.024. In 1872, the last French census to include religion, only 23,424 Jews lived in Paris of a total Jewish population of 49,439. Another 40,812 Jews remained in Alsace-Lorraine. Szajkowski, "Growth of Jewish Community," pp. 304, 314.

94. As one editorialist noted in *L'Univers israélite*, "Judaism is not a nationality, and when one is a good Jew, one is a good Frenchman," Ben-Ammi, *UI*, November 1, 1907, p. 204.

95. France kept no records of immigrants according to religion, but only accord-

ing to nationality. The estimate quoted in the text is that of Michel Roblin on the basis of estimates of the proportion of Jews among total immigrants to France from Eastern European countries. See Roblin, *Les Juifs de Paris*, p. 73.

96. ACIP, B 79; Minutes of the Administrative Council, March 12, 1907, AA 19; *UI*, March 22, 1907, pp. 12–13; *AI*, March 21, 1907, pp. 89–91. For further information on the Union Libérale and its reforms, see my *The Jews in Post-Dreyfus France*, ch. 2, pp. 54–59; Plaut, *Growth of Reform Judaism*, pp. 64–65; Jacob Petuchowski, *Prayerbook Reform in Europe* (New York, 1968), pp. 77–80.

97. Ben-Ammi, "Après la séparation: A Paris," *UI*, Nov. 1, 1907, pp. 199–200.

98. ACIP, B 79.

99. This consequence was noted by contemporaries. See René Drefus, "Le Bilan de la séparation des Eglises et de l'état," lecture given at the Ecole des Hautes Etudes Sociales, Paris, 1911, JTS, France, Box 20, No. 460, and "De l'organisation administrative du Judaisme français," JTS, France, Box 19, 01924, No. 432.

100. Georges Wormser, *Français Israélites*, p. 57; "Rapport sur un projet d'organisation centralisée . . . . ," JTS, Box 19 01924, No. 436.

101. Reports of Annual General Assembly of the Paris Consistory, 1907–1939, HUC and YIVO; Electoral list, Nancy, 1906, CAHJP, ZF 766; and Marseille, 1911, ZF 842.

102. *Ibid.*, and *UI*, November 11, 1910, pp. 338–39.

103. "De l'organisation administrative. . . ." JTS, France, Box 19, 01924, No. 432.

104. Roblin, *Les Juifs de Paris*, pp. 73, 183–86. Roblin relies on figures of total immigration to France and on the census of Jews in Paris, conducted in 1942 under the German occupation.

2. The Golden Age of Symbiosis

1. Joan Roland, *The Alliance Israélite Universelle and French Foreign Policy in North Africa, 1860–1918, passim*; MAE, E Levant, "Palestine, 1918–1929," 10 (May-Sept. 1918):106.

2. *AI*, July 26, 1906.

3. C.C., Minutes, July 20, 1906, HM 1070, CAHJP.

4. B.M., "La Nouvelle revision," *UI*, June 22, 1906, p. 360.

5. Eugen Weber, *Action Française*, pp. 3, 13.

6. *Ibid.*, pp. 53–55, 83, 42. For a discussion of Lazare's role in bringing the facts of the Dreyfus Affair to light, see Michael Marrus, *The Politics of Assimilation*, pp. 180–87.

7. *American Jewish Yearbook*, 12 (5671, 1910–1911):116; *UI*, Feb. 11, 1910, p. 694.

8. Spire, *Quelques Juifs et demi-juifs* (Paris, 1928), 2:156.

9. The *UI*, though, did publish a report on anti-Semitism in Germany. Aug. 27, 1909, pp. 749–53; Sept. 3, 1909, pp. 783–86. Similar conclusions about the attitude of French Jewry toward anti-Semitism in pre-World War I France were drawn by A. Alperin, "Anti-Semitic Propaganda in France on the Eve of the War" [Yid-

dish], in *Yidn in Frankraykh* 2:264–65 and Jacob Fink, *Yahaduth Zarfath* [French Jewry], p. 11.

10. *UI*, Feb. 11, 1910, p. 694.

11. Cited in Weber, p. 83.

12. C.C., Minutes of April 9, 1906; July 9, 1906; July 20, 1906; June 28, 1907; November 4, 1907; November 11, 1907, HM 1070 and 1071, CAHJP.

13. C.C., Minutes, April 9, 1906; July 9, 1906; November 11, 1907; February 5, 1908, HM 1071. A copy of the report, undated, may be found in the archives of the Jewish Theological Seminary, France, Box 20, 09124, #518.

14. C.C., Minutes, April 9, 1906.

15. JTS, France, Box 20, 01924, #518.

16. The opposition to the religious orientation of the report was led by Rothschild, C.C., Minutes, November 4, 1907.

17. *UI*, December 27, 1907, p. 459.

18. C.C., Minutes, February 5, 1908, HM 1071.

19. "Les passeports pour la Russie," *UI*, March 2, 1906, pp. 758–59; "Rapport de M. Levaillant sur certaines formalités imposées par le gouvernment russe aux Israélites français voyageant ou résidant en Russie," October 5, 1909, 19 pp., Brandeis I lc. Reprinted in *UI*, February 11, 1910, pp. 685–90 and February 18, 1910, pp. 716–20.

20. C.C., Permanent Section, Minutes, March 8, 1909; "Rapport de M. Levaillant"; Z. Szajkowski, "The European Aspect of the American-Russian Passport Question," *AJHQ*, 46, no. 1 (September 1956):95–96.

21. "Rapport," *ibid.*, p. 7; Szajkowski, *ibid.*, p. 96.

22. C.C., Permanent Section, Minutes, November 15, 1909.

23. *American Jewish Yearbook*, 12 (5671, 1910–11):115. The League of Rights of Man also protested the situation.

24. *Ibid.*, p. 116; *UI*, January 7, 1910, p. 534. *Journal officiel, Chambre des députés, Débats parlementaires*, pp. 3779–80.

25. C.C., Minutes, November 18, 1912 and December 23, 1912. The letter addressed by Raymond Poincaré, the Minister of Foreign Affairs, to the President of the League of the Rights of Man, noting the government's reasons for its inactivity on the issue, was published by *Le Temps*, October 11, 1912. Further unsuccessful efforts of the league were reported in *Le Temps*, February 8, 1914. For the Alliance's intervention, see the letter of AIU to the Ministers of Commerce and Foreign Affairs, June 13, 1916, AIU, L.239, ff. 321–26 and MAE, Guerre 1914–1918, 1198 Sionisme, May 1916–April 1917, pp. 13–16.

26. C.C., Minutes, November 18, 1912 and December 23, 1912. For American Jewish efforts on this issue, see Naomi W. Cohen, "The Abrogation of the Russo-American Treaty of 1832," pp. 3–41 and *Not Free to Desist*, pp. 54–80.

27. *UI*, March 14, 1913, p. 6; cited and commended in *Union Scolaire*, 134 (June–July 1913), p. 3.

28. M. Vexler, "M. Bergson à l'Académie," *UI*, February 20, 1914, pp. 501–6.

29. "Les mariages civils entre Israélites," *UI*, May 4, 1906, pp. 135–37; *AI*, January 17, 1907, pp. 17–19; M. Weill, vice president of the Administrative Commission of Temples, "Rapport sur la situation de la location des places," December

18, 1908, Brandeis V 3d. The study revealed that in most temples in Paris approximately 50 percent of the seats were not rented, especially in the higher-priced categories. Comments on the spread of anti-clericalism can be found in the remarks of Baron Gustave de Rothschild at the 1907 exercises of the Paris Consistory, JTS, France, Box 20, 01924, #513 and in the discussion of rabbinical reports on local communities, C.C., Minutes, March 29, 1909, HM 1071, CAHJP. Cf. Mathieu Wolff, "L'Hébreu," *UI*, February 10, 1911, pp. 682–86.

30. R. M., "Appel du Consistoire de Paris," *UI*, March 26, 1909, p. 37.

31. The constitution of the *minyan* was on the agenda of the 1907 meeting of the Association of French Rabbis. Cf. *Union du Rabbinat Français*, February 10, 1907, Brandeis I 12b. The reduction of the minyan to seven was proposed in a report of E. Sechès, who noted that "on the one hand, this number is the maximum that one can demand and obtain in the provinces . . . and on the other, it is the minimum with which to satisfy the need for an assembly which merits that name." Of the seven, he suggested that women could contribute three. "Rapport," May 24, 1907, Brandeis I 12b; JTS, France, Box 20, #589. Rabbi Joseph Lehmann introduced another proposal after 1909 to count women in the *minyan* while retaining its number at ten. JTS, France, Box 20, #589. On the other hand, Rabbi Maurice Liber rejected reforms in the *minyan* as irrelevant to the major problem: attracting people to religious services and inspiring real participation on their part. "De la restauration du culte public," April 5, 1910, 29 pp., JTS, France, Box 20, #542.

32. Association of French Rabbis, Circular, December 3, 1911, Brandeis I 12b.

33. *Ibid.*, and ACIP, January 22, 1911, BB 86.

34. Proposals submitted to the Association of French Rabbis, JTS, France, Box 20, #583; C.C., Minutes, June 21, 1909, HM 1071; R.M., "Sauvons le Judaîsme," *UI*, February 25, 1910, pp. 741–46.

35. C.C., Minutes, March 29, 1909; Maurice Liber, "De la restauration," JTS, Box 20, #542.

36. C.C., Permanent Section, Minutes, July 20, 1908. A survey of the annual reports of the Paris Consistory reveals a progressive dimunition in the number of Jewish day schools and an increase in the percentage of students of immigrant origin.

37. M. Vexler, "Notre Jeunesse," *UI*, July 18, 1913, pp. 437–41.

38. Mathieu Wolff, "Le Réveil juif et la province," *UI*, July 4, 1913, pp. 130–31.

39. It appeared from 1913 to 1939 under the direction of Rabbi Jules Bauer and enjoyed the active collaboration of Aimé Pallière, a semi-convert to Judaism.

40. The two issues, edited by Nahum Slousch, appeared in 1913 and 1914. Cf. "Le Cercle Hebraea et la Révue Hébraique," *UI*, September 26, 1913, pp. 230–32.

41. André Spire, *Poèmes Juifs* in *Versets* (Paris, 1908); cf. Paul Jamati, *André Spire* (Paris, 1962), pp. 62–71. On the Jewish themes in the early works of Jean-Richard Bloch, see Denise Goitein, *Jewish Themes in Selected French Works*, p. 195. For a contemporary review of Fleg's *Ecoute Israël*, see M. Vexler, "Ecoute Israël," *UI*, December 19, 1913, pp. 285–90. Fleg's poetry was well-received by French Jews, partly because his subjects were Biblical rather than contemporary. See Fink, *Yahadut Zarfat*, p. 37. On Henri Franck, see J. Durel, *La sagesse d'Henri Franck, poète-juif* and André Spire, *Quelques Juifs et demi-juifs*, 2:107–69.

42. Spire, *Souvenirs à bâtons rompus*, pp. 1–34.

43. André Spire, *Quelques Juifs* 1:xi; *Souvenirs à bâtons rompus*, pp. 35–36; Jamati, pp. 51–56; Ch. Lehrmann, "Du symbolisme au sionisme," *Révue des Cours et Conférences*, June 15, 1938 (Paris, 1938), pp. 465–79; Fink, p. 33. Zangwill's *Chad Gadya* was published in French in 1904 by Péguy in *Cahiers de la Quinzaine* (Sér. VI, 3ᵉ cahier).

44. Cited in Jamati, *André Spire*, p. 71.

45. Edmond Fleg, *Pourquoi je suis juif*, pp. 1–25.

46. Jean Toulat, *Juifs mes frères* (Paris, 1963), p. 64. See also Edmond Fleg, *ibid.*, pp. 30–50.

47. Invitation to first meeting of "Les Amis du Judaîsme," Brandeis, Nonconsistoire.

48. *Ibid.*, and report of first meeting, *UI*, June 6, 1913, pp. 302–5.

49. Hadamard declared at the first meeting that the society was of a nature to rally all types; therefore he himself, a Jew only because of anti-Semitism, and hence a rather lukewarm Jew, was happy to join. *Ibid.*, p. 303.

50. *UI*, February 20, 1914, p. 509.

51. *Ibid.*, p. 304.

52. Roblin, p. 109.

53. For a study of the Rothschild family, see Jean Bouvier, *Les Rothschild* (Paris, 1967).

54. Roblin, *Les Juifs de Paris*, pp. 110–17.

55. For example, André Spire's family ran a glove and shoe factory for generations. See Spire, *Souvenirs*, pp. 15–16; Jean-Richard Bloch's . . . *et compagnie* (Paris, 1917) describes the Simmel family, who leave Alsace after the defeat of 1871 to reestablish themselves and their textile factory on French territory.

56. In February,1906, a month randomly selected, the *Univers israélite* listed 9 Chevaliers de la Légion d'Honneur, 4 Officiers de la Légion d'Honneur, 19 Officiers d'Instruction Publique, 44 Officiers d'académie, 10 Chevaliers du merite agricole, one Officier du merite agricole, 2 military appointments, 2 military medals, 7 appointments of lycée instructors, and one Inspecteur d'Académie of the Académie de Paris.

57. Spire, *Souvenirs*, p. 50; Joel Colton, *Léon Blum* (New York, 1966), pp. 12–13.

58. *UI*, October 6, 1905, p. 88; *American Jewish Yearbook*, 8 (New York, 5667, 1906–1907): pp. 12–13.

59. M. Vexler, "Bergson à l'Académie," *UI*, February 20, 1914, p. 506.

60. André Spire, cited in *Chalom*, July, 1924.

61. Alain Silvera, *Daniel Halévy and His Times*, pp. 216–17.

62. René Johannet, *Péguy et ses Cahiers*, p. 157; Silvera, *ibid.*, p. 127.

63. Silvera, *ibid.*, p. 127.

64. *Ibid.*, pp. 171–72.

65. Spire, *Souvenirs*, p. 153.

66. Silvera, pp. 45–47.

67. His statement on the rootedness of native Jewry in France was well received by French Jews. See Maurice Barrès, *Les diverses familles spirituelles de la France*, p.

67. Léon Blum, *Souvenirs sur l'Affaire*, pp. 88–89; Silvera, *Daniel Halevy*, pp. 140–141; *UI*, February 23, 1917, p. 524; March 2, 1917, pp. 543–46; March 9, 1917, p. 570. Richard Cohen has informed me that French Jewish leaders used Barrès's endorsement in their appeals to the Pétain government in 1940.

68. Barrès, *ibid.*, p. 77.

69. *Le Judaïsme français et la guerre* (Paris, 1918), a collection of articles published in the *Univers israélite* during the war, stressed the fidelity of French Jews to Alsace in no fewer than seven separate articles.

70. *UI*, December 11, 1914, p. 66.

71. H. Prague, "L'Allemagne et les Israélites russes," *AI*, June 10, 1915, p. 93; *Les Juifs et la guerre*, pp. 18–32.

72. ACIP, Minutes, November 10, 1914, AA 19.

73. List of the chaplains 1916, Brandeis, I 11b; Sylvain Halff, "The Participation of the Jews of France in the Great War," *AJYB*, 21 (1920): 89–90. The regiments in which Jews predominated were in the army of the Orient, where Algerian Jews served. The decision to provide religious ministrations to German prisoners of war was taken only after it was made certain that Catholic priests and Protestant ministers were doing the same. Doubtlessly, the French rabbinate did not wish to fuel anti-Semitic contentions that French Jews were pro-German. See C.C., Rapport Moral, 1915, Brandeis I 1d.

74. C.C., Circular letter to chaplains, November 1, 1916, Brandeis I ii b.

75. Report of Grand Rabbi Alfred Lévy, November 11, 1917, Brandeis I ii b.

76. Sylvain Halff, pp. 89–90; *UI*, January 1, 1915, pp. 159–70; Barrès, *Les diverses familles*, pp. 92–93.

77. A report of the Alliance Israélite had noted the success of German propaganda among American Jews. "Rapport du 3 juin 1915," AIU, Angleterre II D 26, Politique extérieure, 1915; Cf. Chouraqui, *Cent ans d'histoire*, p. 216.

78. *UI*, March 16, 1917, p. 591; Circular of the Committee, AIU, France I D 3. Members of the Committee were Georges Leygues, S. Lévi, A. Meillet, Georges Raphael Lévy, J. Bigart, Jacques Schapiro, Victor Basch, E. Boutroux, Paul Boyer, F. Buisson, Alfred Croiset, Victor Delbos, Emile Durkheim, Fournol, Franklin-Bouillon, J. Hadamard, Israël Lévi, Lévy Bruhl, E. Lavisse, E. de Margerie, Edouart Masse, Ferdinand Meyer, E. Meyerson, Gaston Millaud, Pierre Mille, Marius Moutet, Dr. A. Netter, René Pinon, Paul Raphael, Salomon Reinach, Charles Richet, L. Rosenthal, J. H. Rosny, Eugène Sée, Albert Wahl.

79. The introduction of the word "Juif" in the title of the Committee was an unusual step. It may reflect the realization that the Jews to whom the Committee's activity was directed, particularly the Jews of the neutral U.S., did not refer to themselves as Israelites. Fund-raising letter of the French Information and Action Committee, January 1916, AIU, France I D 3.

80. Original draft, ACIP, B 100 (1915); the final version was printed in *UI*, October 8, 1915, and *AI*, September 30, 1915. See also Z. Szjakowski, ed. *Jews, Wars and Communism* (New York: Ktav, 1972), 1:49–52. For the original draft, see Appendix, p. 279.

81. Fund-raising letter, AIU, France I D 3.

82. *UI*, May 19, 1916, p. 269.
83. Extracts of letters addressed by Basch to [Marius] Moutet, 1916, AIU, France I D 3.
84. Letter from Serroy, March 8, 1916, AIU, France IV D 16.
85. *UI*, March 16, 1917, p. 591; *AI*, October 7, 1915, p. 161.
86. Judaeus, "Propagande," *UI*, November 26, 1915, pp. 288–90.
87. Letter of Jacques Hadamard to Prof. Volterra of Italy, April 3, 1916, MAE, Guerre 1914–1918, 1197 Sionisme, Oct. 1914–April 1916, p. 202.
88. Letter to French Ambassador, Washington, August 7, 1915, MAE, Guerre 1914–1918, 1197 Sionisme, pp. 83–85.
89. Letter of Jan. 12, 1916, MAE, Guerre 1914–1918, 1197 Sionisme, p. 121b.
90. Letter from Minister of Foreign Affairs to Consul General of France in N.Y., Feb. 12, 1916, MAE, Guerre 1914–1918, 1197 Sionisme, p. 140.
91. Letter from Homberg to Minister of Finances, Feb. 21, 1916, MAE, Guerre 1914–1918, 1197 Sionisme, pp. 148–49.
92. Telegram from André Tardieu, March 1, 1918, MAE, Guerre 1914–1918, Sionisme 1201, March–May 1918, p. 1.
93. "Report on the Jewish Question and Zionism," MAE, E Levant, Palestine 1918–1929, May–Sept. 1918, p. 106.
94. "Charles Péguy," *UI*, January 1, 1915, pp. 151–52.
95. *UI*, October 19, 1917, pp. 145–47. Similar sentiments were expressed in *UI*, February 23, 1917, pp. 520–21 and *AI*, December 2, 1915, pp. 194–95.
96. *UI*, July 16, 1915, p. 417; April 7, 1916, pp. 104–6. There were several articles on the *Libre Parole*; for example, *UI*, October 6, 1916, pp. 44–46.
97. *UI*, December 10, 1915, pp. 340–41. Though the *UI* did not refer to *La Croix* by name, doubtless it had it in mind. Published by the Assumptionists, it was a vigorous organ of anti-Semitism. For a history of its anti-Semitic activity through the period of the Dreyfus Affair, see Pierre Sorlin, *La Croix et Les Juifs*.
98. *AI*, October 11, 1971, p. 163.
99. The municipality of Nice wrote to Rabbi Bauer to associate itself with his protest. *UI*, April 9, 1915, pp. 73–75.
100. *UI*, July 1, 1915, pp. 358–65. The following week the *UI* repeated his arguments and protested the censorship of Hervé's articles while anti-Semitic articles were freely passed by the censors.
101. *UI*, February 18, 1916, pp. 600–601; Sylvain Halff, pp. 78–79.
102. *AI*, June 24, 1915, pp. 102–103.
103. *UI*, "Les Juifs russes de Paris," December 3, 1915, pp. 318–20. *Le Temps* noted of the vote of the Municipal Council that "rightly or wrongly it is thought that the vote was aimed at the Russian refugees and that this campaign is inspired by sentiments hostile to Jews." *AI*, December 2, 1915, pp. 194–95. Police reports also commented upon the concern which the vote evoked among immigrant Russian Jews and added that 59 immigrant men of draft age had applied for passports between November 20 and December 7. Police report, Dec. 12, 1915, Police Archives, 241.155-A-B-B1-B2.
104. Circular of the Committee, Brandeis Non-consistoire. For the decision to

sponsor a *Livre d'Or* of French and foreign Jews, see ACIP B 101 (1916) and *UI*, November 16, 1917.

105. Spire, *Les Juifs et la guerre*, pp. 42–61; Bulletins of Paris Jewish Workers' Fund to Support the Jewish War Victims, Bund Archives; Appeal of Bund, printed in *UI*, January 22, 1915, pp. 264–66, and January 29, 1915, pp. 288–90.

106. *UI*, February 19, 1915, pp. 365–66.

107. *La Renaissance Juive*, April 28, 1916, p. 1.

108. ACIP, Minutes, December 16, 1915, AA 20.

109. Members of the board of directors included Madame Gubbay and Madame Liber, Eugène Sée, and Sylvain Lévi of the Alliance Israélite Universelle, Messrs. Novochesky, Léonard Rosenthal, Landsmann, and Schapiro, Rabbis Alfred Lévy, Israël Lévi, J. H. Dreyfuss, and Emmanuel Weill, and Professors Emile Durkheim, Jacques Hadamard, and Albert Wahl, and Elie Eberlin. *UI*, February 11, 1916, pp. 571–72.

110. *UI*, November 15, 1915, pp. 220–21.

111. For the Treaty of Berlin and its subversion by the Romanian government, see Oscar Janowsky, *The Jews and Minority Rights (1898–1919)*, pp. 257, 372.

112. Spire, *Les Juifs et la guerre*, p. 133.

113. "nos préoccupations actuelles sont pour ainsi dire exclusivement concentrées sur le sort de nos coreligionnaires russes dont nous voudrions . . . assurer l'égalité des droits." Letter of AIU, September 16, 1915 to Cyrus Adler of the American Jewish Committee, AIU, Etats-Unis I C 1; Chouraqui, p. 217.

114. Letter, July 23, 1915, AIU L.238 ff. 384–387; Chouraqui, *Cent ans d'histoire*, p. 217.

115. Letter of AIU to Minister of Foreign Affairs, July 16, 1918, AIU, L.241 ff. 469–70; Chouraqui, *ibid.*, pp. 220, 468–69. See also letter of AIU to Minister of Foreign Affairs, June 18, 1916 in criticism of Russian treatment of Jews in the war zone. MAE Guerre 1914–1918, 1198 Sionisme, May 1916–April 1917, p. 19.

116. Letters of AIU to Lucien Wolf, June 30, 1916, AIU, L.239 ff. 318–83; Chouraqui, *ibid.*, p. 217.

117. Letter of AIU to Minister of Foreign Affairs, July 16, 1918, AIU, L.241 ff. 469–70; Chouraqui, *ibid.*, pp. 220, 468–69.

118. A special edition of the *UI* was devoted to the emancipation of the Jews in Russia. The June 29, 1917, issue of the same periodical contained letters from the Chief Rabbi of France and from Emile Durkheim rejoicing in the emancipation. From Durkheim: "The Russian Revolution seems to me to have suppressed the Jewish problem in Russia. Moreover, the Jews are assured of their assimilation to other religious confessions; they will enjoy the same rights; their martyrdom has come to an end." *UI*, June 29, 1917, p. 368.

119. For an elaboration of the position of the Alliance on Jewish rights in Eastern Europe, see its pamphlet *La question juive devant la conférence de la paix* (Paris, 1919); Chouraqui, *Cent ans d'histoire*, pp. 227–30; Naomi Cohen, *Not Free to Desist*, pp. 115–16; Oscar Janowsky, pp. 283–308.

120. Report, June 27, 1920, pp. 17–18, Marshall Papers, AJA, Box 55.

121. *Paix et droit*, March, 1921, pp. 1–3.

122. The treaty with Poland was at issue. *UI*, May 16, 1919, p. 240.

123. C.C., Minutes, May 26, 1919, HM 1072, CAHJP.

124. ACIP, Minutes, February 9, 1915, AA19; March 11, 1919, April 25, 1919, AA20; Circular appeal of C.C., May 1, 1919, Brandeis I 1 b.

125. Circular appeal of C.C., May 1, 1919, Brandeis I 1 b.

126. Halff, p. 94.

127. Circular appeal of C.C., May 1, 1919, Brandeis, I 1 b.

128. *Union Scolaire*, March, 1921, p. 6; Minutes of the Comité des Dames Inspectrices, Feb. 28, 1919, p. 145, CAHJP, INV 1077.

129. *UI*, December 6, 1918, pp. 302–3; "Déclaration du grand-rabbin de France," *UI*, August 8, 1919, pp. 528–29.

130. C.C., Permanent Section, Minutes, September 19, 1919, HM 1073, CAHJP.

131. Archives départmentales de France, Moselle, 2V 85 and 2V 86.

3. The Immigrant Challenge

1. For population statistics on Jewish immigration, see Salo Baron, *Steeled by Adversity*, p. 280 and Lloyd P. Gartner, *The Jewish Immigrant in England*, p. 274.

2. See Zosa Szajkowski, "The European Attitude to East European Immigration, (1881–1893)," *PAJHS*, 49 (1951–52): 127–62.

3. Marrus, pp. 157–62.

4. Zosa Szajkowski, *Etuden tsu der geshikhte fun ayngevanderten yiddishen yishuv in Frankraykh* (Paris, 1937), p. 21. For the Aliens Act of 1905, see Lloyd P. Gartner, pp. 48–49; Bernard Gainer, *The Alien Invasion* (London: Heinemann, 1972).

5. "L'émigration russe vers Paris," *UI*, April 6, 1906, pp. 80–81. The Comité des Ecoles also noted the continual growth in the number of foreign students in the Jewish communal schools. Minutes, March 20, 1906, INV 1077, CAHJP.

6. Letter from local committee of Nancy to president of the Alliance Israélite Universelle, April 11, 1907, AIU France IX D 53.

7. Zosa Szajkowski, for example, estimates in his *Etuden* 100,000 Eastern European Jews in Paris in 1914, while extrapolations from Michel Roblin's figures yield 21,000 Eastern European Jews in Paris at that time. Szajkowski, "European Attitude," p. 24; Michel Roblin, *Les Juifs de Paris*, p. 73.

8. Reports of L'Asile israélite de Paris, 1906–1907, 1909, 1911.

9. Extrapolations from statistics of Roblin, *Les Juifs*, pp. 67–73.

10. Institut national d'études démographiques, *Français et immigrés*, Cahier #19, (Paris, 1953), pp. 10–11; Cahier #20 (Paris, 1954), pp. 188–189.

11. Georges Mauco, *Les Etrangers en France*, pp. 546–547.

12. Police Archives, Paris, B^A 263, Municipal Elections, 1907, Report of April 22, 1907 and posters from the campaign.

13. *La Cité*, 8, 29 (January 1909):455–56.

14. Police report, July 28, 1911, Police Archives, Paris, 241.155-A-B-B¹-B².

15. See, for example, Joseph Lugand, *L'immigration des ouvriers étrangers en*

France et les enseignements de la guerre; Mauco, *Les Etrangers en France*; and Jean Pluyette, *La Selection de l'immigrant en France et la doctrine des races.*
16. Mauco, *Les Etrangers*, pp. 312, 467, 558.
17. Reports of *L'Asile de nuit et de jour*, 1925, 1928, 1930, 1931, 1932, 1934, 1936; report of *Assistance par le travail*, *La Nouvelle Aurore*, June 20, 1924, p. 11; *Naye presse*, January 27, 1935, p. 3; Jacob Fink *Yahadut Zarfat*, p. 58.
18. An analysis of a representative sample of the estimated 35,000 Jews who were naturalized in France between 1924 and 1935 reveals that 80.3 percent were Eastern Europeans (42.2 percent from Poland alone), 15.8 percent were from the Levant, and 3.9 percent from Western Europe. A. Menes, "Yidn in Frankraykh," *YIVO Bleter*, 11 no. 5 (May 1937):336–39, 355. Other sources of demographic data include HIAS-HICEM, *Ten Years of Jewish Emigration, 1926–1936* (Paris, 1936); Ida Benguigui, "L'immigration juive à Paris entre les deux guerres," AIU, Ms. 527; M. Moch, "Le Judaïsme en France," unpub. report; M. Dobin, "Yiddishe Immigranten Arbeter in Pariz, 1923–28," *YIVO Bleter*, 3, nos. 4–5 (April–May 1932):385–403; Roblin, *Les Juifs de Paris*; 1931 report of *Oeuvre d'Assistance par le travail*, YIVO.
19. *Français et immigrés*, Cahier No. 19, p. 318.
20. *Ibid.*, p. 17.
21. A. Menes, p. 338.
22. Moch, p. 18.
23. Menes, "Yidn in Frankraykh," p. 355; Z. Szajkowski, "Jewish Communal Life in Paris," [Yiddish], *Yidn in Frankraykh*, 2 (New York, 1942): pp. 207–8.
24. *Yiddish Hantbuch* (Paris, 1937), p. 90; Fink, *Yahadut Zarfat*, p. 58; Ezekiel Kornhendler, *Yidn in Pariz* (Paris, 1970), p. 199.
25. Letter from Minister of Public Instruction to President of *Ligue Française pour la Défense des Droits de l'Homme et du Citoyen*, February 17, 1908, B 82, 1908.
26. *Yiddish Hantbuch*, p. 96.
27. Roblin, p. 157; *UI*, May 6, 1927, pp. 109–10; *Yiddish Hantbuch*, p. 100. For a sociological analysis of two generations of Belleville Jews, see Charlotte Roland, *Du Ghetto à l'occident.*
28. *Revue OSE*, August 1937, pp. 26–27.
29. Roblin, p. 129.
30. Szajkowski, "Jewish Communal Life in Paris," p. 208.
31. Roblin, p. 130.
32. Pierre Aubery, *Milieux juifs de la France contemporaine* (Paris, 1957), p. 40; Roblin, p. 131; A. H. Navon, *Joseph Perez*, p. 159.
33. *PH*, March 12, 1939, p. 18.
34. *La Tribune juive* (Strasbourg), April 6, 1934, p. 260.
35. *PH*, March 12, 1939, p. 18.
36. Jacques Biélinky, "Les Juifs étrangers en France," *UI*, February 4, 1927, p. 689.
37. *Ibid.*
38. *UI*, February 4, 1927, pp. 688–89.
39. Letter, December 18, 1933 to Jacques Biélinky, YIVO, Biélinky Archive.

40. *NP*, January 11, 1937, p. 4; Nathan Netter, the rabbi of Metz, estimated the number of Eastern European immigrant families in his city at greater than 600; see his *Vingt siècles d'histoire d'une communauté juive: Metz et son grand passé*, p. 516. The census of 1931 listed a total of 8,310 Jews in Strasbourg. See *La Tribune juive*, August 9, 1935, p. 582.

41. *Ibid.*

42. *PH*, March 12, 1939, p. 18.

43. *UI*, February 4, 1927, pp. 689–90.

44. *La Nouvelle Aurore*, March 20, 1924, p. 7; Menes, *Yidn in Frankraykh*, p. 338.

45. *UI*, March 23, 1928, p. 847; April 20, 1928, p. 115.

46. *Parizer bleter*, November 21, 1924; Parti Communiste français, *L'importance de la M.O.E. et les diverses immigrations*, 1930.

47. Report of Rabbi Metzger, ACIP, B112.

48. A. Frumkin, *Jewish Daily Forward*, August 31, 1912.

49. Brandeis IV 10 b.

50. *Ibid.*

51. Szajkowski, *Etuden*, p. 22; *Der Yid in Pariz*, June 21, 1914.

52. *Association israélite pour la protection de la jeune fille*, Exercice 1919; *Official Report* of Jewish International Conference on Suppression of Traffic in Girls and Women (London, 1910), pp. 114–16.

53. 1,321 children came from families of five persons, 929 from families of six, 508 from families of seven, 100 from families of eight, 30 from families of nine, 48 from families of from ten to twelve. It should be pointed out that the total figures provided for various categories—living conditions, family size, and location of dwelling—do not coincide. Jacques Biélinky, *Revue OSE* (August 1937), pp. 26–27.

54. The total sample of children numbered 335. *Revue OSE* (February 1938), pp. 11–14.

55. Reports on courses of religious instruction in Paris area, 1930 and 1931, JTS, Box 17.

56. Registration lists of the Ecole Zadoc Kahn and of courses of religious instruction of the rue des Tournelles and the rue Nobel were analyzed. Addresses were cross-checked, so that the father of several children would not be counted more than once. While it could be argued that children enrolled in courses of religious education do not represent the anti-religious, radical members of the immigrant Jewish community, there seems to be little difference between the occupational distribution of this sample and the estimates for the entire immigrant community found in E. Speiser's *Calendrier juif*. According to Speiser's figures, 61% of all Eastern European Jewish immigrants in Paris in 1911 worked in artisan trades, 28% were engaged in commerce, 3% in the liberal professions, and 8% in miscellaneous occupations. Moreover, in this period organized workers were but a small fraction of the working population. The sample may underrepresent those prosperous merchants who would refrain from sending their children to what were essentially charity schools. ACIP, B 81 (1907), B 83 (1908), B 85 (1909).

57. For complete statistics, see Appendix.

58. There are two Yiddish-language articles on the professional distribution of

Eastern European immigrant Jews in France during the interwar period. M. Dobin's "Di professies fun di yiddishe immigranten in Pariz," *YIVO Bleter*, 4, no. 1 (August 1932): 22–42, is based on an analysis of the occupations of applicants to the organization *Aide par le travail*. Since the clients of this organization were looking for employment, shopkeepers and other merchants are virtually absent. Menes's "Yidn in Frankraykh," pp. 329–55, makes extensive use of the highly fallible name-counting method, isolating Jewish-sounding names in such sources as Bottin's *Annuaire du commerce et de l'industrie*. Since it is unclear what proportion of Jews were listed in the sources utilized, the statistics are subject to further error. Michel Roblin's figures on Paris Jewry rely on similar sources as well as a 1941 police census. Using war-time material to provide information on Jewish occupational distribution in the 1930s can lead to serious distortions, for Jewish economic life during the German occupation was dislocated. I have also made use of a survey of the professional distribution of the fathers of 538 children served by *La Colonie Scolaire*, published in the *Almanach juif* (Paris, 1931); a survey published in the *Revue OSE* (February 1938), p. 14; and original reports of the *Oeuvre d'Assistance par le travail aux immigrants juifs*, YIVO.

59. Menes, "Yidn in Frankraykh," p. 339. Other surveys confirm this estimate. Extrapolations from Roblin's figures for Polish Jews in 1926 lead to the conclusion that 40.8 percent of those earning their living in the clothing industry were artisans and façonniers, the rest merchandisers and their employees. Roblin, pp. 102–3.

60. *Ibid.*

61. Menes, "Yidn in Frankraykh," p. 339; Dobin, "Di professies," p. 23.

62. Extrapolations from raw data, *Almanach juif.*

63. Extrapolations from raw data, *Revue OSE* (February 1938), p. 14.

64. Dobin, "Di professies," pp. 23–24; *Oeuvre d'Assistance par le Travail*, YIVO, France.

65. Dobin, *ibid.*, p. 24; YIVO, France.

66. Menes, "Yidn in Frankraykh," p. 339.

67. Menes, *ibid.*, p. 339; Dobin, "Di professies," p. 24; YIVO, France.

68. Menes, *ibid*; Dobin, *ibid.*, and *Almanach Juif; Revue OSE.*

69. Dobin, "Di professies," p. 23; YIVO, France.

70. *Asile israélite, Exercice* 1909, pp. 13–14; *Crèche israélite, Exercice* 1911, pp. 26–27.

71. *PH*, September 20, 1933, p. 3.

72. ACIP, B 112 (1922).

73. YIVO, France.

74. *UI*, February 4, 1927, pp. 688–91; *NP*, January 11, 1937, p. 4; *PH*, March 12, 1939, p. 18.

75. Roblin, pp. 98–99, 129.

76. Menes, "Yidn in Frankraykh," p. 341.

77. Roblin, pp. 98–129.

78. *UI*, February 4, 1927, pp. 689–90.

79. For studies of similar patterns among immigrant Jews in the U.S. and Great Britain, see Moses Rischin, *The Promised City* (New York: Harper, 1970) and Lloyd Gartner, *The Jewish Immigrant in England.*

80. ACIP, B 79; *UI*, November 25, 1921, pp. 205–6; *Menorah*, December 8, 1923, p. 364; *Association cultuelle sephardite de Paris, Exercice*, 1930, 1931.

81. *La Revue israélite*, May 1924, p. 14; Circular appeal of *Ozer Dalim*, April 1, 1927, JTS, Box 17; *PH*, December 21, 1932, p. 3.

82. *Français et immigrés*, Cahier 19, p. 108; "Italians and Poles of Catholic background settled in a Catholic country, react with respect to religion in France as though they were not in the presence of the same religion."

83. *Moral report of Association cultuelle israélite dite "Accoudas [sic] Hakehilos,"* Annual General Assembly, December 15, 1913, HUC, France, Box 47.

84. *Ibid.*, and *Der Yid in Pariz*, April 20, 1912.

85. ACIP, B 101 (1916).

86. Without Jewish education, one writer commented, the children of immigrants would grow up neither Jews nor Gentiles. Sacrifices would have to be made to ensure the Jewishness of the younger generation. *Der Yid in Pariz*, September 20, 1912.

87. ACIP, *Exercice*, 1906–1914.

88. Article 10, Statutes of the *Association de l'Ecole "Talmud Torah" des Israélites Russes et Polonais*, HUC, France, Box 47.

89. For example, the Talmud Thora de Montmartre, flyer n.d., JTS, France, Box 17. *Di Moderne tsayt*, October 2, 1908, called for progressive national education.

90. For a survey of societies conducted by YIVO in the 1930s, see Szajkowski, "Jewish Societies in Paris in 1939," pp. 218–30.

91. *Français et immigrés*, Cahier no. 20, pp. 200–201.

92. Szajkowski, "Jewish Societies," pp. 219–20.

93. *Ibid.*, pp. 221–27; the records of three *landsmanshaften, L'Humanité des ouvriers du lle arrondissement*, established in 1908, the *Ershte hevra fun Poilishe Yidn*, established in 1897, and the *Société des enfants d'Israël de David*, minutes and correspondence book, 1905–1923, YIVO, France. See also, Charlotte Roland, pp. 251–52 and *PH*, August 10, 1934, p. 3.

94. *Der Yid in Pariz*, November 20, 1912.

95. *UI*, April 18, 1913, p, 135.

96. *Der Yid in Pariz*, February 20, 1913.

97. *Ibid.*, and Report of commission of the Federation of Jewish Societies, Brandeis, Non-consistoire.

98. *Ibid.*

99. *Ibid.*

100. *Asile israélite de nuit et de jour, Exercice*, 1906–1932; *UI*, January 15, 1915, pp. 240–41; A.A., "Jewish Organizations and Institutions in Paris," [Yiddish], *Yidn in Frankraykh*, p. 253.

101. *Asile israélite de nuit et de jour, Exercice*, 1932, p. 119.

102. *UI*, November 11, 1910, pp. 261–65.

103. *La Solidarité—soupe populaire du IVe arrondissement*, YIVO, France, 75.

104. Zosa Szajkowski, "150 Years of the Jewish Press in France," [Yiddish], p. 243.

105. *Di Moderne tsayt*, September 25, 1908.

106. *Der Yiddisher arbeter*, for example, lasted from 1911 to 1914. Cf. Szajkowski, p. 247.

107. M. Waldman, "Vegen Yiddish-literarishen tsenter in Pariz," pp. 253–54.

108. E. Kornhendler, p. 242; Szajkowski, *Unzer Shtime*, March 31, 1939, p. 1.

109. *Der Yid in Pariz*, May 20, 1912; flyer, January 3, 1912, Bund Archives.

110. Flyer, n.d., and flyer, July 9, 1912, Bund Archives.

111. Flyers, Bund Archives.

112. *Di Moderne tsayt*, January 17, 1909; *Der Yid in Pariz*, May 20, 1912, May 26, 1912, June 20, 1912; J. Tchernoff, *Dans le creuset de la civilisation*, 2:280–81.

113. "Sixteen Years of Yiddish Theater in Paris," [Yiddish], *Parizer leben*, February 2, 1923; Zosa Szajkowski, "Yiddishe Theater in Frankraykh," p. 289.

114. Flyers, Bund Archives; *Di Moderne tsayt*, January 17, 1909; *Der Yid in Pariz*, June 20, 1912.

115. Flyers, Bund Archives; Tchernoff, *Dans le creuset*, 2:280–81.

116. Szajkowski, "150 Years," p. 243; *Français et immigrés*, Cahier no. 20, p. 202.

117. Report of Daniel Charney, YIVO, France.

118. *Ibid.*, and Szajkowski, "150 Years," pp. 245–269.

119. Circular of *Kultur Verayn*, December, 1919, YIVO, France, 75; *Arbeter shtime*, September 19, 1925, December 12, 1925, January 23, 1926.

120. D. Rappaport, "Di Parizer Kultur-Lige," *Parizer leben*, January 19, 1923, p. 3.

121. Bundist Circular, January 1926, YIVO, France 75; "The Destruction of the Bundist Fraction in the Paris Kultur-Lige," *Arbeter shtime*, January 23, 1926, p. 1; Raphael Ryba, "Yiddishe sotsialistisher farband 'Bund' " *Unzer tsayt* (Nov–Dec. 1947): 159–62; David Diamant, "Di Kultur-geselshaftleche Bevegung funem Yiddishen Yishuv in Frankraykh far di Yorn 1937–1957," *Ikuf Almanach* (New York, 1961), p. 125; my own interview with F. Schrager, President of ORT of France and former secretary of the *Kultur-Lige*, October 31, 1972.

122. *Arbeter shtime*, February 5, 1927.

123. Diamant, "Di Kultur-geselshaftleche," pp. 132–33; Szajkowski, "Yiddishe Theater," pp. 312–14.

124. Waldman, "Vegen Yiddish-literarishen," pp. 255–57 and *Yizkor Buch tsum Andenk fun 14 Umgekumene Parizer Yiddishe Shrayber* [Memorial Book to the Memory of 14 Paris Yiddish Writers], eds. B. Shlevin, M. Shulstein, G. Koenig, Y. Spero (Paris, 1946) esp. pp. 12–13.

125. Szajkowski, "Jewish Communal Life in Paris," p. 245.

126. *NP*, January 11, 1934, p. 6; March 23, 1934.

127. Daniel Charney, Report on Yiddish Culture in Paris [Yiddish], YIVO, France; Y. Lerman, *Ikuf Almanach*, p. 172; Szajkowski, "Jewish Communal Life in Paris," p. 240.

128. *Ibid.*

129. Szajkowski, "Jewish Communal Life in Paris," pp. 212–14, 239, 243–44; Diamant, "Di Kultur-geselshaftlech," p. 132.

130. *Almanach Juif*, p. 80; Federation of Jewish Societies, *Rapport moral et financier 1935–36*, pp. 9–10; Szajkowski, "Jewish Communal Life in Paris," p. 210; *La Nouvelle Aurore*, November 15, 1924, p. 13.

131. A. Alperin complained in *Parizer haynt*, March 4, 1932, p. 1 of the need to maintain closer contact with the provinces.

132. FSJ, *Rapport moral*; program of *Université Populaire Juive*, 1931–32, YIVO, France; Report of FSJ, YIVO, France.

133. *Chalom*, February, 1933, p. 19.

134. Program of UPJ, 1931–1932, YIVO, France.

135. Pamphlets of *La Colonie Scolaire*, YIVO, France; *Menorah*, June 1, 1930, p. 169.

136. *La Colonie Scolaire, Exercice* 1934, YIVO, France.

137. *PH*, January 20, 1937, p. 3.

138. *PH*, December 19, 1937, p. 3.

139. *NP*, January 11, 1937, p. 4; *PH*, February 9, 1933, p. 3; *La Tribune juive*, August 24, 1928, pp. 521–23; September 21, 1928, pp. 592–93.

140. Daniel Charney, Report, YIVO, France; Szajkowski, "Jewish Communal Life in Paris," p. 240.

141. *Parizer bleter*, November 21, 1924.

142. Report of M. Gomelsky, January 28, 1927, CZA Z4 3589 I. Articles in *Parizer haynt* were devoted to the problem of mixed marriages among the children of immigrant Jews. *PH*, April 1, 1932, p. 3; February 3, 1933, p. 3.

143. Yossel Tsucker, *A Fremd Lebn* (Warsaw, 1939), p. 14.

4. The Jewish Labor Movement

1. For a history of the Bund, see Henry Tobias, *The Jewish Bund in Russia*. On the early years of the Jewish labor movement, see Ezra Mendelsohn, *Class Struggle in the Pale* (Cambridge: Cambridge University Press, 1970).

2. Tobias, *ibid.*, pp. 140, 239.

3. *Ibid.*, pp. 50–57., and Moshe Mishkinsky, "The Jewish Labor Movement and European Socialism," pp. 289–91.

4. Tobias, *ibid.*, pp. 160–176, 200–206; Mishkinsky, *ibid.*, pp. 291–92.

5. Henry Tobias and Charles Woodhouse, "Primordial Ties and Political Process in pre-Revolutionary Russia: the Case of the Jewish Bund," pp. 339–340.

6. Michel Roblin, *Les Juifs de Paris*, p. 168; Raphael Ryba, "Der entvicklungsveg fun Parizer Bund," *Unzer shtime*, December 7, 1947. A leaflet in the Bund Archives in New York dated January 13, 1912, however, announces the tenth-anniversary celebration of the group, "Kempfer."

7. Zosa Szajkowski, *NP*, October 1, 1934, p. 4; N. Frank, *PH*, June 24, 1934, p. 3. For a discussion of the anarcho-syndicalist tendency of the French labor movement, see Frederick Ridley, *Revolutionary Syndicalism in France* and Peter Stearns, *Revolutionary Syndicalism and French Labor: A Cause without Rebels*.

8. Zosa Szajkowski, *Di professionnelle bevegung tsvishen di Yiddishe arbeter in Frankraykh biz 1914*, pp. 59–62.

9. *Ibid.*, pp. 98–117. Szajkowski's work draws upon the records of the Jewish *Syndicat des casquettiers*, founded in 1896. I was not able to consult those records in depth as they were only recently deposited in the CAHJP.

10. Leaflets of Jewish sections of furrier union, bakers' union, shoe workers' union, leather workers' union, and garment industry, Bund Archives; *Der Agitator*, November 7, 1908, p. 8; *Der Yiddisher arbeter, passim.*

11. Lorwin, *The French Labor Movement* (Cambridge: Harvard University Press, 1954) p. 42.

12. *Der Yiddisher arbeter*, October 5, 1912; Szajkowski, *Professionelle*, p. 72.

13. Szajkowski, *Professionelle*, pp. 165–75.

14. *Ibid.*, pp. 68–69.

15. Letter of A. Losovsky, n.d., to secretary of CGT, Russian Institute, Columbia University, C.U.1.1.3.2.

16. *Ibid.*

17. *Ibid.*, and Szajkowski, *Professionelle*, pp. 37–40. See also a police report of April 7, 1911, about a meeting of 600 Jewish workers protesting the anti-Semitic propaganda of a syndical leader. Police Archives, Paris, 241.155-A-B-B¹-B².

18. For the attitude of the CGT to political action, see Ridley, *Revolutionary Syndicalism in France* pp. 88–98; Stearns, *Revolutionary Syndicalism and French Labor.* p. 21.

19. Ms. of Charles Matline, secretary of the Capmakers' Union, communicated to me by Matline; Szajkowski, *Professionelle*, p. 126. Losovsky returned to Russia after the Revolution and became the vice-commissioner of the Foreign Ministry of the USSR before being purged by Stalin.

20. Losovsky Mss., Russian Institute, 1.1.3.2.

21. Letter of A. Losovsky, October 9, 1911, Bund Archives.

22. In his letter, Losovsky had claimed that there were 40,000 immigrant Jewish workers in Paris—an inflated estimate. *Ibid.; Der Yiddisher arbeter*, November 17, 1911; Szajkowski, *Professionelle*, p. 46.

23. Szajkowski, *ibid.*, pp. 78–79.

24. *Ibid.*, p. 79.

25. *Ibid.*, p. 74

26. Leaflets, Bund Archives.

27. Lists of principal manufacturers and contractors in the garment industry in the years 1906–1918 reveal the percentage of Jews as ranging from 21% to 55%. Police Archives, Paris, BA 1394, BA 1376.

28. My own interview with David Diamant, director of the *Institut Historique Maurice Thorez*, October 27, 1972; and with Charles Matline, secretary of the Capmakers' Union, October 13, 1972 (see above, note 19).

29. *Der Yid in Pariz*, November 20, 1912.

30. Police Report, March 10, 1913, Police Archives, Paris, BA 1394; *Der Yiddisher arbeter*, October 18, 1913; Szajkowski, *Professionelle*, p. 142.

31. *Der Yiddisher arbeter*, May 1, 1912.

32. Contracts, n.d. and November 4, 1912, Losovsky Mss., Russian Institute, 1.1.3.2; *Rapports de la Fédération des Syndicats Ouvriers de la Chapellerie Française* (Paris, 1912), available in the archives of the Capmakers' Union, Paris; 1912 tariffs

and descriptions of contracts in INV 2761, CAHJP; Szajkowski, *Professionelle* pp. 141–47; Letter of the cooperative, entitled L'Union, INV 2761, CAHJP.

33. *L'Humanité*, March 13, 1913; Szajkowski, *Professionelle*, p. 196.

34. Police report, March 12, 1913, Police Archives, Paris, BA 1394.

35. Police reports, March 12, 1913, September 16, 1916, October 3, 1916, Police Archives, Paris BA 1394; April 7, 1911, July 2, 1914, Police Archives, 241.155-A-B-B¹-B².

36. Police report, March 19, 1916, Police Archives, Paris, Bᴬ 1394.

37. Police report, September 22, 1916, *Ibid.*

38. *L'Humanité*, September 16 and 18, 1916.

39. M. Lauzel, *Ouvriers juifs de Paris* (Paris, 1912), p. 20.

40. See, for example, the demand for suppression of façonnerie in the *Compte Rendu, Rapport des Travaux du 6me Congrès* of the Fédération d'Industrie des Travailleurs de l'Habillement (Limoges, 1906), pp. 22–23 and in the Fédération des Syndicats ouvriers de la Chapellerie Française, *XIVe Congrès National* (1909), pp. 22.

41. Szakowski, *Professionelle*, p. 197. For anti-foreigner sentiment in the French labor movement, see also pp. 83, 89.

42. Resolutions of the General Assembly of Labor Commission of Capmakers' Union, July 4, 1911, Russian Institute 1.1.3.2.; A. Losovsky, "A bas le travail à domicile," *L'Ouvrier Chapelier*, February 1, 1912.

43. *Der Yiddisher arbeter*, April 11, 1914.

44. *Ibid.*, August 9, 1913; my own interview with Jaques Léderman, secretary of the handbag (maroquinerie) union on November 2, 1972. Several strikes of 1912 within the garment industry were broken by using façonniers. Police Archives, Bᴬ1394 12000–40.

45. *Parizer yiddishe voch*, July 14, 1916.

46. Police Archives, Paris, Bᴬ 1394, Bᴬ 1406, Bᴬ 1376.

47. Police report, June 8, 1916, A.N. F⁷ 13.943.

48. Szajkowski, *Naye presse*, October 11, 1934.

49. Police reports, October 3, October 10, October 22, 1916, Police Archives, Paris, Bᴬ 1394.

50. *Di Yiddishe tribune*, October 17, 1915.

51. Police reports of April 28, 1915, May 21, 1915, August 11, 1915, February 12, 1916, April 19, 1916, May 27, 1916, June 23, 1916, A.N. F⁷ 13.943.

52. *Ibid.*, February 23, 1915.

53. *Ibid.*, May 21, 1915.

54. *Ibid.*, March 27, 1915.

55. *Ibid.*, March 19, 1916, Police Archives, Paris Bᴬ 1423.

56. Bulletins of Paris Jewish Workers' Fund, Bund Archives; police report, May 15, 1916, A.N., F⁷ 13.943.

57. Memorandum of the Jewish Workers' Committee to Aid Jewish Victims of the War (another name for the Fund) to the Congress of Syndicates of the Department of the Seine, May 1916, A.N., F⁷ 13.943.

58. *Ibid.*

59. *Ibid.*

60. *La Renaissance juive*, March 2, 1917, p. 6.

61. Szajkowski, *Unzer shtime*, November 5, 1938, p. 2. The author notes that protest by French socialists and the fear of American Jewish displeasure prevented the implementation of the expulsion plan.

62. Police report, June 20, 1915, A.N., F⁷ 13.943.

63. *Ibid.*, and circulars in French and Yiddish, Brandeis, Non-consistoire; Szajkowski, *Unzer shtime*, October 22, 1938, pp. 2, 4.

64. Police report, December 13, 1915, A.N., F⁷ 13.943.

65. Lorwin, *French Labor Movement*, pp. 56–58. For a detailed history of the birth of the Communist labor movement in France, see Annie Kriegel, *Aux origines du communisme français* (Paris, 1964).

66. Police reports, December 27, 1919, based on *L'Humanité* article of November 4, 1919, A.N., F⁷ 13.943; police reports of December 28, 1919, February 7, 1920, March 4, 1920, Police archives, Paris, 241.155 R; Szajkowski, May 31, 1938, p. 14.

67. Police reports, March 11, March 15, March 29, April 26, 1920, May 9, 1927, Police Archives, Paris, 241.155 R.

68. *Morgenstern*, June 29 and July 27, 1929; *PH*, May 28, 1935, p. 3; *Unzer shtime*, June 3, 1938.

69. Lorwin, *French Labor Movement*, pp. 60–61; Ridley, *Revolutionary Syndicalism in France*, pp. 77–79; Stearns, *Revolutionary Syndicalism and French Labor*, p. 22.

70. *PH*, April 22, 1935, p. 3; *Unzer shtime*, January 25, 1936.

71. *Unzer shtime*, January 11, 1936; January 25, 1936.

72. *Compte rendu officiel des travaux du XIIe Congrès National*, Lille, 1921, pp. 79–81.

73. *Ibid.*, p. 81.

74. Report of the Third Congress of the CGTU (Paris, 1925), pp. 411–12; for the establishment of the Yiddish Intersyndical Commission in July of 1923, see *Arbeter shtime*, January 1, 1924; Jacques Lederman, "The Organized Jewish Labor Movement between the Two World Wars," [Yiddish], *Combattants de la Liberté* (Paris, 1948), p. 38 erroneously cites 1924 for its reestablishment.

75. Reports of second through seventh congresses of CGTU, 1925–1933; PCF, *L'Importance de la M.O.E. et les diverses immigrations*, pp. 3–4; Union des syndicats ouvriers de la région Parisienne (CGTU), *Du travail ou du pain!* pp. 27–28.

76. PCF, Third National Congress (Paris, 1925), p. 393.

77. *Arbeter shtime*, September 1, 1924; PCF, Report of Fifth National Congress (Lille), June 19–26, p. 14.

78. *Cahiers du Bolchévisme*, Special number, July 28, 1926, p. 1539.

79. Report of Third Congress of CGTU (Paris, 1925), p. 415.

80. Report of Fifth Congress of Unions of the Seine (January–February 1925), pp. 30–31.

81. PCF, *L'Importance de la M.O.E.*, pp. 81–82.

82. PCF, Sixth National Congress of PCF, Saint-Denis (1929), p. 37; similarly, PCF, *Résolutions adoptées par la conférence nationale* (March 1930), pp. 23–24.

83. *Cahiers du Bolchévisme*, 7, Special number (May 1932), *Thèses et résolutions du VIIe Congrès du PC*, p. 69.

84. CGTU, *Contre la xénophobie*, p. 10.

85. PC (Region Parisienne), Rapport d'organisation pour la Conférence de la région Parisienne (February 1932), pp. 20–22.

86. *Yiddish Hantbuch* (Paris, 1937), p. 102; Szajkowski, "Fun Yiddishen arbeterleben in Pariz," p. 235.

87. Lederman, "Organized Jewish Labor Movement," p. 40; *Arbeter shtime*, December 4, 1926, October 8, 1927, March 10, 1928, p. 3; January 12, 1929, p. 3; *Emes*, July 18, 1931, p. 4.

88. *Journal officiel*, August 12, 1932, p. 8818; July 17, 1934, pp. 7352–7355; August 1, 1935, pp. 8368–8370; Lederman, *ibid.*, p. 41.

89. Maurin, *La Main d'Oeuvre immigrée sur le marché du travail en France* (1933), pp. 27–28; CGTU, *Programme 1935*, pp. 41–42; Reports of Congresses of CGTU, 1925–1933.

90. PCF, *L'Importance de la M.O.E.*, p. 81; PCF, *Rapport d'organisation*, p. 21.

91. *Der Morgen*, August 17, 1933, p. 4.

92. *NP*, February 2, 1934, p. 6.

93. *Ibid.*, June 21, 1934, p. 4; September 28, 1934, p. 3; July 24, 1935, p. 6. *PH*, September 23, 1934, p. 3; September 27, 1934, p. 3; March 6, 1935, p. 1.

94. *NP*, August 27, 1935, p. 5; *PH*, March 30, 1935, p. 3; September 24, 1935, p. 3; Broadside of *Syndicat des entrepreneurs et artisans de la confection du vêtement* (n.d.) and 1937 appeal to Ladies' garment *façonniers*.

95. Szajkowski, "Fun yiddishen arbeter leben in Pariz," p. 233 and "Jewish Communal Life in Paris," p. 236.

96. *Ibid.*, and Lederman, "Organized Jewish Labor Movement," p. 48.

97. *NP*, March 13, 1937, p. 1.

98. Lorwin, *French Labor Movement*, pp. 74–75.

99. Letter from Paris Region of the CP to Medem Farband and Left Poalei Zion, seeking cooperation with the two groups and expressing continued concern for Jewish workers, even though the foreign-language commissions had been abolished, *NP*, July 9, 1937, p. 1. Jewish Communists interviewed either had no memory of the abolition of the language sections of the Party or denied that they were abolished. David Diamant insisted that there had merely been a change of name and not of function. My interview with him, October 27, 1972.

100. *NP*, September 9, 1937, p. 6; September 30, 1937, p. 3; September 28, 1937, p. 6.

101. *Unzer shtime*, March 17, 1939.

102. *NP*, February 14, 1939.

103. *Unzer shtime*, January 28, 1939.

104. *Arbeter shtime*, December 18, 1926.

105. *La Renaissance juive*, March 2, 1917, p. 6; Police report, February 5, 1917, A.N. F7 13.943; *L'Humanité*, March 6, 1917, p. 6.

106. Brochure of *Gesellschaft frayunt fun di yiddishe arbeter tsugabshuln*—Paris (*Kultur-Lige*), YIVO archives.

107. *NP*, January 11, 1934, p. 6 and March 23, 1934, p. 5.

108. "Why we don't participate in the '*klal-yisrael*' action against anti-Semitism in Germany," [Yiddish], August, 1935, Bund Archives.

109. *Arbeter vort*, March 15, 1928, p. 3.

110. Leaflet of *Arbeter Ring*, December 1933, Bund Archives.

111. *Der Kampf*, January–February, 1930, pp. 40–41, *Archion Ha-avodah* [Labor Archive], Tel Aviv.

112. *Arbeter shtime*, May 25, 1929, p. 5.

113. *NP*, January 31, 1934.

114. *Der Morgen*, August 24, 1933, p. 4.

115. *Arbeter shtime*, April 2, 1927.

116. Leaflet, December 1933, Bund Archives.

117. Minute book of "Arbetslozen comitet fun 20 arrondissement," YIVO archives, France; *Arbeter vort*, January 16, 1932, p. 1.

118. Leaflet of *Arbeter Ring*, December, 1933, Bund Archives; records of *Arbeter gesellshaft*, France, YIVO archives; *Unzer shtime*, February 29, 1936, p. 4.

119. Leaflets announcing two mass protests against the Beilis Trial, n.d. and October 17, 1913, Bund Archives. For a study of the Beilis Trial, see Maurice Samuel, *Blood Accusation* (New York: Knopf, 1966).

120. Appeals, n.d., 1911, and 1914, in Yiddish, Bund Archives.

121. Leaflets, n.d., and August 25, 1933, Bund Archives.

122. Raphael Ryba, *Unzer tsayt*, Special Issue, 1947, p. 161.

123. The nature of Communist influence has been described as a series of concentric circles, with those who vote Communist and read the Communist press in the outer circles. See Annie Kriegel, *Les communistes français*, pp. 11–26. In 1937 the *Naye presse* published 8,000 copies, down from its peak of 15,000 copies. The Friends of the *Naye presse* counted 2,500 members.

124. *Arbeter shtime*, April 27, 1929, p. 5; David Diamant, *Yidn in Shpanishn Krieg*, pp. 364–77. There were 155 Jewish families in France who sent volunteers to Spain.

125. Minute book of the *Arbetslozen comitet*, entries of January 17, 1934 and March 31, 1934, YIVO archives, France.

126. This was the case particularly in the handbag union in the mid-1930s, when the leadership refused to conduct business in Yiddish. *Unzer shtime*, April 7, 1936, August 15, 1936, p. 4, September 12, 1936. Jacques Lederman reported that French workers were invited to meetings of his union, the handbag union. Interview, November 2, 1972.

127. My interview with David Diamant, October 27, 1972; Charles Matline, October 13, 1972; Jacques Lederman, November 2, 1972; Boris Chubinski, January, 1972.

128. Annie Kriegel, *Le Pain et les roses*, p. 252.

5. Immigrants and Natives, 1906–1933

1. ACIP, GG50, GG55, GG60, GG65, GG75, GG76, GG240, GG246, GG170, GG172, GG174, GG177, GG188, GG140, GG142, GG144, GG145, GG148, GG150 (marital records, 1906–1925). Marital records kept by each consis-

torial temple indicate name and place of birth of the marital partners. I analyzed the records of 1,627 marriages and attempted through the examination of names to include as immigrants those persons of Eastern European origin born in France. The temples studied were the Victoire, Nazareth, Tournelles, and Buffault temples. Most of the intermarriages took place in the Nazareth temple, located in a mixed neighborhood, and the Tournelles synagogue in the heart of the immigrant quarter. The vast majority of such marriages involved an immigrant male and a native female, perhaps because the number of available immigrant females was insufficient for the immigrant male population. It was impossible to carry the study beyond 1925 because consistorial records after that date were unfortunately closed to me. It appears from the data of 1922–1925 that the percentage of immigrant–native marriages was falling as the immigrant community grew in size and more single females were available for marriage. Examination of all Paris marriages in the mid-1920s revealed that 6% were between native Frenchmen and foreigners. William Oualid, *L'Immigration ouvrière en France*, p. 11.

2. Pierre Abraham, *Trois frères*, pp. 42–43.
3. B.I., "La tolérance ne suffit pas," *UI*, September 21, 1906, p. 10.
4. *UI*, February 20, 1925, p. 515.
5. ACIP, *Exercice* (1926), p. 7.
6. Minutes of General Assembly, May 25, 1913, ACIP, B 94 (1913).
7. *UI*, July 3, 1925, p. 334.
8. Ben-Ammi, "La peur du jargon," *UI*, July 28, 1913.
9. *UI*, July 27, 1928, pp. 560–61.
10. Minutes of the consistorial subcommission, January 18, 1916, ACIP, B 101 (1916).
11. *Ibid.*
12. *Der Nayer zhournal*, October 31, 1913, pp. 11–12.
13. *Di Moderne tsayt*, December 13, 1908.
14. *PH*, March 3, 1933, p. 3.
15. *Pariz*, April 12, 1915.
16. Reports of Comité de Bienfaisance, 1906–1912; Minutes, 1887–1910.
17. *Le 70me Anniversaire de la Bienfaisance Israélite* (1913), p. 9.
18. Police Archives, Paris, 241.155-A-B-B¹-B².
19. Comité de Bienfaisance, Minutes, February 14, 1906.
20. Minutes, March 14, 1906.
21. Letter of Comité de Bienfaisance to Alliance Israélite Universelle, February 7, 1906, AIU, France I H 1.
22. Comité de Bienfaisance, Minutes, May 21, 1913.
23. Minutes, July 9, 1913.
24. Minutes, January 21, 1914.
25. *Ibid.*
26. In the Middle Ages Jewish communities controlled the entry of new Jews into the community in order to protect the economic and political security of prior residents. This control grew logically out of the corporate responsibility borne by the community for tax collection and the economic creativity of the Jewish group in the given place. After the mass expulsion of the Jews from Spain in 1492, numerous

Jewish communities refused to accept the refugees or accepted them only grudgingly. For one example, see Cecil Roth, A *History of the Marranos*, p. 223.

27. Esther Panitz, "In Defense of the Jewish Immigrant, 1881–1924," *American Jewish Historical Quarterly*, 53 (December 1963): 99–130; Naomi W. Cohen, *Not Free to Desist*, pp. 37–53.

28. For Jewish opposition to the Aliens Act, see John Garrard, *The English and Immigration*, pp. 120–133, and Bernard Gainer, *The Alien Invasion* (New York, 1972), p. 149.

29. Letter from the local committee of the AIU of Nancy to AIU, Paris, March 30, 1906, AIU, France IX D 53.

30. *Ibid.*

31. *Ibid.*, April 11, 1907, AIU, France IX D 53.

32. M. Liber, "Sur la règlementation de l'immigration," Brandeis, France IV 3 c. Born in Warsaw in 1884, Maurice Liber was brought to France at the age of four. Schooled at the Ecole Rabbinique, he adopted the mentality of, and identified with, the native community.

33. *Ibid.*

34. *UI*, September 26, 1913, p. 679.

35. Letter from the local committee of the AIU of Nancy to AIU, Paris, January 16, 1908, AIU, France IX D 53.

36. Letter of the Office Central de Philanthropie Israélite, April 20, 1914, HUC, France, Box 47.

37. Records of the Fondation Rothschild, ACIP, BB 87 (1911–1920).

38. Reports of Hôpital Fondation de Rothschild, 1905–1907, 1910–1912, 1928–1930, HUC.

39. *UI*, January 26, 1906, pp. 606–7; December 17, 1909, pp. 421–26.

40. Appeal of L'Atelier, 191–, JTS, France, Box 17.

41. Arrêté consistorial portant constitutions d'un tribunal rabbinique (Beth Dinn) dans la communauté israélite de Paris, n.d., JTS, France, Box 19.

42. Report of Louis Helbronner on the civil status of Russian Jews in France, JTS, France, Box 22; ACIP, B 95 (1913); *Observation de M. Tchernoff sur les actes d'état civil des Juifs russes en France*, n.d., Brandeis, France I 4 a.

43. *UI*, January 31, 1908, pp. 613–17.

44. Louis Weill, "Divorce des israélites russes en France," *UI*, October 8, 1909, pp. 110–15; October 15, 1909, pp. 142–47; October 22, 1909, pp. 174–78; October 29, 1909, pp. 204–9; November 5, 1909, pp. 236–40; November 12, 1909, pp. 274–77.

45. ACIP, Minutes, February 13, 1912.

46. ACIP, Minutes of Juridical Commission, February 12, 1912, B 91 (1912).

47. ACIP., Minutes, March 12, 1912; letter of president of ACIP to Chief Rabbi of C.C., March 22, 1912, ACIP, BB 88 (1912–1913).

48. Letter of president of ACIP to Chief Rabbi of C.C., March 22, 1912, ACIP, BB 88 (1912–1913).

49. C.C., Minutes, March 26, 1912.

50. Note to S.S., Avocat à la Cour d'Appel de Paris, from N. Zarine, Consul général, November 20, 1912, ACIP, B 92 (1912).

51. *Der Yid in Pariz*, March 20, 1913.

52. *Ibid.*

53. ACIP, Minutes of the Administrative Section, December 9, 1913, B 96 (1914).

54. *Ibid.*

55. *UI*, April 28, 1916, pp. 210–11.

56. Circular, May 15, 1916, Brandeis, Non-consistoire.

57. Bulletin of Oeuvres des Orphelins Israélites de la Guerre, October, 1915, Brandeis, Non-consistoire; Comité de Bienfaisance, Minutes, 1911–21; Comité des Dames Inspectrices, Minutes, October 15, 1914, January 12, 1915, June 12, 1918, November 5, 1918, INV 1077, CAHJP.

58. "Pour la protection des juifs russes," *UI*, May 5, 1916, pp. 231–32.

59. *UI*, November 30, 1917, pp. 294–95.

60. *UI*, December 8, 1916.

61. *Union Scolaire*, March, 1921, p. 6.

62. Letter from Narcisse Leven, August 27, 1914, American Jewish Committee, France-AIU 1912–1929. Marshall forwarded the request to Felix Warburg, president of the American Joint Distribution Committee. See Chouraqui, *Cent ans d'histoire*, p. 219.

63. Report of November 27, 1914, AIU, France IV D 16.

64. Letters from the Benbanaste and Mantal families of Belfort, December, 1915 and January, 1916, AIU, France II D 6.

65. Letters of April 15, 1918 and April 20, 1918 to Rozanès in Report of M. Garih, Association Orientale de Paris, Brandeis, Non-consistoire.

66. *UI*, December 25, 1914, pp. 124–25; January 8, 1915, p. 202.

67. Circular, May 15, 1916, Brandeis, Non-consistoire.

68. The Comité de Bienfaisance, for example, enlisted no immigrant collaborators but continued to dispense relief to individual immigrants and funds to immigrant organizations like the Asile de Nuit and the Volontaires Russo-roumains. Comité de Bienfaisance, Minutes, 1911–1921. Within the immigrant community, there were independent charitable institutions, particularly among the politically conscious members of the working class. A "Paris Jewish Workers' Fund to Support Jewish Victims of the War," for example, was set up by Bundists in Paris in October 1915, with sections in the various Jewish trades. It published a bulletin listing contributions and stressed the need to "keep the money in our own hands" rather than donating it to middle-class organizations which had no concern for workers. Bulletin No. 5, October 15, 1916, p. 1, Bund Archives; Police reports, May 15 and 27, 1916, A.N. F[7] 13.943.

69. Minutes of the Comité de Protection des Emigrants Israélites, April 22, 1920, ACIP, B 108 (1920).

70. *Ibid.*

71. Minutes of the Comité de Protection des Emigrants Israélites, December 7, 1924, YIVO, France; Minutes of the Comité de Bienfaisance, October 15, 1924, Minute Book, 1921–1934.

72. 1930 report of Comité Central d'Assistance aux Emigrants Juifs, France, YIVO.

73. Report of Comité Central d'Assistance, 1932, France, YIVO; HIAS-HICEM, *Ten Years of Jewish Emigration 1926–1936*, mimeographed (Paris, 1936), pp. 6–8, 10–11.

74. *Ibid.*, p. 6 and 1932 report of Comité Central d'Assistance, France, YIVO.

75. Comité de Bienfaisance, Minutes, January 11, 1927, Minute Book 1921–1934.

76. *Der Morgen*, November 28, 1933, p. 3.

77. Comité de Bienfaisance, Minutes, March 17, 1931 and April 21, 1931, Minute Book, 1921–1934.

78. *Ibid.*, December 17, 1933.

79. *Ibid.*, January 13, 1935, Minute Book 1934–1937.

80. *Ibid.*, October 4, 1936.

81. *Ibid.*, February 17, 1935.

82. *Ibid.*, June 15, 1939, Minute Book 1938–1947.

83. *UI*, February 22, 1907, pp. 710–11.

84. Comité de Bienfaisance, Minutes, October 20, 1910.

85. Lloyd Gartner, *The Jewish Immigrant in England*, pp. 227–29.

86. Yves Rodet, *L'Immigration des travailleurs étrangers en France* (Paris, 1924), p. 206.

87. *L'Humanité*, February 3, 1907. See also *UI*, February 22, 1907, pp. 710–11.

88. *Ibid.*

89. Letter of Minister of Public Instruction to the Director of Primary Education of the Seine, November 29, 1907, ACIP, B 80 (1907); letter of Minister of Public Instruction to president of the League of the Rights of Man, February 17, 1908, ACIP, B 82 (1908).

90. *Ibid.* and *UI*, February 22, 1907, pp. 712–13. One of the schools in question was transformed into a regular public school in 1921 when the number of Jewish pupils had fallen. E. Weill, "Rapport moral et religieux relatif à l'année 1921," Brandeis, France IV 17 c; letter from the Association pour le développement de l'instruction élémentaire et professionnelle to the president of the ACIP, January 28, 1921, ACIP, B110 (1921). At the urging of members of the rabbinate, the ACIP decided to encourage Jewish families in the area to send their children in greater numbers to this school because of the opportunity it afforded for Sabbath observance and to ask the Inspectaire Primaire of the fourth arrondissement to withhold his final decision on the school. ACIP, Minutes, February 7, 1921.

91. *UI*, February 22, 1907, p. 713.

92. Georges Batault, "Les solutions du problème juif; nationalisme ou assimilation," *Mercure de France*, April 15, 1921, pp. 338–39.

93. *La Nouvelle Aurore*, October 31, 1924, p. 5.

94. J. Biélinky, "Les émigrants juifs à Belleville," *UI*, October 15, 1926, pp. 167–69; *La Nouvelle Aurore*, June 15, 1925, p. 14.

95. *UI*, October 22, 1926, p. 217.

96. *Ibid.*

97. Minutes of Commission d'Inspection, March 19, 1907, ACIP, B80 (1907); report on number of children in consistorial schools, B 80 (1907); Association consistoriale israélite de Paris, *Exercices*, 1905–1914; Report, 1913, ACIP, B 93 (1913).

98. Report of Rabbi Haguenau, May, 1920, ACIP, B 108 (1920); letter of secretary-general of the Comité des Ecoles to Baroness Edmond de Rothschild, January 9, 1923, ACIP, BB 92 (1921–1923); report of ACIP, n.d. but internal evidence indicates mid-1930s, JTS, France, Box 17.

99. Emphasis mine. Letter, September 1, 1907, ACIP, B 83 (1908).

100. Minutes of Comité des Ecoles, October 15, 1907, ACIP, B 80 (1907).

101. Ibid., June 18, 1913, p. 235. INV 1077, CAHJP.

102. Administrative commission of the Ecole Rabbinique, 1908–1914, Minutes, January 3, 1911, May 7, 1913; Ibid., 1919–1939, Minutes, January 6, 1932, June 23, 1937, C.C. 4 B 6. La Tribune juive noted in 1927 that French Jewry had to rely on foreign born Jews to maintain its own rabbinate. TJ, May 20, 1927, p. 289.

103. Zosa Szajkowksi has noted that even the lycée students were mostly of immigrant origin, "Jewish Communal Life in Paris," [Yiddish], Yidn in Frankraykh, 2:241.

104. Report, ACIP, B 83 (1908).

105. PH, May 29, 1932, p. 1.

106. ACIP, Exercice (1932), p. 4.

107. Ibid. (1927), p. 7 and (1930), p. 4. Reports of ACIP, September 28, 1930 and September 25, 1932, JTS, France, Box 17.

108. M. Liber, "Rapport à M. le Grand-Rabbin de Paris sur l'année scolaire 1929–1930," November 30, 1930, Brandeis, France IV 20 b.

109. ACIP, Exercise (1926), p. 7.

110. Joseph Bonsirven, Juifs et chrétiens, p. 28.

111. ACIP, Exercice (1927), p. 8.

112. UI, December 20, 1907, pp. 421–26; March 13, 1908, pp. 805–10.

113. ACIP, Minutes, June 5, 1907, AA 19; Minutes of the Financial Section, November 10, 1908, ACIP, B 83 (1908); letter to Université Populaire Juive, May 21, 1912, ACIP, BB 88 (1912–1913).

114. Letter of administrative and financial section of ACIP to AIU, January 27, 1922, ACIP, BB 92 (1921–1923).

115. Broadside of Acceuil Fraternel Israélite, JTS, France, Box 17.

116. UI, March 26, 1926, pp. 13–14; June 11, 1926, p. 313; June 25, 1926, p. 382.

117. Union Scolaire, 28, no. 159 (January 1929).

118. Ibid.

119. Le Volontaire Juif, February–March, 1932, p. 2.

120. Jules Meyer, "Contre le particularisme," Union scolaire, 33, no. 187 (April 15, 1933):22.

121. Ibid. and no. 158 (January 1928):3–4.

122. Interview with Adolphe Caen, president of the Union Scolaire, TJ, November 30, 1934, p. 967.

123. N. Frank, PH, March 15, 1933.

124. Proposed statutes of ACIP, (1909), JTS, France, Box 20, 01924, No. 494; minutes of ACIP, May 11, 1909, AA 19.

125. Statutes of consistories of Chalons-sur-Marne and Le Havre, JTS, France, Box 20, Nos. 489 and 468.

126. ACIP, Minutes, May 27, 1919, Extraordinary General Assembly, 1919, pp. 13–14; *UI*, June 13, 1919, pp. 346–47.

127. Letter of J. Landau to Chief Rabbi J. H. Dreyfuss, n.d., and letter from Sidlowski, Lubetzki, et al., August 11, 1911, JTS, France, Box 17; ACIP, Minutes, June 27, 1911 and December 5, 1911, AA 19; Minutes of Sous-commission de la boucherie, October 24, 1911, Brandeis, France, I 10 c.

128. ACIP, Minutes, December 5, 1911, AA 19.

129. Minutes of the Religious Section, ACIP, B 95 (1913); minutes of ACIP, June 4, 1913, B 95 (1913).

130. ACIP, Minutes, December 9, 1913, B 96 (1914).

131. ACIP, Special meeting of Bureau du consistoire, December 30, 1912, B 93 (1912).

132. Minutes of Religious Section, ACIP, B 95 (1913).

133. *Ibid.*

134. "Note pour M. le Préfet," April 20, 1934, and letter of G. Samuel, president of the Consistoire israélite de la Moselle to Préfet de la Moselle, February 13, 1934, A.D., Moselle 2V 86 10³.

135. Letter of G. Samuel, A.D. Moselle 2V 86 10³.

136. Commissaire de Police to M. le Commissaire Central à Metz, September 19, 1934, communicated to Préfet de la Moselle, *Ibid.*

137. Decision of Tribunal de Metz, November 28, 1934. The case was appealed and the decision of the lower court sustained by the Paris Cour de Cassation, December 5, 1936. *Ibid.*

138. Minutes of Administrative and Financial Section, June 7, 1921 and March 14, 1922, ACIP, B 110 (1921) and B 112 (1922).

139. Comité de Bienfaisance, Minutes, October 20, 1925, Minute Book 1921–34.

140. *Ibid.*, January 24, 1928.

141. *Ibid.*, October 13, 1926.

142. C.C., Minutes, December 21, 1926 and April 5, 1927, HM 1072, CAHJP.

143. C.C., Minutes of Permanent Section, March 17, 1927, HM 1073, CAHJP.

144. *Ibid.*, May 12, 1927 and May 31, 1927.

145. C.C., Minutes, January 25, 1939; Article 9, Statutes of C.C., (1939), HUC, France, Box 52.

146. ACIP, *Exercice* (1926), p. 6.

147. *Ibid.*, (1929), pp. 12–13.

148. *Ibid.*, p. 7.

149. *Ibid.*, p. 13.

150. "L'élargissement du Consistoire de Paris," *UI*, March 28, 1930, p. 809.

151. The Council was enlarged to 24, and one-sixth of that number could now be foreigners. The 20 remaining members would serve as Parisian representatives to the C.C., which still did not permit foreign delegates. ACIP, *Exercice* (1930), pp. 14, 17.

152. *TJ*, December 4, 1931, p. 751.

153. William Oualid, *L'Immigration ouvrière en France*, pp. 46–47.

154. *UI*, October 9, 1931, p. 136.

155. *UI*, January 30, 1925, p. 437; Rapport à l'Assemblée Générale de l'Association Ohel Jacob, concernant son activité pendant la période 1926–27, AIU, France I H 1.

156. Letter of Ohel Jacob to ACIP, February 1, 1928, Brandeis, France, IV 8 b.

157. Rapport à l'Assemblée Générale de l'Association Ohel Jacob.

158. *Ibid.* and letter of ACIP, 1928, to Ohel Jacob, Brandeis, France, IV 8 b.

159. Meeting of representatives of ACIP and of Ohel Jacob, March 19, 1928, Brandeis, France, IV 8 b.

160. Notes de M. Adolphe Caen sur "Les Consistoires et les Etrangers," (1931), Brandeis, France, IV 3 c.

161. *Ibid.*

162. *Ibid.*

163. Notes du secretariat: *Exposé* (1931), Brandeis, France, IV 3 c.

164. Police Report, August 29, 1929, Police Archives, Paris, 241.155-A-B-B[1]-B[2].

165. Notes du secretariat.

166. *Ibid.*

167. *Ibid.*

168. When the Pavée synagogue, built by Agoudas HaKehillos, was dedicated in 1914, no consistorial rabbi was present. A Yiddish paper then pointed out that in London the Chief Rabbi of England himself had spoken in Yiddish at the dedication of an immigrant yeshiva "to indicate that he was also the rabbi of the foreign Jews." The President of the Paris Consistory was reported to have said: "We have absolutely no interest in synagogues where foreign rabbis will preach in jargon. . . . In France one must be French." *Der Yid in Pariz*, July 20, 1914.

169. *Menorah*, February 26, 1930, p. 9.

170. *PH*, May 17, 1934.

171. Asiles de Nuit et de Jour, *Exercice* (1932), p. 123.

172. Comité de Bienfaisance, Minutes, November 30, 1934, Minute Book 1934–1937.

173. J. Biélinky, "Les Juifs en France," *La Conscience des Juifs*, November 11, 1935, pp. 12–13.

174. J. Biélinky, *Revue OSE*, February 2, 1937, p. 30.

175. *PH*, June 27, 1934.

176. ACIP, *Exercice* (1928), p. 7.

177. *PH*, March 3, 1933, p. 3; May 17, 1934, p. 3.

178. *Ibid.*, May 6, 1934, p. 1; October 9, 1934, p. 1.

6. The Infiltration of Zionism

1. M. Mirtil, "L'Union des juifs de France." Ms. in the Biélinky Archive, YIVO; published in *Les Cahiers du renouveau* (April, 1935), pp. 136–137.

2. The German rabbinate, for example, issued an anti-Zionist statement in

response to preparations for the First Zionist Congress, and Jewish public opinion forced Herzl to relocate in Basle, Switzerland. See Alex Bein, *Theodore Herzl*, pp. 220–22; Walter Laqueur, *A History of Zionism*, p. 103; and Ben Halpern, *The Idea of the Jewish State*, pp. 144–45.

3. Ben-Ammi, "Le Sionisme et l'histoire juive," *UI*, August 23, 1907, p. 714.

4. R.T., a regular columnist for *UI* declared, "If Israel wishes to remain one of the important factors of history, it must hold fast to its moral and philanthropic role and live life in common with other citizens in the countries where it has found a refuge and a homeland." *UI*, January 14, 1910, p. 557. Another contributor noted that Judaism was never stronger than when the Jews ceased being a nation. J. Cohen, *UI*, January 21, 1910, pp. 581–88.

5. R.M., *UI*, January 14, 1910, pp. 549–50.

6. Maurice Vexler, "Le Sionisme en France," *UI*, September 12, 1913, p. 632.

7. *Ibid.*, pp. 632–33.

8. Report of speech by Mlle. Schach, *UI*, June 11, 1915, p. 288.

9. A.N., F⁷ 13.943, M.2123 U, June 9, 1917. The committee was composed of Marcel Bernfeld, a Romanian subject; Enric Braunstein, a Romanian student in Paris; Jacob Jacobson, a Russian subject; and Léon Algazi, a Romanian student at the *Ecole Rabbinique*. See also *UI*, June 11, 1915, p. 286 and Enric Braunstein, "Rapport sur la politique générale de l'Organisation Sioniste de France," November 1919, CZA A 93/6.

10. *La Renaissance Juive*, May 12, 1916.

11. Article by André Spire, with his typed emendations, CZA A 93/1, pp. 43–44.

12. Letter January 26, 1916, MAE, Guerre 1914–1918, Sionisme 1200 Jan.–Feb. 1918, p. 205.

13. The support of the *Ligue des Droits de l'Homme* for Zionism was officially announced December 1, 1918. A.N., F⁷ 13.943, Report of December 18, 1918. See also *UI*, December 20, 1918, pp. 354–55 and *Les Cahiers des Droits de l'Homme*, July 25, 1922. Letter of October 7, 1916, from Marc Jarblum to Kaplansky describes his recruitment activity among French socialists. Kaplansky IV 104.17, Archion Ha'avoda (Labor Archive), Tel-Aviv. Marc Jarblum (1887–1972) came to Paris as a student in 1907 and became a leader of Poalei-Zion. During the 1930s he edited two Poalei-Zion papers in France, *Unzer vort* and *Di Naye tsayt*. He was a member of the Central Bureau of Poalei-Zion and of the Va'ad Hazioni. During World War II he was active in the resistance in France and Switzerland. He settled in Israel in 1955. *Encyclopedia Judaica*, 9:1287.

14. The size of the audience was estimated by the police informer. Report of August 9, 1915, A.N. F⁷ 13.943. A similar theme was echoed in the appeal of the Zionist group of the 18th *arrondissement*. *La Renaissance Juive*, April 14, 1916.

15. *UI*, January 19, 1917, p. 407.

16. A.N., F⁷ 13.943.

17. Meetings of January 23, 1916; May 7, 1916; November 26, 1916; January 21, 1917; December 16, 1917; December 15, 1918 as reported by police agents. A.N., F⁷ 13.943.

18. Police report of meeting January 23, 1916. Five hundred were in attendance. A.N., F⁷ 13.943.

19. A.N., F⁷ 13.943. This dossier of classified police information includes surveillance not only of Zionists but also of Bundists and of minor Jewish groups.

20. 7672 Source Norbert, February 27, 1919; P.2997 U, December 3, 1918, A.N., F⁷ 13.943.

21. P.2858, September 14, 1918 and P.2981 U, November 26, 1918, A.N., F⁷ 13.943.

22. *La Renaissance Juive*, April 14, 1916 and May 5, 1916; Police reports, A.N., F⁷ 13.943; N. Hermann, "Zionism in France during the War." (Yiddish) *Almanach Juif* (Paris, 1931), p. 44. The sections were located in the 3rd, 4th, 9th, 10th, 18th, and 20th *arrondissements*.

23. Rapport sur la Politique générale de l'Organisation Sioniste de France, November 1919, CZA A 93/6, p. 8.

24. A.N., F⁷ 13.943.

25. *UI*, September 15, 1916, p. 686.

26. Letter from Marc Jarblum to Kaplansky, ca. August–September 1916, Kaplansky IV 104 17, Labor Archive, Tel-Aviv. Zosa Szajkowski, "150 Years of Jewish Press in France," 2:62.

27. For a discussion of Jewish diplomacy at the Versailles peace deliberations and the mediating role of such American Jewish notables as Louis Marshall and Cyrus Adler between representatives of Western and Eastern European Jewry, see Naomi Cohen, *Not Free to Desist*, pp. 102–22. Other studies of Jewish negotiations for minority rights include Oscar Janowsky, *The Jews and Minority Rights, 1898–1919*; Jacob Robinson, *Das Minoritäten Problem und seine Literatur*; and Kurt Stillschweig, *Die Juden Osteuropas in den Minderheitsvortragen*.

28. Cohen, *ibid.*, p. 116.

29. Alliance Israélite Universelle, *La Question juive devant la Conférence de la Paix*. The French government was sympathetic to the Alliance's point of view. In a memo to his superior, Gabriel Puaux, director of the Services d'Information et de Presse, André Spire responded negatively to a government spokesman's qualifications of minority rights with the terms "to guarantee the rights of minorities until they can blend themselves [*se fondre*] with the majority population." "The Quai D'Orsay," Spire replied, "must be ignorant of the first word of the Jewish question to allow such a phrase in a letter destined to defend the actions of France regarding this question. The Jews of Eastern Europe exhibit a marked ethnic personality which they desire to defend against assimilation and it mocks their demands to speak to them of fusion with the races which have persecuted and massacred them." Letter from Spire to Gabriel Puaux, July 18, 1919, CZA A 93/5.

30. Letter from Leo Motzkin to Israel Cohen, August 24, 1919, CZA Z4/1791 II.

31. Leonard Stein, *The Balfour Declaration*, pp. 589–601; *UI*, November 23, 1917, pp. 265–66 and February 15, 1918, p. 553.

32. Readers' letters to *UI* were critical of the hostile or indifferent tone that most correspondents of the paper, with the notable exception of Aimé Pallière, had taken toward the Balfour Declaration. See *UI*, November 23, 1917, pp. 265–66; November 30, 1917, pp. 289–92; and January 18, 1918, pp. 467–68. In a note addressed by the Secretariat of the Alliance Israélite to members of the Central Committee on February 18, 1917, objections were raised to Zionism on both practical

and ideological grounds. Palestine could not, it was claimed, absorb the masses of Jews, who, in any case, would make poor farmers. Zionism played into the hands of anti-Semites. Only the Jews of Russia and Poland consider themselves, and wrongly, a nation. The solution of the Alliance was to encourage the emancipation of Jews in all countries and equal civil rights for Jews in Palestine. A.I.U. France I.G.3. The fear that Zionism would strengthen the hands of anti-Semites was confirmed by the fact that Urbain Gohier, one of France's most prominent anti-Semites since the days of the Dreyfus Affair, announced himself in favor of obligatory Zionism. *UI*, January 18, 1918, pp. 457–60.

33. Article by André Apire, CZA A 93/1, p. 472.

34. Report of Sylvain Lévi, MAE, Palestine 1918–1929, E13, Feb.–July, 1919; also E12, Jan.–Feb. 1919, p. 179. On Rothschild's role in Lévi's appearance, see Evyatar Friesel, "Baron Edmond de Rothschild and the Zionists, 1918–1919," pp. 127–29.

35. Yiddish was seen as a German language and hence an entering wedge for German cultural and political influence. AIU, France II D 6 bis; *UI*, March 14, 1919, pp. 7–8. On Rothschild's preparation of the speech, see Friesel, "Baron de Rothschild," p. 128.

36. A.I.U., France II D 6 bis for Sylvain Lévi's account of his speech at the Peace Conference. See also André Chouraqui, *L'Alliance Israélite Universelle* (Paris, 1965), pp. 223–27 and Minutes of 46th Session of the Supreme Council of the Allies, Chouraqui, pp. 476–80.

37. *Le Peuple Juif*, March 7, 1919, pp. 3–4. The Zionist student group also protested Lévi's speech. *Le Peuple Juif*, March 14, 1919, p. 11. For Spire's reaction, see his memoirs, *Souvenirs à batons rompus*, p. 109.

38. Minutes of Permanent Section of Central Consistory, March 17, 1919, HM 1073, CAHJP.

39. *Ibid.*, March 17, 1919.

40. *Ibid.*, March 24, 1919; C.C. Minutes, March 24, 1919, HM 1072, CAHJP.

41. AIU, France II D 6 bis. This was the only text of the Central Consistory resolution I was able to locate, as it was not preserved in the archives of the Consistory itself. An anonymous hand-written explanatory note describes the text as a proposed declaration drawn up by Israël Lévi, which was to have been submitted for approval to the Central Consistory in March 1919. According to this note, Baron Edmond de Rothschild declared that he was opposed to any public declaration. Since a statement drawn up by Israël Lévi *was* adopted on March 24, 1919, by the Central Consistory, it appears likely that this served, at the least, as the basis for the final version.

42. Minutes of Permanent Section of Central Consistory, May 12, 1919, HM 1073. A leader of the Keren Kayemeth branch in Strasbourg, commenting on the restrictions placed on the French rabbinate: "Recently I have found a dedicated collaborator in . . . the person of Rabbi Berman of Dijon. Unfortunately, Rabbi Berman cannot do what he wants. In his community he confronts the opposition of two to three of his coreligionists. . . . The rabbi of a French community is the fifth wheel of a wagon or, to put it better, a chamber valet, who must play the tune the commu-

nity pipes." Letter from Léon Salomon of Strasbourg to Adolph Pollak, Berlin, March 18, 1923, CZA Z4/2146.

43. *Le Peuple juif,* October 8, 1920, p. 8.

44. Note, signed J.G., February 26, 1919, MAE Palestine 1918–1929, Carton E 13, Feb.–July 1919.

45. *Parizer leben,* February 16, 1923, p. 2. See also *La Terre retrouvée,* April 15, 1939, p. 10.

46. As early as February 1917, the secretariat of the Alliance sent a 15-page note to the members of the Central Committee, objecting to Zionism. AIU, France I G 3. Jacques Bigart, the secretary-general of the Alliance, in a letter of May 3, 1918, to Joseph Nehama of Salonica, raised the familiar objections to Zionism and added that it would be futile to combat Zionism at the moment because the movement was so violent. Hence, his policy of waiting until the injustice could be revealed through a series of events. AIU, France I G 3 and Chouraqui, *L'Alliance Israélite,* pp. 221, 470–72. Expressions of neutrality were published in the Annual Report presented to the Extraordinary Annual Meeting of June 27, 1920 and again in the form of a resolution of the Central Committee, AIU, France XI A 81; *Paix et droit,* December 20, 1922, p. 12. The Alliance, it was maintained, could not take a position on an issue which divided Israelites themselves. The resolution was circulated in draft form to the members of the Central Committee, inviting their comments. One member noted that it was hypocritical of the Alliance to claim neutrality on the issue. The Alliance had taken a stand on whether the Jews were a nation seeking to reestablish themselves in a kingdom or a religious body, and had come down on the side of the latter definition and hence in opposition to Zionism. AIU, France I G 4. Letter, probably from Salomon Cahen, December 12, 1922. Alfred Berl, a prominent collaborator of the Alliance and a notorious anti-Zionist, demanded that the last sentence of the resolution, which stated that "the Alliance viewed with satisfaction all that would be done in that country (Palestine) for the economic, moral, and intellectual development of the Israelites," be struck, since it violated the position of absolute neutrality. The sentence was deleted. AIU, France I G 4, Letter of December 11, 1922.

47. Letter from S. Lehmann to the President of the Alliance, June 30, 1918, AIU, France I G 5. For articles sympathetic to Zionism, see *UI* May 10, 1918, pp. 197–200 and May 17, 1918, pp. 227–29.

48. *Paix et droit,* March, 1921, pp. 2–3; April, 1921, p. 4; January, 1922, pp. 5–6.

49. *Le Peuple juif,* June 25, 1920, p. 9.

50. The names of 78 prominent Jewish personalities were already on the list, including that of Rabbi Isaïe Schwartz of Strasbourg, later (in 1939) to become Chief Rabbi of France. Keren Hayesod directed its appeal to non-Zionists, and the funds collected were used for development in Palestine. Letter of February 9 and 10, 1922, AIU, France I G 5.

51. Letters of September 1 and 3, 1922, AIU, France I G 5.

52. Extraordinary Session of the Alliance Israélite, October 25, 1922, Marshall Papers, Box 157, AJHA.

53. The first demand was stated in a letter of February 1, 1921, from Nahoum to

Jacques Bigart, secretary-general of the Alliance, recounting his reply to James de Rothschild's desire for a more sympathetic attitude on the part of the Central Committee of the Alliance toward Zionism. AIU, France I G 5. The second was raised by M. Sée at the Extraordinary Session of the Alliance, October 25, 1922, Marshall Papers, Box 157, AJHA.

54. Interview with M. Canet, July 1, 1927, MAE, E Levant 1918–1929, Palestine 29, 1926–1929, p. 123. Similar sentiments were expressed in a meeting of January 21, 1926, *ibid.*, pp. 5–6 and in a letter of the Alliance, April 6, 1923, MAE, E Levant 1918–1929, Sionisme 28, July 1922–December 1925, pp. 44–45.

55. For example, from October 1, 1925 until September 30, 1926 contributions to the Keren Kayemeth in France totaled 256,932.70 francs. More than half of the contributions (139,866.65 francs) came from Alsace-Lorraine. *La Terre promise*, October 25, 1926, p. 8. The philanthropic definition of Zionism was first suggested in France by Fernand Corcos, a Zionist of an old Sephardic family. See his "Le Bilan du Sionisme Français," *Menorah*, June 15–July 1, 1927, pp. 188–91.

56. Appeal of Keren Hayesod, printed in *Menorah*, October 15, 1922 p. 61 and February, 1923, pp. 177–78.

57. The article was signed Judaeus, the *nom de plume* of Rabbi Liber. *UI*, August 25, 1922, pp. 509–13. Interview with Rabbi Schilli, October 18, 1972.

58. Resolution of the Association of French Rabbis, General Assembly 1923. The resolution was adopted with only one dissenting vote. Special Collections, Brandeis, I 12 b. See *Menorah*, July 29, 1923.

59. *Ibid.*

60. *UI*, August 21, 1925, pp. 525–27; *Menorah*, September 1, 1925, and September 15, 1925, p. 267.

61. M. Liber, *UI*, August 21, 1925, p. 525. Italics in original.

62. *La Terre promise*, July 24, 1925, p. 6. For information on Pallière (1875–1949) see his autobiographical work *Le Sanctuaire Inconnu* (Paris, 1926) and *EJ*, 13:43.

63. *Menorah*, September 1, 1925 and September 15, 1925, p. 267; *La Tribune juive* (Strasbourg), April 9, 1926, p. 202; CZA Z4/3232 II.

64. The distinction was drawn by Ben Halpern, *The Idea of the Jewish State*, pp. 131–33.

65. Letter of Leo Motzkin to F. Rosenblüth, March 12, 1929, and April 2, 1929, CZA L9/111. Motzkin had stressed in his talks with Rabbi Lévi the importance for the Zionist Organization of having French Jewry represented by suitable and authoritative personalities.

66. Letters of Leo Motzkin to F. Rosenblüth, April 2, 1929, and to Rabbi Israël Lévi, July 12, 1929, CZA L9/111.

67. Letter of Sylvain Lévi to Leo Motzkin, May 17, 1929, CZA L9/111.

68. Unsigned letter of S. Brodetzky, April 19, 1929, CZA Z4/3362.

69. Letter of Leo Motzkin to Stein of the Zionist Executive, London, May 14, 1929, labeled strictly confidential, CZA L9/111.

70. Letter of Israël Lévi to Leo Motzkin, July 5, 1929, CZA L9/111.

71. Letter of Leo Motzkin to Israël Lévi, July 12, 1929, CZA L9/111. See also Joel Colton, *Léon Blum: Humanist in Politics*, p. 476; André Blumel, *Léon Blum:*

juif et sioniste, pp. 11–12. In 1932 Blum wrote an article for the New York Yiddish paper, *Der Tag*, reprinted in *Parizer haynt*, September 19, 1932, in which he stressed the compatibility of Zionism with French patriotism. He suggested that the many French Jews who were afraid of working for Jewish causes because they feared this would arouse anti-Semitism erred in their approach.

72. Letter of Motzkin to Lévi, July 12, 1929, CZA L9/111.

73. Letter of Jewish Agency Executive to Dr. A. Auerbach, Keren Hayesod, Paris, July 4, 1935, CZA Z4/3362.

74. Letter of Léopold Metzger of the Regional Union of Zionists of Eastern France to the Zionist Organization, London, October 17, 1935, CZA Z4/3233; letter from the Organization Department of the Jewish Agency to the *Fédération des Sociétés Juives*, July 16, 1935, CZA Z4/3362; letter from Israël Jefroykin to Dr. Werner Senator, March 16, 1936, CZA S29/679; letter from Leo Motzkin to Israël Lévi, July 12, 1929, CZA L9/111; letter, probably from Dr. A. Auerbach to Lauterbach, July 3, 1935, CZA Z4/3362.

75. *La Terre retrouvée*, October 25, 1931, pp. 14, 19.

76. Report of the Keren Hayesod, June, 1935, CZA Z4/3233.

77. Letter from the Regional Union of Zionists of Eastern France to the Zionist Organization, London, December 29, 1934, CZA Z4/3233.

78. For an account of the Passfield White Paper, see Walter Laqueur, *A History of Zionism*, 492–93.

79. Minutes of the Annual Session of the Alliance Israélite, November 5, 1930. American Jewish Committee Archives, France A.I.U., 1930–1933.

80. Oscar I. Janowsky, *Foundations of Israel* (Princeton: Van Nostrand, 1959), pp. 146–47.

81. Jacob Kaplan, "Un sermon sur le sionisme," *UI*, April 16, 1937, pp. 489–90. See also *Bulletin du Centre de Documentation et de Vigilance*, no. 28 (April 8, 1937), pp. 1–2.

82. *Samedi*, July 8, 1939, p. 4.

83. *La Terre retrouvée*, June 1, 1939, p. 5. The 1939 White Paper limited Jewish immigration to Palestine to 75,000 over the next five years, after which it would be dependent on Arab approval. Jewish purchase of land in Palestine was also severely restricted. For an account of the White Paper, see Walter Laqueur, *The Israel-Arab Reader* (New York: Citadel, 1969), pp. 64–75 and *A History of Zionism*, pp. 528–33. Only the *Union Patriotique des Français Israélites* called upon French Jews, as Frenchmen first and foremost, not to protest British policy in Palestine. *La Terre retrouvée*, June 1, 1939, p. 20.

84. CZA S5 1708, S 5 1741.

85. For a more extended discussion of Alsatian Zionism, see my *The Jews in Post-Dreyfus France*, dissertation, Columbia University, 1975, pp. 358–59.

86. Editorial of *La Revue littéraire juive*, March, 1927. The editorial committee included Fernand Corcos, Edmond Fleg, Henry Marx, R. R. Lambert, Yvonne Netter, Maxa Nordau, and Hillel Zlatopolsky. See also, the letter of C. Rivline, *Union Scolaire*, November 15, 1931, p. 5. Grand Rabbi Julien Weill attributed considerable importance to the role of Zionism in the cultural revival among French

Jewry. J. Weill, "La Renaissance religieuse dans le Judaisme," p. 94. See also Rabbi R. Hirschler, *Kadimah*, Special no., 5693, p. 49; Rabbi Haguenau, "Le Sionisme," (1921 sermon), in *Discours et Prières*, p. 176.

87. Notes du Secrétariat, Paris Consistory, Special Collections, Brandeis University Library, IV 3 c, pp. 1–2.

88. *UI*, April 18, 1927, pp. 869–70.

89. For information on these and other French Jewish periodicals, see Zosa Szajkowski, "150 years of Jewish Press," pp. 236–308.

90. Cf. *Menorah* (1922–1933). *Menorah* received a subsidy from the Zionist Organization in London. Letter of L. Camhy, editor of *Menorah*, to Leo Motzkin, September 9, 1929, CZA L9/235. See also *La Tribune juive* (Strasbourg, 1926–1939); *Kadimah* (Mulhouse, 1930–1936); *Chalom* (1924–1934), the organ of the *Union Universelle de la Jeunesse Juive*, and *Cahiers juifs* (1933–1936) of Paris and Alexandria.

91. *La Terre retrouvée*, May 1, 1937, p. 6.

92. CZA Z4/3233.

93. Letter from A. Rywkind of *Organisation Sioniste de France* to Lauterbach, December 4, 1936, CZA S5/2198.

94. A comment by Rywkind: "Having taken issue with Dr. Weizmann and grossly attacked N. Goldmann, as well as the Zionist funds, *Samedi* has become impossible for us." *Ibid.* However, both *Samedi* and *Affirmation* were pro-Zionist. See *Affirmation*, April 21, 1939, p. 6; August 18, 1939, p. 1. Commemorating the national past was even invoked as a rationale for the nonreligious to observe Jewish holidays. J. Chender, "La question religieuse," *Affirmation*, July 7, 1939, p. 6. *Samedi* was highly critical of French Jewish indifference to Arab terrorism and even called in 1938 for a Jewish state in Palestine as "the only hope for the Jewish people." *Samedi*, February 12, 1938, p. 2. See also September 19, 1936, pp. 1, 6; April 11, 1936, p. 8; August 14, 1937, pp. 1, 2.

95. *L'Univers israélite* noted the enthusiastic reception of the film "La Nouvelle Palestine" in Strasbourg and Bordeaux. *UI*, April 6, 1923 and May 11, 1923. See also *La Terre retrouvée*, March 20, 1929, p. 11; Report of Regional Union of Zionists of Eastern France, February 21, 1935, CZA Z4/3233; *La Terre retrouvée*, October 15, 1928, p. 19, and January 25, 1934, p. 24; *Menorah*, May 1, 1925, p. 147.

96. A. Alperin, "Jewish Organizations and Institutions in Paris," p. 256.

97. Letter from Maurice Levinson to Zionist Federation of France, October 5, 1931, CZA F11/13.

98. 1937 Report of Regional Union of Zionists of Eastern France, CZA S5/2229.

99. *Ibid.*, and Report of Regional Union of Zionists of Eastern France, February 21, 1935, CZA Z4/3233.

100. Minutes of Directing Committee of Zionist Federation of France, May 14, 1928, CZA L9/275.

101. Letter from the President of the Consistory of Moselle, March 4, 1937, to Regional Union of Zionists of Eastern France, rejecting Zionist offers of cooperation in Jewish educational activities with the comment that the religious courses as constituted were completely satisfactory. CZA S29/68.

102. In giving advice to those who wished to establish a similar group in Poland the leaders of France-Palestine suggested that any evidence that the society was founded at Zionist initiative should be avoided. CZA L9/281.

103. *Menorah*, December 1, 1925, p. 347. For an interview with Godart, see *Chalom*, January 15, 1930, pp. 4–6. For Godart's pro-Zionist activities, see *La Terre retrouvée*, January 25, 1934, p. 10. Godart also served as president of the Keren Kayemeth in France. Henri Hertz was responsible for France-Palestine's day-to-day activity. Cf. CZA L9/281 and letter of Nahum Goldmann to David Ben-Gurion, November 24, 1935, CZA Z4/3232 III.

104. "J. F.," "La Nouvelle mission de France-Palestine," *La Terre retrouvée*, December 25, 1935, pp. 6–7.

105. *Le Peuple juif*, October 31, 1919, pp. 1–3.

106. Meeting of Directing Committee of the Zionist Federation of France, May 14, 1928, CZA L9/275.

107. Report of 1935, probably of Regional Union of Zionists of Eastern France, CZA Z4/3233.

108. *Ibid.*

109. Letter from N. Halpern and A. Goldstein of Keren Hayesod to the Zionist Organization Executive, London, June 17, 1931, CZA Z4/3362; Letter of Jewish Agency Department of Organization to Jefroykin, June 23, 1939 and letter of N. Hermann to Jewish Agency, Zurich, July 1937, CZA S29/67a.

110. Michel Roblin, *Les Juifs de Paris*, p. 174. Szajkowski also remarks that the Federation of Jewish Societies was under Zionist influence during the 1930s. Szajkowski, "Jewish Communal Life in Paris," p. 219.

111. For Pallière's influence, see Chapter 7 under "The UUJJ."

112. A typical Pallière statement on Zionism: "In becoming Frenchmen, the Jews of France did no less remain Jews, and just as they rebel at the idea of seeing anyone suspect the purity of their patriotism, they should no more support the thought that they could be accused, in any way, of denying Judaism, its faith, its traditions, its hopes. And that is why the new opportunities which have opened in Palestine must find them united with their brothers of the whole world in the desire to profit from the marvelous possibilities offered for the realization of the age-old ideal of Israel." *Foi et réveil*, No. 11, 1920, p. 69. See also "La Route de Jerusalem," *UI*, November 30, 1917, pp. 289–92; "Les Leçons du Congrès d'Amérique," *UI*, February 3, 1919, pp. 545–48; *La Palestine nouvelle*, No. 5 (March 1, 1919), p. 4; *La Terre promise*, July 24, 1925, pp. 6–7; "Sionisme et U.U.J.J.," *Chalom*, January 1927, p. 305.

113. Confidential letter of Aimé Pallière to Zionist Organization Executive, July 24, 1927, CZA Z4/3232 II.

114. Aimé Pallière, "Sionisme et U.U.J.J.," *Chalom*, May 1927, pp. 3–5; A. L. Grajevsky, "Idéologie Sioniste," *Chalom*, May 1927, pp. 22–25; "Zionism has but one goal, the renaissance of Judaism. It is our duty to aid in the realization of that ideal."

115. Confidential letter of Aimé Pallière, July 24, 1927, CZA Z4/3232 II.

116. Letter of J. Castel to Zionist Organization Executive, May 30, 1927, CZA Z4/3232 II. The international Zionist leadership sought closer, more direct contact

with the UUJJ and found its program "still so vague and many-sided." Memo of G. Stolar to F. Rosenblüth, August 17, 1927, CZA Z4/3232 II. In 1927, they considered the UUJJ to be the most important and most popular Jewish association in Paris, which kept Jewish youth in Jewish surroundings and supplied them with palatable doses of Jewish culture. Confidential Report on French Zionism, CZA Z4/3232 II.

117. *Chalom*, June, 1929, p. 20.

118. "L'élargissement du Consistoire de Paris," *UI*, March 28, 1930, pp. 809–10.

119. *Samedi*, October 15, 1938, p. 5.

120. *La Terre retrouvée*, October 25, 1931, pp. 14, 19; Report of the Keren Hayesod, June, 1935, CZA Z4/3233.

7. Toward a New Pluralism

1. Philip G. Altbach, "The International Student Movement," p. 158.

2. For a discussion of German youth movements, see Walter Laqueur, *Young Germany: A History of the German Youth Movement* and George L. Mosse, *The Crisis of German Ideology*, pp. 171–89.

3. Aline Coutrot, "Youth Movements in France in the 1930's," pp. 25–26.

4. *Ibid.*, pp. 26–27; 32.

5. Chanoch Rinott, "Major Trends in Jewish Youth Movements in Germany," pp. 77–95 deals with the Zionist tendencies of the German Jewish youth movements, as does Chaim Schatzker's "The History of the 'Blau-Weiss': The Path to Zionism of the First German Jewish Youth Movement," pp. 137–168. See also Walter Gross, "The Zionist Students' Movement," pp. 143–164, Eliyahu Moaz (Mosbacher), "The Werkleute," pp. 165–182. For an analysis of the major umbrella youth organization of German Jews, which was neutral in orientation but included Zionists, see Herbert Strauss, "The Jugendverband," *Leo Baeck Institute Yearbook*, 6 (1961):206–35.

6. The Union de la Jeunesse Israélite existed as early as 1906 and was subsidized by the Paris Consistory. Letter, June 26, 1907, ACIP, BB 85 (1907–1909). The Association des Jeunes Juifs was established in 1912 by young Russian immigrants, assisted by André Spire. It published a monthly bulletin entitled "Les Pionniers." JTS, France, Box 22; Letter to Paris Consistory, ACIP, B 91 (1912). See also André Spire, *Les Juifs et la guerre*, pp. 137–42.

7. The *Naye presse*, Feb. 6, 1934, p. 5 noted that a celebration of the Jewish Communist youth group drew 400 young people aged 16–18 and a large number between the ages of 13 and 15. The Bundist youth group, Skif, established in 1935, held regular activities. See *Unzer shtime*, Jan. 25, 1936, p. 1 and Michel Roblin, *Les Juifs de Paris*, p. 171. The *Yiddish Hantbuch* of 1937 listed 19 Jewish youth groups, pp. 120–123.

8. N. Frank, *PH*, July 21, 1933, p. 3.

9. *NP*, Jan. 11, 1934, p. 6; Report of Daniel Charney on Yiddish culture in Paris, YIVO Archives, France.

10. "Appel à la jeunesse israélite," *UI*, November 28, 1919, pp. 222–25. The goal of the founders was to establish a "society for education and religious propaganda," pp. 222–23.

11. *Ibid.*, p. 222.

12. Programs of Chema Israel, 1919–20 to 1933–34, JTS, France, Box 17. A report of one of the Sunday lectures, given by Aimé Pallière, noted that the hall was standing room only. *UI*, December 23, 1921, pp. 302–4.

13. *UI*, April 17, 1922, pp. 39–40 and November 30, 1923, p. 289.

14. Programs of Chema Israel, 1919–20, 1920–21, 1924–25, 1928, 1930, 1932–33, JTS, France, Box 17.

15. "L'Oeuvre de Chema Israel," descriptive circular, 1930, JTS, France, Box 17.

16. *UI*, May 13, 1921, announces the existence of a section in Lyon, pp. 82–83. See also "L'Oeuvre de Chema Israel," JTS, France, Box 17.

17. *Ibid.* The branches were in Bayonne, Belfort, Besançon, Bordeaux, Forbach, Lille, Lunéville, Lyon, Marseilles, Metz, Mulhouse, Nice, Nîmes, and Rouen. See also the *Bulletin du Chema Israel*, December, 1928, describing activities in Metz. Stationery from 1932 and 1933 also listed 14 sections in the provinces, with Thionville replacing Bordeaux, JTS, France, Box 17.

18. A report on the subject was proposed for 1932. *Kadimah*, June 12, 1931, p. 7.

19. The lecture on Shalom Aleichem was a notable, and early, exception. On only one occasion, the announcement of a meeting to be presided over by Grand Rabbi Aisenstadt, the Consistory-recognized rabbi of the Russian Jewish community, was publicity conducted in Yiddish as well as French. Circular, July, 1928, JTS, France, Box 17. Most history and literature courses focused on subjects acceptable to Western tastes—e.g., the Golden Age of Jewry in medieval Spain, the history of the Jews in France, Biblical and Talmudic literature. Circulars, JTS, France, Box. 17.

20. *Bulletin de Chema Israel*, May 1928, p. 14.

21. Names of committee members did not exceed 10 percent of Eastern European origin. *Bulletin de Chema Israel*, May 1930, p. 13; May 1928, p. 14.

22. CC, Permanent Section, Minutes, May 20, 1930 notes an allocation of 2,000 francs a year to Chema Israel. From its founding Chema Israel had enjoyed the collaboration of French rabbis and the use of Consistory facilities for its meetings and courses. CAHJP, HM 1073. By 1926 the UUJJ had defined its pro-Palestinism and its goal of cultivating Jewish sentiment through a variety of means, of which religion was only one. *Chalom*, October, 1926, pp. 9–11.

23. *UI*, June 3, 1927, p. 243.

24. *Chalom*, May 15–June 15, 1928, p. 12.

25. *UI*, June 3, 1927, p. 243.

26. "Lettre de Paris," *Kadimah*, June 12, 1931, p. 7.

27. Letters, November 21, 1932 and November 14, 1933. JTS, France, Box 17.

28. The last schedule of programs dates from 1933–34. The *Bulletin de Chema Israel* was published for the last time in 1934. JTS, France, Box 17.

29. *La Tribune juive*, July 20, 1928, p. 441.

30. *Chalom*, August 15–September 15, 1928, p. 15

31. *Ibid.*, and June, 1931, p. 23

32. Confidential report on French Zionism (1927), CZA Z4/3232 II.

33. *Chalom*, July, 1927, p. 13.

34. Aimé Pallière, "L'U.U.J.J. et l'esprit religieux," *Chalom*, February, 1929, p. 2. See also Meyerkey (pen name of Meyer Levyne), "Chronique parisienne," *Chalom*, April 15, 1927, p. 19: "Even as unbelievers, they want to be Jews. This proves that we are at least as much a people as a religion; that one is a child of Israel as long as one does not break ethnically one's ties with Israel."

35. Pallière was conscious of this return to an earlier definition of Judaism. The question of whether a Jewish organization was religious or not, he noted, revealed the extent of assimilation among French Jews. "It would have astonished the Jews of former times; Jewish people, Jewish religion; these elements for them could not be separated." *Chalom*, March 1928, p. 4.

36. *Chalom*, July 1927, pp. 12–13.

37. *Ibid.*, p. 13.

38. Confidential letter of Pallière to Z. O. Executive, July 24, 1927, CZA Z4/3232 II.

39. *Chalom*, October 1926, p. 9.

40. Confidential report on French Zionism (1927). Pallière was reported to be most anxious to turn the UUJJ into a friendly Zionist body, but other leaders, particularly Nehama, opposed taking such a step. CZA Z4/3232 II; *Menorah*, September 1, 1928, p. 239.

41. Lecture of Léon Berman, as reported by Jaime Azancot, "Le Judaisme de demain," *Chalom*, February 1929, pp. 18–19.

42. *Chalom*, October 1926, p. 11. Because of its critical stance toward the type of assimilation which followed the emancipation of French Jewry, the UUJJ printed articles refuting the received myths of French Jewish history. See, for example, "L'Abbé Grégoire contre la synagogue: Essai de vérité historique," *Chalom*, June 1931, pp. 4–7.

43. *Chalom*, October 1926, p. 10. An appeal in *Chalom*: "Young Jews, learn Hebrew! A language is a soul. There would be no France without the beautiful French language—no Judaism without Hebrew." *Chalom*, December 1927–January 1928, p. 16.

44. W. Rabinovitch, "Rapport sur le travail de la section de Paris," *Chalom*, August 1927, p. 7.

45. Statutes of UUJJ, *Chalom*, October 1926, p. 11.

46. *Ibid.*, p. 9.

47. *Ibid.*, pp. 9–10.

48. *Ibid.*, pp. 9, 11.

49. *Chalom*, July, 1926, pp. 15–16. Lambert later became the editor-in-chief of the *Univers israélite* and, under Vichy, the interim president of the Union Génerale des Israélites Français. See *L'Activité des organisations juives en France sous l'occupation* (Paris, 1947), p. 113 and *passim*.

50. *Chalom*, January 1928, p. 21.

51. Confidential letter of Pallière to Z.O. Executive, July 24, 1927, CZA Z4/3232 II.

52. *Chalom*, May 15–June 15, 1928, p. 12.
53. *Chalom*, June 15–July 15, 1928, pp. 20–21.
54. Ben-Ammi, "Pourquoi je ne suis pas U.U.J.J.-iste," *UI*, August 3, 1928, pp. 581–83.
55. Meyerkey, "Lettre ouverte à M. le Grand-Rabbin de France," *La Tribune juive*, August 31, 1928, pp. 542–43.
56. "Après le Congrès de l'U.U.J.J.," *UI*, August 24, 1928, p. 628.
57. Meyerkey, *La Tribune juive*, August 31, 1928, pp. 540–41.
58. *Chalom*, February 1929, pp. 15–16; September 1928, pp. 6–7.
59. "Do you doubt that through its courses in Hebrew and Jewish history, its youth activities, and its action on behalf of Palestine, the UUJJ saves, and leads back to Israel, a large number of souls," queried the UUJJ, *Chalom*, February 1929, pp. 15–16.
60. Aimé Pallière, "Au carrefour," *Chalom*, January 1934, pp. 1–5. Pallière called for a religious revival and patience on the part of Jews as a response to Nazism. In addition, he rejected the notion of a Jewish nationalism in France which might define Jewish political interests as contrary to French interests, as Rabinovitch had done. The following month Rabinovitch was no longer listed as Editorial Secretary on the masthead of *Chalom*. Subsequently, more native Jews, and fewer immigrants, began to appear as contributors to the journal.
61. The accent on the spiritual became increasingly stronger within the pages of *Chalom* during 1933 and 1934. Pallière, the editor, had begun to find Zionism more pragmatic and less idealistic than he had hoped.
62. Maxime Piha, "Assimilés et renégats," *Cahiers juifs*, no. 2 (March–April, 1933), p. 94.
63. The Eclaireurs Israélites de France, hereafter referred to as the EIF, continues in existence, having celebrated its fiftieth anniversary in 1973.
64. EIF, *Historique* (undated pamphlet). A cordial interview with Denise Gamzon, widow of Robert Gamzon, on September 13, 1972, provided much information on Gamzon's life and on the evolution of the Jewish scout movement. For further biographical information on Gamzon, see Isaac Pougatch, *Robert Gamzon*.
65. EIF, Minutes of the Conseil Directeur des Chefs et Commissaires, hereafter abbreviated as CD, May 8, 1924.
66. Even several years later the establishment of Jewish scout troops was seen as a safeguard against the allure of proselytizing groups. For example, in 1930 the EIF learned that Protestants were attempting to proselytize among immigrant Jews in the 20th arrondissement, and concluded that "it would be necessary to set up troops in that quarter." EIF, CD, Minutes, November 20, 1930.
67. EIF, CD, Minutes, November 29, 1926.
68. *Ibid.*, Minutes, March 20, 1927. Rabbi Maurice Liber, perhaps the most vociferously anti-Zionist member of the Central Committee, remained staunchly opposed to the federation.
69. *Ibid.*, Minutes, October 4, 1927.
70. EIF, General Assembly, October 9, 1930.
71. EIF, CD, Minutes, May 14, 1927.
72. *Ibid.*, June 30, 1927.

73. *Ibid.*, October 21, 1928.
74. *Ibid.*, October 20, 1930.
75. *Ibid.*, February 25, 1933; *La Terre retrouvée*, December 25, 1932, p. 18. The vote on the resolution was 40–4.
76. Letter to Mme. Gamzon, mother of Robert Gamzon, February 20, 1933, cited in EIF, CD, Minutes, February 25, 1933.
77. Argument advanced by M. Hait, scout leader from Mulhouse, of immigrant origin. EIF, CD, Minutes, February 25, 1933.
78. *Ibid.*, and April 30, 1933. The spokesmen for the troop leaders were Robert Gamzon and M. Hait. See also R. Gamzon, "Le scoutisme israélite," *Le Rayon*, December 15, 1927, pp. 12–13 for a similar argument.
79. EIF, CD, Minutes, February 25, 1933.
80. *Ibid.*
81. Mme. Helbronner, EIF, CD, *Ibid.*
82. *Ibid.*, April 30, 1933.
83. Mmes. Geismar and Bumsel, *Ibid.*
83. *Ibid.*, June 19, 1933.
85. *Ibid.*
86. *Ibid.*, November 21, 1933 and March 27, 1934.
87. *Ibid.*
88. EIF, *Historique.*
89. EIF, General Assembly, November 9, 1930; Edmond Fleg, "L'Eclaireur d'Israël," in *La Voix d'Israël: Conférences israélites* (Paris, 1932), pp. 165–70.
90. EIF, *Historique:* "The German refugees brought a richer and livelier conception of Judaism into the movement." Mme. Gamzon also stressed the impact of the German Jewish refugees upon the movement, noting that native Jewish youth were more reponsive to the refugees than to immigrants from Eastern Europe because they felt a common cultural bond with the former. Interview, September 13, 1972.
91. EIF, *Historique:* Report to the Central Committee, EIF, CD, Minutes, February 3, 1935.
92. EIF, *Historique; Affirmation*, February 24, 1931, p. 7.
93. EIF, typescript manual, p. 18.
94. EIF, CD, Minutes, February 1, 1936.
95. EIF, typescript manual, p. 16.
96. EIF, CD, Minutes, February 12, 1930.
97. EIF, typescript manual, p. 16.
98. EIF, CD, Minutes, November 11, 1934.
99. EIF, General Assembly, December 20, 1937.
100. *Ibid.*
101. EIF, CD, Minutes, June 10, 1933. There was some prejudice in the movement against troop leaders of immigrant origin, especially if they had not become naturalized French citizens. Alsatian Jews were found to be most sensitive on this issue. See EIF, CD, Minutes, June 22, 1929.
102. *Ibid.*, November 11, 1934. A member of the Central Committee had also commented in a letter of February 22, 1933 to Gamzon's mother: "One of the goals of the EIF is, in effect, the Gallicization of the former [the immigrants] as much as

the Judaization of the assimilated through scoutism." Cited in EIF, CD, Minutes, February 25, 1933.

8. The Futile Struggle for Leadership

1. Robert F. Byrnes, *Anti-Semitism in Modern France*, 1:110–14; 125–36. See also pp. 18–26.

2. Ralph Schor, "Xénophobie et Extrème Droite: L'Exemple de *l'Ami du Peuple* (1928–1937)," pp. 116–44.

3. It was not until the 1930s that such titles as J. Boissel's *Le Juif, poison mortel* (Paris, 1935) and Louis-Marie Ferré's *Le Racisme et la question juive* (Chauny, 1939) appeared. They contrasted sharply with earlier works like Raymond Chatel's *La Conjuration mondiale judéo-sociale-boche* (Loingres, 1920) and A. L. de la Franquerie de Beslon's *Une nouvelle manoeuvre judéo-maçonnique* (Toulouse, 1928).

4. A. Alperin, "Anti-Semitism in France," p. 270.

5. Alperin, "Anti-Semitism in France," pp. 275–76; *Centre de documentation et de vigilance*, Bulletin 75, (December 1, 1938), mimeographed, pp. 6–7; Pierre Lazareff, *Deadline*, p. 198.

6. Lazareff, *ibid.*, pp. 99–110.

7. Alperin, "Anti-Semitism in France," pp. 270–71.

8. See Robert Soucy, "Le Fascisme de Drieu La Rochelle," pp. 61–84 and "Romanticism and Realism in the Fascism of Drieu La Rochelle," pp. 69–90; also William R. Tucker, "Politics and Aesthetics: The Fascism of Robert Brasillach," pp. 605–617.

9. One editorial in *La Tribune Juive* of Strasbourg blasted French critics who absolved the Tharauds of antisemitism. How, it asked, can critics ignore the Tharauds' approval of Nazism? *TJ*, December 1, 1933, p. 823.

10. *Le Matin*, September 30, 1938. Lazareff, *Deadline*, pp. 198–200; *Le Droit de vivre*, January 1934, p. 2. For an analysis of the French Right during this period, see Charles Micaud, *The French Right and Nazi Germany* (New York, 1964).

11. Interview between Philippe Serre, Undersecretary of State and delegates of the Paris Consistory, February 11, 1938, cited in Ida Benguigui, "L'immigration juive à Paris entre les deux guerres," unpub. thesis for Diplôme d'Etudes superieures, AIU, Ms 527, 1965, pp. 98–99.

12. Minute book of the Unemployment Committee of the 20th Arrondissement (Belleville Club), Yiddish, January 31, 1934, YIVO France.

13. *Les Cahiers des Droits de l'Homme*, May 30, 1931; *Le Populaire*, May 7, 1931; Alperin, "Anti-Semitism in France," p. 274; *Kadimah*, 4, no. 1 (December 1933): 8–9; *Archives israélites*, February 22, 1934, p. 17.

14. On Stavisky, see John M. Sherwood, *George Mandel and the Third Republic*, pp. 137–38 and Weber, *Action Française*, pp. 320–324.

15. For Vallat's remarks, see below and *Journal officiel*, June 7, 1936, p. 1327; Colton, *Léon Blum: Humanist in Politics*, p. 144.

16. *UI*, April 7–14, 1933, p. 24.

17. A. Berl, *Paix et droit*, January 1936, p. 2.

18. Jacques Maritain, *Les Juifs parmi les nations*, p. 22.

19. *La Tribune juive*, May 12, 1933.
20. *Ibid.*, December 22, 1933, pp. 887–88 and August 31, 1934, p. 687.
21. *Ibid.*, April 5, 1935.
22. *Ibid.*, January 13, 1939, p. 24.
23. *Union Scolaire*, December 15, 1931, p. 3.
24. ACIP, *Exercice 1934* (May, 1935), p. 14.
25. *PH*, May 27, 1935, p. 3; *NP*, May 28, 1935, p. 5; *Pariz*, May 30, 1935. David Weinberg, who was allowed access to the records of the Paris Consistory, reports that the notes for the speech which he found there were different from and harsher than the printed version of the speech and the speech as delivered. Weinberg, *A Community in Crisis*, pp. 76, 95–96. The *Univers israélite* did not print the text of Rothschild's speech and reported only that it drew much applause.
26. Declaration of the *Union Patriotique des Français Israélites*, printed in *Kadimah*, 4, no. 5 (May 1934):25; cf. also *Kadimah*, 4, no. 7 (June 22, 1934):20.
27. *La Tribune juive*, October 12, 1934, pp. 815–16.
28. *Ibid.*, September 18, 1935, pp. 657–58; *Kadimah*, 4, no. 5 (May 1934):25.
29. *Kadimah*, May 1, 1931, p. 14; July 24, 1939, p. 12; April 29, 1932, pp. 17–18.
30. *La Conscience des juifs*, May 1936, p. 5.
31. Jacques Rozner, "La lutte contre l'antisemitisme implique la lutte contre le fascisme," *Le Droite de vivre*, 2, no. 14 (July–August 1933):5; Pierre Créange, *Epitres aux juifs*, p. 161; *Racisme? Non, LICA* (Paris, n.d.), p. 3.
32. Bernard Lecache, *Pour tuer l'antisemitisme* (Paris n.d.), p. 11 and "Pas d'exclusivisme dans la lutte contre l'antisemitisme," *Kadimah*, October–November 1932, pp. 55–56.
33. *Ver Kemft kegn antisemitizm?* (Paris, 1933), p. 11.
34. J. Chomsky, *PH*, November 4, 1934, p. 3; see also N. Frank, *PH*, October 26, 1934, p. 3.
35. A. Alperin, *PH*, May 29, 1935, p. 1.
36. *Ibid.*, August 10, 1934, p. 1.
37. *Ibid.*, May 5, 1935, p. 1; May 6, 1935, pp. 1, 3; May 24, 1935, p. 1; June 7, 1935, p. 3.
38. FSJ, *Rapport moral et financier 1935–36* (Paris, 1936), pp. 24–25.
39. *PH*, September 17, 1932, p. 3; *Parizer morgenblatt*, September 17, 1932, p. 3; *Kadimah*, 2 no. 20 (August–September 1932):8–9.
40. *PH*, June 3, 1935, p. 1; *Pariz*, June 21, 1935.
41. *PH*, July 8, 1932, p. 1; *UI*, August 13, 1932, pp. 517–19; September 23, 1932, p. 711.
42. *La Terre retrouvée*, December 25, 1932, p. 3.
43. *PH*, February 1, 1933, p. 3; March 8, 1933, p. 3; January 28, 1934, p. 4; February 2, 1934, p. 1.
44. Opposition to an international Jewish defense organization was voiced by Sylvain Lévi of the Alliance at the Biennial Reunion of the Jewish Associations, Paris, June 27, 1932. Archives of the American Jewish Committee, Europe; letter of J. Bigart to Dr. N. Goldmann, n.d., AIU, France II D 6 bis.
45. *PH*, March 29, 1933, p. 3; April 5, 1933, p. 1; May 17, 1933, p. 3.

46. *Le Volontaire juif,* 3, no. 26 (September–December 1933):6–7; 5, no. 37 (July–August 1935):6; FSJ, *Rapport Moral . . . 1935–36,* p. 18. For further information on the boycott movement, see Moshe Gottlieb, "Boycott, Anti-Nazi," *Encyclopedia Judaica,* 4:1280–82.

47. *Journal officiel,* December 24, 1934, pp. 12,590–99.

48. *PH,* December 7, 1934, p. 1; December 8, 1934, p. 1; December 9, 1934, p. 1; December 10, 1934, p. 1.

49. *Ibid.,* December 30, 1934, p. 1; February 1, 1935, pp. 1, 3; June 26, 1935, p. 1; July 8, 1935, p. 3.

50. *Parizer morgenblatt,* October 6, 1932, p. 1; *PH,* January 10, 1933, p. 1; February 23, 1933, p. 3.

51. *NP,* March 6, 1934, p. 6.

52. *Ibid.,* March 22, 1934, p. 5.

53. *Ibid.,* January 26, 1934; May 5, 1934, p. 3.

54. *Ibid.,* February 20, 1934, p. 6.

55. Appeal in Yiddish, "To all Jewish Workers and Toilers," Bund Archives; D. Diamant, *Ikuf Almanach,* p. 130; *NP,* July 22, 1934, p. 3.

56. Appeal, "To all Jewish Workers," Bund Archives.

57. *PH,* August 26, 1934, p. 4.

58. *NP,* August 18, 1934, p. 5; Diamant, *Almanach,* p. 130.

59. P. Schrager, *NP,* June 18, 1935, p. 3.

60. *Ibid.,* July 12, 1935, p. 3. A number of studies of the French Popular Front have appeared in recent years. Among them are Louis Bodin and Jean Touchard, *Front populaire 1936*; Daniel Brower, *The New Jacobins*; Jacques Chambaz, *Le Front populaire pour la paix, la liberté et le pain*; and Claude Willard et al., *Le Front populaire* (the latter two from a Communist perspective) and Daniel Guérin, *Front populaire, révolution manquée* and Georges Lefranc, *L'Expérience du Front populaire.*

61. *NP,* April 8, 1935, p. 2; April 12, 1935, p. 5; April 17, 1935, p. 4.

62. *Ibid.,* March 28, 1937, p. 7; April 16, 1938, p. 3.

63. *Ibid.,* September 17, 1936, p. 2.

64. *Ibid.,* October 11, 1935, p. 2.

65. *PH,* July 30, 1935, p. 1; *NP,* July 30, 1935 and July 31, 1935, pp. 1–2.

66. *PH,* July 30, 1935, p. 1.

67. *PH,* September 16, 1935, p. 1.

68. FSJ, *Rapport Moral . . . 1935–36,* p. 20; *PH,* August 7, 1935, p. 1; August 8, 1935, p. 1; September 21, 1935, p. 1.

69. *PH,* September 26, 1935, pp. 3–4; October 2, 1935, p. 1.

70. *NP,* October 8, 1935, p. 1; October 9, 1935, pp. 1–2; *PH,* October 10, 1935, p. 3.

71. *Unzer shtime,* January 4, 1936.

72. *NP,* December 12–December 16, 1935, p. 1.

73. *Naye tsayt,* January 17, 1936, p. 1, 6.

74. *Ibid.,* February 28, 1936, p. 21; *PH,* March 5, 1936, pp. 1, 3; *Unzer shtime,* February 29, 1936, p. 2.

75. *PH,* February 17, 1936, p. 3; May 10, 1936, p. 4; May 20, 1936, p. 1; *Naye*

tsayt, March 13, 1936, p. 1; March 20, 1936, p. 5; *NP*, March 1, 1936, pp. 3–4.

76. *NP*, December 29, 1935, p. 4.

77. Brochure of *Centre de Liaison*, 1938, YIVO, France; *NP*, February 7, 1936, p. 1.

78. Handbill in Yiddish signed by Bernard Lecache and André Wurmser urging Jews to protest PH's anti-Popular Front stand in the elections, YIVO, France; *NP*, April 28, 1936, p. 5; May 4, 1936, p. 1; *PH*, May 2, 1936, p. 1; May 7, 1936, p. 1.

79. *NP*, August 26, 1935, p. 4.

80. *PH*, September 2, 1936, p. 3.

81. *PH*, March 27, 1937, p. 3; "Appeal of the Standing Committee of Medem Farband and Left Poalei-Zion to reestablish the United Labor Front on the Jewish Street," [*Yiddish*], Bund Archives.

82. *NP*, March 21, 1937, p. 1.

83. *Ibid.*, March 26, 1937.

84. *Ibid.*, April 21, 1937, p. 1; April 22, 1937, p. 3; April 26, 1937, p. 4.

85. *NP*, June 14, 1937, p. 1; Weinberg, *A Community in Crisis*, p. 158.

86. I. Lerman, *NP*, November 18, 1937, p. 3.

87. *NP*, April 24, 1938, p. 1; April 25, 1938, p. 1.

88. M. Jarblum, *PH*, April 8, 1938, p. 3.

89. *Ibid.*, May 8, 1938, p. 1; May 11, 1938, p. 1; May 15, 1938, p. 1; *Samedi*, October 30, 1937, p. 5; November 6, 1937, p. 5; May 21, 1938, p. 7.

90. *NP*, April 26, 1938, p. 1; Weinberg, *A Community in Crisis*, pp. 159–61.

91. *PH*, December 26, 1938, p. 3; Weinberg, *ibid.*, p. 165.

92. *NP*, May 13 and 14, 1938, p. 1; *Unzer shtime*, June 1937 and April 1938, May 8, 1938, May 21, 1938.

93. This remark followed an attack on Louis Bertrand, who was sympathetic to Nazism because of his view that it would protect France from Bolshevism. *UI*, March 6, 1936, p. 371.

94. *Paix et droit*, March 1933, p. 10; PH, April 2, 1933, p. 1.

95. *Le Volontaire juif*, 3, no. 24 (May–June 1933); 5–6; *UI*, June 23, 1933, pp. 321–22. Police report on opposition of Central Consistory and Alliance to the boycott, March 30, 1933, Police Archives 241-155-1-B.

96. Judaeus, "La persécution des juifs en Allemagne et le devoir des Juifs français," *UI*, March 31, 1933, p. 838.

97. *AI*, June 8, 1933, p. 86.

98. *PH*, August 10, 1934, p. 1.

99. C.C., Permanent Section, Minutes, November 21, 1934, HM 1073, CAHJP.

100. *PH*, August 24, 1934, p. 4.

101. Police report, April 7, 1933, Police Archives, Paris, 241.155-1-B.

102. *Le Matin*, April 7, 1933; *La Victoire*, April 7, 1933; Police report on protest meeting, April 5, 1933, Police Archives, Paris, 241.155-1-B.

103. *UI*, March 20, 1936, p. 411; June 26, 1936, p. 630.

104. C.C., Permanent Section, Minutes, February 21, 1935, HM 1072, CAHJP.

105. *Ibid.*, Minutes, June 2, 1935; C.C., Minutes, June 24, 1935, HM 1072, CAHJP.

106. C.C., Permanent Section, December 31, 1935; C.C., Minutes January 28, 1936.

107. A fund-raising letter sent by the *Centre de Défense et de Vigilance* on October 1, 1936, appealed for support "dans une action qui exige le ralliement immédiat de toutes les forces saines du judaïsme français et qui pour être efficace doit rester discrète. Les manifestations bruyantes des groupements ou d'individus isolés, sans qualité pour representer le judaïsme français, ne font qu'aggraver le mal au lieu d'y porter rémède." Archives of Maurice Moch, Paris. See also *UI*, June 26, 1936, p. 630; *American Jewish Yearbook*, 39:316.

108. Mimeographed *Bulletin du Centre de Défense et de Vigilance*, archives of Maurice Moch, Paris.

109. *UI*, October 2, 1936, p. 54.

110. Arieh Tartakower and Kurt Grossmann, *The Jewish Refugee* (New York: Institute of Jewish Affairs, 1944), p. 133; W. Rosenstock, "Exodus 1933–1939," *Leo Baeck Institute Yearbook*, 1 (1956):380; Comité pour la défense des droits des Israélites en Europe centrale et orientale, *La défense des droits et de la dignité des réfugiés et apatrides Israélites et non-Israélites en France en 1934, 1935, et 1936*, mimeographed, report of October 16, 1935, pp. 56–57.

111. Ministry of Interior to Prefects of Haut-Rhin, Bas-Rhin, and Moselle, July 1, 1933, Report, Préfecture de Police, Direction de l'Administration et de la Police Générales, November 10, 1933; Police report, October 24, 1933; Letter, October 19, 1933 from Ministry of Foreign Affairs to Ministry of the Interior, Police Archives, Paris, 241.155-1-A.

112. John H. Simpson, *The Refugee Problem*, p. 188; Comité pour la défense . . . , p. 41.

113. Simpson, *ibid.*, p. 301.

114. *American Jewish Yearbook* 40:183.

115. Decree Law of May 2, 1938, *Journal officiel*, pp. 4967–69.

116. *Appel en faveur de nos frères victimes de l'anti-semitisme allemand*, April 10, 1933, JTS, France, Box 17; *Paix et droit*, March 1933, p. 6; *UI*, March 31, 1933, p. 383; *AI*, March 30, 1933, p. 50.

117. *La Tribune juive*, March 30, 1934, p. 761.

118. Police report, November 1933, Police Archives, 241.155-1-A.

119. *PH*, May 4, 1933, p. 1; May 13, 1933, p. 3.

120. Letter, Lambert to Prefect of Police, November 23, 1933, Police reports, November 23, 1933 and November 27, 1933. Police Archives, Paris, 241.155-1-A. An earlier report of November 21, 1933 described a police investigation of the quarters of the Comité as requested by Robert de Rothschild, who had "sought the expulsion from French territory of several refugees." The Communist propaganda conducted by the refugees seems to have consisted largely of protesting against the Comité's treatment of the refugees.

121. André Spire, "J'accuse le Comité National de Secours," YIVO, France 75; *PH*, March 15, 1934, p. 3.

122. *AI*, June 8, 1933, p. 86.

123. *PH*, April 8, 1933, p. 3.

124. Georges Wormser describes William Oualid's contacts with important gov-

ernmental figures and the successful results. Oualid, a member of both the Paris Consistory and the Alliance, was active in refugee work. Wormser, *Français Israélites*, pp. 144–45.

125. Raymond-Raoul Lambert, *UI*, October 12, 1934, p. 65.

126. *UI*, July 28, 1933, p. 480; December 22, 1933, pp. 438–40; *AI*, March 21, 1935, pp. 27–28.

127. Interview with M. Modiano, president of CRIF, cited in Benguigui, "L'immigration juive," p. 86; report of Comité de défense . . . , Centre de Documentation Juive Contemporaine, 6753.

128. *Comité pour la défense* . . . , p. 21.

129. *Ibid., passim.*

130. *Ibid.*, pp. 11–13.

131. *Ibid.*, p. 41.

132. Lecture of General Brissaud-Desmaillet, June 13, 1935, *ibid.*, pp. 62–63.

133. *Ibid.*, pp. 48–52, 57; Letter of Minister of the Interior, November 26, 1935, *ibid.*, pp. 62–63.

134. Letter of Justin Godart, November 27, 1933, *ibid.*, p. 17.

135. *Ibid.*, p. 71.

136. *Ibid.*, pp. 71–72.

137. Emphasis in original. Letter from R. R. Lambert to Robert Schumann, February 21, 1938, AIU.

138. C.C., Permanent Section, Minutes, October 24, 1935, HM 1073, CAHJP.

139. *Journal officiel*, June 7, 1936, p. 1327.

140. Colton, *Léon Blum*, p. 195.

141. Blumel, *Léon Blum*, p. 9; Lazareff, *Deadline*, p. 88; Colton, *ibid.*, p. 145.

142. *Kadimah*, June 22, 1934, p. 20; *Chalom*, March 1934, p. 20; *NP*, June 20, 1936, p. 3; July 1, 1936, p. 1; *PH*, June 14, 1936, p. 4; *Samedi*, September 19, 1936, p. 6; Créange, *Epitres aux juifs*, p. 163; Zachariah Shuster, "As Léon Blum Began to Reign," pp. 312–13.

143. *PH*, February 17, 1934, p. 3; March 11, 1934, p. 1; *Le Volontaire juif*, IV, 27 (January–March 1934), p. 7; *La Tribune juive*, April 17, 1936, p. 235.

144. *Naye tsayt*, May 15, 1936, p. 3; *PH*, June 14, 1936, p. 4.

145. *Samedi*, September 19, 1936, p. 6.

146. *PH*, June 14, 1936, p. 4.

147. *Le Droit de vivre*, May 25, 1934, p. 2.

148. *Souvenirs sur l'Affaire* (Paris, 1937), p. 97.

149. *PH*, July 1, 1936, p. 3; January 23, 1937, p. 1; *NP*, July 1, 1936, p. 1.

150. *PH*, January 22, 1937, p. 4.

151. *Ibid.*, January 24, 1937, p. 1.

152. *Ibid.*, January 25, 1937, p. 1. Rabbi Louis-Germain Lévy of the Union Libérale spoke instead, apparently on his own initiative since his congregants were prominent in the *Union Patriotique*. He was greeted by a mixture of anti-Semitic heckling and applause. The meeting closed with a Nazi salute.

153. *Chalom*, October 1933, pp. 18–19.

154. *Kadimah*, 4, no. 5 (May 1934): 27–28.

155. *Samedi*, November 13, 1937, p. 2.

156. *Ibid.*, June 5, 1937, p. 1.
157. *PH*, September 17, 1938, p. 3; *La Tribune juive*, October 21, 1938, pp. 637–38; *Samedi*, September 24, 1938, p. 3.
158. *Unzer shtime*, October 8, 1938; *Samedi*, November 5, 1938, p. 6.
159. For example, *La Tribune juive*, June 24, 1938, p. 385.
160. Le Matin, Nov. 19, 1938, p. 1; *Samedi*, November 26, 1938, p. 1.
161. My interview with Henri Schilli, October 18, 1972. According to Schilli, Weill's remarks referred only to the plan to resettle Jewish refugees on Madagascar.
162. *Unzer shtime*, November 13 and November 17, 1938, p. 1.
163. Union des sociétés juives de France, *Les Immigrés juifs dans les journées de septembre* (Paris, 1938), pp. 3–5.
164. *Ibid.*
165. *PH*, December 30, 1938, p. 3.
166. For a more detailed account of this period, see Weinberg, A *Community in Crisis*, pp. 175–91.
167. *UI*, December 2, 1938, p. 161.
168. *Samedi*, November 26, 1938, p. 2.
169. *Ibid.*, October 8, 1938, p. 1.
170. *Affirmation*, February 24, 1939, p. 4; January 13, 1939, p. 5.
171. *Samedi*, October 29, 1938, p. 6.
172. *PH*, October 16, 1938, p. 3 and December 30, 1938, p. 3.
173. *Ibid.*, October 16, 1938, p. 3.
174. *Affirmation*, May 19, 1939, p. 6; May 26, 1939, p. 7; *Samedi*, March 18, 1939, p. 1.
175. *Samedi*, December 12, 1938, p. 2.
176. *PH*, August 27, 1939, p. 4.
177. *NP*, August 25, 1939, September 2, 1939, pp. 1–6; Weinberg, A *Community in Crisis*, pp. 203–05.

Bibliography

Archival Material

American Jewish Archives, Cincinnati
Louis Marshall Papers: Box 55 & 157 Relations with Alliance
    Israélite Universelle

Archion Ha'avodah [Labor Archive], *Tel-Aviv*
Kaplansky Archive, IV 104 17 Correspondence with Marc Jarblum

Archives of the Alliance Israélite Universelle, Paris.
France I C 1 Material on Anti-Semitism, 1861-present
      I D 2 World War I
      I D 3 Comité d'Action auprès des Juifs des pays neutres
      I G 3–5
      I H 1 Correspondence with member societies
      I ID 6 and IID6 bis World War I
      IV D 16 Intervention with French governmental represen-
      tatives
      V A 40 Lazard, Lucien 1910–17
      VIII E 13, 15, 18 Schools
      IX A 67 Changes in statutes, 1922
      IX A 81 Central Committee, 1868– 1931
      IX D 53 Russian and Romanian emigration
      XI A 81
      XI D 57 Prostitution
Etats-Unis I C 1

Archives of the American Jewish Committee, New York
Folders entitled "France/Alliance Israélite" and "Europe"

Brandeis University—Special Collections
France—Boxes I–V. A rich collection of consistorial and non-consis-
    torial material, including communal reports.

Bund Archives, New York
Broadsides and leaflets of Di Kemfer (1904–1914) and the Paris
    Medem Farband (1920s and 1930s).

Central Archives for the History of the Jewish People, Jerusalem
HM 1070 Minutes of the Central Consistory, 1905–1914
HM 1071 Minutes of the Permanent Section of the Central Consis-
    tory, 1905–1914
HM 1072 Minutes of the Central Consistory, 1919–1939
HM 1073 Minutes of the Permanent Section of the Central Consis-
    tory, 1919–1936
ZF 766 Nancy Liste électorale 1906
ZF 842 Marseille Liste électorale de la communauté 1911
ZF 137 Miscellaneous letters, 1898–1925
ZF 348 Congrès Juif Mondial
ZF 346 Anordnung des Israelitschen Hilfskomitet, Strasbourg
ZF 362 Paris, 1938 Statuts de la Caisse Israélite de prêts.
INV 2761 Chambre syndicale des ouvriers Casquettiers de Paris,
    1896–1931 (mostly from period preceding 1918)
INV 1077 Minutes of Comité des Ecoles, Paris. 1908–1928; corre-
    spondence of Comité des Ecoles, Paris, 1907–1914; Comité
    des Dames Inspectices, Paris, 1906–1923

Central Zionist Archives, Jerusalem
Z4 The Zionist Organization/The Jewish Agency for Palestine Cen-
    tral Office, London. Correspondence with French Zionist or-
    ganizations and reports of French Zionist elections.

Z4 691	Z4 2077
1220	3232I-II-III
1791II	3233
2146	3362
215/19	3589
218/17	3729
222/21	3731
222/38	Comité des délégations juives, *1919–24*
226/21-22	Z4 1791 Z4 2651 Z4 4127
231/24-25	2077 1808I 2510

L9 Presidency of the Zionist General Council, Paris (1925–33),
       under the leadership of Leo Motzkin
L9 110 + 111
       274–281 Correspondence of Motzkin regarding French Zionism
       346 Letters to French government
       244 J. Schramek, correspondence, 1927–29
       89 18th Zionist Congress
       303 Hehaloutz
S5 Organization Department of the Executive of the Zionist Organi-
       zation and the Jewish Agency for Palestine (from 1933)
S5 1809, 1708, 1678, and 1741 Results of Zionist elections in
       France and Alsace
       2198
       2229
S25 Political Department (from 1921) S25 578
S29 Section for the organization of non-Zionists (from 1929)
       67a and 68
F11 Files of French Zionist federations, particularly material relating
       to Zionist elections in France.
       13– 16; 17; 21–24
Personal Papers
A68 Justin Godart
A79 Isaac Naiditch
A93 André Spire
A303 Marc Jarblum

Centre de Documentation Juive Contemporaine, Paris
Mimeographed material on refugee committees in Paris

Comté de Bienfaisance Israélite de Paris
Minute books (Délibérations): 1887–1910; 1911–1921; 1921–1934;
       1934– 1937; 1938– 1947

Consistoire Central (*Union des Associations Cultuelles Israélites de
       France et d'Algérie*), *Paris.*
2B1 Minutes of Permanent Section 1907–1913
2B3 Minutes of Permanent Section, 1936– 1939

4B6 Administrative Commission of the Ecole Rabbinique, 1908– 14;
       1919– 39

Consistoire Israélite de Paris (ACIP)
AA19 Register of the deliberations of the Administrative Council,
       1906– 1915
AA20 1915– 1922
B79-B112 General Correspondence; relations with civil and religious
       authorities, 1906–1922 BB85-BB92 Correspondence, 1906–
       1923
GG50 (1906–7); GG55 (1912–13); GG56 (1913–14); GG60 (1919);
       GG65 (1922)
GG75 + 76 (1925)
       Marriage registers of the Temple de la rue de Nazareth
GG140 (1906–8); GG142 (1911–12); GG144 (1914–19); GG145
       (1919–20); GG148 (1921–23); GG150 (1924–25)
       Marriage registers of the Temple de la rue de la Victoire
GG170 (1906–7); GG172 (1912–13); GG174 (1915–17); GG177
       (1919–20); GG188 (1925)
       Marriage registers of the Temple de la rue des Tournelles
GG240 (1912–19); GG246 (1924–25)
       Marriage registers of the Temple de la rue Buffault

Eclaireurs Israélites de France, Paris
Historique, 1923– 1937
Minutes and correspondence, 1923– 37

France: Archives Nationales.
F[19] 11.017 Separation of church and state
F[19] 11.158 Statutes of religious associations, 1906–1923
F[19] 11.159–11.160 Attribution of religious property after the separa-
       tion, 1906–1923.
F[7] 13.943 Police surveillance of Jewish organizations, 1915–1935.
France: Archives Départementales
Moselle 2V 85 + 86
       Relations of the departmental consistory and the government

France: Ministère des Affaires Etrangères
Guerre 1914–1918 Sionisme 1197 (1914–1916)

1198 (1916– 1917)
1199 (1917)
1200 (Jan.–Feb. 1918)
1201 (Mar.–May 1918)
E Levant 1918–1929 Palestine 10 (May–Sept. 1918)
11 (Oct.–Dec. 1918)
E 312 4 (Jan.–Feb. 1919)
E 313 4 (Feb.–July 1919)
E 314 4 (1919– 1920)
Sionisme 16 (1921–1922)
Palestine 28 (1922–1925)
29 (1926– 1929)

Hebrew Union College, Cincinnati: Special Collections
Box 44–45 Alliance Israélite Universelle
46   Consistoire Israélite de Paris
47   Jews in France, societies
48   Paris, Bienfaisance israélite
50   Consistoire de Paris, Caisse de la communauté
51   Consistoire Central
52   Union des associations cultuelles israélites de France
61   Consistoire israélite de Colmar, Metz, and Strasbourg
63   Jews in France—miscellaneous
66   Jews in Lyons, Nancy, Nice, Mulhouse, Carpentras, Vesoul

Archives of the Jewish Theological Seminary, New York.
France, Boxes 17, 19, 20, 22 Uncatalogued.

Archives of Maurice Moch, Paris: Private collection.
Material concerning the Centre de documentation et de vigilance

Police Archives, Paris.
241.155 Sundry police reports on Jewish and refugee organizations, 1907–1939
BA 1372 Ebenistes, 1891–1909
BA 1376 Habillement, 1917–1918
BA 1394 Ouvriers Tailleurs, 1901–1918
BA 1406 Ouvriers Tailleurs, 1876–1919

BA 1407 Ouvriers Tailleurs, 1917–1919
BA 1408 Ouvriers Tailleurs, 1919
BA 1423 Chambre Syndicale de l'Habillement, 1909–1918
BA 263 Municipal Election, Quartier St. Gervais, 1907
BA 287 Municipal Election, Quarter St. Gervais, 1908

Russian Institute, Columbia University, New York.
1.1.3.2 3 folders containing material on A. Losovsky

Syndicat des casquettiers, Paris.
Material on early years of the union.

YIVO, New York.
Yidn in Frankraykh; Bielinky Archives

Newspapers and periodicals

Affirmation, weekly (1939)
Der Agitator, anarchist (1908)
L'Ancien combattant juif (1938–39)
Arbeter fraynt, anarchist (1927–29)
Arbeter shtime, communist bi-weekly (1923–29)
Arbeter vort—Belgia-Frankraykh, Poalei-Zion weekly (1928–1936)
Archives israélites, weekly (1840–1935)
Bené-Mizrah, published by the Association de la jeunesse israélite
    orientale (Paris) and the Université populaire juive (1930–31)
Le Blé, monthly bulletin of the patronage de la jeunesse israélite
Bulletin de Chema Israel (1925–1934)
Bulletin du Comité des délégations juives (1919–1925)
Bulletin de la LICA (1929–1931)
Bulletin de presse sioniste-revisionniste (1934)
Bulletin de l'Union Patriotique des Français Israélites (1935–1936)
Les Cahiers des droits de l'homme (1900–1939)
Cahiers juifs, bi-monthly (Alexandria-Paris), (1933–1936)
Les Cahiers du renouveau (1934–1939)
Chalom (1924–1934)

Connaître (1924–1925)

La Conscience des Juifs (1934–1938)

Le Droit de vivre, published by LICA (1932–1939)

L'Echo sioniste (1917–1922)

Eliacin, published by the Eclaireurs Israélites de France (1932–1933)

L'Emancipation juive (1916–1917)

Emes, communist weekly and later twice weekly (1930–1932)

Foi et réveil, religious quarterly (1913–1938)

Le Foyer nouveau (1924)

Geserd, monthly devoted to publicity for the Jewish colony in
        Birobidzhan (1934–1935)

L'Humanité

Di Idishe tribune (1915)

La Jeunesse juive (1926–1929)

Le Juif (Strasbourg) (1920–1921)

Kadimah (Mulhouse) (1930–1936)

Klorkayt, Trotskyite monthly (1930–1931)

Le Matin

Menorah (formerly *l'Illustration juive*) (1922–1933)

Di Moderne tsayt (1908–1909)

Der Morgen, communist thrice weekly (1933)

Morgenstern, Bundist bimonthly (1929)

Di Naye presse, communist daily (1934–1939)

Naye tsayt, published by Poalei-Zion (1936)

Der Nayer journal (Paris, Warsaw, New York) (1913)

Der Nayer veg, revisionist (1926–1927, 1930)

La Nouvelle aurore, Zionist (1922–1926)

Ordo (German language) (1938)

Paix et droit, published by the Alliance Israélite Universelle
        (1921–1939)

Palestine (1927–1928)

Palestine économique (1936)

La Palestine nouvelle (1918–1919)

Palestine—Nouvelle revue juive, monthly (1927–1931)

Pariser Tageblatt, German daily published by refugees (1935–1938)

Pariz, weekly (1935)

Parizer bleter (1924–1926)

Parizer haynt, daily (1926–1939)

Parizer handels tsaytung (1933)

Parizer leben (1923)

Parizer morgenblatt, daily (1932)

Parizer vochenblatt (1933–1934)

Parizer yiddishe voch (1916)

Parizer yiddishe tsaytshrift (1936)

Le Peuple juif, published by the Fédération sioniste de France (1906–1921)

Races et racisme, bimonthly (1937–1939)

La Renaissance juive (1916–1917)

Le Rayon, monthly publication of the Union Libérale Israélite (1912–1939)

La Reconstruction juive, monthly publication of ORT (1930)

Le Réveil israélite (1919–1920)

Revue hébraique (1913–1914)

La Revue israélite, monthly (1923–1924)

La Revue juive (1924)

Revue juive de Génève (Geneva) (1932–1939)

Revue littéraire juive, monthly (1927–1931)

Revue OSE, monthly (1937–1940)

Samedi, weekly (1936–1939)

Shem—Revue d'action hébraique (1939)

Souvenir et science: Revue d'histoire et de littérature juives (Strasbourg) (1930–1933)

Le Temps

La Terre promise, bimonthly Zionist publication (1925–1928)

La Terre retrouvée, monthly publication of Keren Kayemeth l'Yisrael (1928–1939)

La Tribune juive (Strasbourg) (1926–1939)

La Tribune juive (Paris), organ of Russian Jews (1919–1924)

Union scolaire (1913–1934)

L'Univers israélite (1844–1939)

Unzer shtime, Bundist paper (1935–1939)

Le Volontaire juif (1931–1935)

Der Yid in Pariz (1912–1914)
Yunget vort, monthly publication of youth section of Medem Farband (1931)

Printed Primary Sources

Agathon. *Les Jeunes gens d'aujourd'hui*. Paris, 1913.

Algemayne Entsiklopedi. Paris, 1939.

Almanach juif. Paris, 1931.

Alliance Israélite Universelle. *Bulletin de l'Alliance Israélite Universelle*. Paris, 1905–1913.

—— *La Question juive devant la Conférence de la Paix*. Paris, 1919.

Association consistoriale israélite de Paris. *Exercice*. Paris, 1907–1935.

Association cultuelle israélite de Marseille. *Exercice*. Marseille, 1907.

Association culturelle sephardite de Paris. Paris, 1930–1931.

Association des dirigeants d'oeuvres juives de Paris. Paris, 1932.

Association israélite pour la protection de la jeune fille. Paris, n.d.

Association philanthropique de l'Asile de nuit, de jour, et de la crèche israélite. Paris, 1906–1938.

Banager, Jacques. *Israël et les évenements actuels*. S.l., 1936.

Baron, Jean-Marie. *La grande découverte; les juifs et le sang B*. Paris, 1938.

Barrès, Maurice. Les *Déracinés*. Paris, 1897.

—— *Les diverses familles spirituelles de la France*. Paris, 1917.

—— *Scènes et doctrines du nationalisme*. Paris, 1925.

Beauplan, Robert de. *Un problème de l'heure: le drame juif*. Paris, 1939.

Benda, Julien. *La Jeunesse d'un clerc*. Paris, 1936.

Beracha, Sammy. *A la recherche d'un patrie*. Paris, 1931.

Berneri, C. *Le juif antisemite*. Paris, 1935.

Berr, Michel. *Appel à la justice des nations et des rois*. Strasbourg, 1801.

Blank, Ruben. *Adolf Hitler, ses aspirations, sa politique, sa propagande et les protocols des sages de sion*. S.l., n. d.

Bloch, Jean-Richard. . . . *et compagnie*. Paris, 1917.

Blum, Léon. *Souvenirs sur l'Affaire*. Paris: Gallimard, 1935.

Boissel, J. *La crise ouvrière juive* Paris, 1938.

—— *Le Juif, poison mortel*. Conférence donnée à la salle des centraux le 4 janvier 1935.

Bonsirven, Joseph. *Juifs et chrétiens*. Paris, 1936.

—— "Chronique de Judiasme français." *Etudes*. Paris, 1936.

—— "Le juif réassimilant l'israélite." Paris, 1937.

—— "Y a-t-il en France un réveil de l'antisemitisme." Paris, 1935.

Bucard, Marcel. *L'Emprise juive*. Paris, 1938.

—— *Programme et moyens d'action du mouvement syndical*. S.l., 1935.

Cahen, Edmond. *Juif, non!* . . . *Israélite*. Paris: Librairie de France, 1930.

Cahiers du Bolchévisme. Thèses et rèsolutions adoptées par le Ve Congrés du PCF, Lille, 1926, Numéro spécial, July 28, 1926.

——. Thèses et résolutions du VIIIe Congrès du Parti Communiste. Paris, March 1932. Numéro spécial, May 1932.

Céline, Louis-Ferdinand. *Bagatelles pour un massacre*. Paris, 1937.

Centre de recherches de solutions au problème juif. *Memorandum sur une solution du problème des réfugiés*. Paris, 1938.

CGTU, *Contre la xénophobie*. Paris, 1931.

Chandan, K. S. *Le problème juif, facteur de la paix mondiale*. Paris, 1933.

Chatel, Raymond. *La conjuration mondiale judéo-sociale-boche*. Loingres, 1920.

Claudel, Paul. *Le Père humilié*. Paris, 1920.

——et al. *Les Juifs*. Paris, 1937.

Clouard, Henri. *La Cocarde*. Paris, 1910.

La Colonie Scolaire. *Oeuvre pour la protection de l'enfance, 1926–1936*. Paris, 1936.

—— *Activité*. Paris, 1929 and 1933.

Comité d'Assistance aux Réfugiés. Paris, 1939.

Comité Central d'assistance aux émigrants juifs. *Rapport annuel*. Paris, 1934.

Comité de Bienfaisance Israélite. *Assemblée générale*. Paris, 1905–1908; 1911–1937.

Comité des Délégations juives auprès de la Conférence de la Paix. Paris, 1919.

Comité français pour la protection des intellectuels juifs persécutés. *La Protestation de la France contre les persécutions antisemites*. Paris, 1933.

Comité hébreu de libération nationale. Paris, n.d.

Comité pour la défense des droits des israélites en Europe centrale et orientale. *La défense des droits et de la dignité des réfugiés et apatrides Israélites et non-Israélites en France en 1934, 1935, et 1936*. Mimeographed. Paris, 1936.

—— *La défense des droits et de la dignité des réfugiés et apatrides*. Paris, n.d.

Conférence de la jeunesse juive de France. S.l., 1938.

La Conférence mondiale des anciens combattants juifs. Paris, 1935.

Congrès Mondial Juif. *La France et le Congrès Mondial Juif*. S.l., 1934.

Consistoire israélite de Nancy. *Réponses au questionnaire relatif à la séparation*. Nancy, 1906.

Créange, Pierre. *Epitres aux juifs*. Paris, 1937.

Debré, S. "The Jews of France." *Jewish Quarterly Review*, 2 (April 1891):367–435.

Delassus, Henri. *La question juive*. S.l., 1911.

Der Folksfront. Paris, 1935.

"Devant la question juive." *Grande Revue*. Paris, 1939.

Dior, Raymond A. "Les Juifs." Special issue of *Crapouillot*, September 1936.

Dreyfuss, J. H. *Israël et la France*. Paris, 1933.

Drumont, Edouard. *La France juive*. Paris: Marpin et Flammarion, 1886.

Eberlin, E. *La double tare*. Paris: Editions SNIE, 1935.

Engelmann, S. *Application au culte israélite de la loi de séparation*. Pamphlet, S.l., n.d.

Ershte Alveltliche Yiddishe Kultur Kongres, Sept. 17–21, 1937. Paris, n.d.

Fédération des sociétés juives. *Rapport moral et financier, 1935–1936*. Paris, 1936.

Fédération des syndicats ouvriers de la chapellerie française, *XIVe Congrès National*, 1909.

Fédération d'Industries des Travailleurs de l'Habillement, *Compte Rendu, Rapport des travaux du VIe Congrès*. Limoges, 1906.

—— *Compte Rendu Officiel des Travaux du XIIe Congrès National*. Lille, 1921.

Fédération Nationale des Cuirs et Peaux, *Sixième Congrès National*. Fougères, 1909.

—— *Septième Congrès National*. Graulhet, 1911.

Ferré, Louis-Marie. *Le Racisme et la question juive*. Chauny, 1939.

Fisher, Joseph. *Un peuple renaît*. Paris, 1939.

Fleg, Edmond. *Ecoute, Israël*. Paris. 1913.

—— *Pourquoi je suis juif*. Paris, 1928.

—— *Israël et moi*. Paris, 1928.

Frank, N. *Parizer Motiven*. Paris, 1924.

Frankel, I. *Vi azoy tsu vern a frantsoyz*. Paris; L. Beresniak, n.d.

George, Waldemar. *L'Humanisme et l'idée de patrie*. Paris, 1936.

Ginsburger, M. *Les juifs à Ribeauvillé et à Bergheim*. Strasbourg, 1939.

Goemare, Pierre. *Quand Israël rentre chez soi*. Paris, 1924.

Groos, René. *Enquête sur le problème juif*. Paris, 1935.

—— *Réponse à M. Paul Lévy*. Paris, 1921.

Haguenau, David. *Discours et prières*. Paris, 1921.

Halévy, Léon. *Résumé de l'histoire des juifs modernes*. Paris: Lecointe et Duvey, 1828.

Halphen, Achille-Edmond. *Receuil des lois, décrèts, ordonnances, avis du Conseil d'Etat, arrêtés et reglements concernant les Israélites depuis la révolution de 1789*. Paris, 1851.

Hertz, Henri. "La France et la Palestine," *Bulletin d'Etudes du Consistoire Central*. Lyon, 1941.

HIAS-HICEM. *Ten Years of Jewish Emigration 1926–1936*. Paris, 1936.

—— *Four Years of Jewish Migration 1927–1930*. Paris, 1931.

Jarblum, Marc. *Les Juifs russes et la guerre*. Paris, 1916.

Josse, Prosper and Rossillon, Pierre. *L'Invasion étrangère en France en temps de paix.* Paris, 1936.

Jouhandeau, Marcel. *Le Péril juif.* Paris, 1939.

Kadmi-Cohen. *Nomades.* Paris, 1929.

—— *Apologie pour Israël par un juif.* Paris, 1937.

Kaplan, Jacob. *Racisme et Judaisme.* Paris, 1940.

Kornhendler, Ezekiel. *A Kol in Midbar.* Paris, 1935.

Kultur Lige. *10 Yor Kultur Lige.* S.l., 1932.

Lacambre-Mialet. *Français, vous êtes trahis.* Paris, 1938.

Laforgue, René. *L'Influence d'Israël sur la pensée moderne.* Paris, 1935.

La Franquerie de Beslon, A. L. de. *Une nouvelle maneouvre judéo-maçonnique.* Toulouse, 1928.

Lamberlin, R. *Le Péril juif.* Paris, 1924.

Lauzel, M. *Ouvriers juifs de Paris.* Paris, 1912.

Lecache, Bernard. *Vous n'êtes pas des esclaves.* Paris, 1937.

—— *Pour tuer l'antisemitisme.* Paris, n.d.

Lerman, Y. *Far der Fartaydikung fun unzer folk.* Paris, 1938.

Leroy-Beaulieu, Anatole. *Les Juifs et l'antisemitisme: Israël chez les nations.* Paris, 1893.

Levaillant, Isaie. "La génèse de l'antisemitisme sous la troisième république." *REJ,* 53 (1907): lxxvi-c.

Lévy, Jacob. *Les Doubles-Juifs.* Paris, 1927.

Lévy, Roger. *Une université nouvelle.* Paris, 1919.

Livian, Marcel. *La Régime juridique des étrangers en France.* Paris, 1936.

Manuel, Albert. *1914–1918: Les Israélites dans l'armée française.* Angers, 1921.

Marcovici-Cléja, Simon. *Le Problème juif mondial; son acuité, sa solution definitive.* Paris, 1938.

Maritain, Jacques. *Les Juifs parmi les nations.* Paris, 1938.

Mater, André. *Le Régime des cultes.* Paris, 1909.

Maurin. *La Main d'oeuvre immigrée sur le marché du travail en France.* Paris: CGTU, 1933.

Maurras, Charles. *Au Signe de Flore.* Paris, 1933.

Milie, Pierre, et al. *Union ORT pour la propagation du travail in-*

dustriel et agricole parmi les juifs; exposition international des arts et techniques, Paris, 1937.

Millet, Raymond. *Trois millions d'étrangers en France.* Paris: Librairie de Medecis, 1938.

Mossé, Benjamin, ed. *La Révolution française et le rabbinat français.* Avignon, 1890.

Moyen, François. *Le Culot des juifs.* Paris, 1939.

Navon, A. *Les 70 ans de l'Ecole Normale Israélite Orientale (1865–1935).* Paris, 1935.

—— *Joseph Perez.* Paris, 1925.

Netter, Nathan. *La Patrie absente et la patrie retrouvée. Sermons et allocutions patriotiques.* Metz, 1929.

Oualid, William. *L'Immigration ouvrière en France.* Paris, 1927.

PCF (Région Parisienne). *Rapport d'organisation pour la conférence de la Région Parisienne.* February, 1932.

——*Résolutions adoptées par la conférence nationale du PCF (Mars, 1930).* Paris, 1930.

—— *VIe Congrès National du PCF (Mars-Avril 1929), Saint-Denis: Manifeste, Thèses et Résolutions.* Paris, 1929.

—— *Ve Congrès National du PCF, Lille, 19–26 juin 1926: Rapport moral du comité central.*

—— *L'Importance de la MOE et les diverses immigrations.* S.l., 1930.

Pallière, Aimé. *Le Sanctuaire inconnu.* Paris, 1926.

Paraf, Pierre. *Israël—Histoire d'un peuple: Israël 1931. Paris, 1931.*

Péguy, Charles. *Notre jeunesse.* Paris, 1910.

Pour nos enfants. Exercice 1931, 1935, 1937. Paris, n.d.

Proust, Marcel. *A la recherche du temps perdu.* Paris, 1914–1922. English edition, New York: Random House, 1934.

Racisme? Non, LICA. Paris, n.d.

Reinach, Théodore. *Histoire des israélites depuis l'époque de leur dispersion jusqu'à nos jours,* 5th edition. Paris: Hachette, 1914.

—— *Les Juifs et la Révolution française,* Resumé de la conférence faite à l'Université populaire juive de Paris, le 16 mai 1909. Paris, 1909.

La Révolution française et l'émancipation des juifs. 8 vols. Paris, 1968.

Rolland, Romain. *Jean-Christophe,* trans. Gilbert Cannan. New York, 1910–1913.

Rollin, Henri. *L'Apocalypse de notre temps: les dessous de la propagande allemande d'après les documents inédits.* Paris, 1939.

Rouffet, Raoul. *La France en attente: Dictature ou révolution.* Paris, n.d.

Salomon-Koechlin, Louis. *Le Temps de la raison.* Paris, 1939.

Schwob, René. *Moi juif.* Paris, 1928.

Société de secours aux Juifs des Territoires de l'Ancien Empire Russe. *Rapport* Paris, 1920–21, 1921–22, 1922–23.

Le 70me Anniversaire de la Bienfaisante Israélite. Paris, 1913.

Speiser, E. *Calendrier juif.* Paris, 1911.

Spire, André. *Les Juifs et la guerre.* Paris, 1918.

—— *La Question juive devant la conférence de la paix.* Zurich, 1919.

—— *Quelques juifs et demi-juifs.* 2 vols. Paris, 1928.

—— *Versets: Et vous riez—Poèmes juifs.* Paris, 1908.

Steinhardt, N. and Neuman, Em. *Illusions et réalités juives.* Paris, 1937.

Tama, Diogène. *Transactions of the Paris Sanhedrim.* London, 1807.

Tchernoff, J. *Dans le creuset des civilisations.* 4 vols. Paris: Rieder, 1938.

Thiéry, Adolphe. *Dissertation sur cette question: est-il des moyens de rendre les juifs plus heureux et plus utiles en France.* Paris, 1788.

Tsucker, Yossel. *A Fremd Leben.* Warsaw, 1939.

Union des Associations cultuelles israélites, *Assemblée ordinaire.* Paris, 1908–1917, 1919–1939.

Union des sociétés juives de France. *Les Immigrés juifs dans les journées de septembre.* Paris, 1938.

Union des syndicats ouvriers de la Région Parisienne (CGTU). *Du Travail ou du pain!* S.l., 1930.

Vanikoff, Maurice. *La Commemoration des engagements volontaires des juifs d'origine étangère 1914–1918.* S.1., 1932.

Verdavainne, G. *Israël, nation sans territoire contre la nation française.* Paris, 1937.

——*Israël, nation des parasites contre la classe ouvrière.* Paris, 1938.

Ver fartaydigt di ayngevanderte? Paris, 1938.

Ver kemft kegn antisemitizm? Paris, 1933.

Viguier, Laurent. *Les Juifs à travers Léon Blum.* Paris, 1938.

Virebeau, Georges. *Les Juifs et leurs crimes.* Paris, 1938.

Viviorke, V. *Mizrach un Ma'ariv.* Paris, 1936.

La voix d'Israël. Conférences israélites. Paris, 1932.

Weill, Julien. "La renaissance religieuse dans le judaïsme," *La Renaissance Religieuse.* Paris, 1928.

Wurmser, André. *Variations sur le renégat.* Paris, 1937.

Yiddish Folkskich. *Rapport.* Paris, 1931.

Yiddish Hantbuch. Paris: Naye Presse, 1937.

Zérapha, Georges. *Notre combat contre l'antisemitisme.* Paris, 1936.

Secondary Sources

Abraham, Pierre. *Trois Frères.* Paris, 1971.

L'Activité des organisations juives en France sous l'occupation. Paris, 1947.

Albert, Phyllis. "Le rôle des consistoires israélites vers le milieu du xixè siècle." *REJ,* 130 nos. 2–3–4 (April-December 1971): 231–54.

—— *The Modernization of French Jewry: Consistory and Community in the Nineteenth Century.* Hanover, New Hampshire: University Press of New England, 1977.

Alperin, A. "Yiddishe gezelshaftn un institutsies in Pariz in 1939" (Jewish Organizations and Institutions in Paris) *Yidn in Frankraykh,* ed. E. Tcherikower, 2:248–80. New York: 1942.

—— "Di antisemitishe propaganda in Frankraykh erev der milchome," *Ibid.,* 2:265–280.

Altbach, Philip. "The International Student Movement," *Journal of Contemporary History* 5, no. 1 (1970):156–174.

Anchel, Robert. *Napoléon et les juifs*. Paris, 1928.

—— *Les Juifs de France*. Paris, 1946.

Arendt, Hannah. *The Origins of Totalitarianism*, 2nd edition. New York: Meridian Books, 1958.

Aubery, Pierre. *Milieux juifs de la France contemporaine à travers les écrivains*. Paris: Plon, 1957.

Baron, Salo. "Ghetto and Emancipation." *Menorah Journal*, 14 (June 1928):515–26.

—— "Newer Approaches to Jewish Emancipation," *Diogenes*, 29 (Spring 1960):56–81.

—— *A Social and Religious History of the Jews*, 3 vols. New York: Columbia University Press, 1937.

Bauer, Jules. *L'Ecole rabbinique de France*. Paris: Presses Universitaires de France, 1930.

Bein, Alex. *Theodore Herzl*. New York: Atheneum, 1970.

Bellanger, Claude, Jacques Godechot, Pierre Guirol, and Fernand Terron. *Histoire générale de la presse française*. 3 vols. Paris, 1969–1972.

Benguigui, Ida. "L'Immigration juive à Paris entre les deux guerres." Unpub. thesis for Diplome d'études supérieurs. Paris. 1965.

Berman, Léon. *Histoire des juifs de France des origines à nos jours*. Paris: Librairie Lipschutz, 1937.

Blum, Léon. *L'Histoire jugera*. Montreal: Editions de l'Arbre, 1945.

Blumel, André. *Léon Blum: juif et sioniste*. Paris: Editions de La Terre retrouvée, 1951.

Bodin, Louis, and Jean Touchard. *Front populaire 1936*. Paris, 1972.

Bouvier, Jean. *Les Rothschild*. Paris: P.U.F., 1967.

Brower, Daniel. *The New Jacobins*. Ithaca: Cornell University Press, 1968.

Buthman, William. *The Rise of Integral Nationalism in France*. New York: Columbia University Press, 1939.

Byrnes, Robert F. *Antisemitism in Modern France*, vol. 1. New Brunswick, N.J.: Rutgers University Press, 1950.

Chambaz, Jacques. *Le Front populaire pour la paix, la liberté et le pain*. Paris, 1961.

Chavagnes, René de. "Le juif au theatre." *Mercure de France* (Paris, 1910), pp. 16–34.

Chavardes, Maurice. *Le 6 fevrier 1934: la République en danger*. Paris: Calmann-Lévy, 1966.

Chouraqui, André. *Cent ans d'histoire: l'Alliance israélite universelle et la renaissance juive contemporaine* (1860–1960). Paris, 1965.

Cohen, Naomi W. "The Abrogation of the Russo-American Treaty of 1832." *Jewish Social Studies*, 25, no. 1 (January 1963): 3–41.

———*Not Free to Desist*. (Philadelphia: Jewish Publication Society, 1972).

Colton, Joel. *Léon Blum: Humanist in Politics*. New York: Random House, 1966.

Combattants de la liberté (French and Yiddish), published by the Commission Intersyndicale Juive auprès de la CGT. Paris, n.d.

Coutrot, Aline. "Youth Movements in France in the 1930's." *Journal of Contemporary History*, 5, no. 1 (1970): 23–35.

Cuddihy, John Murray. *The Ordeal of Civility*. New York: Basic Books, 1975.

Curtis, Michael. *Three against the Third Republic*. Princeton: Princeton University Press; 1959; reprint, Greenwood, 1976.

Dalby, Louise. *Léon Blum: Evolution of a Socialist*. New York: Thomas Yoseloff, 1963.

Dansette, Adrien. *Religious History of Modern France*, trans. John Dingle. 2 vols. New York: Herder, 1961.

Debré, Moses. *The Image of the Jew in French Literature 1800–1908*. New York: Ktav, 1970.

Desmarest, Jacques. *La politique de la main d'oeuvre en France*. Paris, 1946.

Diamant, D., and M. Bahel. *Vingtième anniversaire de la Presse Nouvelle 1934–1954*. Paris, 1954.

Diamant, D. *Yidn in Shpanishn Krieg 1936–1939*. Warsaw: OJFS-NAJ, 1967.

Dobin, M. "Di professies fun di yiddishe emigranten in Pariz. *YIVO Bleter*, 4, no. 1 (August 1932):22–42.

——"Yiddishe immigranten arbeter in Pariz, 1923–1928." *YIVO Bleter*, 3, nos. 4–5 (April–May 1932):385–403.

Durel, J. *La Sagesse d'Henri Franck, poete-juif.* Paris, 1931.

Dvoretzky, Mark. "Ha-Sotsiologia shel yahadut Zarfat b'tkufah haahronah." (1963), 3–12.

Earle, Edward Meade. *Modern France.* Princeton: Princeton University Press, 1951; reprint, Russell, 1964.

Feigelson, Ralph. *Ecrivains juifs de la langue française.* Paris, 1960.

Fernberg, Babeth Grace. *Treatment of the Jewish Character in the 20th Century Novel of France, Germany, England, and the U.S. (1900–1940).* Stanford University dissertation, 1943.

Fink, Jacob. *Yahadut Zarfat: kovez masot u-ma'amarim.* Paris: Machberoth, 1951.

Friesel, Evyatar. "Baron Edmond de Rothschild and the Zionists, 1918–1919" [Hebrew], *Zion*, 38 (1973):122–36.

Gartner, Lloyd. *The Jewish Immigrant in England, 1870–1914.* Detroit: Wayne State University Press, 1960.

Gay, Peter. "Encounter with Modernism: German Jews in German Culture, 1888–1914," *Midstream*, 21, no. 2 (February 1975):23–65.

George, Waldemar. *Les Artistes juifs de l'Ecole de Paris.* Alger, 1959.

Girard, Patrick. *Les Juifs de France de 1789 a 1860.* Paris: Calmann-Lévy, 1976.

Glasberg, Victor M. "Intent and Consequences: The 'Jewish Question' in the French Socialist Movement of the late Nineteenth Century." *Jewish Social Studies*, 36, no. 1 (January, 1974):61–71.

Goitein, Denise. *Jewish Themes in Selected French Works between the Two World Wars.* Unpublished dissertation, Columbia University, 1967.

Goldberg, Harvey. *Jean Jaurès.* Madison: University of Wisconsin Press, 1962.

Gordon, Milton. *Assimilation in American Life.* New York: Oxford University Press, 1964.

Gourfinkel, Nina. *L'Autre patrie*. Paris, 1953.

Gross, Walter. "The Zionist Students' Movement," *Leo Baeck Institute Yearbook*, 4 (1959):143–64.

Grossman, Edward. *Antisemitism, Zionism, and Jewish Opinion in France, 1886–1914*. Senior Honors Thesis, Harvard University.

Grossmann, Kurt, and Arieh Tartakower. *The Jewish Refugee*. New York: Institute of Jewish Affairs, 1944.

Guérin, Daniel. *Front populaire, révolution manquée*. Paris, 1970.

Hagani, Baruch. *L'Emancipation des juifs*. Paris, 1928.

Halff, Sylvain. "Les Juifs dans la vie économique de la France." *Jüdische Presszentrale* (Zurich), May 17, 1929.

——"The Participation of the Jews of France in the Great War." *American Jewish Yearbook*, 21 (1919–1920):31–97.

Halpern, Ben. *The Idea of the Jewish State*. Cambridge: Harvard University Press. 1961.

Hertzberg, Arthur. *The French Enlightenment and the Jews*. New York: Columbia University Press. 1968.

Hoffmann, Stanley. "Paradoxes of the French Political Community." *In Search of France*. New York, 1963.

Hyman, Paula E. "Joseph Salvador: Proto-Zionist or Apologist for Assimilation," *Jewish Social Studies*, 34, no. 1 (January 1972):1–22.

Ikuf Almanach. New York, 1961.

Isaac, Jules. *Expériences de ma vie*. Paris, 1959.

Jamati, Paul. *André Spire*. Paris, 1959.

Janowsky, Oscar. *The Jews and Minority Rights (1898–1919)*. New York: Columbia University Press, 1933.

Jarblum, Marc. "170 Years of Emancipation" [Hebrew], *Sefer Hashanah shel ha-'itonim*. S.1., 1960.

Jehouda, Josué. *L'Anti-sémitisme, miroir du monde*. Geneva: Editions Synthèse, 1958.

Johannet, René. *Péguy et ses cahiers*. Paris, 1914.

Kahn, Emil. *Au Temps de la République*. Paris, 1966.

Kahn, Frida. *Generation in Turmoil*. Great Neck, N.Y.: Channel, 1960.

Kahn, Léon. *Les Juifs de Paris pendant la révolution*. Paris: Allendorf, 1898.

Kaplan, Jacob. *Les Temps d'épreuve*. Paris: Editions de Minuit, 1952.

Katz, Jacob. *Exclusiveness and Tolerance*. New York: Schocken, 1962.

——*Out of the Ghetto*. Cambridge: Harvard University Press. 1973.

Kelman, C., *Rapport: Congrès du Jubilé de la Fédération des sociétés juives de la France, 1923–1948*. Paris, 1948.

Klatzmann, Joseph. *Le Travail à domicile dans l'industrie parisienne du vêtement*. Paris: Impriménie Nationale, 1957.

Kornhendler, Ezekiel. *Yidn in Pariz*. Paris, 1970.

Kriegel, Annie. *Les Communistes français: Essai d'ethnologie politique*. Paris, 1968.

——*Le Pain et les roses*. Paris, 1968.

——*La Croissance de la CGT (1918–1921)*. Paris, 1966.

——and Becker, Jean-Jacques. *1914: La Guerre et le mouvement ouvrier français*. Paris, 1964.

La Capra, Dominick. *Emile Durkheim: Sociologist and Philosopher*. Ithaca: Cornell University Press, 1972.

Landau, Lazare. "Histoire des Juifs en France." *Revue d'histoire et de philosophie religieuse*, 53 no. 2 (1973): 246–64.

Laqueur, Walter. *A History of Zionism*. New York: Holt, Rinehart, and Winston, 1972.

——*Young Germany: A History of the German Youth Movement* London: Routledge, 1962.

Lazareff, Pierre. *Deadline*. New York: Random House, 1942.

——*From Munich to Vichy*. New York, 1942.

Lefranc, Georges. *L'Expérience du Front populaire*. Paris, 1972.

Lehrmann, Chanan. *L'Elément juif dans la littérature française*. Paris: Albin-Michel, 1960–61. English translation by George Klin. Rutherford, N.J.: Fairleigh Dickinson University Press, 1971.

Leven, Narcisse. *Cinquante ans d'histoire: l'Alliance israélite universelle*, 2 vols. Paris, 1911.

Lichtheim, George. "Socialism and the Jews." *Dissent*, 15 (1968):314–32.

McLelland, J. S., ed. *The French Right from de Maistre to Maurras.* New York: Harper, 1970.

Mandel, A., *Les Temps incertains.* Paris: Calmann-Lévy, 1950.

Manuel, Albert. "Les consistoires israélites de France." *Revue des études juives,* 82 (1926):521–32.

Maoz (Mosbacher), Eliyahu. "The Werkleute," *Leo Baeck Institute Yearbook,* 4 (1959):165–82.

Maritain, Raïssa. *Les grandes amitiés.* New York, 1942.

Marrus, Michael. *The Politics of Assimilation* New York: Oxford University Press, 1971.

Mauco, Georges. *Les Etrangers en France.* Paris: Librairie Armand Colin, 1932.

Méjan, Louis. *La Séparation des églises et de l'état.* Paris, 1959.

Menes, A. "Yidn in Frankraykh," *YIVO Bleter,* 11, no. 5 (May 1937):329–55.

Micaud, Charles. *The French Right and Nazi Germany, 1933–1939.* Durham, N.C.: Duke University Press, 1943.

Milhaud, Darius. *Notes sans musique.* Paris, 1949.

Millner, Joseph. *Yidn in Frankraykh.* Paris, 1952.

Mishkinsky, Moshe. "The Jewish Labor Movement and European Socialism." *Jewish Society through the Ages,* ed. H. H. Ben-Sasson and S. Ettinger, pp. 284–96. New York: Schocken, 1971.

Mosse, George L. *The Crisis of German Ideology.* New York: Grosset and Dunlap. 1964.

Netter, Nathan. *Vignt siècles d'histoire d'une communauté juive: Metz et son grand passé.* Paris, 1938.

——*La Patrie égarée et la patrie renaissante.* Metz, 1947.

——*Cent ans d'histoire d'une société de charité messine: La Jeunesse israélite de Metz, 1838–1938.* Paris, 1938.

Nir-Rafalkes, Nahum. *Vanderungen.* Tel-Aviv, 1966.

Pagès, Emile. *Anthologie des écrivains morts à la guerre 1939–1945.* Paris, 1960.

Petit, Jacques. *Bernanos, Bloy, Claudel, Péguy: quatre écrivains catholiques face à Israël.* Paris, 1972.

Philipson, David. *The Reform Movement in Judaism.* New York, 1907.

Pierrard, Pierre. *Juifs et catholiques français de Drumont à Jules Isaac (1886–1945)*. Paris: Fayard, 1970.

Plamyène, Jean and Lasierra, Raymond. *Les Fascismes français: 1923–1963*. Paris: Editions du Seuil, 1963.

Pougatch, Isaac. *Robert Gamzon*. Paris, 1972.

Prajs. Lazare. *Péguy et Israël*. Paris, 1970.

Rabi, Wladimir. "De 1906 à 1939," *Histoire des Juifs de France*, ed. Bernhard Blumenkranz, pp. 363–88. Toulouse: Privat, 1972.

——*Anatomie du Judaïsme français*. Paris: Editions de Minuit, 1962.

Randall, Earle Stanley. *The Jewish Character in the French Novel 1870–1914*. Menasha, Wisc., 1941.

Rémond, René. *La droite en France: De 1815 à nos jours*. Paris, 1963.

Revel, G. "L'évolution de la population israélite du Bas-Rhin de 1784 à 1953," *FSJU*, 3, no. 9 (October 1954):24–25.

Ridley, Frederick. *Revolutionary Syndicalism in France*. Cambridge: Cambridge University Press, 1970.

Rinott, Chanoch. "Major Trends in Jewish Youth Movements in Germany," *Leo Baeck Institute Yearbook*, 19 (1974):74–95.

Robinson, Jacob. *Das Minoritäten Problem und seine Literatur*. Berlin, 1935.

Roblin, Michel, *Les Juifs de Paris*. Paris: Editions A et J. Picard, 1952.

Roth, Cecil. *A History of the Marranos*. New York: Schocken, 1974.

Ryba, Raphael. "Der entvicklungs-veg fun Parizer Bund," *Unzer shtime*, December 7, 1947.

——"Yiddishe sotsialistisher farband 'Bund' in Frankraykh." *Unzer tsayt*, 3–4 (November–December 1947):159–62.

Roland, Charlotte. *Du Ghetto à l'occident*. Paris: Editions de Minuit, 1962.

Roland, Joan Gardner. *The Alliance Israélite Universelle and French Foreign Policy in North Africa, 1860–1918*. Columbia University dissertation, 1965.

Rosenstock, W. "Exodus 1933–1939: A Survey of Jewish Emigration from Germany," *Leo Baeck Institute Yearbook*, 1 (1956): 373–90.

Ruppin, Arthur. *The Jews in the Modern World*. London: Macmillan 1934; reprint New York: Arno Press.

Savine, G. de Lafonte de. *Etat statistique des juifs en 1914 dans l'armée, la magistrature, les administrations*. Paris, 1914.

Schatzker, Chaim. "The History of the 'Blau-Weiss': The Path to Zionism of the First German Jewish Youth Movement," [Hebrew], *Zion*, 38 (1973): 137–68.

Schlewin, Baruch. *Yidn fun Belleville*. Paris: Farlag, 1948.

Schnurmann, E. *La Population juive en Alsace*. Paris, 1936.

Schor, Ralph "Xénophobie et extrème droite: l'exemple de l'*Ami du Peuple* (1928–1937)," *Revue d'histoire moderne et contemporaine* (Jan.–March 1976):116–44.

Schorsch, Ismar. *Jewish Reactions to German Antisemitism, 1870–1914*. New York: Columbia University Press; Philadelphia, Jewish Publication Society, 1972.

Schwarzfuchs, Simon. *Brève histoire des juifs en France*. Paris, 1956.

Sherwood, John M. *Georges Mandel and the Third Republic*. Stanford: Stanford University Press, 1970.

Shuster, Zachariah. "As Leon Blum Began to Reign," *Menorah Journal*, 24, no. 3 (October–December 1936): 305–15.

Silberner, Edmund. "Anti-Jewish Trends in French Revolutionary Syndicalism." *Jewish Social Studies*, 15, no. 3–4 (July–October 1953); 195–202.

——*Western Socialism and the Jewish Question* [Hebrew]. Jerusalem, 1955.

Silvera, Alain. *Daniel Halévy and his Times*. Ithaca, Cornell University Press, 1966.

Simpson, John Hope. *The Refugee Problem*. London: Oxford University Press, 1939.

Sorlin, Pierre. *La Croix et les juifs*. Paris: Gasset, 1967.

Soucy, Robert. *Fascism in France: The Case of Maurice Barrès*. Berkeley & Los Angeles: University of California Press, 1972.

——"Le Fascisme de Drieu La Rochelle," *Revue d'histoire de la deuxième guerre mondiale*, no. 66 (April 1967):61–84.

——"Romanticism and Realism in the Fascism of Drieu La Rochelle." *Journal of the History of Ideas*, 31 (Jan.–March 1970): 69–90.

Spire, André. *Souvenirs à batons rompus.* Paris, 1962.

Sraer, Eugène. *Les Juifs en France et l'égalité des droits civiques.* Paris, 1933.

Stearns, Peter. *Revolutionary Syndicalism and French Labor: A Cause without Rebels.* (New Brunswick, N.J.: Rutgers University Press, 1971).

Stein, Leonard. *The Balfour Declaration.* New York: Simon and Schuster, 1961.

Stern-Taübler, Selma. "The Jew in Transition from Ghetto to Emancipation." *Historia Judaica*, 2, no. 2 (October 1940): 102–19.

Stillschweig, Kurt. *Die Juden Osteuropas in den Minderheits-Vorträgen.* Berlin, 1936.

Szajkowski, Zosa. *Analytical Franco-Jewish Gazeteer 1939–1945.* New York: Ktav, 1966.

——*Antisemitizm in der frantsoizisher arbeter-bevegung fun Fourierizm bizn soyf fun Dreyfus Affeire 1845–1906.* New York, 1948.

——"Conflicts in the Alliance Israélite Universelle and the Founding of the Anglo-Jewish Association, the Vienna Allianz, and the Hilfsverein," *Jewish Social Studies*, 19, nos. 1–2 (January–April 1957), 29–50.

——"The Conflicts of Orthodoxy and Reform" [Hebrew], *Horeb*, 14, no. 9 (1960):253–92.

——*Etuden tsu der geshikhte fun ayngevanderter yiddishn yishuv in Frankraykh.* Paris: 1937.

——"The European Aspect of the American-Russian Passport Question." *American Jewish Historical Quarterly*, 46, no. 1 (September 1956):86–100.

——"Fun yiddishn arbeter-leben in Pariz." *Di Yiddishe Ekonomik* (May–June 1938):232–49.

—— "The Growth of the Jewish Community in France." *Jewish Social Studies*, 8 (1946).

——"The Impact of the Beilis Case on Central and Western Europe." *Proceedings of the American Academy of Jewish Research,*" 31 (1963):197–218.

———'Jewish Diplomacy," *Jewish Social Studies,* 22, no. 3 July 1960): 131–58.

———*Jews in the French Foreign Legion.* New York: Ktav, 1975.

———*Jews and the French Revolutions of 1789, 1830, and 1848.* New York: Ktav, 1970.

———"150 Years of Jewish Press in France." *Yidn in Frankraykh,* ed. E. Tcherikower, 2:236–308. New York, 1942.

———*Poverty and Social Welfare among French Jews 1800–1880.* New York: Editions Historiques Franco Juives, 1954.

———(S. Fridman). *Di professionelle bevegung tsvishn di yiddishe arbeter in Frankraykh biz 1914.* Paris, 1937.

———"Secular vs. Religious Jewish Life in France." *The Role of Religion in Modern Jewish History,* ed. Jacob Katz, pp. 107–127. New York: Ktav, 1975.

———"Vi azoy dos opteiln di kirch fun der mlukha in 1905 hot bavirkt di yiddishe kehilles in Frankraykh." *Davka,* 5, no. 4 (October–December 1954): 382–91.

———"Yiddishe theater in Frankraykh." *Yiddishe Theater in Europe,* pp. 289–321. New York, 1971.

Szyster, Boruch. *La Révolution française et les juifs.* Toulouse, 1929.

Tal, Uriel. *Christians and Jews in Germany,* trans. Noah Jonathan Jacobs. Ithaca: Cornell University Press, 1975.

Tcherikower, Elias. *Yehudim be'ittot Mahpekha* [Jews in Times of Revolution]. Tel-Aviv, 1957.

Tchernoff, J. *Les Demagogues contre les démocrates.* Paris, 1947.

Themanlys, Pascal. *Un itineraire de Paris à Jerusalem.* Jerusalem, 1963.

Tobias, Henry. *The Jewish Bund in Russia.* Stanford: Stanford University Press, 1972.

———and Charles Woodhouse. "Primordial Ties and Political Process in pre-Revolutionary Russia: The Case of the Jewish Bund." *Comparative Studies in Society and History,* 8, no. 3 (April 1966):331–60.

Tscher-ski, E. "The Dreyfus Affair, the Jewish Labor Immigrants, and the French Jewish Leaders" [Yiddish], *Yidn in Frankraykh*, 2:155–92.

Tsen yor Farband fun Yiddishe Gezelshaftn in Frankraykh. Paris, 1948.

Tsur, Jacob. *Prière du Matin: l'aube de l'état d'Israel*. Paris, 1967.

Tucker, Robert. "Politics and Aesthetics: The Fascism of Robert Brasillach." *Western Political Quarterly*, 15, no 4 (December 1962): 605–17.

Waldman, M. "Vegn yiddish-literarishn tsenter in Pariz." *Pinkes far der forshung fun der yiddisher literatur un presse*. New York, 1965.

Wardi, Charlotte. *Le Juif dans le roman français contemporain (1933–1948)*, Thèse pour le doctorat, Faculté des lettres et des sciences humaines de Paris. June, 1970.

Weber, Eugen. *Action Française*. Stanford: Stanford University Press, 1962.

——*The Nationalist Revival in France*. Berkeley and Los Angeles: University of California Press, 1959).

Weill, Julien. *Zadoc Kahn*. Paris: Alcan, 1912.

Weinberg, David H. *A Community on Trial: The Jews of Paris in the 1930's*. Chicago: University of Chicago Press, 1977.

Willard, Claude, et al. *Le Front populaire*. Paris, 1972.

Wischnitzer, Mark. *To Dwell in Safety*. Philadelphia: Jewish Publication Society, 1948.

Wormser, Georges. *Français Israélites*. Paris: Editions de Minuit, 1963.

Yizkor Bukh tsum Andenk fun 14 Umgekumene Parizer Yiddish Shrayber [Memorial Book to the Memory of 14 Paris Yiddish Writers], ed. B. Shlevin, M. Shulstein, G. Koenig, Y. Spero. Paris, 1946.

Interviews

David Diamant, director of the Institut Historique Maurice Thorez, Paris, October 27, 1972.

M. Frenkel, Bundist, Courbevoie, France, May 8, 1972.

Denise Gamzon, professor of French literature, University of Tel-Aviv, September 13, 1972.

Rabbi Simon Langer, New York City, February 14, 1972.

Jacques Lederman, secretary of the Syndicat des Maroquiniers, Paris, November 2, 1972.

Charles Matline, secretary of the Syndicat des Casquettiers, Paris, October 13, 1972.

Wladimir Rabi, judge and writer, Paris, October 15, 1972.

Rabbi Henri Schilli, director of the Ecole Rabbinique, Paris, October 16, 1972.

P. Schrager, former president of ORT, Paris, November 1, 1972

Boris Chubinski, research associate of YIVO, New York City, January, 1972.

Georges Wormser, banker and former president of the Consistoire de Paris, October 27, 1972.

Index